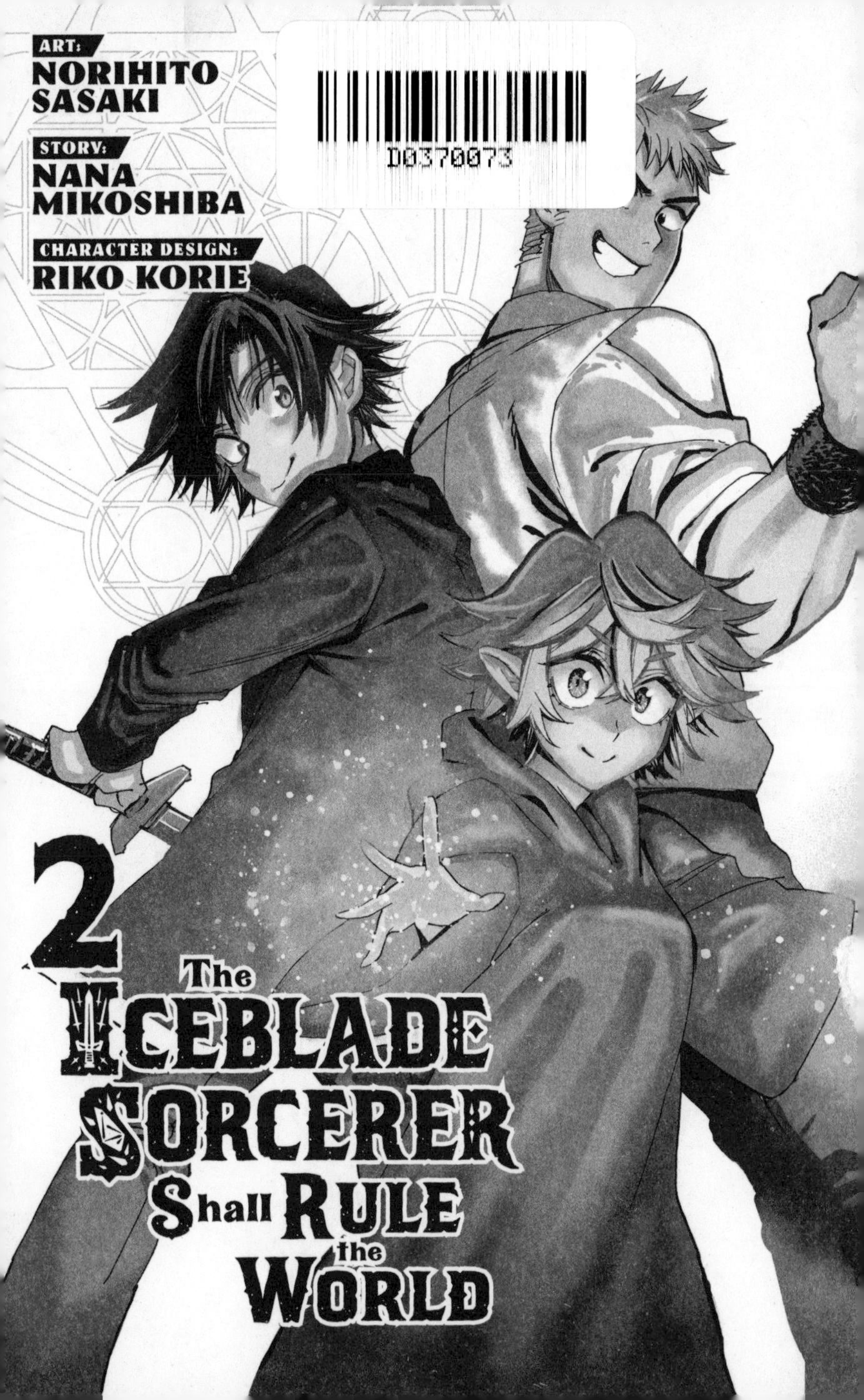
ART:
NORIHITO SASAKI
STORY:
NANA MIKOSHIBA
CHARACTER DESIGN:
RIKO KORIE
2
The ICEBLADE SORCERER Shall RULE the WORLD

CONTENTS

CHAPTER 7   Inertial Control —— 003

CHAPTER 8   The Man in Black —— 023

CHAPTER 9   Blood-Stained Ice —— 041

CHAPTER 10   Someday... —— 059

CHAPTER 11   After the Training —— 077

CHAPTER 12   Master —— 097

CHAPTER 13   Let's Go to Our Clubs! —— 117

CHAPTER 14   Now We're Cookin'! —— 137

CHAPTER 15   Moonlight Drinks —— 157

BONUS STORY   Sweet Time With Rebecca? —— 177

CHAPTER 7 Inertial Control

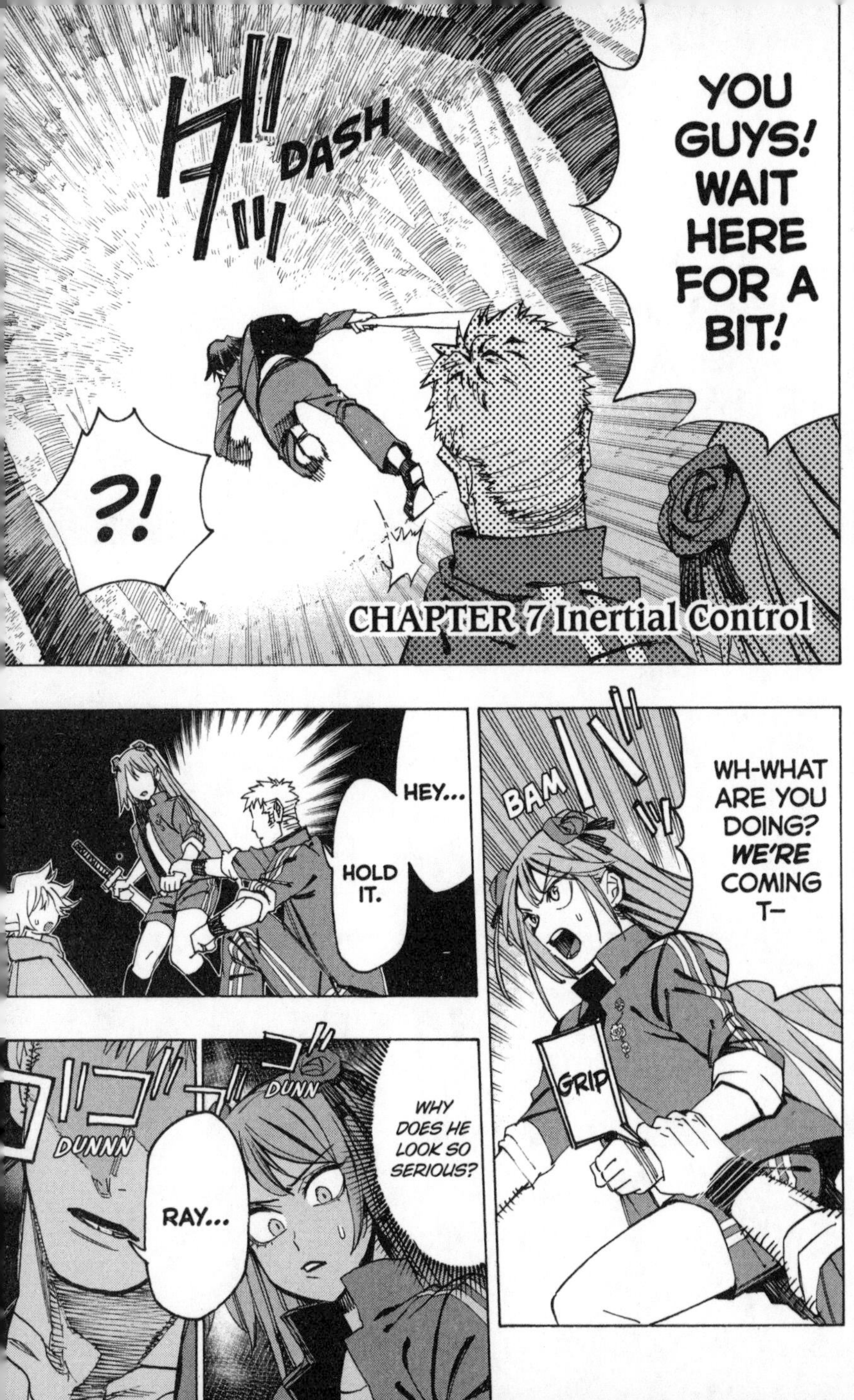
YOU GUYS! WAIT HERE FOR A BIT!
DASH
?!
CHAPTER 7 Inertial Control
BAM
WH-WHAT ARE YOU DOING? *WE'RE* COMING T–
GRIP
HEY...
HOLD IT.
DUNN
WHY DOES HE LOOK SO SERIOUS?
RAY...
DUNNN

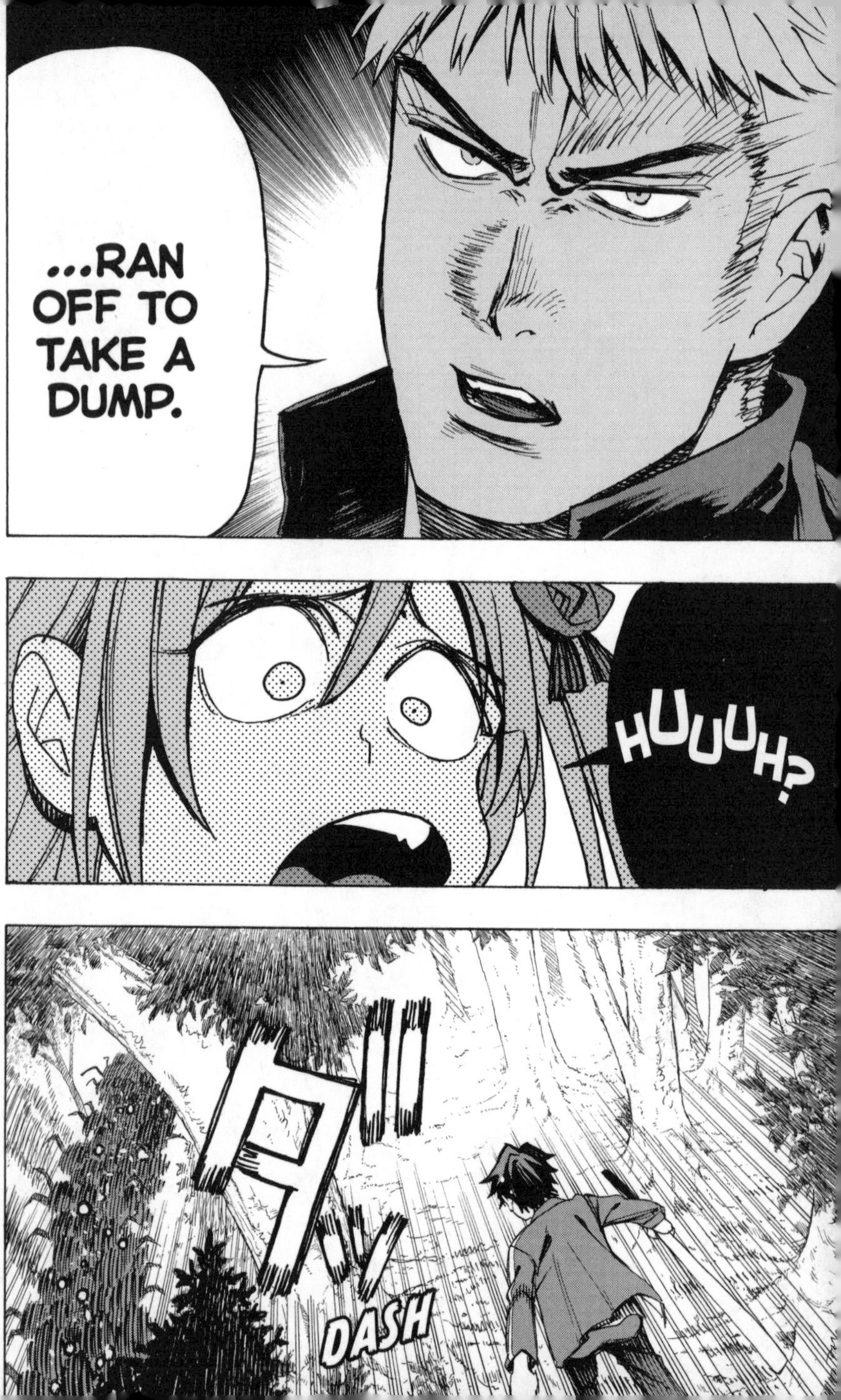
...RAN OFF TO TAKE A DUMP.
HUUUH?
DASH

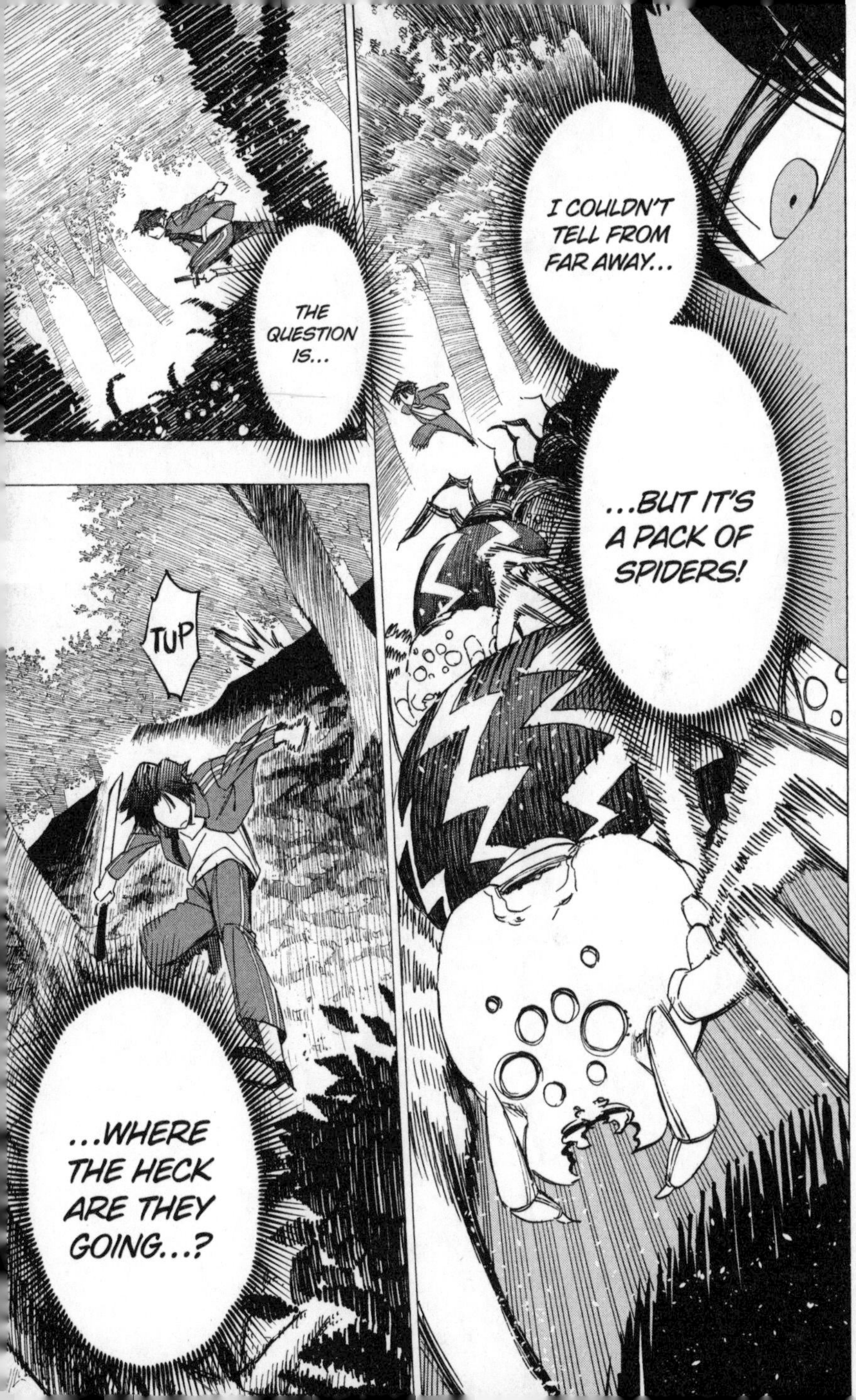
I COULDN'T TELL FROM FAR AWAY...
...BUT IT'S A PACK OF SPIDERS!
THE QUESTION IS...
TUP
...WHERE THE HECK ARE THEY GOING...?

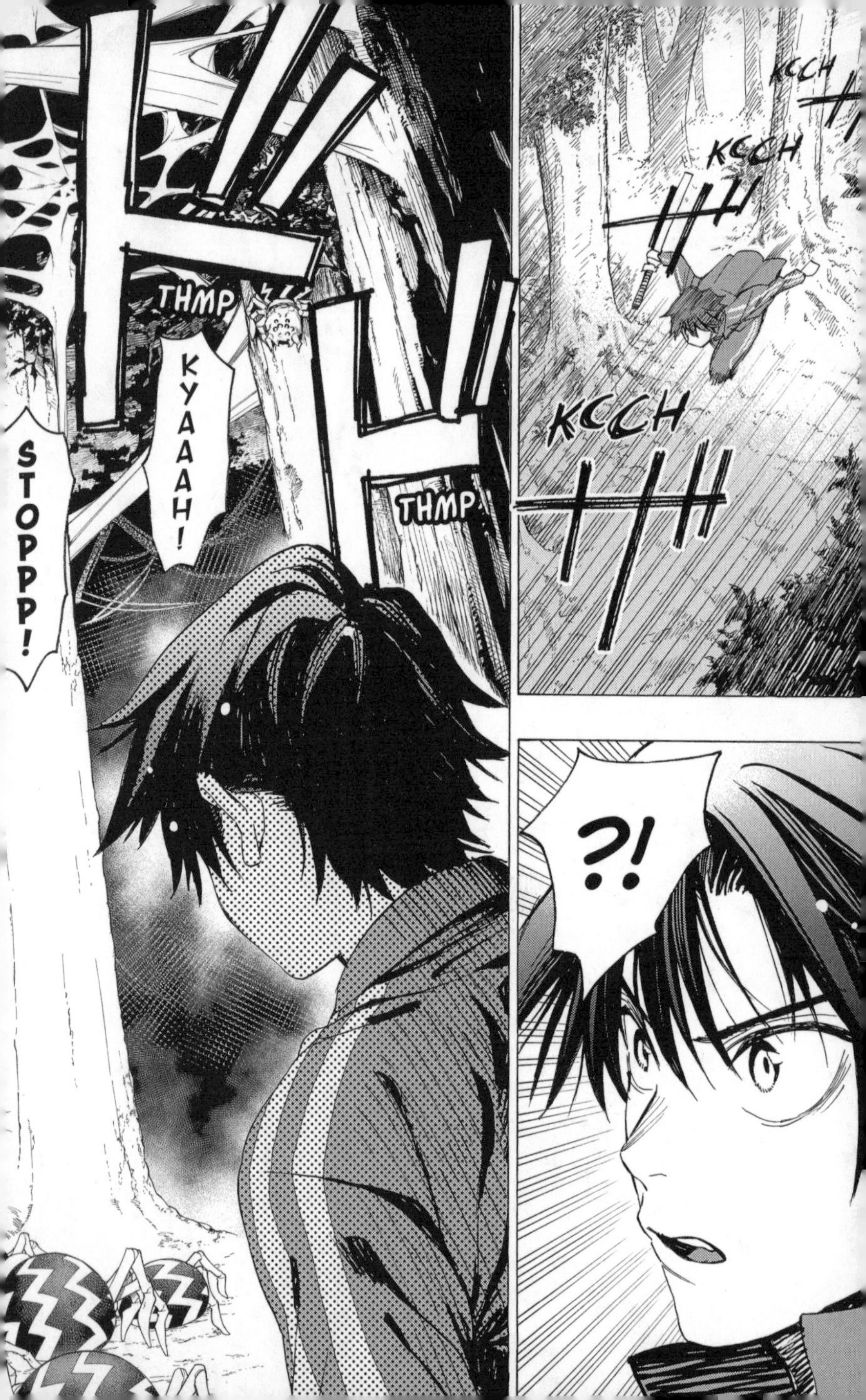
KCCH
KCCH
KCCH
?!
THMP
KYAAAH!
THMP
STOPPP!

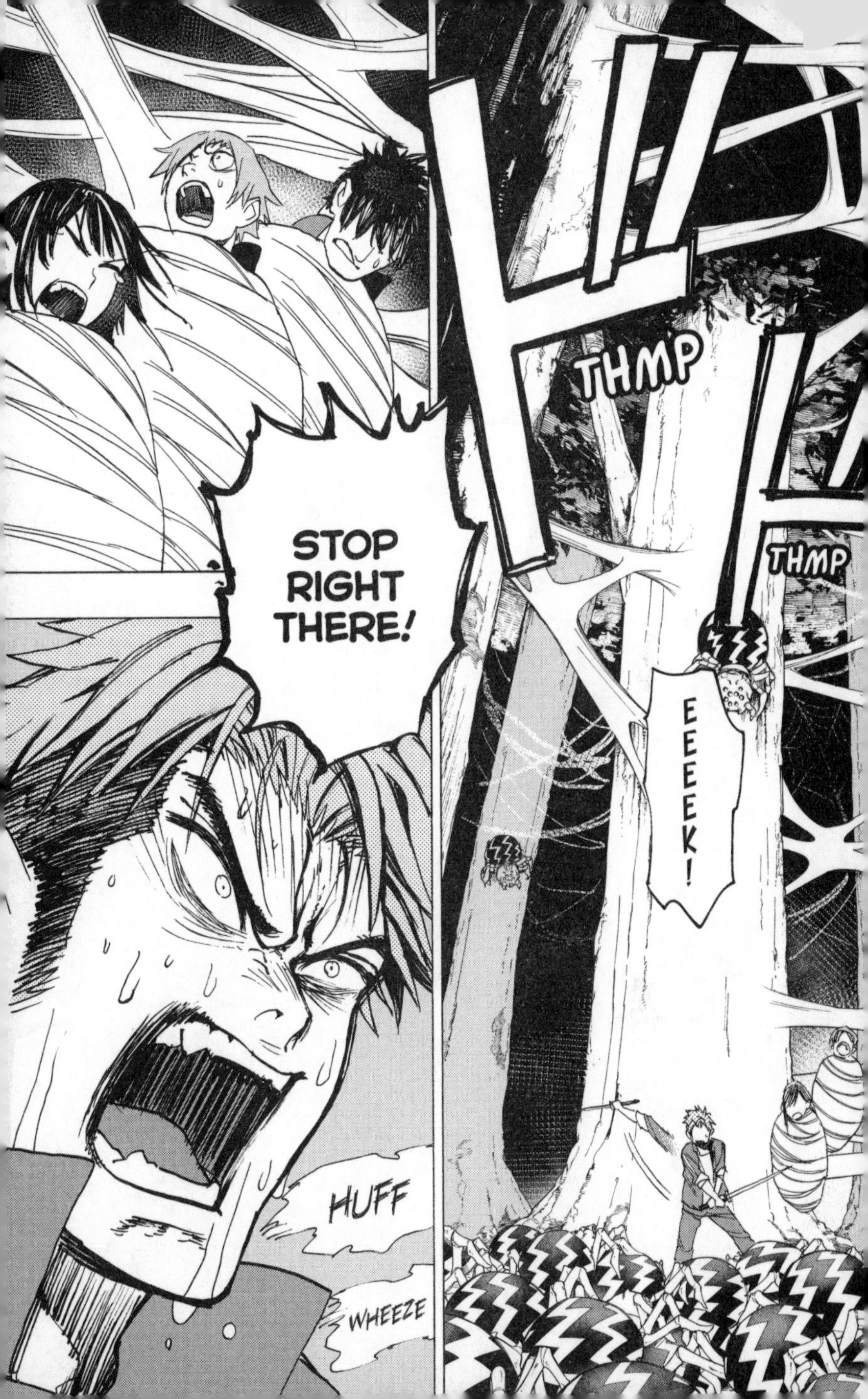
THMP
THMP
EEEEK!
STOP RIGHT THERE!
HUFF
WHEEZE

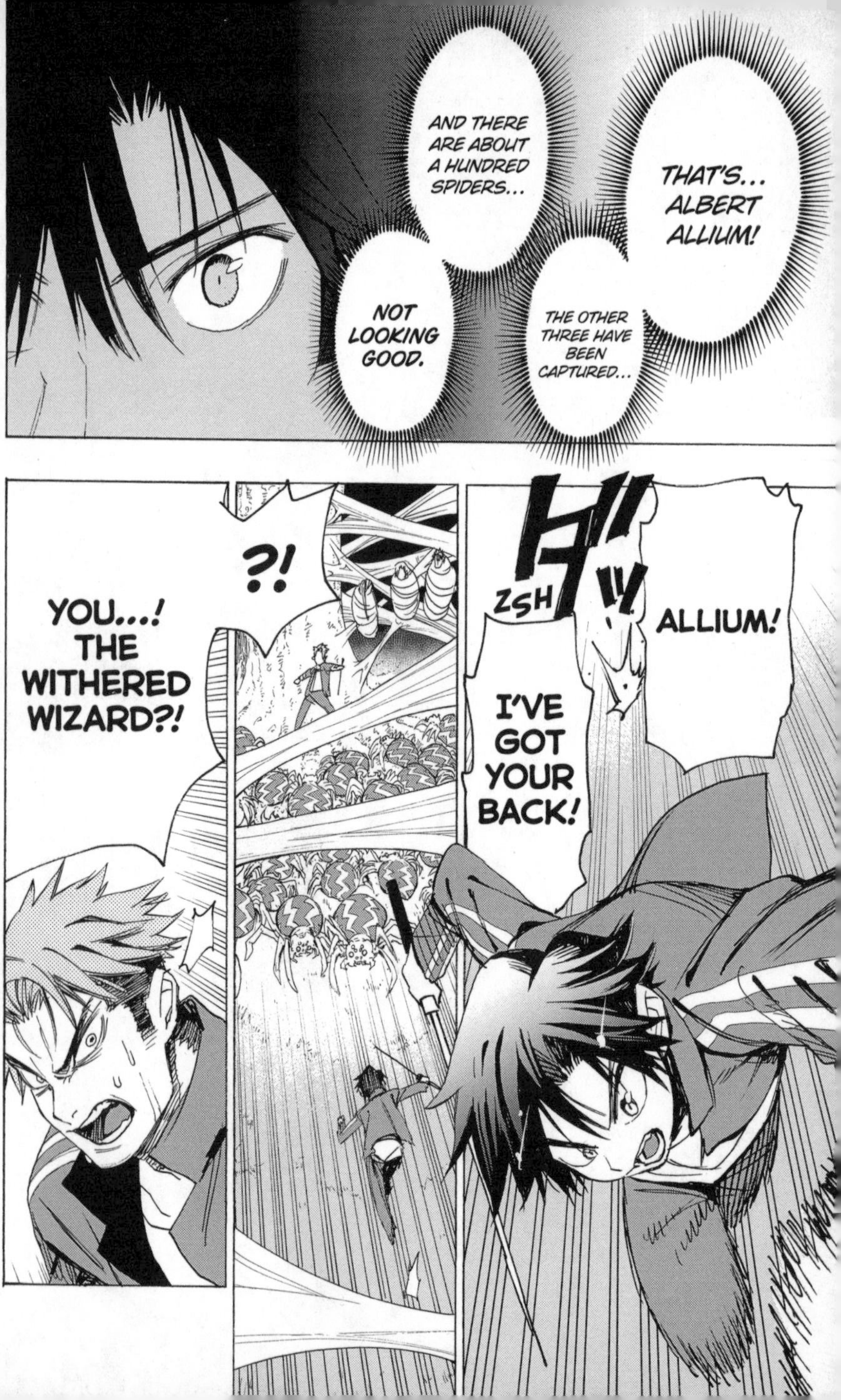
THAT'S... ALBERT ALLIUM!
THE OTHER THREE HAVE BEEN CAPTURED...
AND THERE ARE ABOUT A HUNDRED SPIDERS...
NOT LOOKING GOOD.
ZSH
ALLIUM!
I'VE GOT YOUR BACK!
?!
YOU...! THE WITHERED WIZARD?!

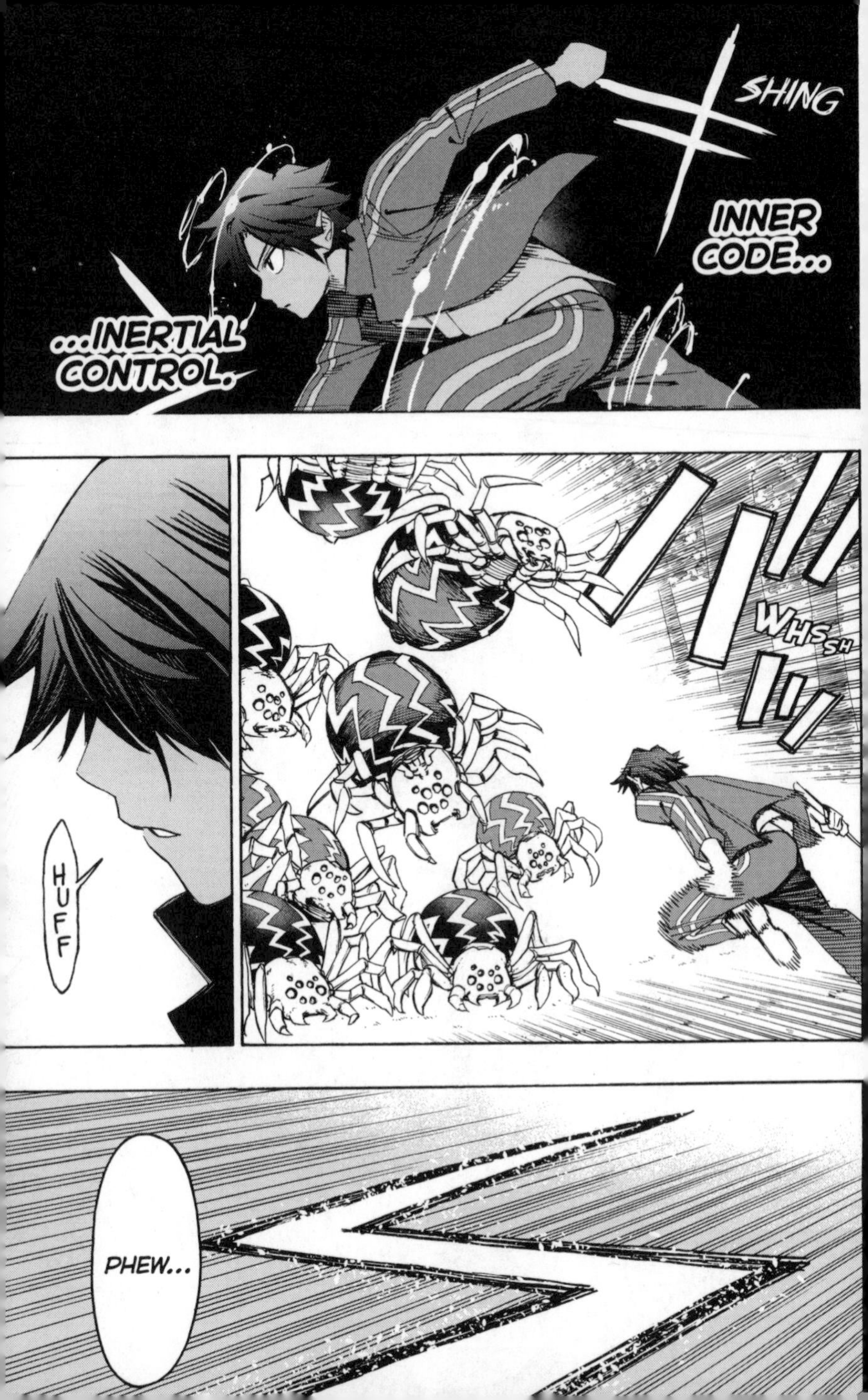
SHING
INNER CODE...
...INERTIAL CONTROL.
WHSSH
HUFF
PHEW...

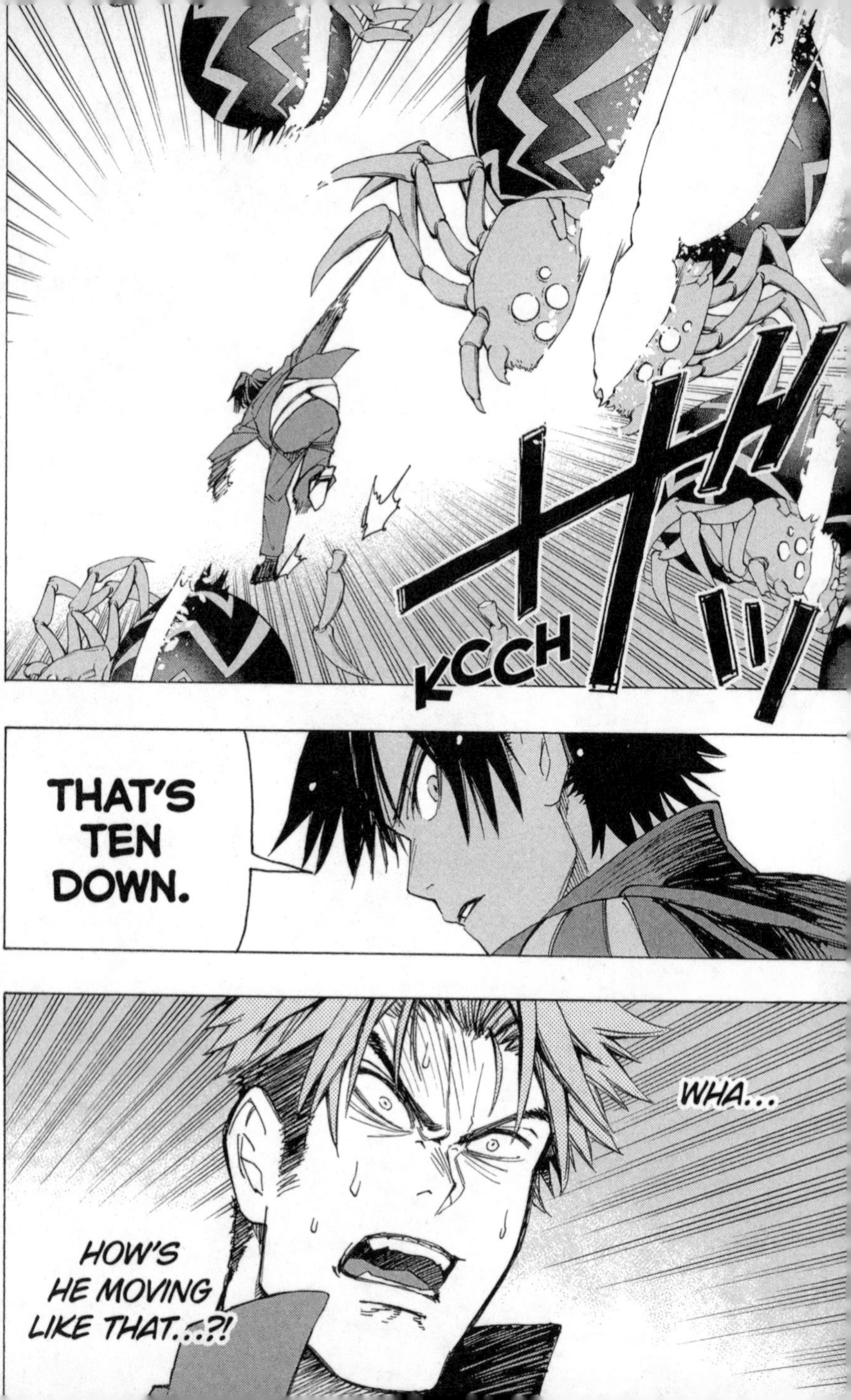
KCCH
THAT'S TEN DOWN.
WHA...
HOW'S HE MOVING LIKE THAT...?!

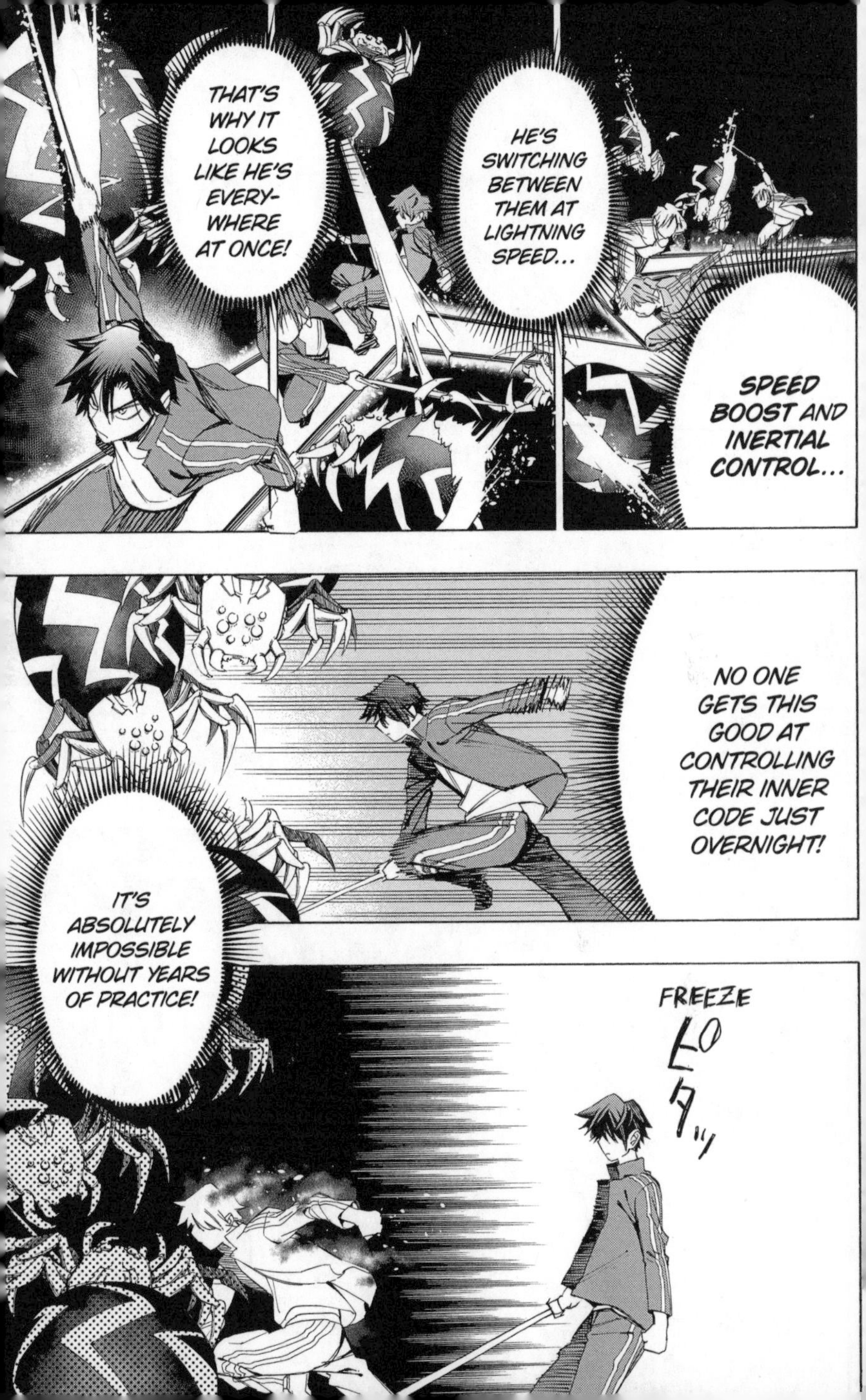
SPEED BOOST AND INERTIAL CONTROL...
HE'S SWITCHING BETWEEN THEM AT LIGHTNING SPEED...
THAT'S WHY IT LOOKS LIKE HE'S EVERY-WHERE AT ONCE!
NO ONE GETS THIS GOOD AT CONTROLLING THEIR INNER CODE JUST OVERNIGHT!
IT'S ABSOLUTELY IMPOSSIBLE WITHOUT YEARS OF PRACTICE!
FREEZE
ピタッ

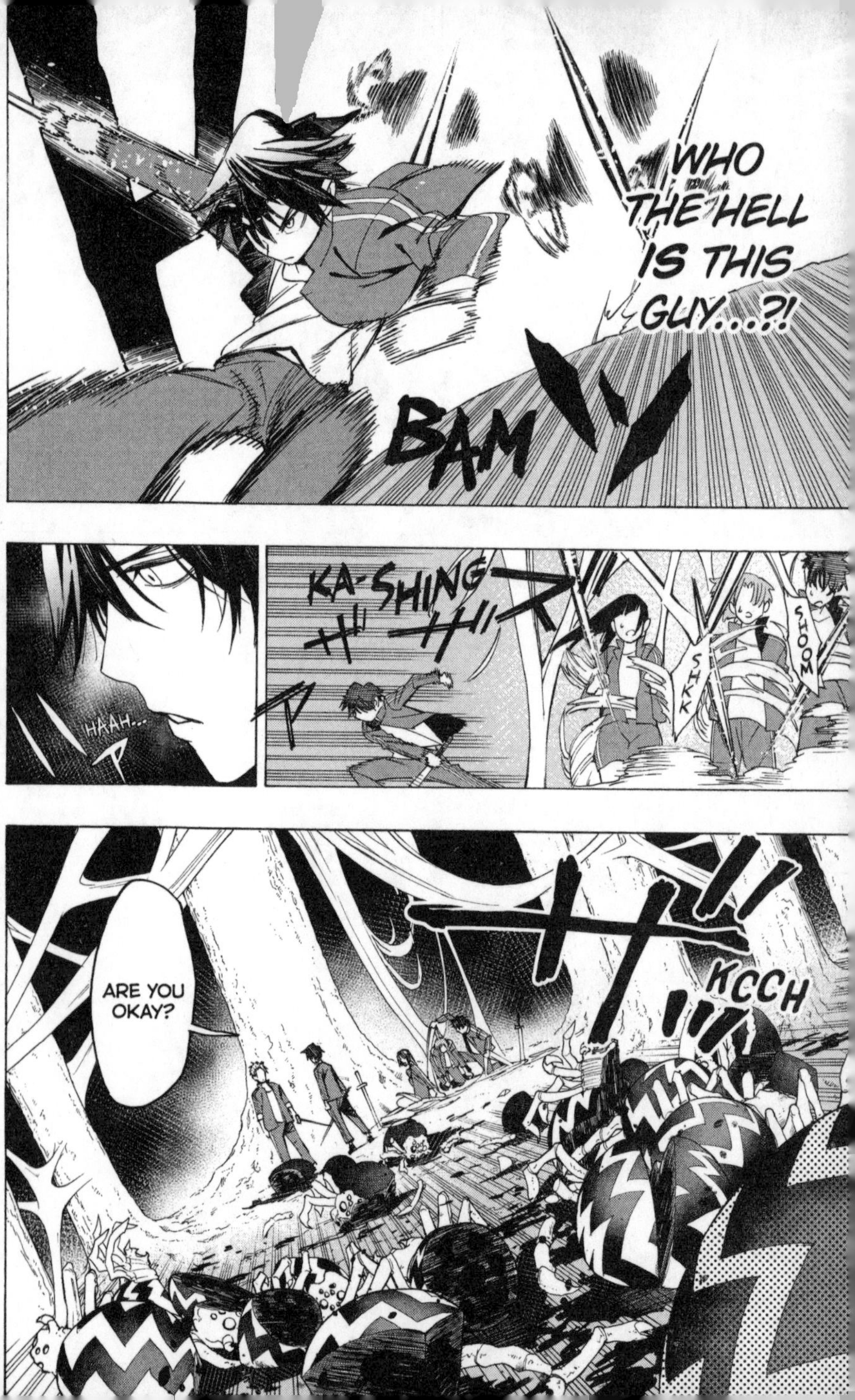
WHO THE HELL IS THIS GUY...?!
BAM
SHOOM
SHKK
KA-SHING
HAAH...
KCCH
ARE YOU OKAY?

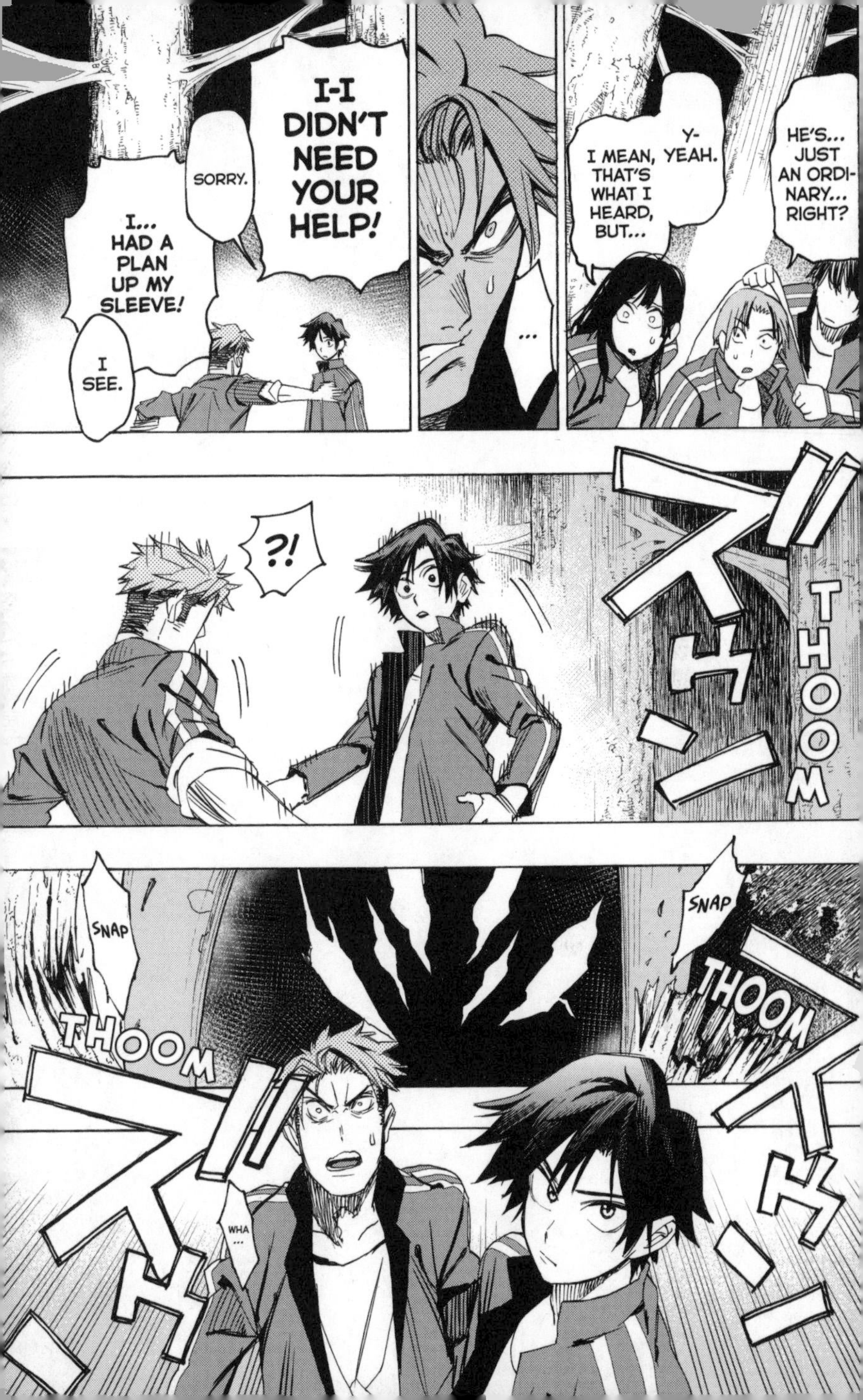
HE'S... JUST AN ORDINARY... RIGHT?
Y-YEAH.
I MEAN, THAT'S WHAT I HEARD, BUT...
...
I-I DIDN'T NEED YOUR HELP!
SORRY.
I... HAD A PLAN UP MY SLEEVE!
I SEE.
THOOM
?!
SNAP
THOOM
SNAP
THOOM
WHA...

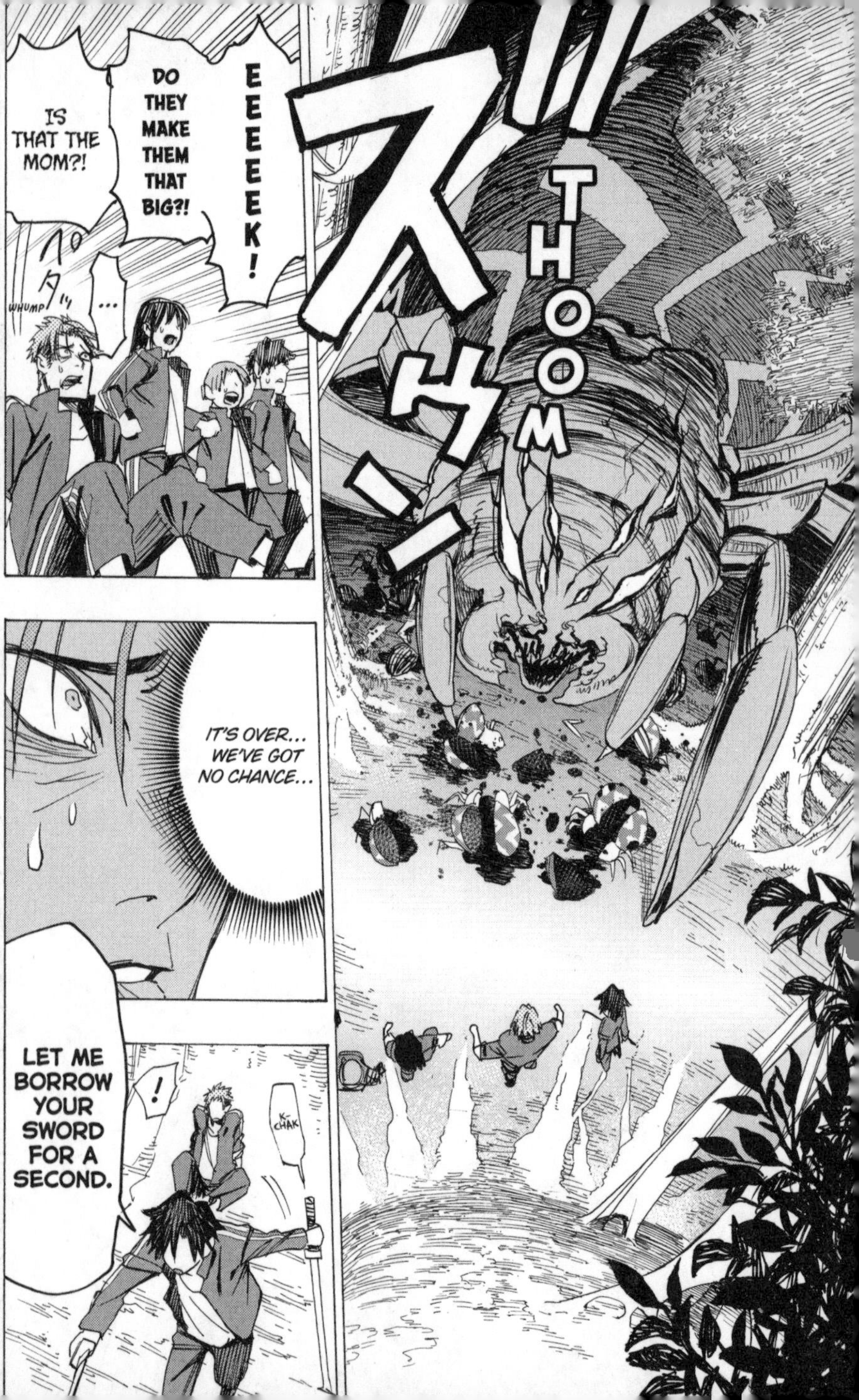

THOOM
EEEEEEK!
DO THEY MAKE THEM THAT BIG?!
IS THAT THE MOM?!
WHUMP
...
IT'S OVER... WE'VE GOT NO CHANCE...
!
LET ME BORROW YOUR SWORD FOR A SECOND.
K-CHAK

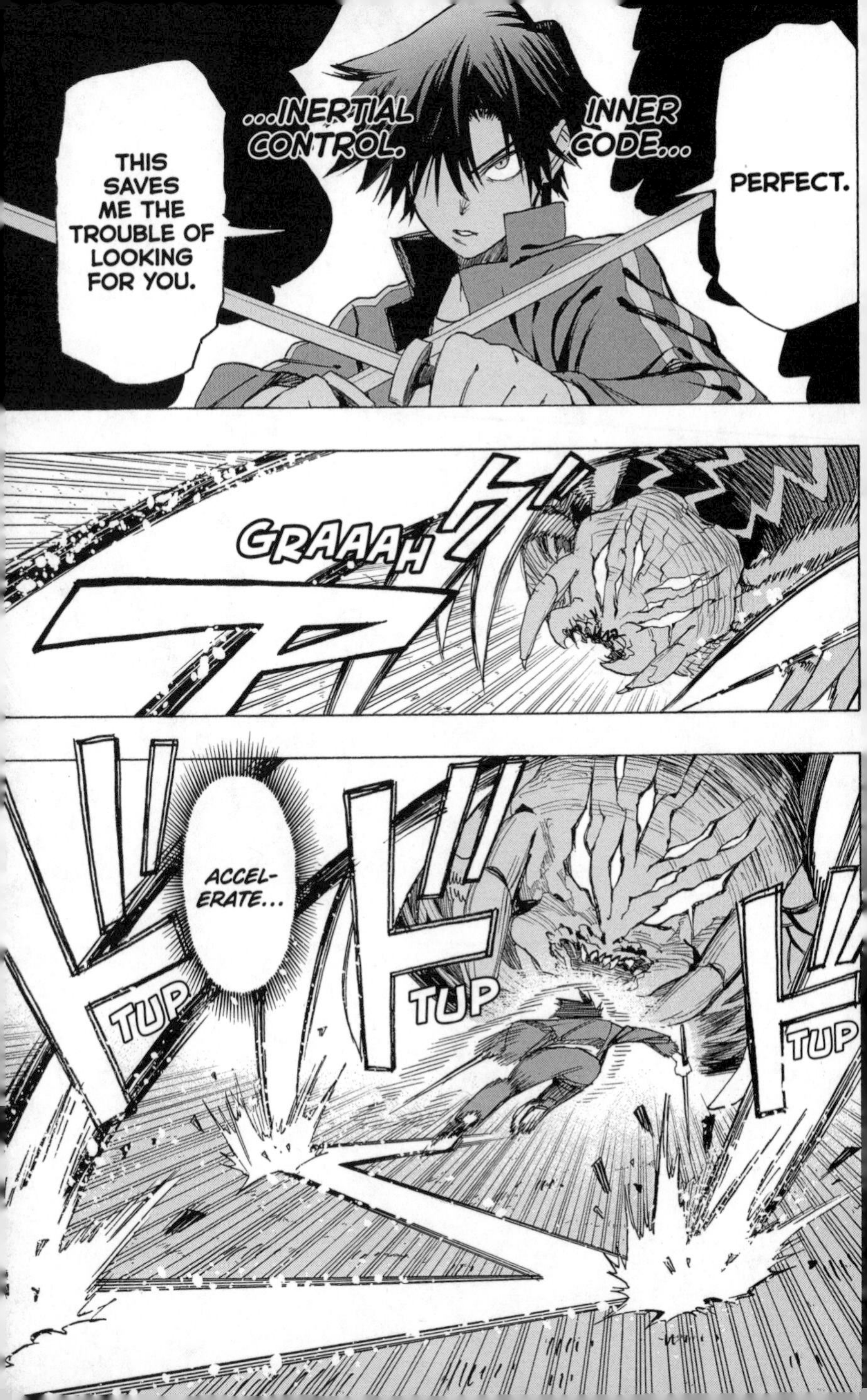
PERFECT.
INNER CODE...
...INERTIAL CONTROL.
THIS SAVES ME THE TROUBLE OF LOOKING FOR YOU.
GRAAAH
TUP
TUP
ACCEL-ERATE...
TUP

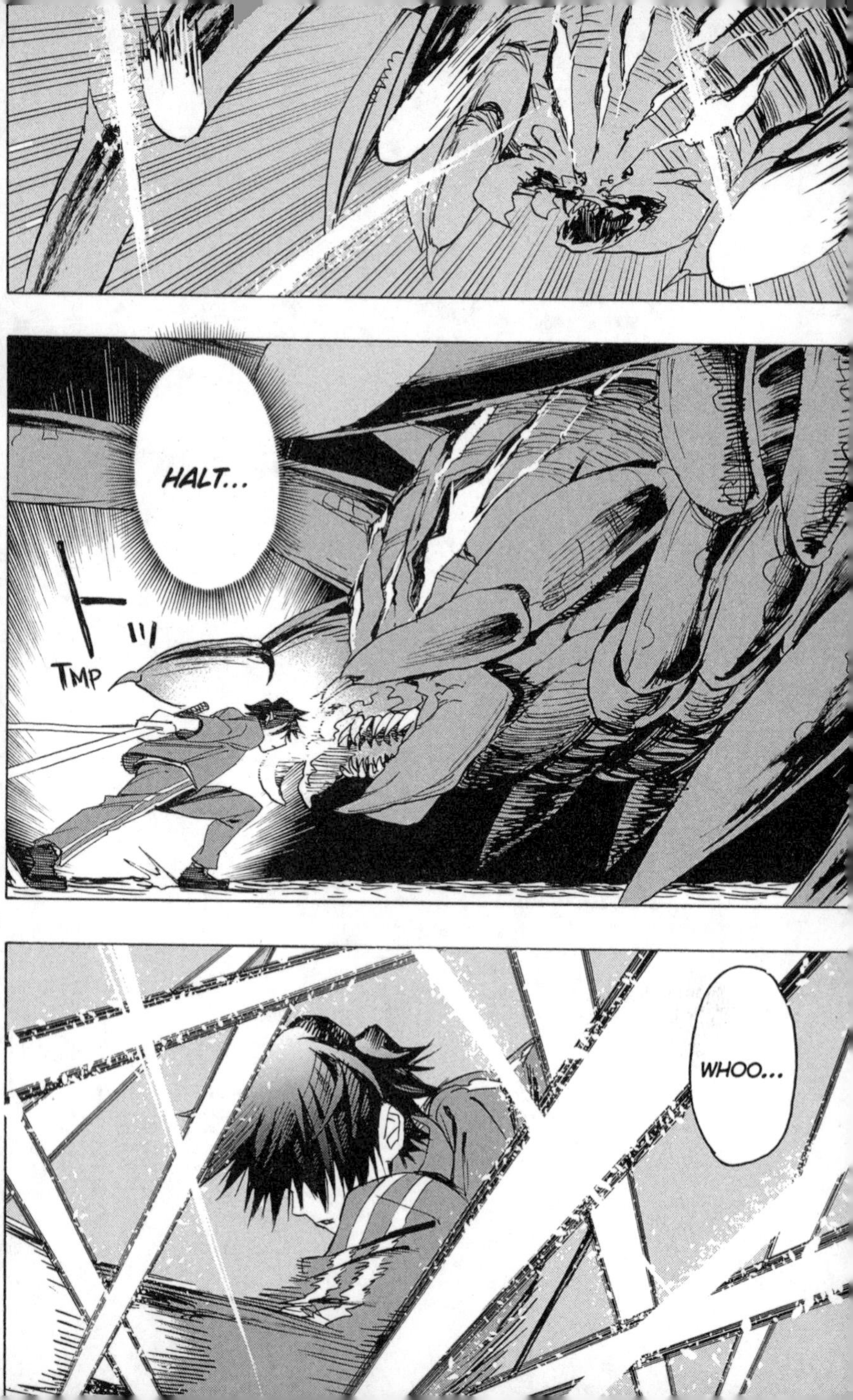
HALT...
TMP
WHOO...

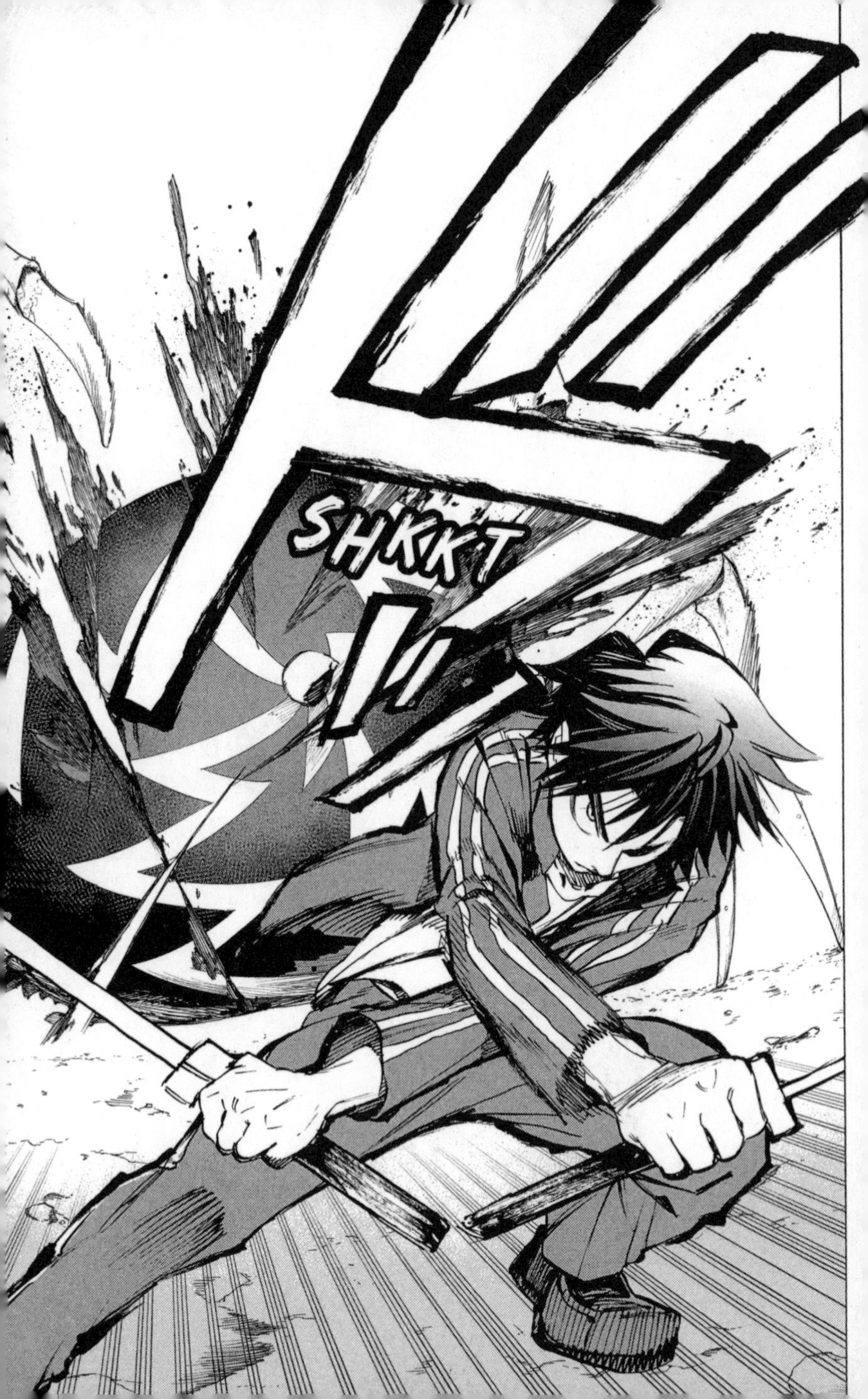
SHKKT

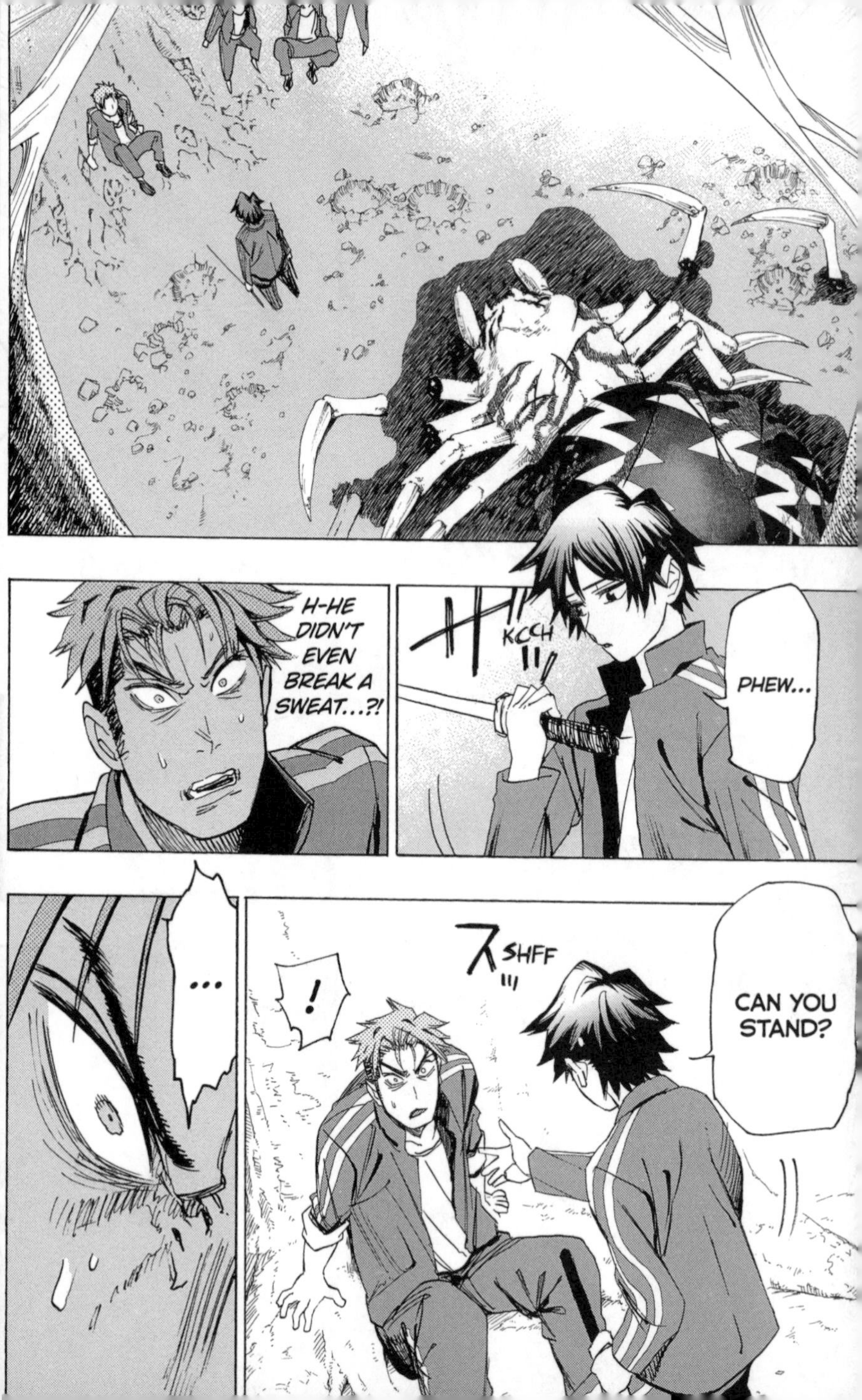
KCCH
PHEW...
H-HE DIDN'T EVEN BREAK A SWEAT...?!
CAN YOU STAND?
SHFF
!
...

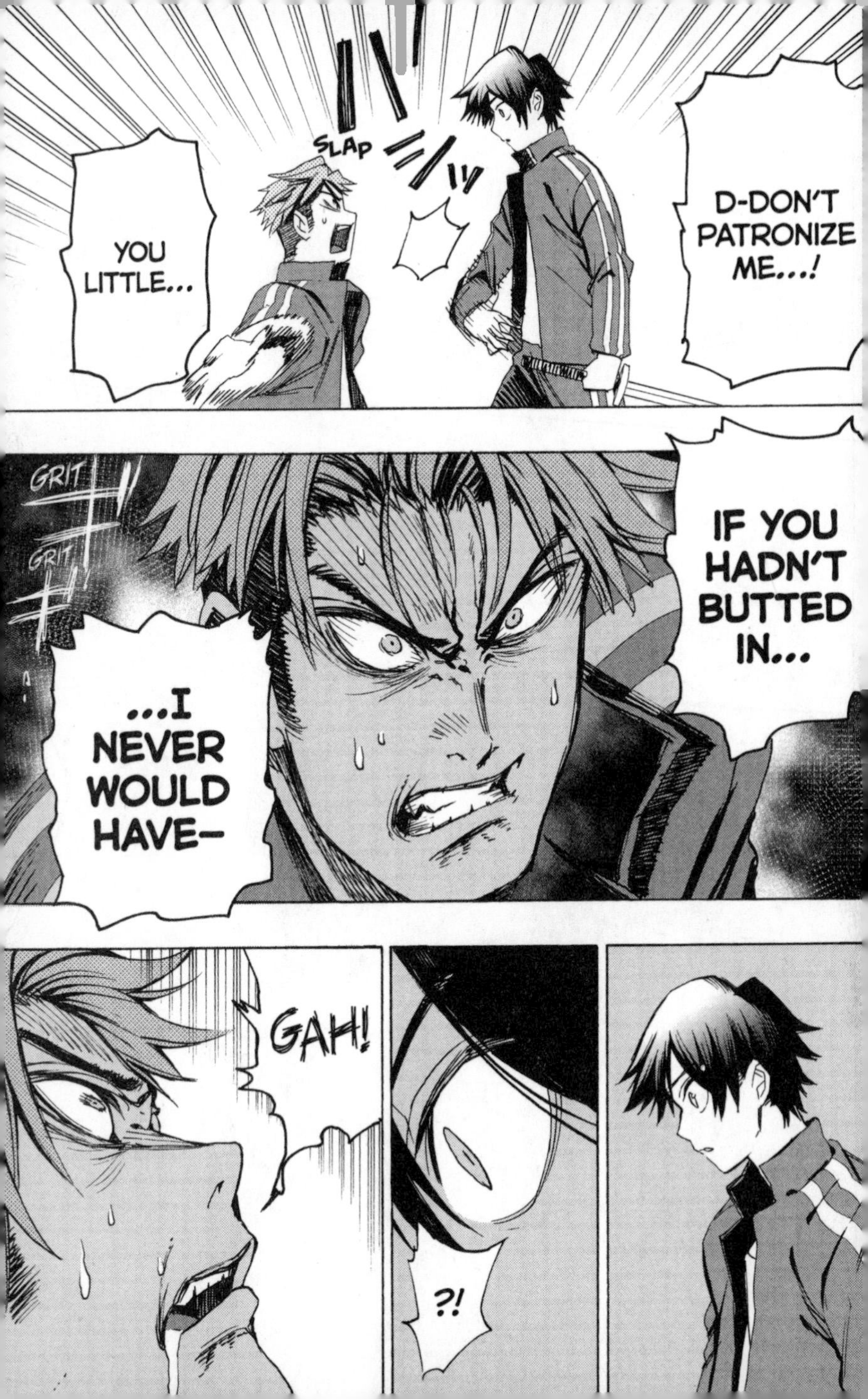
D-DON'T PATRONIZE ME...!
SLAP
YOU LITTLE...
IF YOU HADN'T BUTTED IN...
GRIT
GRIT
...I NEVER WOULD HAVE–
?!
GAH!

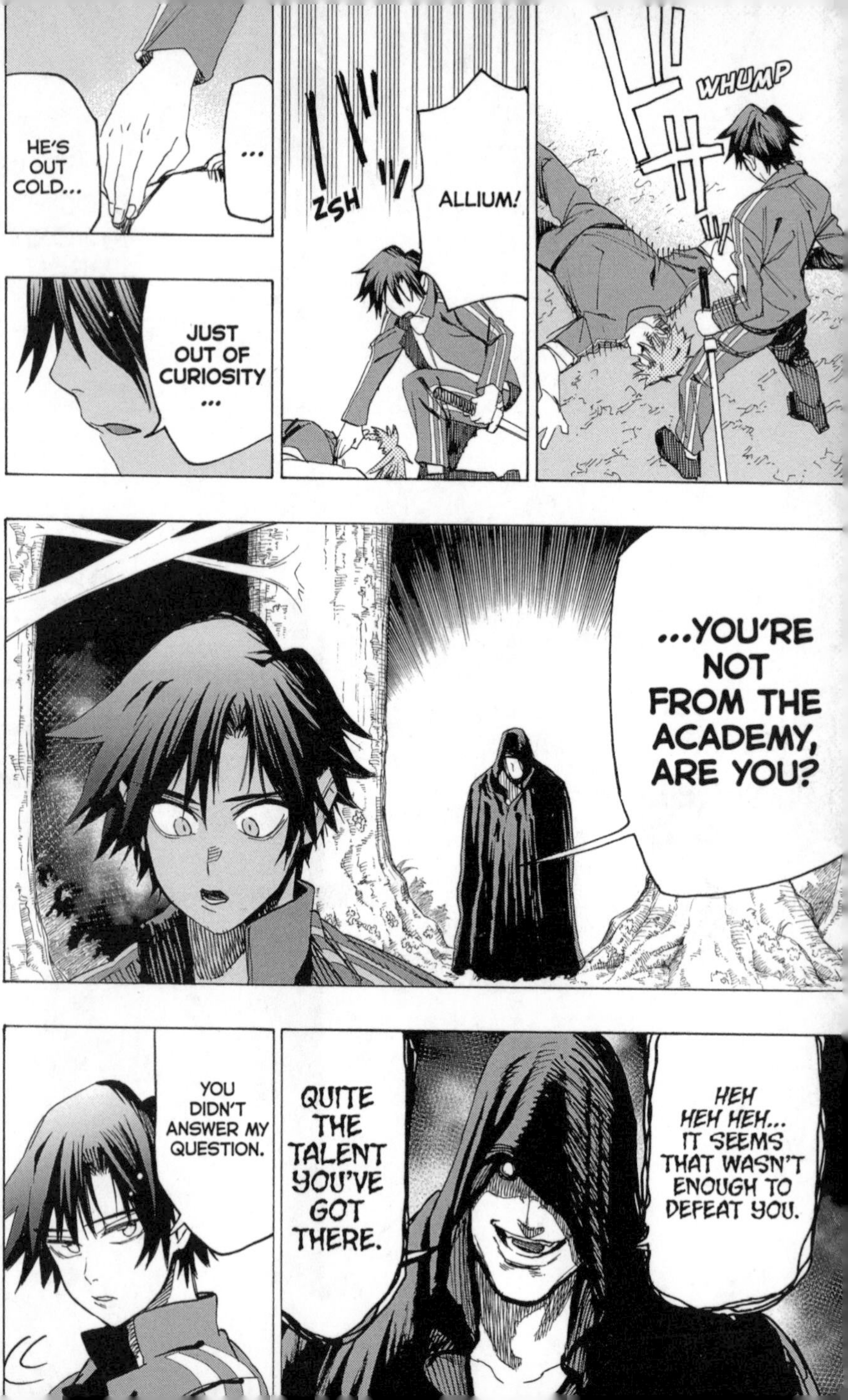
WHUMP
ZSH
ALLIUM!
...
HE'S OUT COLD...
JUST OUT OF CURIOSITY ...
...YOU'RE NOT FROM THE ACADEMY, ARE YOU?
HEH HEH HEH... IT SEEMS THAT WASN'T ENOUGH TO DEFEAT YOU.
QUITE THE TALENT YOU'VE GOT THERE.
YOU DIDN'T ANSWER MY QUESTION.

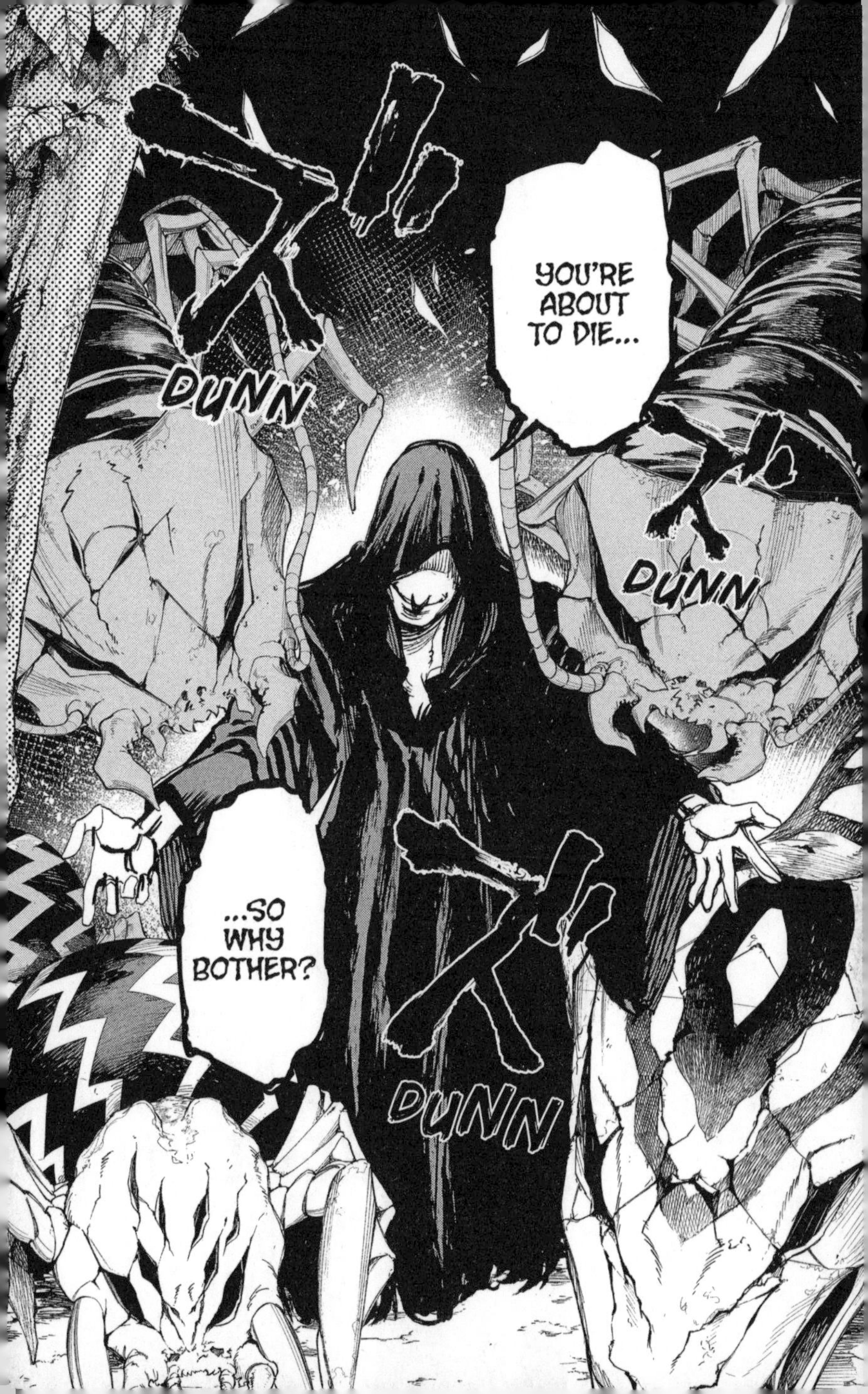
YOU'RE ABOUT TO DIE...
DUNN
DUNN
...SO WHY BOTHER?
DUNN

The
ICEBLADE
SORCERER
Shall RULE
the
WORLD

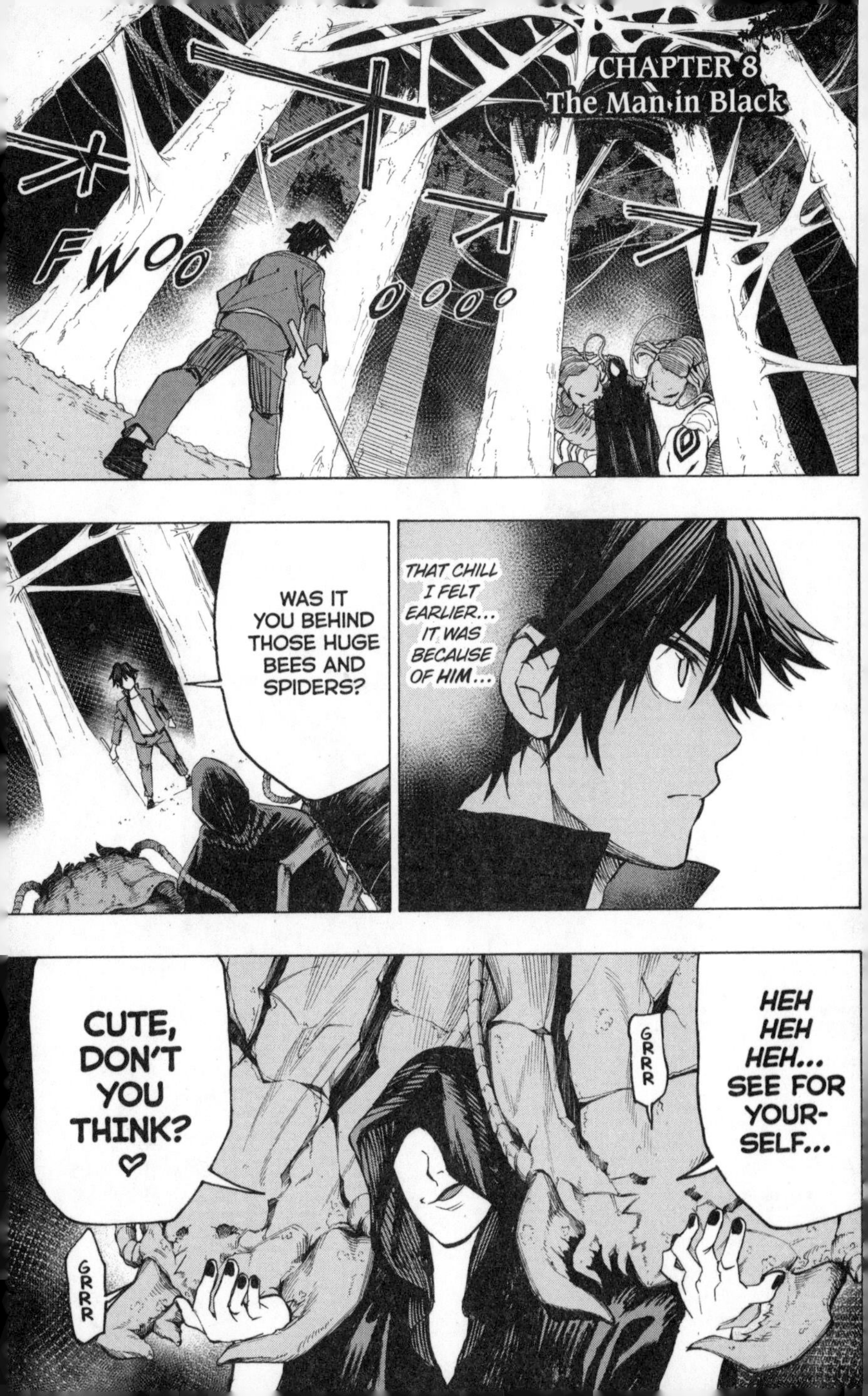
CHAPTER 8
The Man in Black
FWOOOOOOOO
THAT CHILL I FELT EARLIER… IT WAS BECAUSE OF HIM…
WAS IT YOU BEHIND THOSE HUGE BEES AND SPIDERS?
HEH HEH HEH… SEE FOR YOURSELF…
GRRR
CUTE, DON'T YOU THINK? ♡
GRRR

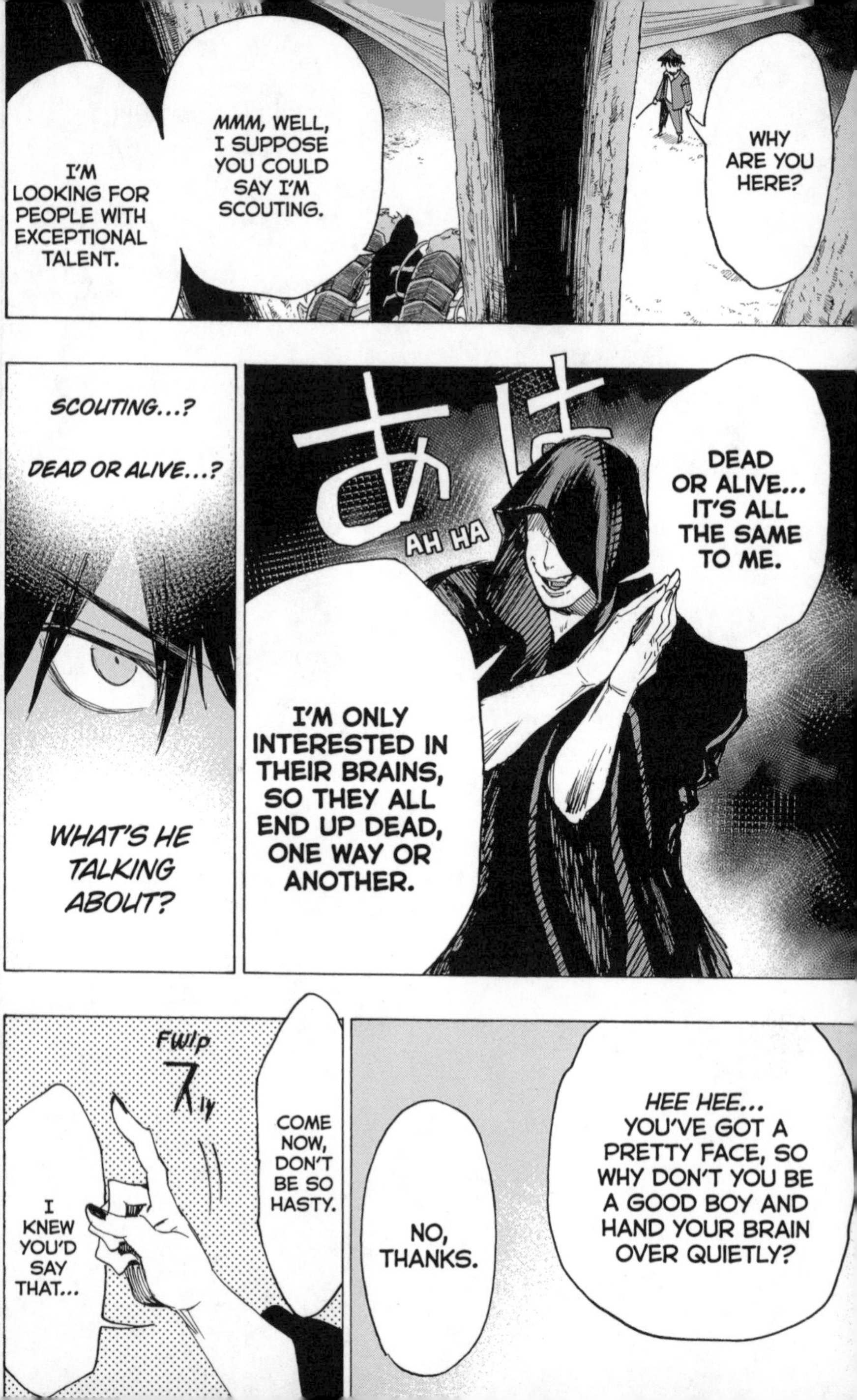
WHY ARE YOU HERE?
MMM, WELL, I SUPPOSE YOU COULD SAY I'M SCOUTING.
I'M LOOKING FOR PEOPLE WITH EXCEPTIONAL TALENT.
あは
AH HA
DEAD OR ALIVE... IT'S ALL THE SAME TO ME.
I'M ONLY INTERESTED IN THEIR BRAINS, SO THEY ALL END UP DEAD, ONE WAY OR ANOTHER.
SCOUTING...?
DEAD OR ALIVE...?
WHAT'S HE TALKING ABOUT?
HEE HEE... YOU'VE GOT A PRETTY FACE, SO WHY DON'T YOU BE A GOOD BOY AND HAND YOUR BRAIN OVER QUIETLY?
NO, THANKS.
COME NOW, DON'T BE SO HASTY.
FWIP
I KNEW YOU'D SAY THAT...

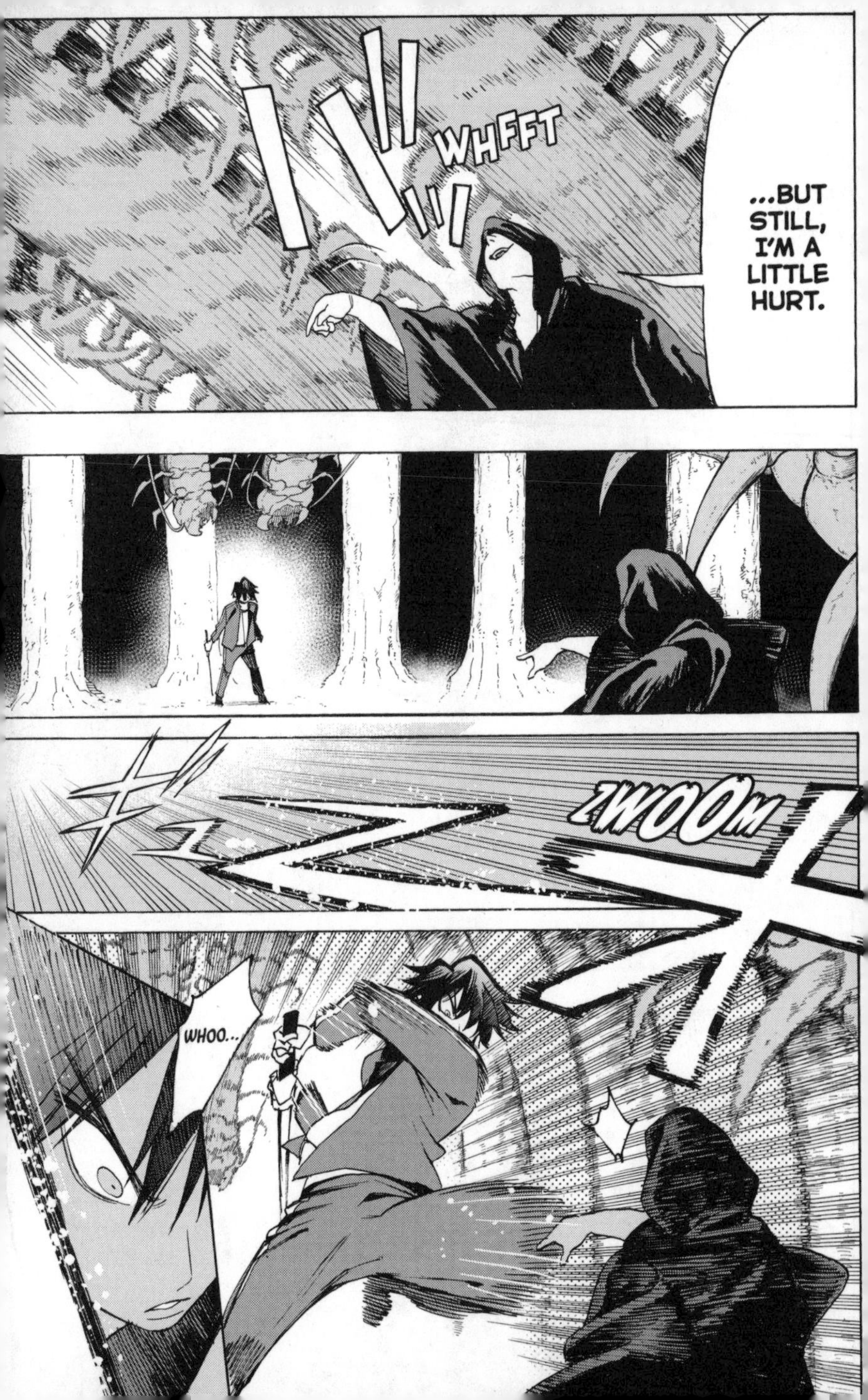
...BUT STILL, I'M A LITTLE HURT.
WHFFT
ZWOOM
WHOO...

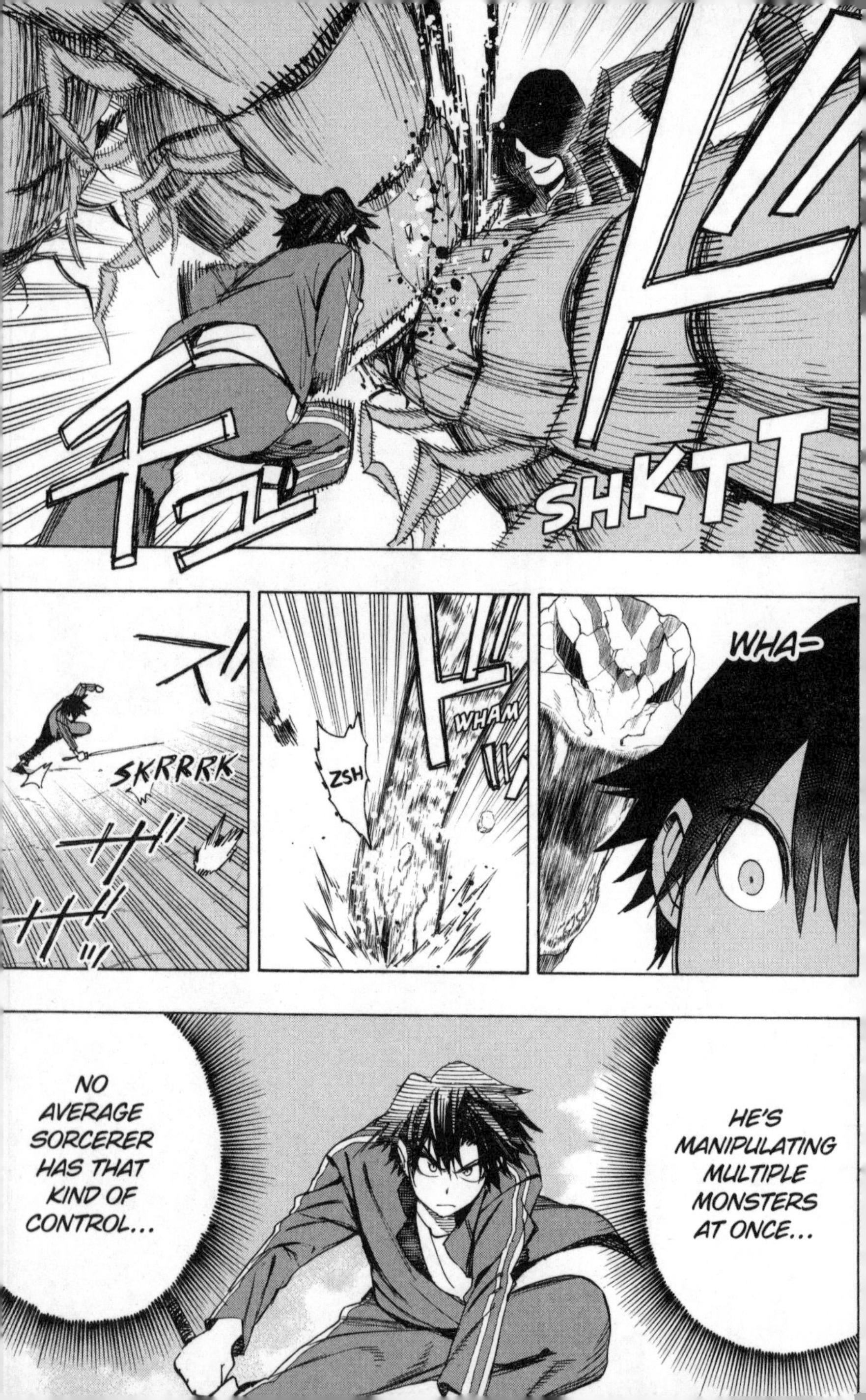
SHKTT
WHA-
WHAM
ZSH
SKRRRK
HE'S MANIPULATING MULTIPLE MONSTERS AT ONCE...
NO AVERAGE SORCERER HAS THAT KIND OF CONTROL...

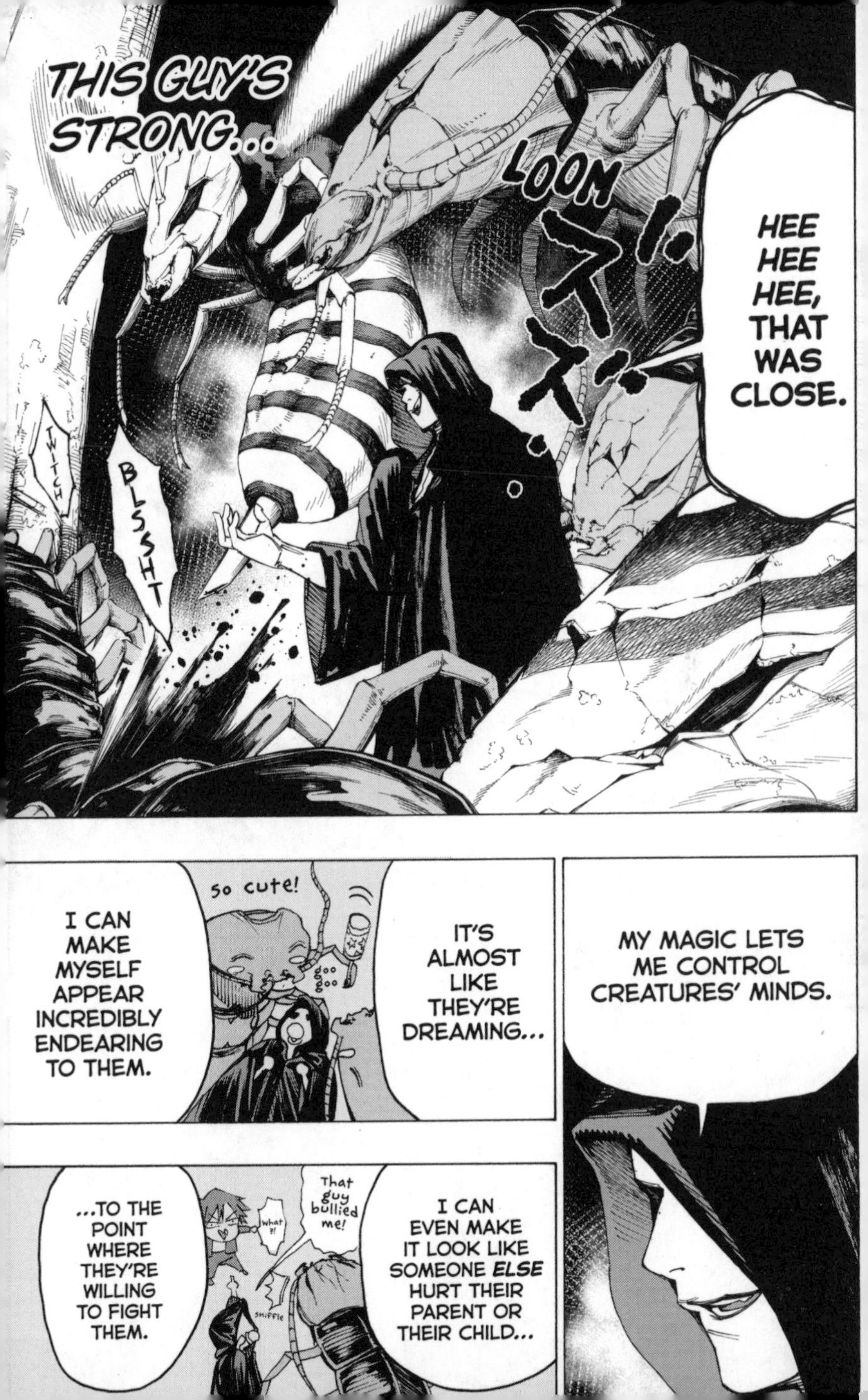
HEE HEE HEE, THAT WAS CLOSE.
LOOM
THIS GUY'S STRONG...
TWITCH
BLSSHT
MY MAGIC LETS ME CONTROL CREATURES' MINDS.
IT'S ALMOST LIKE THEY'RE DREAMING...
so cute!
goo goo
I CAN MAKE MYSELF APPEAR INCREDIBLY ENDEARING TO THEM.
I CAN EVEN MAKE IT LOOK LIKE SOMEONE *ELSE* HURT THEIR PARENT OR THEIR CHILD...
That guy bullied me!
what?!
sniffle
...TO THE POINT WHERE THEY'RE WILLING TO FIGHT THEM.

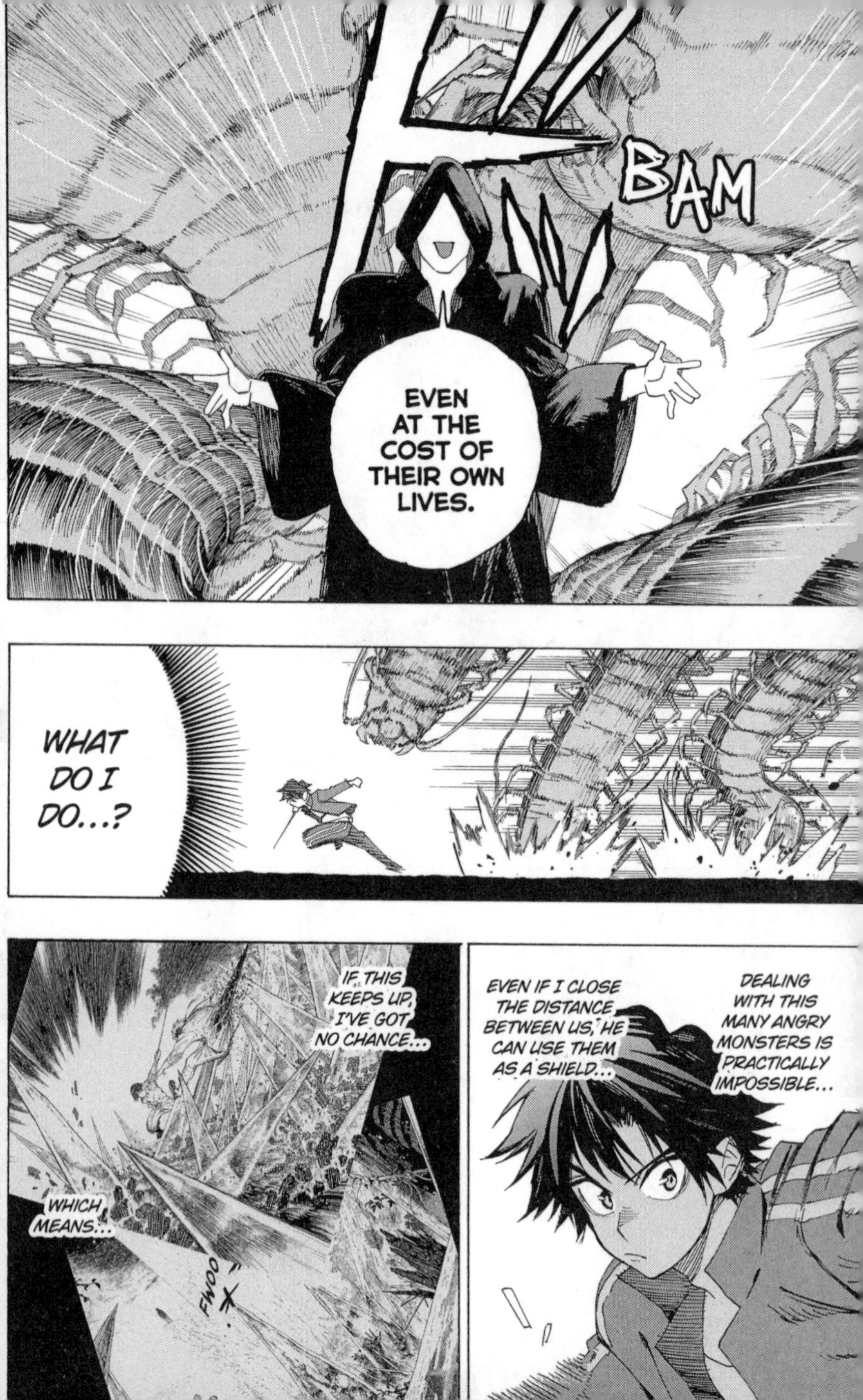
BAM
EVEN AT THE COST OF THEIR OWN LIVES.
WHAT DO I DO...?
DEALING WITH THIS MANY ANGRY MONSTERS IS PRACTICALLY IMPOSSIBLE...
EVEN IF I CLOSE THE DISTANCE BETWEEN US, HE CAN USE THEM AS A SHIELD...
IF THIS KEEPS UP, I'VE GOT NO CHANCE...
WHICH MEANS...
FWOO

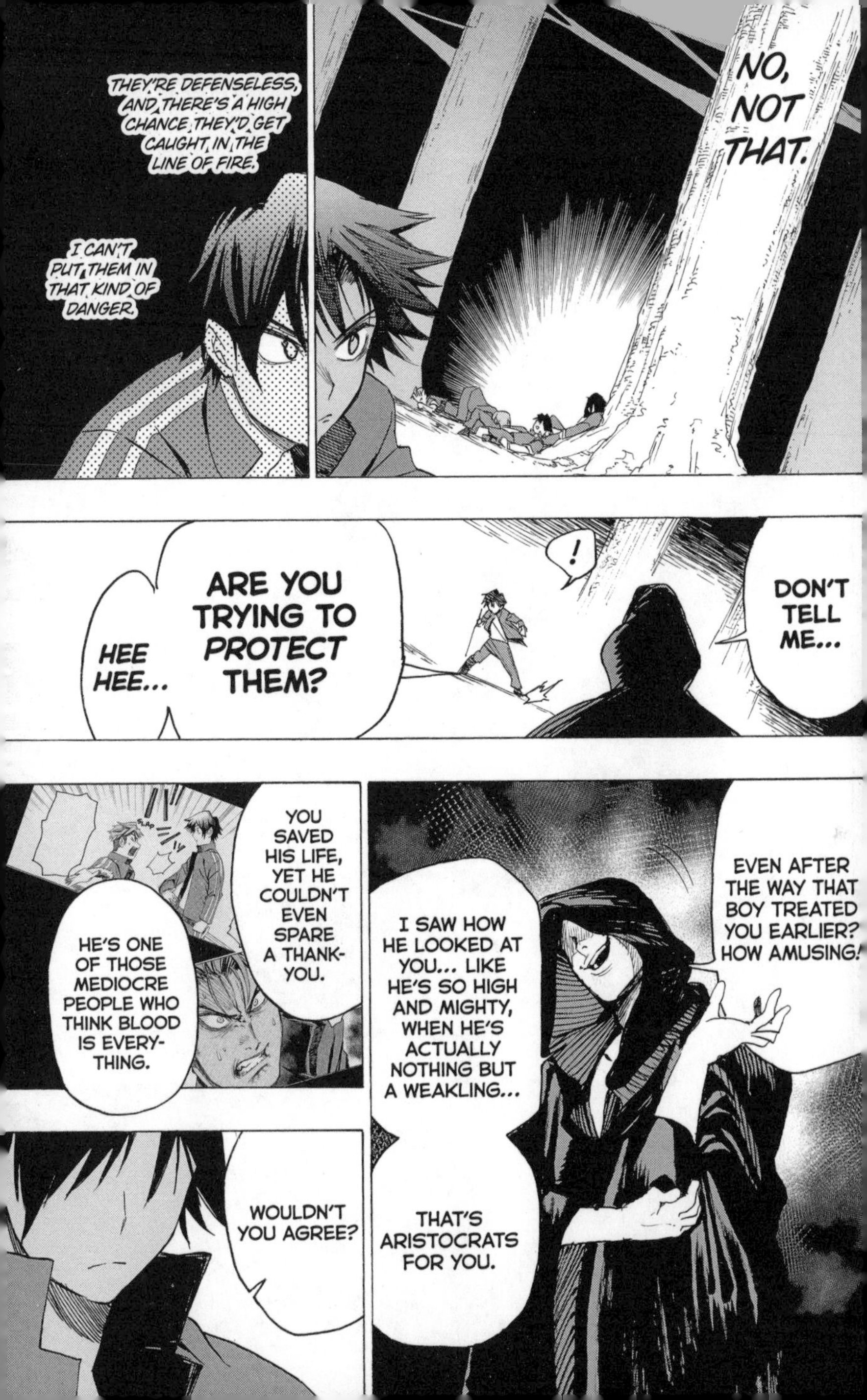
NO, NOT THAT.
THEY'RE DEFENSELESS, AND THERE'S A HIGH CHANCE THEY'D GET CAUGHT IN THE LINE OF FIRE.
I CAN'T PUT THEM IN THAT KIND OF DANGER.
DON'T TELL ME...
!
HEE HEE... ARE YOU TRYING TO *PROTECT* THEM?
EVEN AFTER THE WAY THAT BOY TREATED YOU EARLIER? HOW AMUSING!
I SAW HOW HE LOOKED AT YOU... LIKE HE'S SO HIGH AND MIGHTY, WHEN HE'S ACTUALLY NOTHING BUT A WEAKLING...
THAT'S ARISTOCRATS FOR YOU.
YOU SAVED HIS LIFE, YET HE COULDN'T EVEN SPARE A THANK-YOU.
HE'S ONE OF THOSE MEDIOCRE PEOPLE WHO THINK BLOOD IS EVERYTHING.
WOULDN'T YOU AGREE?

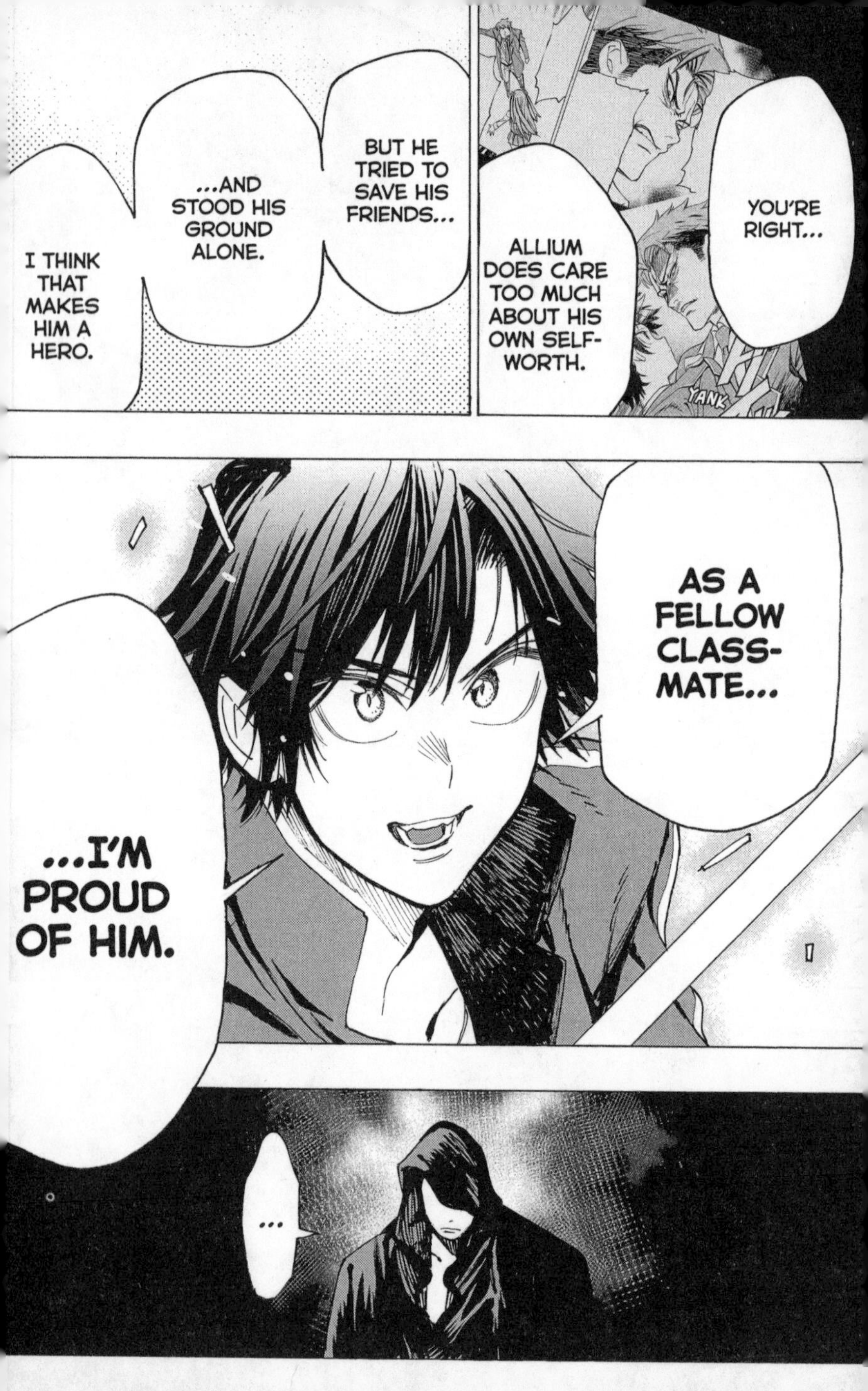
YOU'RE RIGHT...
YANK
ALLIUM DOES CARE TOO MUCH ABOUT HIS OWN SELF-WORTH.
BUT HE TRIED TO SAVE HIS FRIENDS...
...AND STOOD HIS GROUND ALONE.
I THINK THAT MAKES HIM A HERO.
AS A FELLOW CLASSMATE...
...I'M PROUD OF HIM.
...

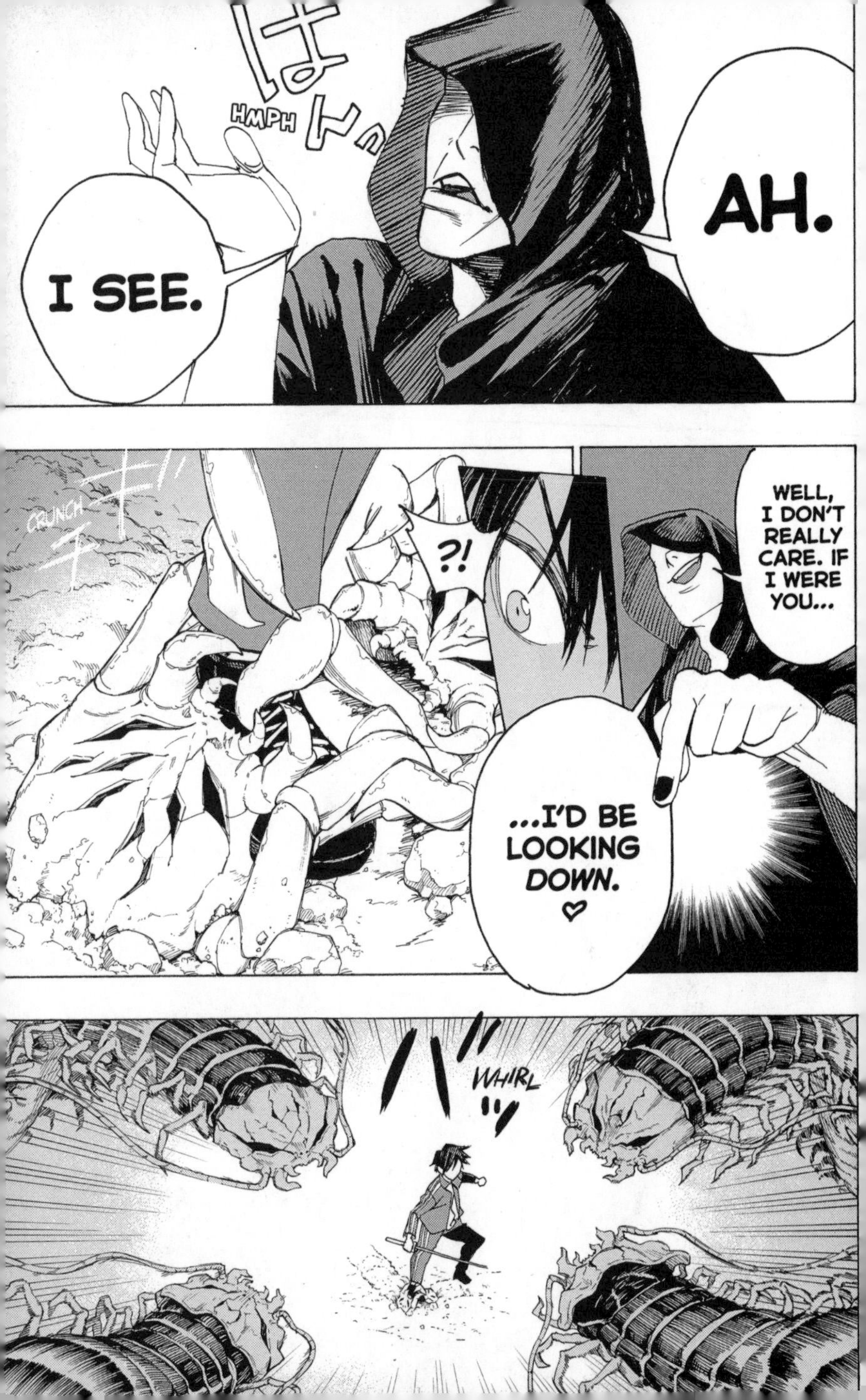
AH.
HMPH
I SEE.
WELL, I DON'T REALLY CARE. IF I WERE YOU...
?!
CRUNCH
...I'D BE LOOKING DOWN. ♡
WHIRL

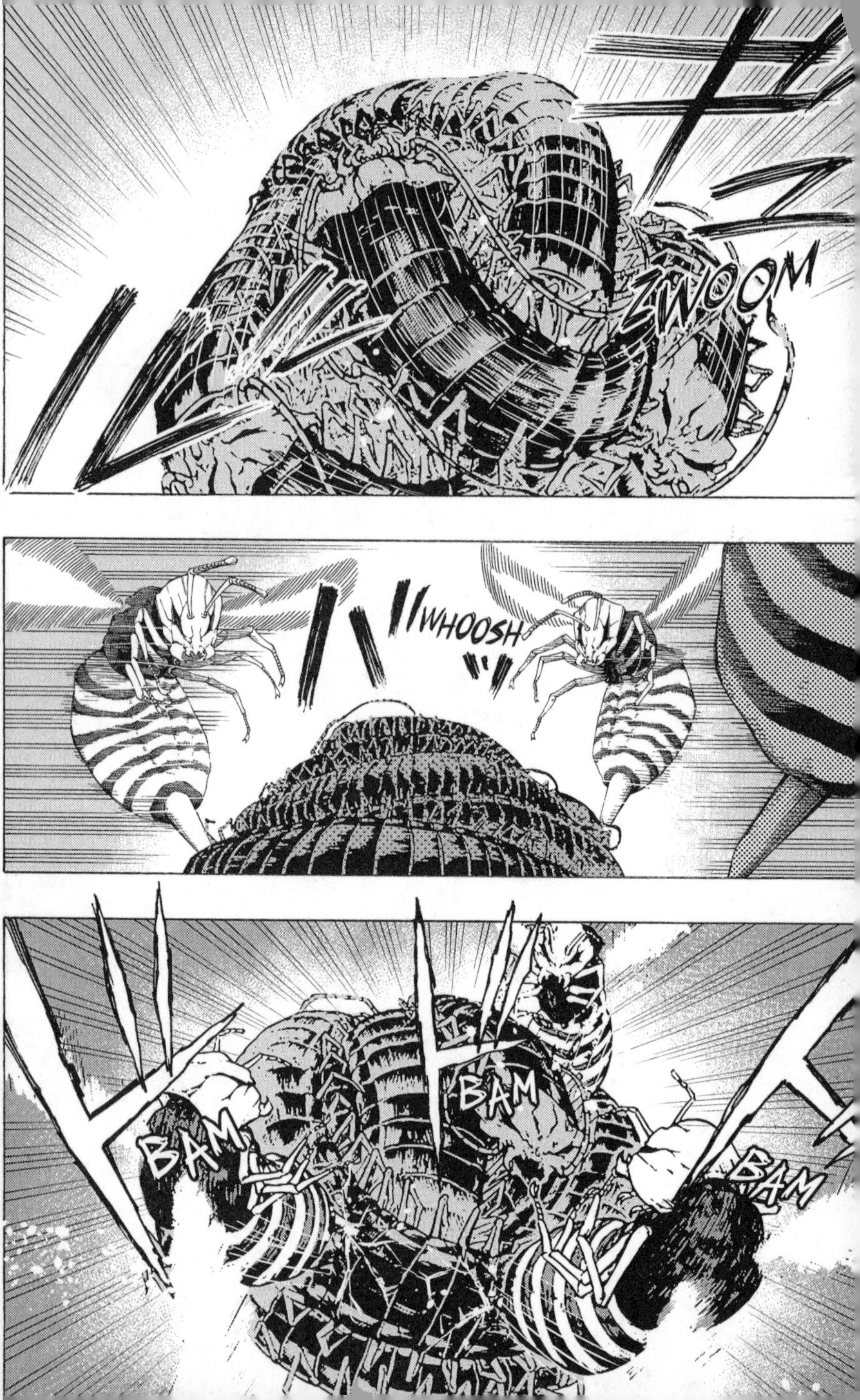
ZWOOM
WHOOSH
BAM
BAM
BAM

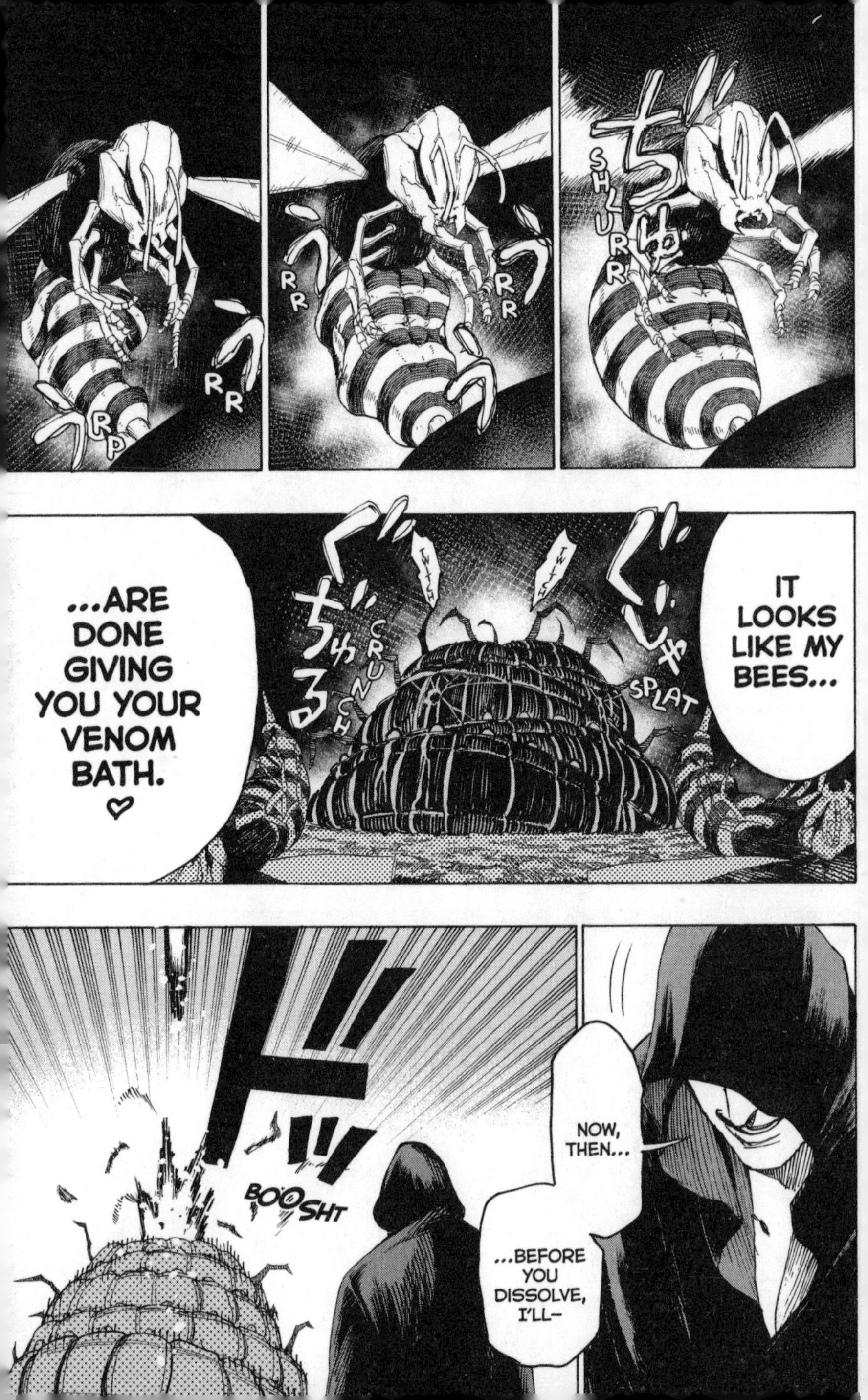
SHLURR
RR
RR
RR
RP
IT LOOKS LIKE MY BEES...
TWITCH
SPLAT
TWITCH
CRUNCH
...ARE DONE GIVING YOU YOUR VENOM BATH. ♡
NOW, THEN...
...BEFORE YOU DISSOLVE, I'LL–
BOOSHT

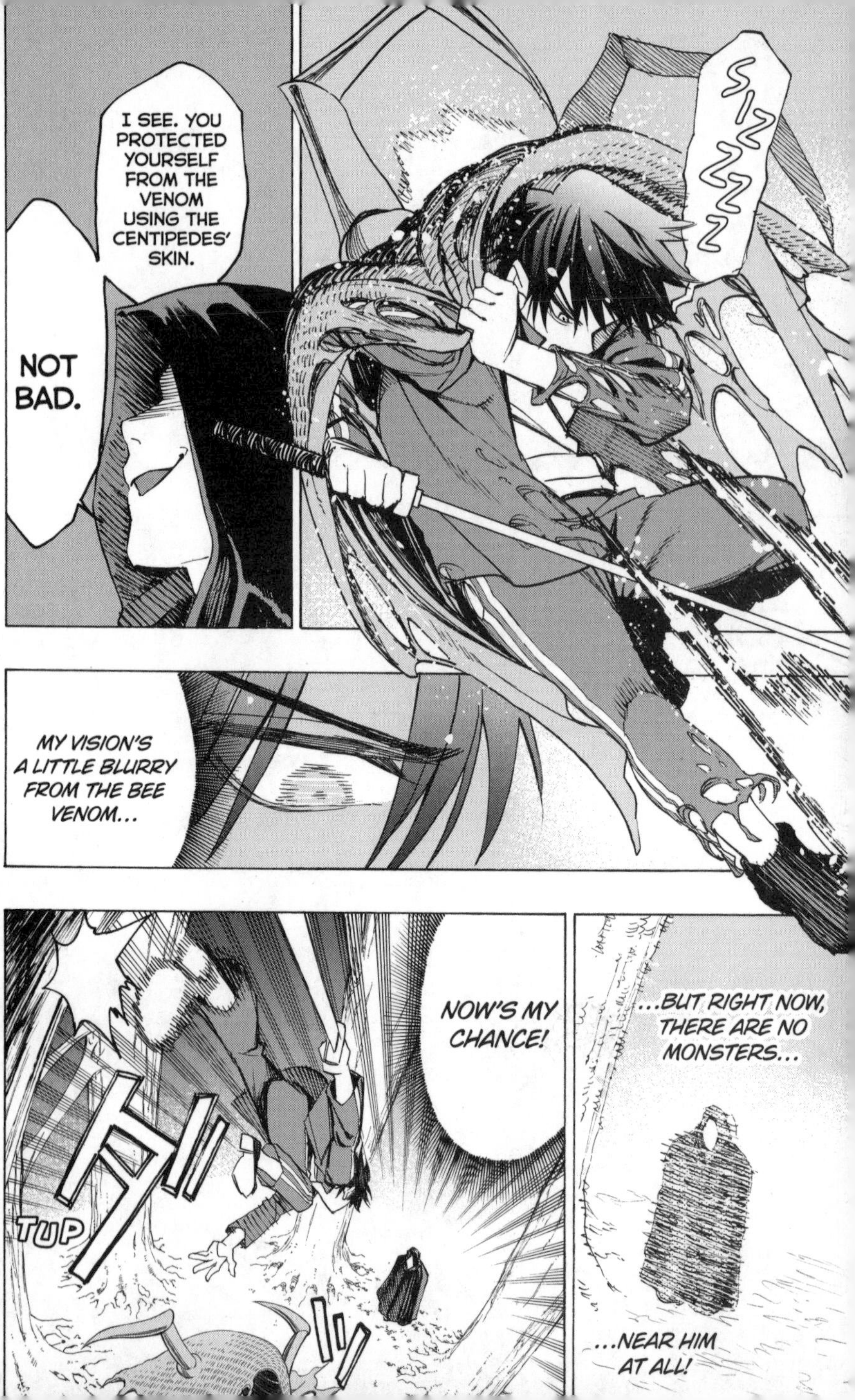
SIZZZZZ
I SEE. YOU PROTECTED YOURSELF FROM THE VENOM USING THE CENTIPEDES' SKIN.
NOT BAD.
MY VISION'S A LITTLE BLURRY FROM THE BEE VENOM...
...BUT RIGHT NOW, THERE ARE NO MONSTERS...
...NEAR HIM AT ALL!
NOW'S MY CHANCE!
TUP

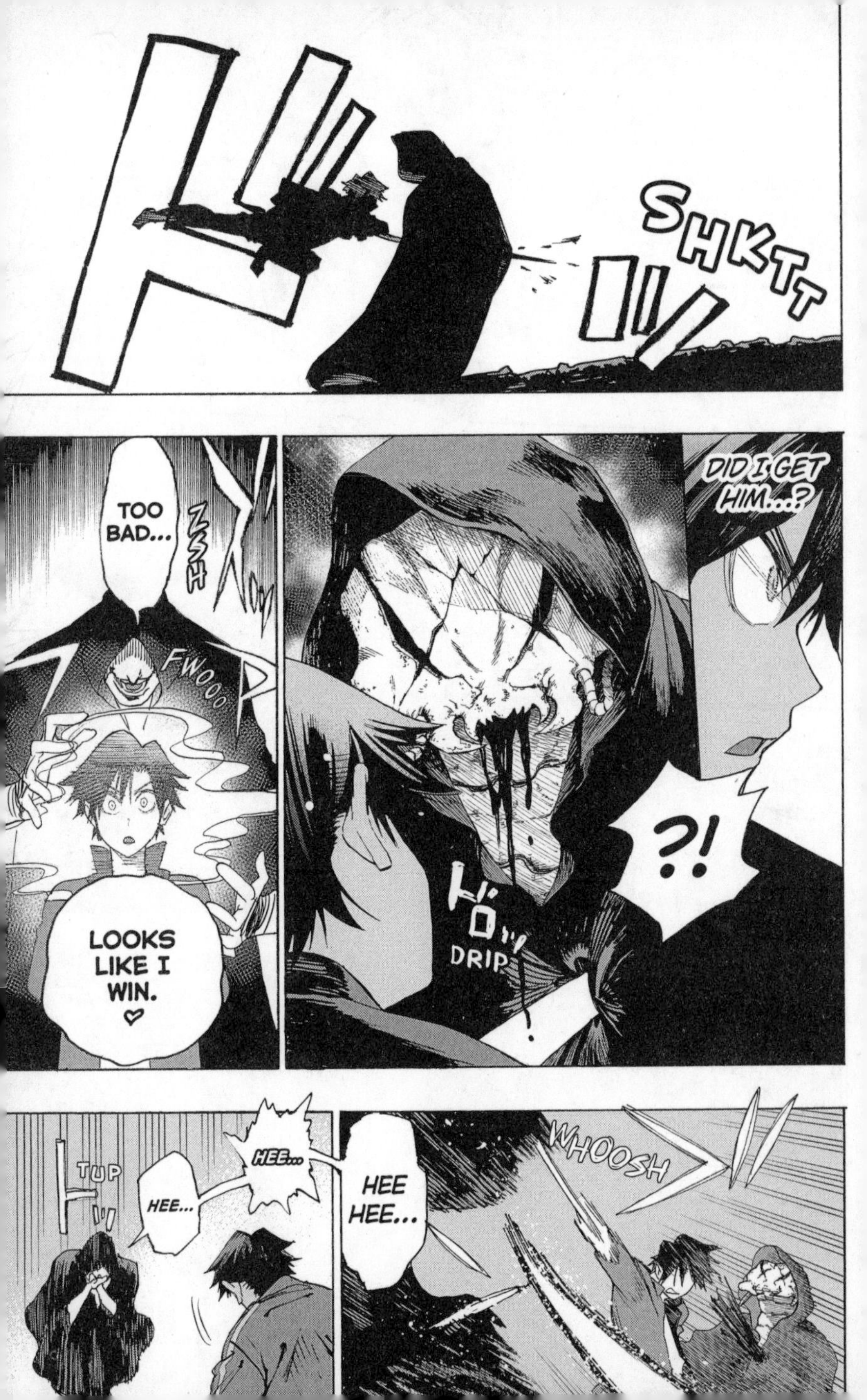
SHKTT
DID I GET HIM...?
?!
DRIP
TOO BAD...
ZWSH
FWOOO
LOOKS LIKE I WIN. ♡
WHOOSH
HEE HEE...
HEE...
HEE...
TUP

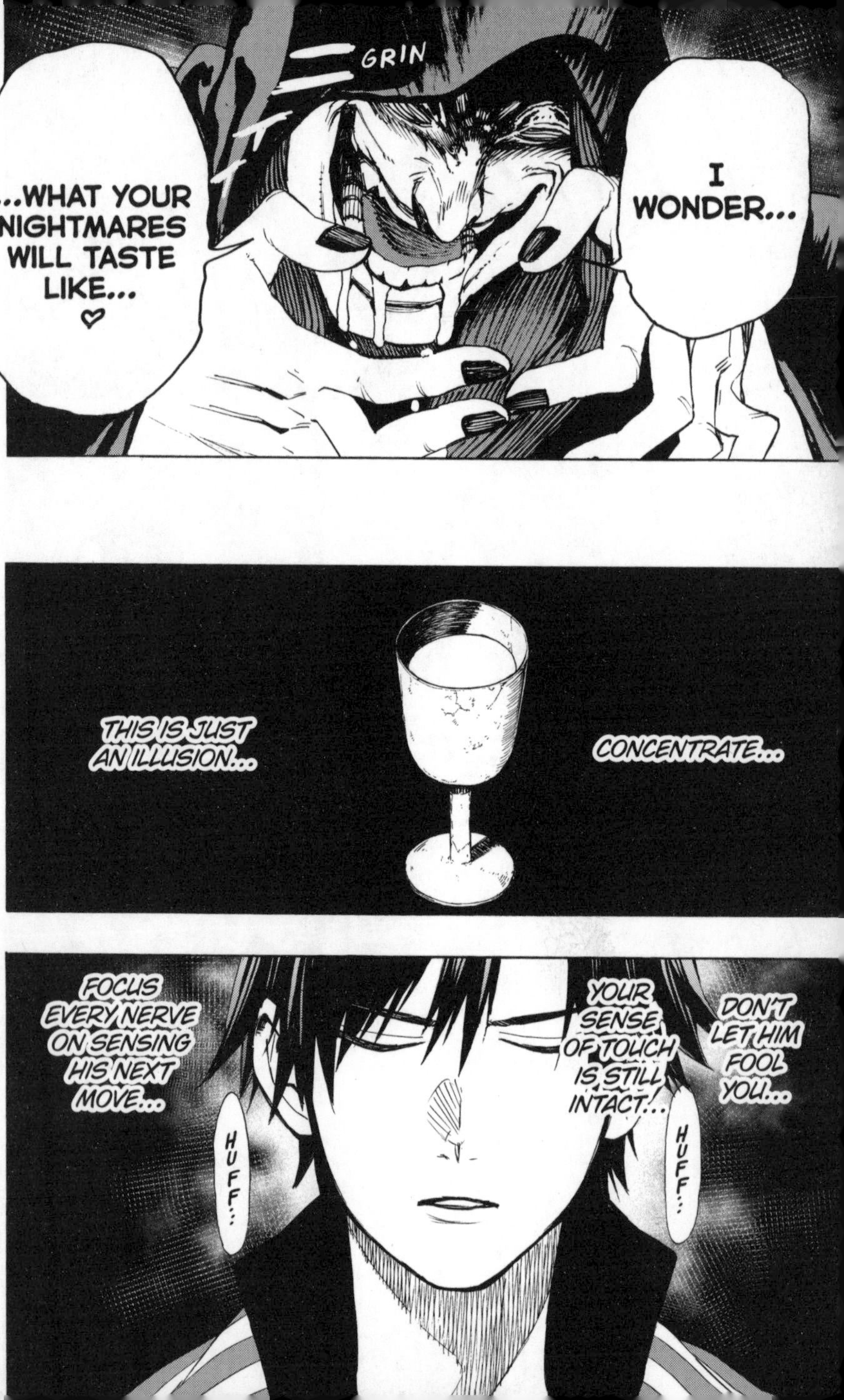
GRIN
I WONDER...
...WHAT YOUR NIGHTMARES WILL TASTE LIKE... ♡
CONCENTRATE...
THIS IS JUST AN ILLUSION...
DON'T LET HIM FOOL YOU...
YOUR SENSE OF TOUCH IS STILL INTACT!...
FOCUS EVERY NERVE ON SENSING HIS NEXT MOVE...
HUFF...
HUFF...

THIS IS AN ILLUSION.
IT ISN'T REAL.
FOCUS.
WHY'D YOU KILL ME?
IT HURTS!
WAA-AH!
I DON'T WANNA DIE...
IT'S ALL...
...YOUR FAULT...
I MISS MY WIFE...
FOCUS.
GIVE ME BACK MY SON!
AAA-AH!
FO-

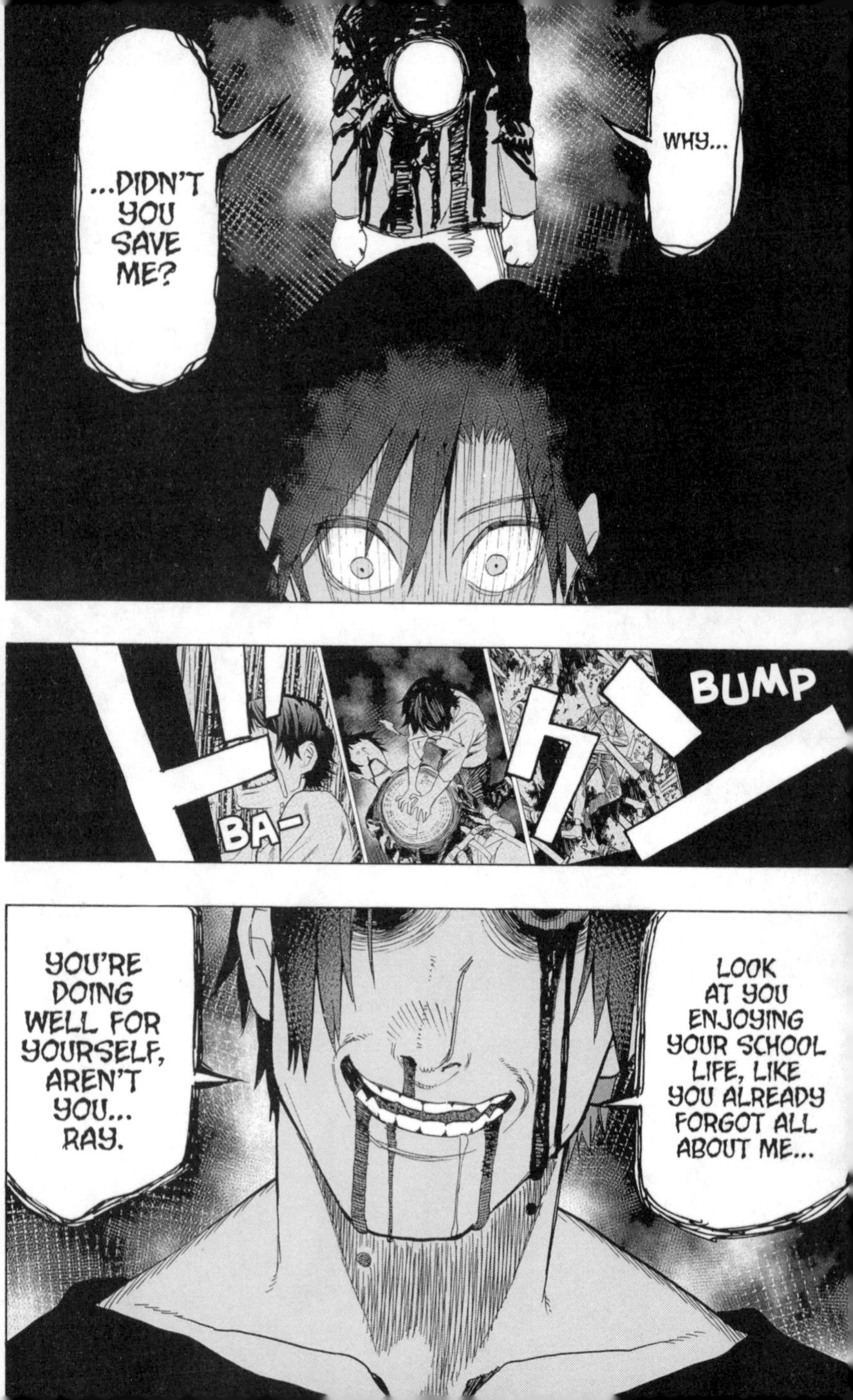
WHY...
...DIDN'T YOU SAVE ME?
BUMP
BA-
LOOK AT YOU ENJOYING YOUR SCHOOL LIFE, LIKE YOU ALREADY FORGOT ALL ABOUT ME...
YOU'RE DOING WELL FOR YOURSELF, AREN'T YOU... RAY.

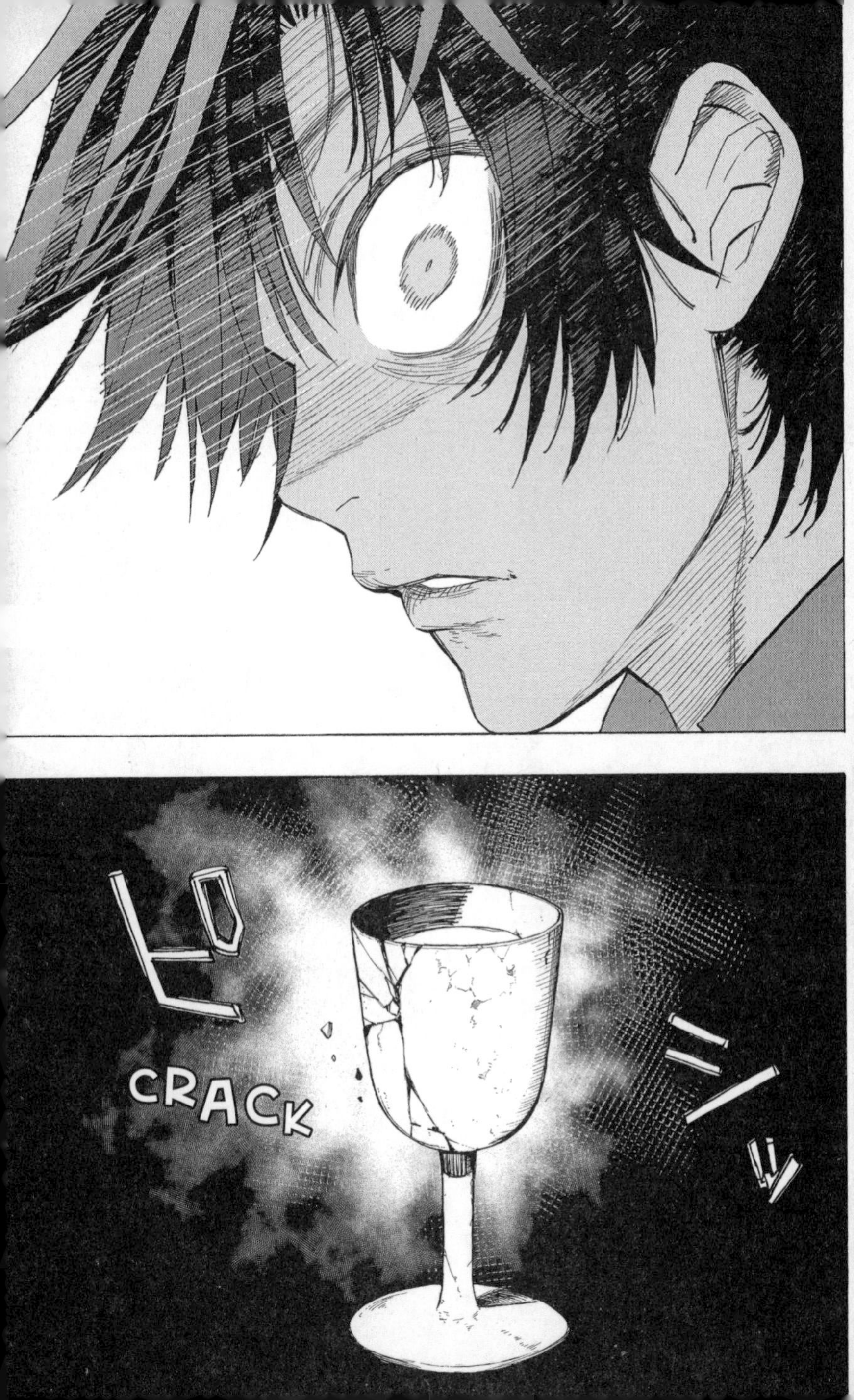
CRACK

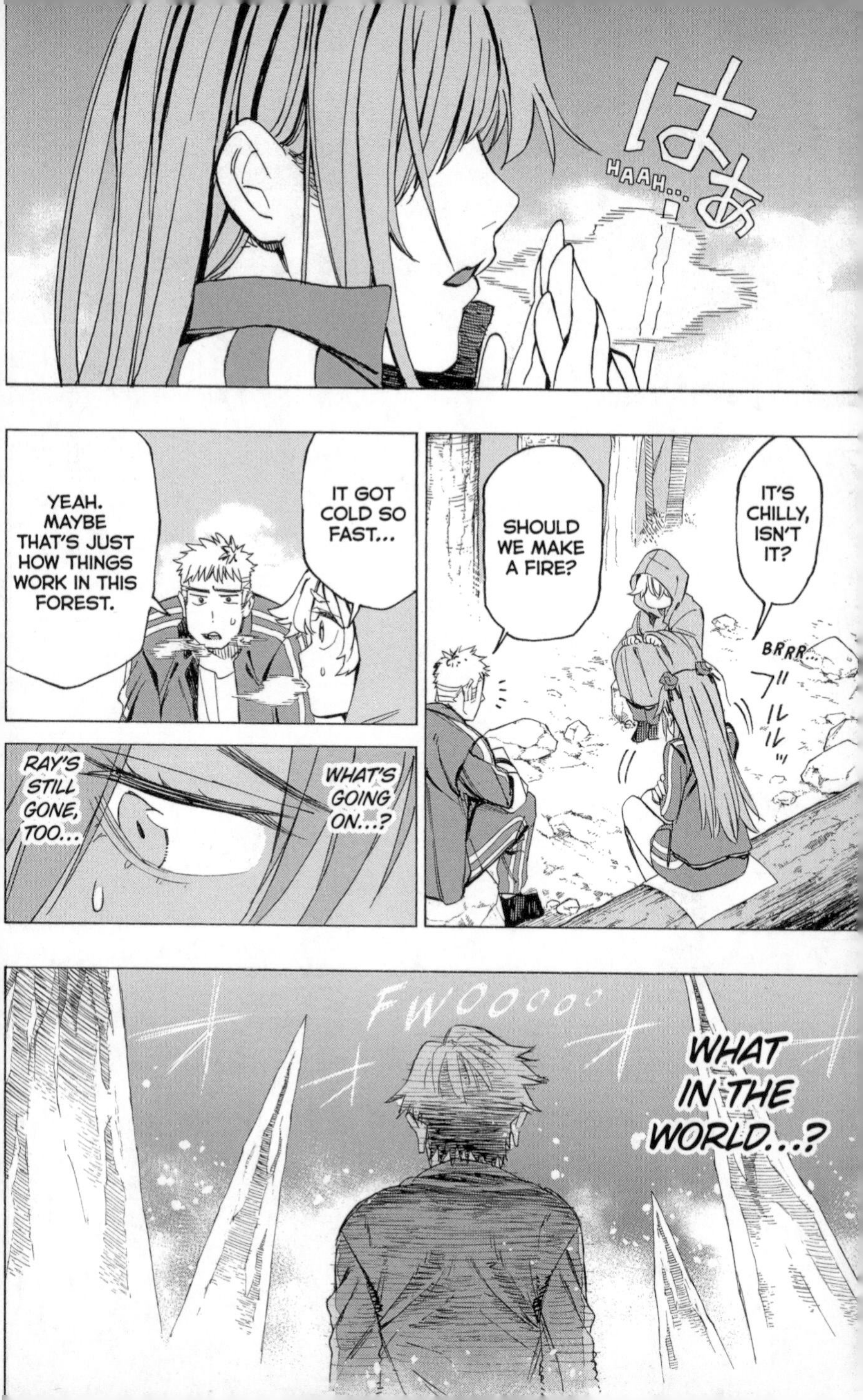
はあ
HAAAH...
IT'S CHILLY, ISN'T IT?
SHOULD WE MAKE A FIRE?
BRRR...
ブルルッ
IT GOT COLD SO FAST...
YEAH. MAYBE THAT'S JUST HOW THINGS WORK IN THIS FOREST.
WHAT'S GOING ON...?
RAY'S STILL GONE, TOO...
FWOOOOO
WHAT IN THE WORLD...?

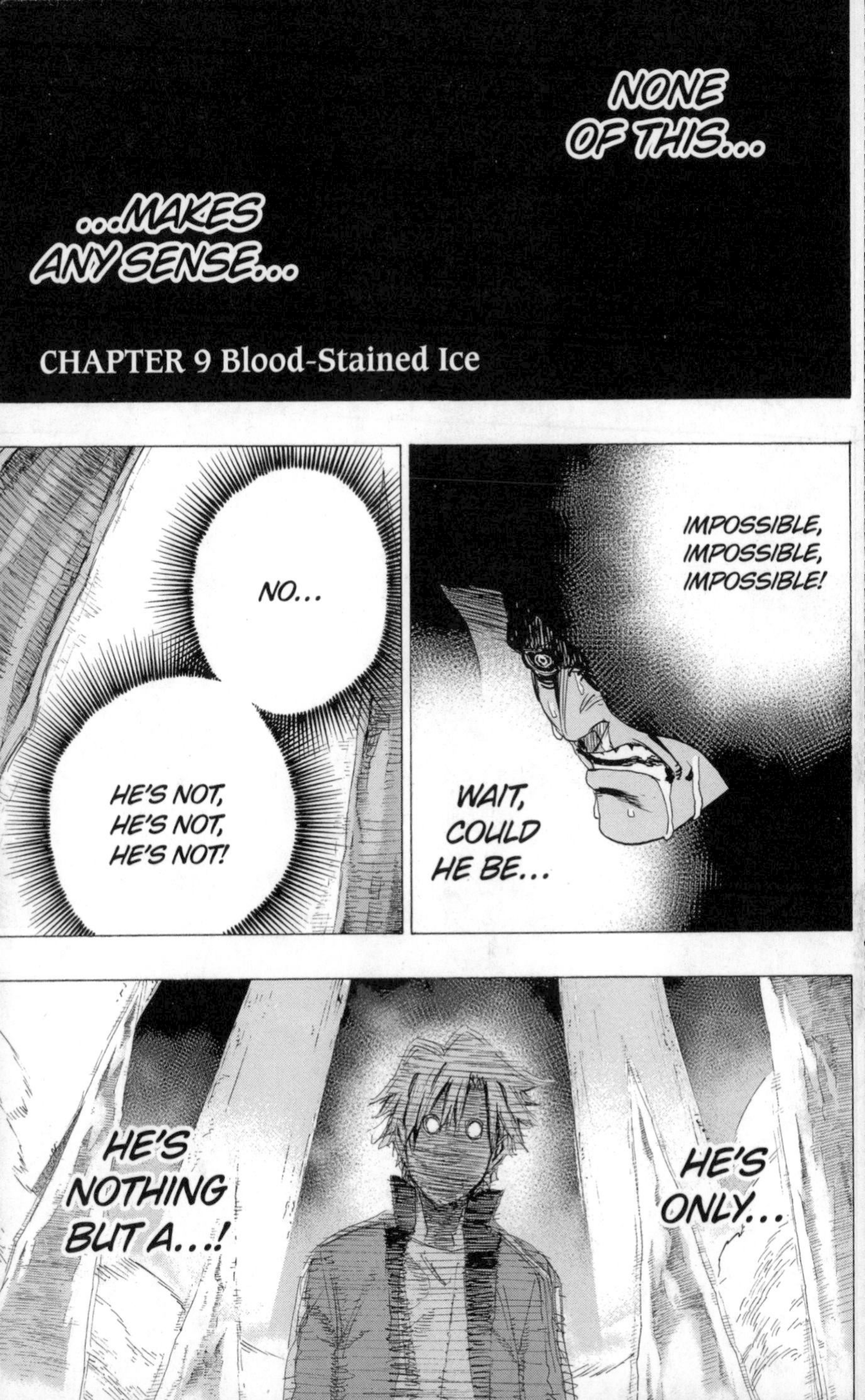
NONE OF THIS...
...MAKES ANY SENSE...
CHAPTER 9 Blood-Stained Ice
IMPOSSIBLE, IMPOSSIBLE, IMPOSSIBLE!
WAIT, COULD HE BE...
NO...
HE'S NOT, HE'S NOT, HE'S NOT!
HE'S ONLY...
HE'S NOTHING BUT A...!

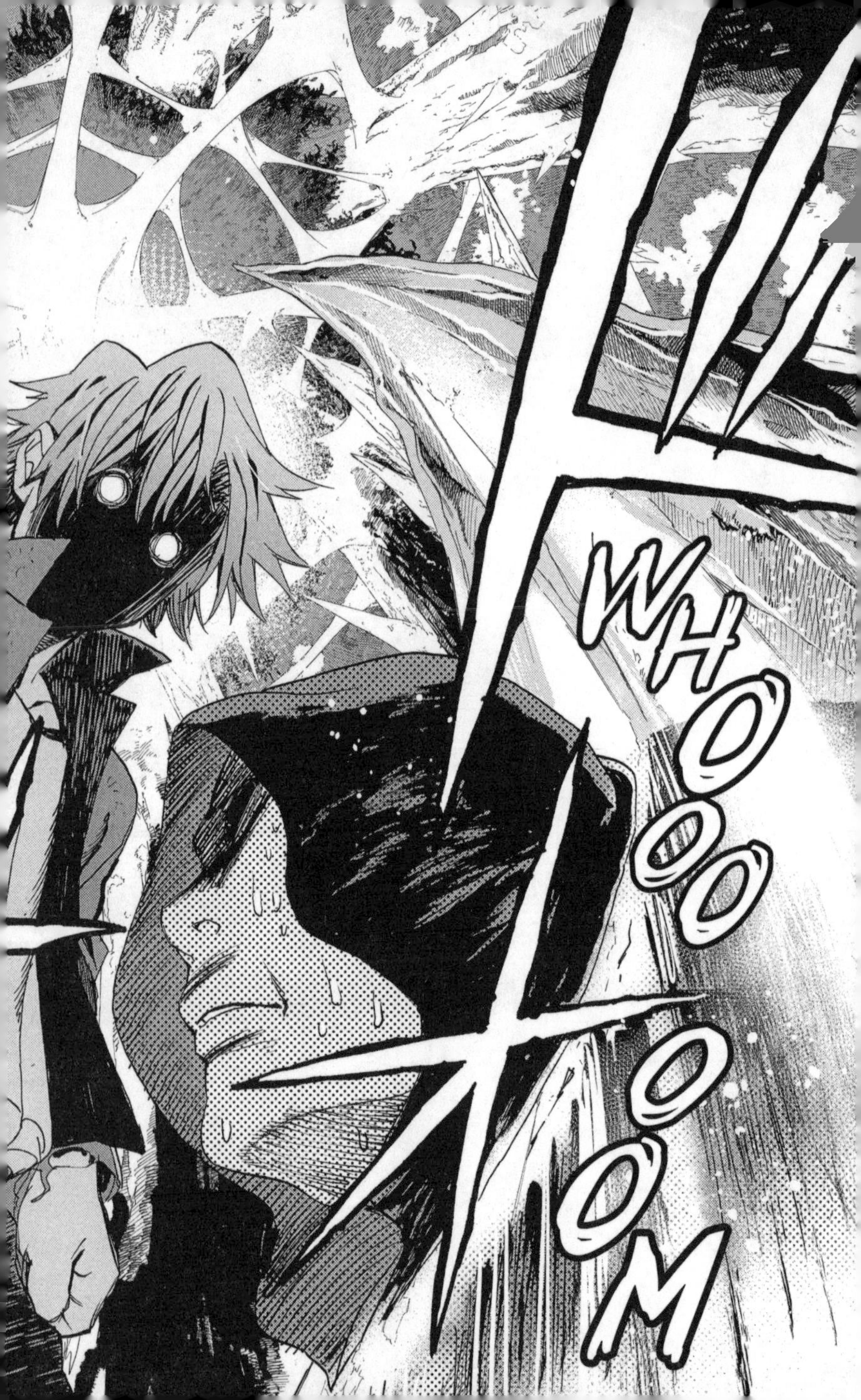
WHOOOOOOM

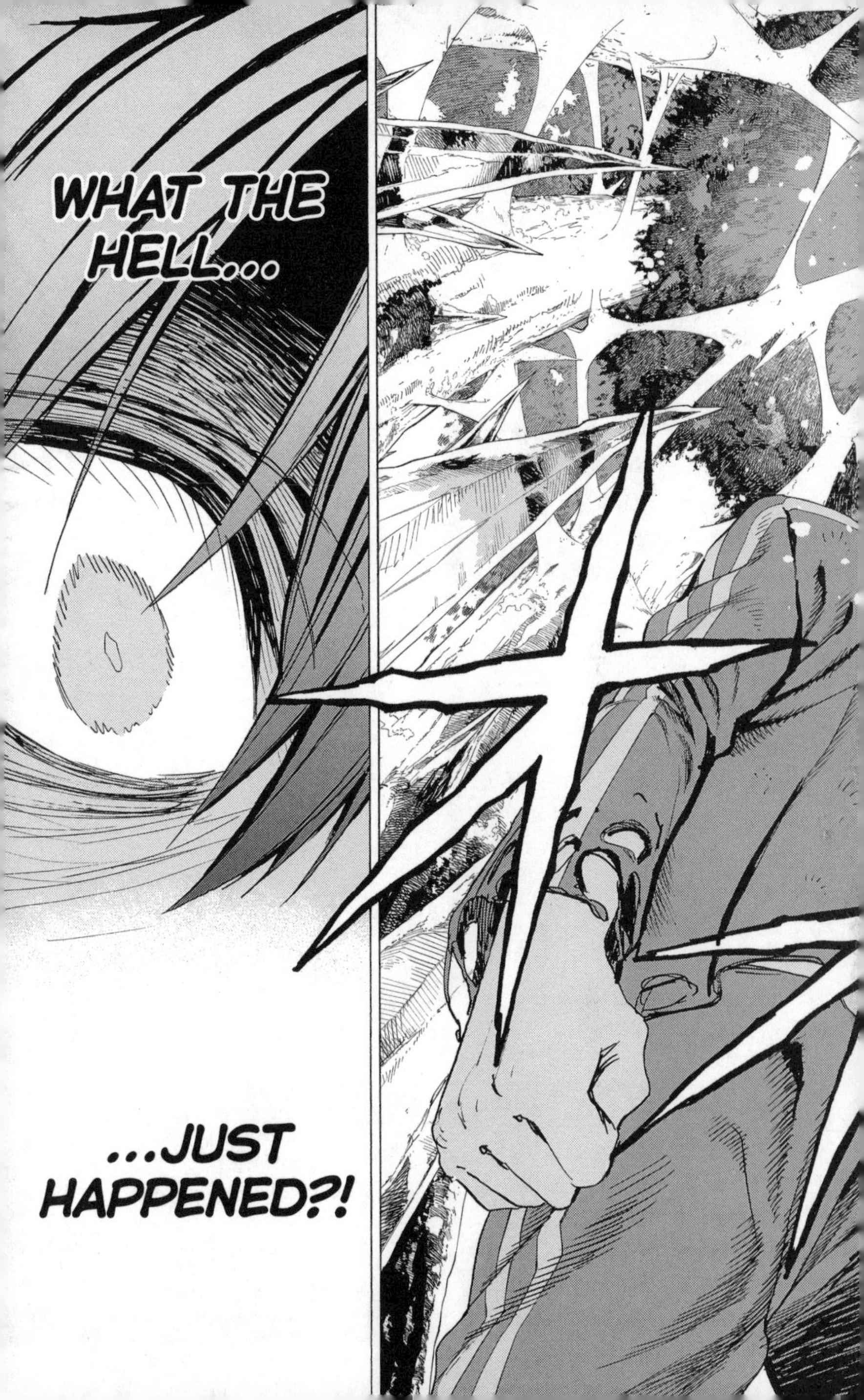
WHAT THE HELL...
...JUST HAPPENED?!

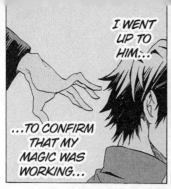

FWOOO
TUP
THAT'S RIGHT... EARLIER...
GRIN
I WENT UP TO HIM...
...TO CONFIRM THAT MY MAGIC WAS WORKING...
THAT'S WHEN I FELT THIS OVERPOWERING DARKNESS COME OVER ME...
IT WAS ONLY A SECOND...
...THE BLINK OF AN EYE.
WHEN I CAME TO...
...THE ENTIRE WORLD...
...HAD TURNED TO ICE.
THERE'S ONLY ONE PERSON...
YOU...
YOU'RE...
...WHO COULD PULL OFF A FEAT LIKE THAT.

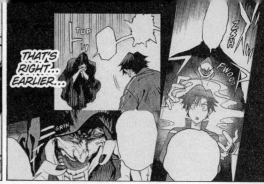

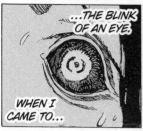

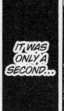

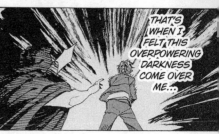

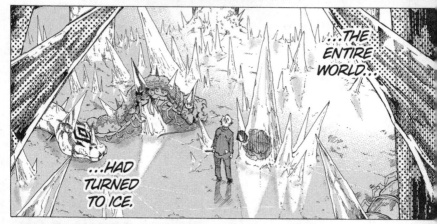

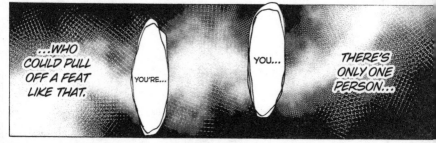

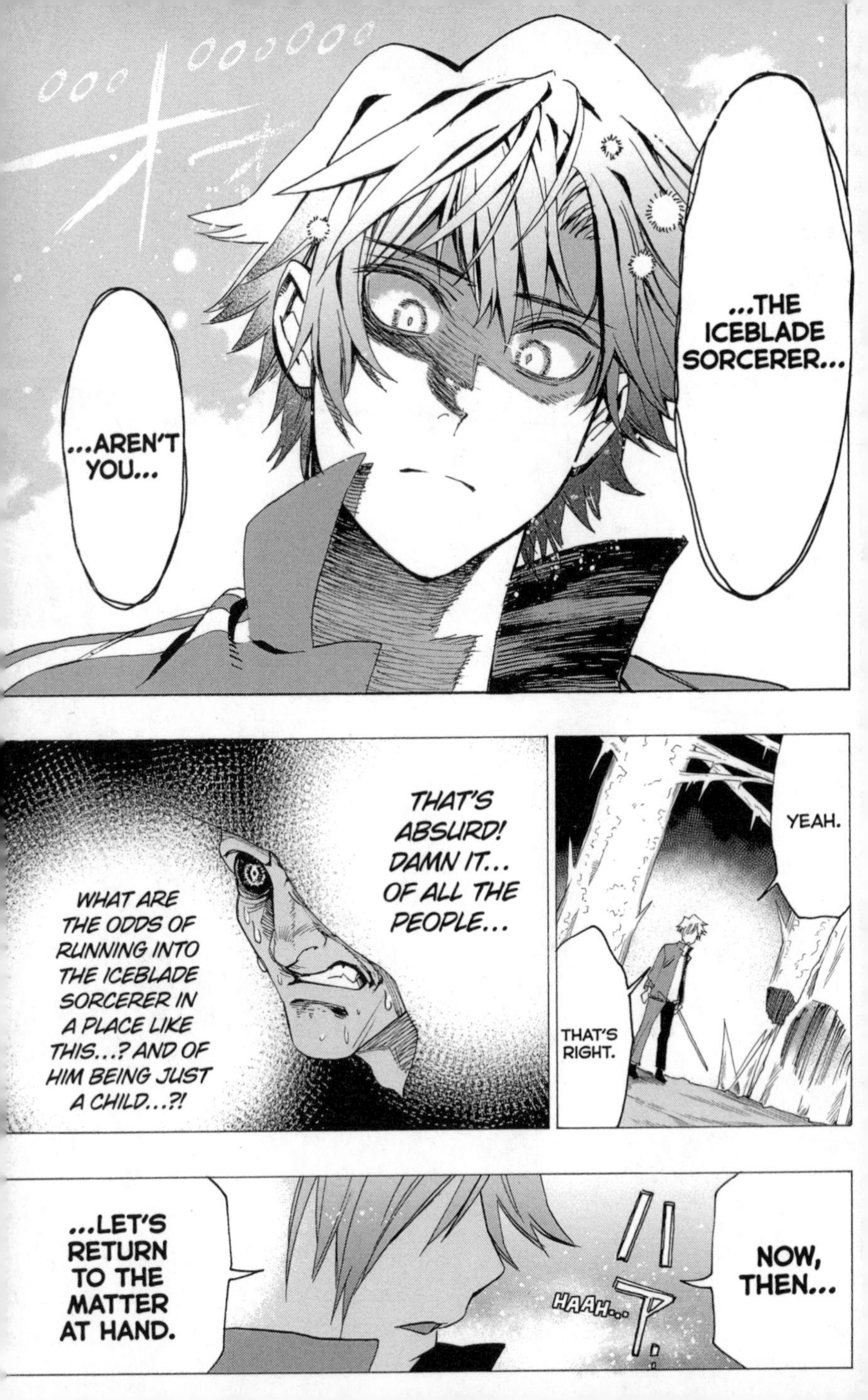
...THE ICEBLADE SORCERER...
...AREN'T YOU...
YEAH.
THAT'S RIGHT.
THAT'S ABSURD! DAMN IT... OF ALL THE PEOPLE...
WHAT ARE THE ODDS OF RUNNING INTO THE ICEBLADE SORCERER IN A PLACE LIKE THIS...? AND OF HIM BEING JUST A CHILD...?!
NOW, THEN...
HAAH...
...LET'S RETURN TO THE MATTER AT HAND.

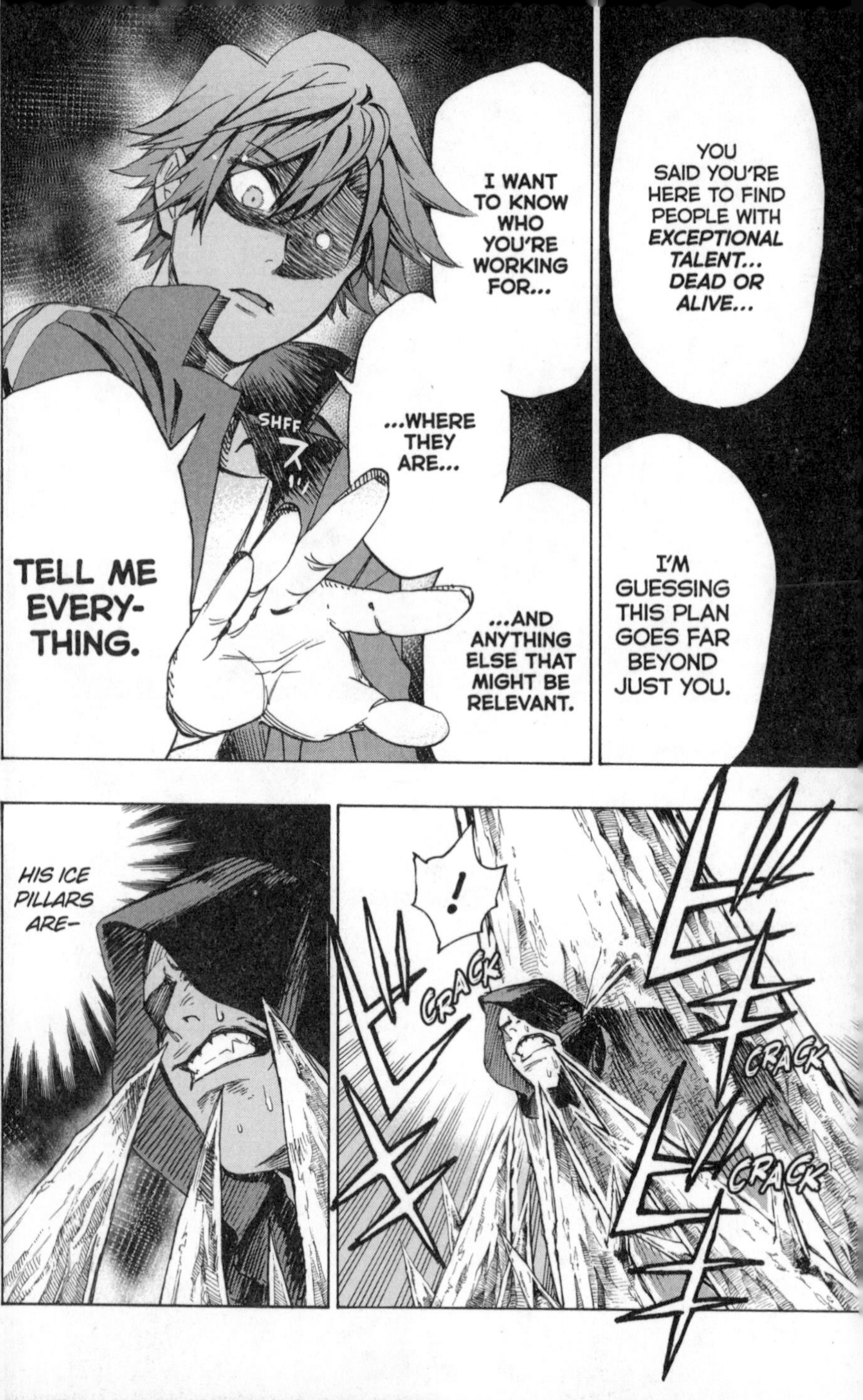
YOU SAID YOU'RE HERE TO FIND PEOPLE WITH *EXCEPTIONAL TALENT... DEAD OR ALIVE...*
I'M GUESSING THIS PLAN GOES FAR BEYOND JUST YOU.
I WANT TO KNOW WHO YOU'RE WORKING FOR...
...WHERE THEY ARE...
...AND ANYTHING ELSE THAT MIGHT BE RELEVANT.
SHFF
TELL ME EVERY-THING.
!
CRACK
CRACK
CRACK
HIS ICE PILLARS ARE-

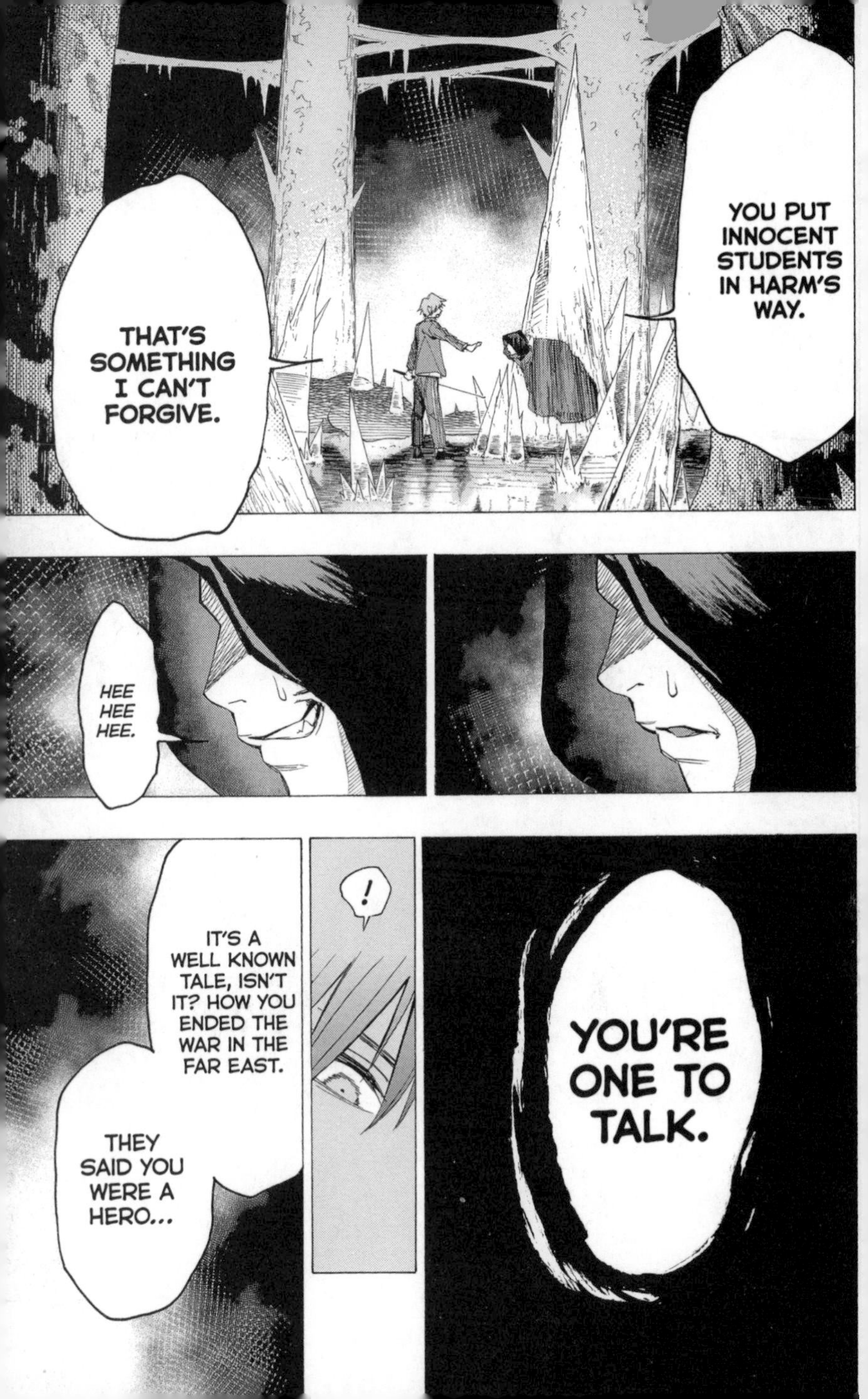
YOU PUT INNOCENT STUDENTS IN HARM'S WAY.
THAT'S SOMETHING I CAN'T FORGIVE.
HEE HEE HEE.
YOU'RE ONE TO TALK.
!
IT'S A WELL KNOWN TALE, ISN'T IT? HOW YOU ENDED THE WAR IN THE FAR EAST.
THEY SAID YOU WERE A HERO...

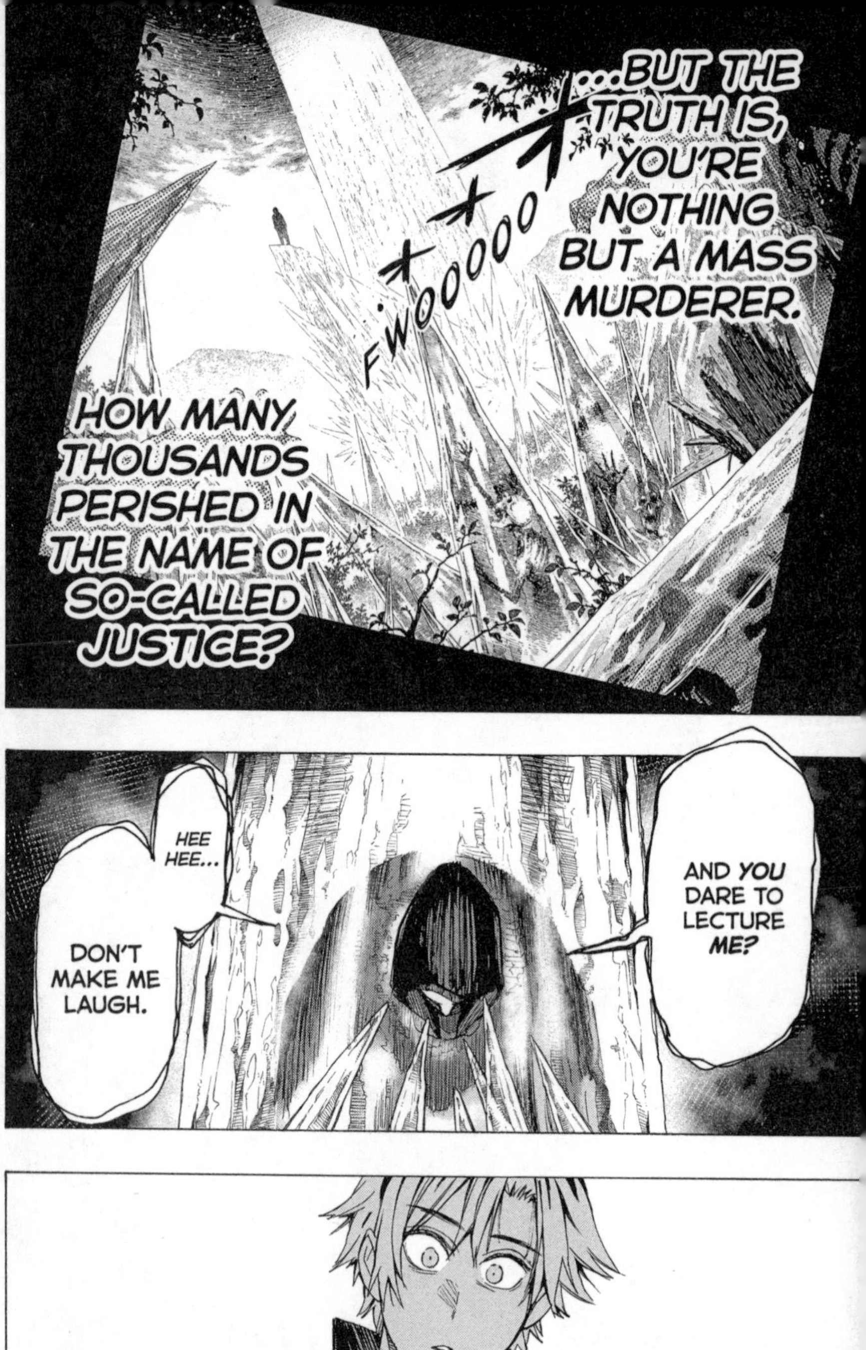
...BUT THE TRUTH IS, YOU'RE NOTHING BUT A MASS MURDERER.
FWOOOOO
HOW MANY THOUSANDS PERISHED IN THE NAME OF SO-CALLED JUSTICE?
AND *YOU* DARE TO LECTURE *ME*?
HEE HEE...
DON'T MAKE ME LAUGH.

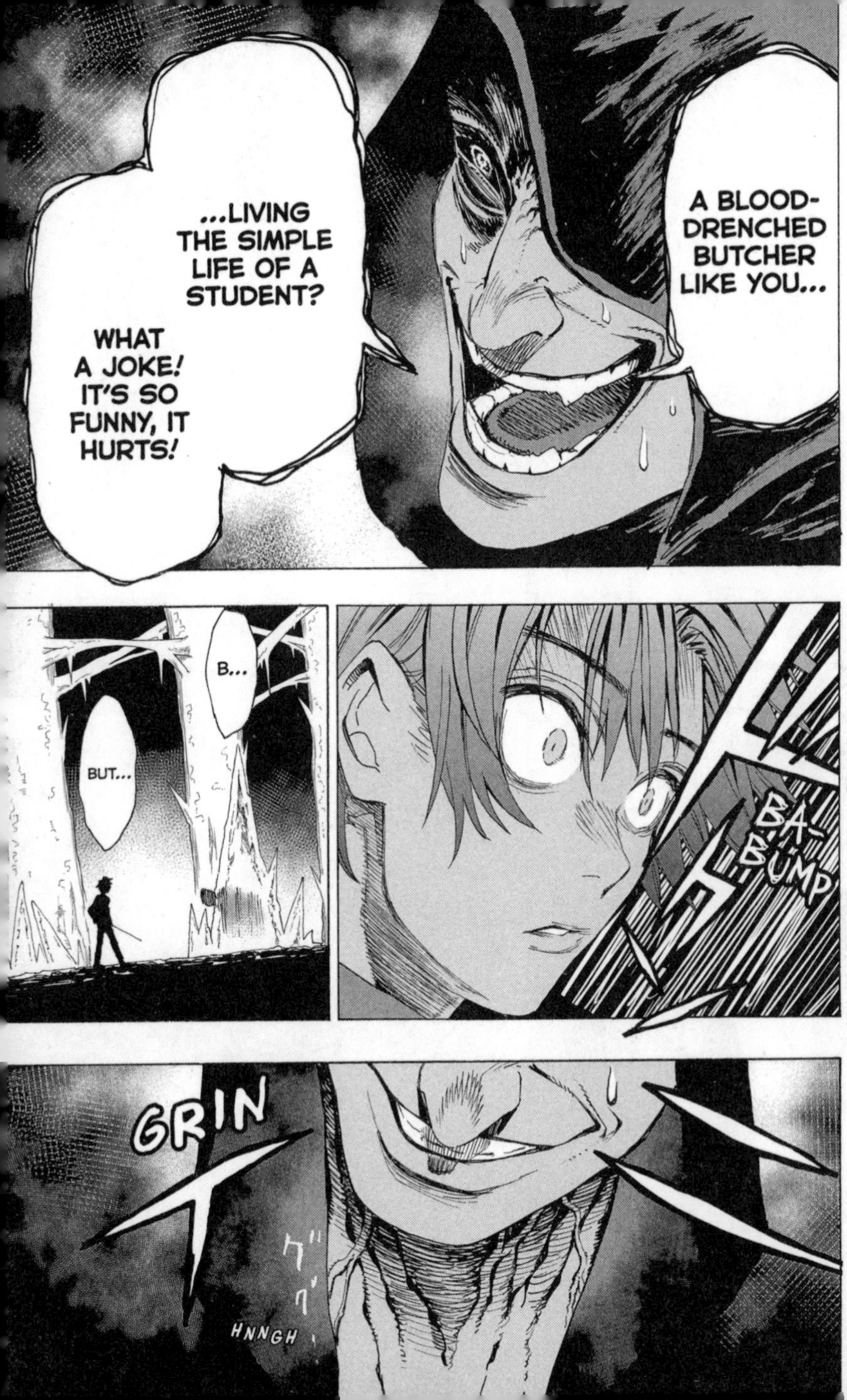
A BLOOD-DRENCHED BUTCHER LIKE YOU...
...LIVING THE SIMPLE LIFE OF A STUDENT?
WHAT A JOKE! IT'S SO FUNNY, IT HURTS!
BA-BUMP
B...
BUT...
GRIN
HNNGH

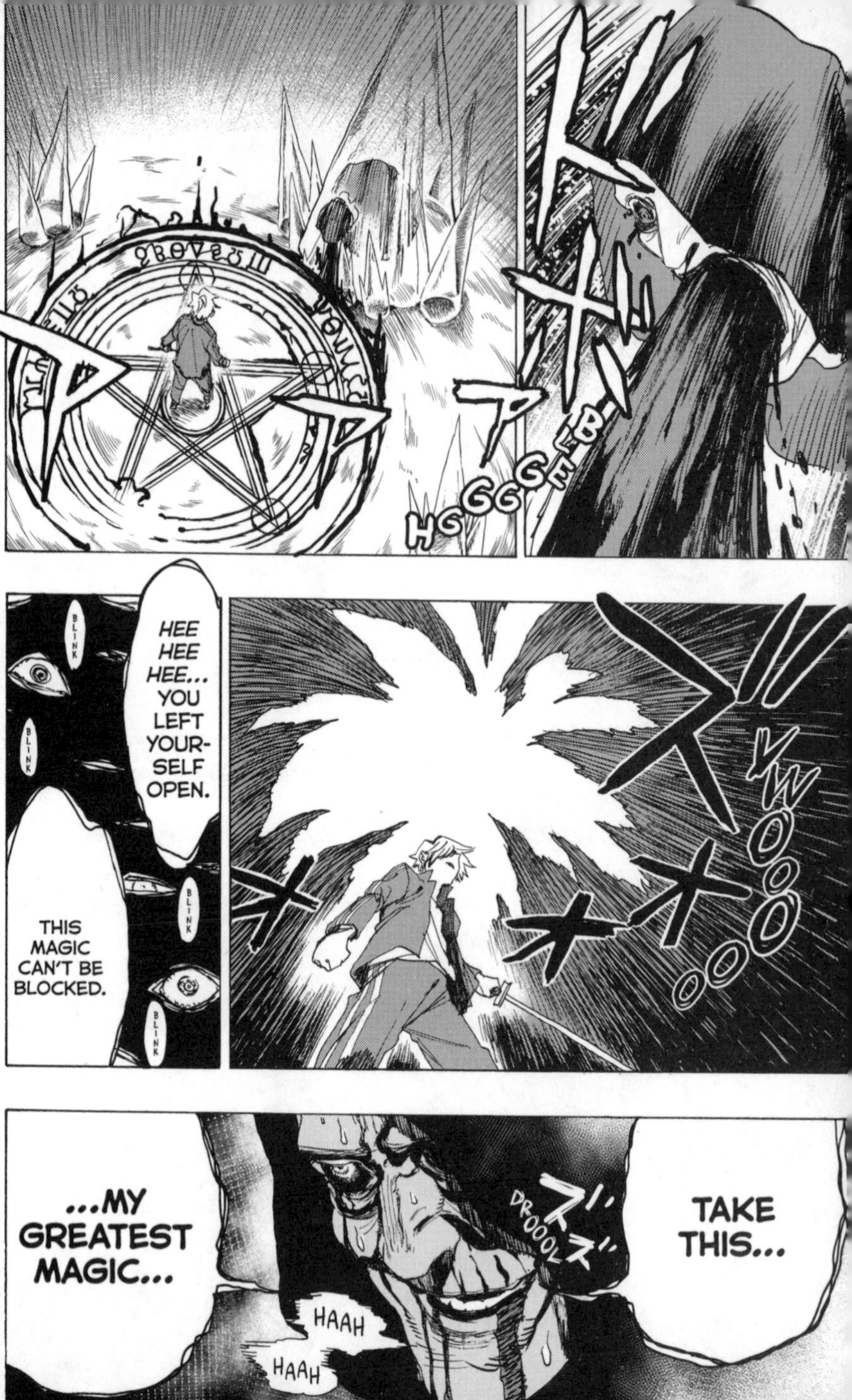
BLEGGGGH
VWOOOOO
BLINK
BLINK
HEE HEE HEE... YOU LEFT YOUR-SELF OPEN.
THIS MAGIC CAN'T BE BLOCKED.
BLINK
BLINK
TAKE THIS...
DROOOL
...MY GREATEST MAGIC...
HAAH
HAAH

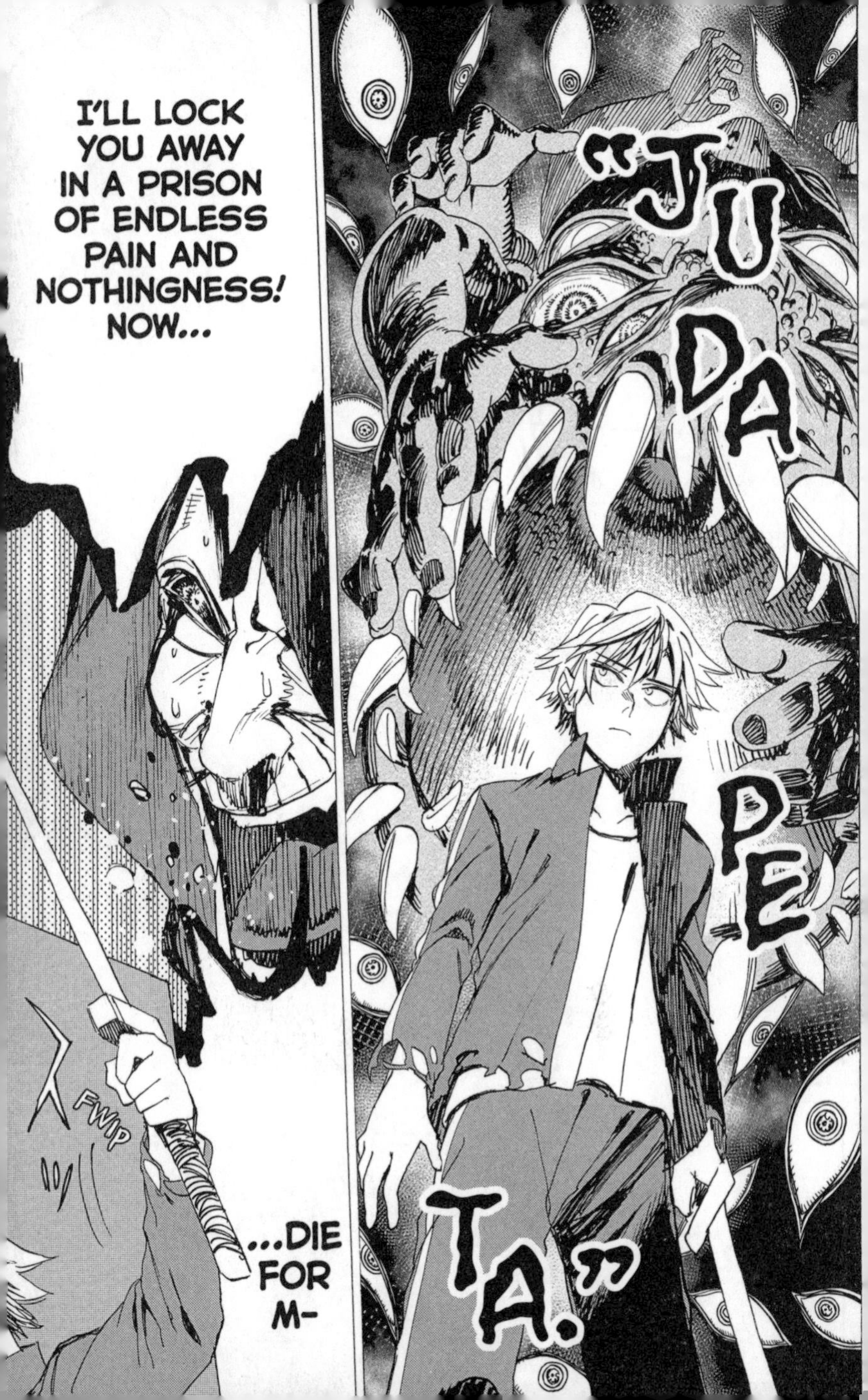
"JU
DA
PE
TA."
I'LL LOCK YOU AWAY IN A PRISON OF ENDLESS PAIN AND NOTHINGNESS! NOW...
FWIP
...DIE FOR M-

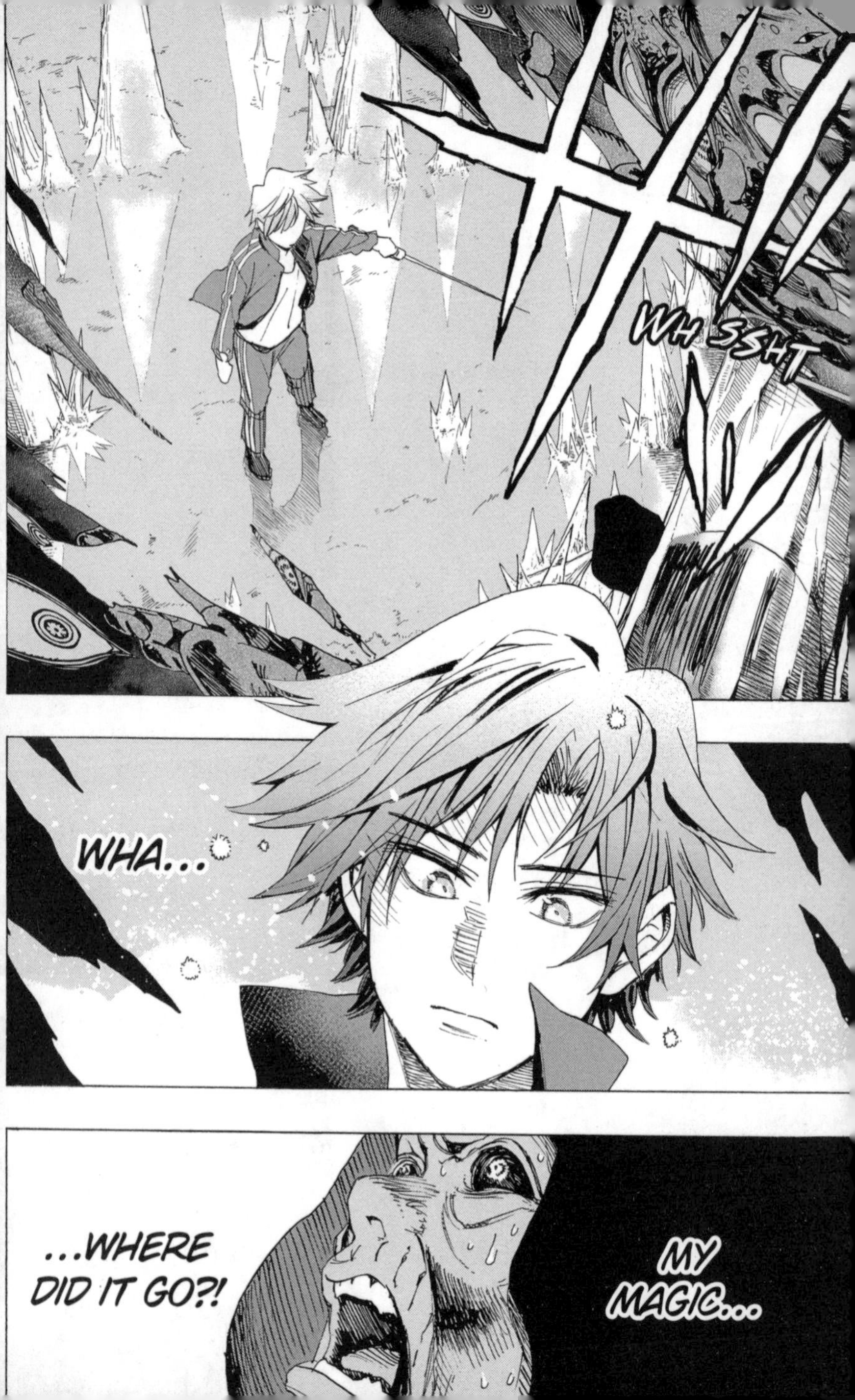
WH SSHT
WHA...
MY MAGIC...
...WHERE DID IT GO?!

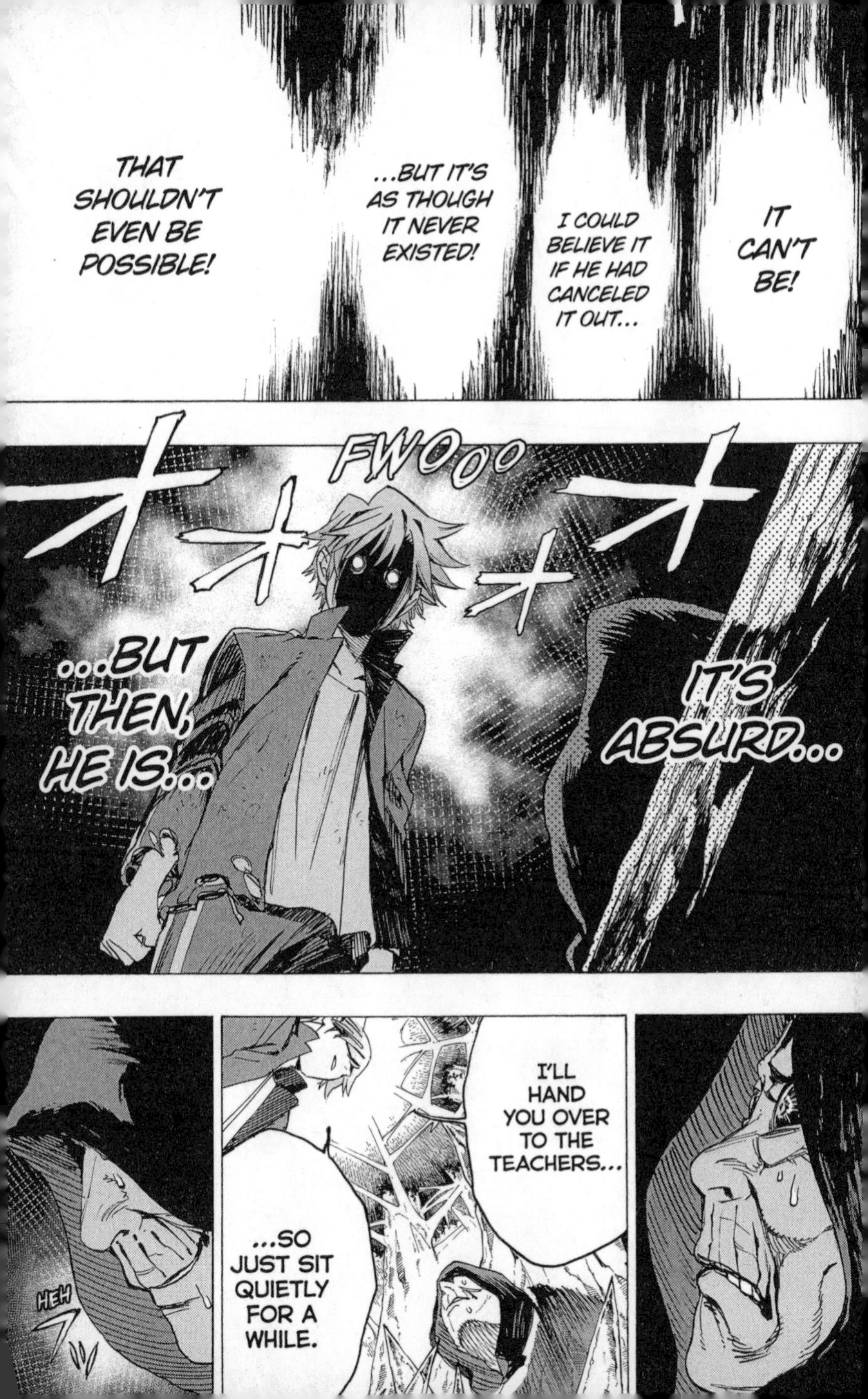
IT CAN'T BE!
I COULD BELIEVE IT IF HE HAD CANCELED IT OUT...
...BUT IT'S AS THOUGH IT NEVER EXISTED!
THAT SHOULDN'T EVEN BE POSSIBLE!
FWOOOO
IT'S ABSURD...
...BUT THEN, HE IS...
I'LL HAND YOU OVER TO THE TEACHERS...
...SO JUST SIT QUIETLY FOR A WHILE.
HEH

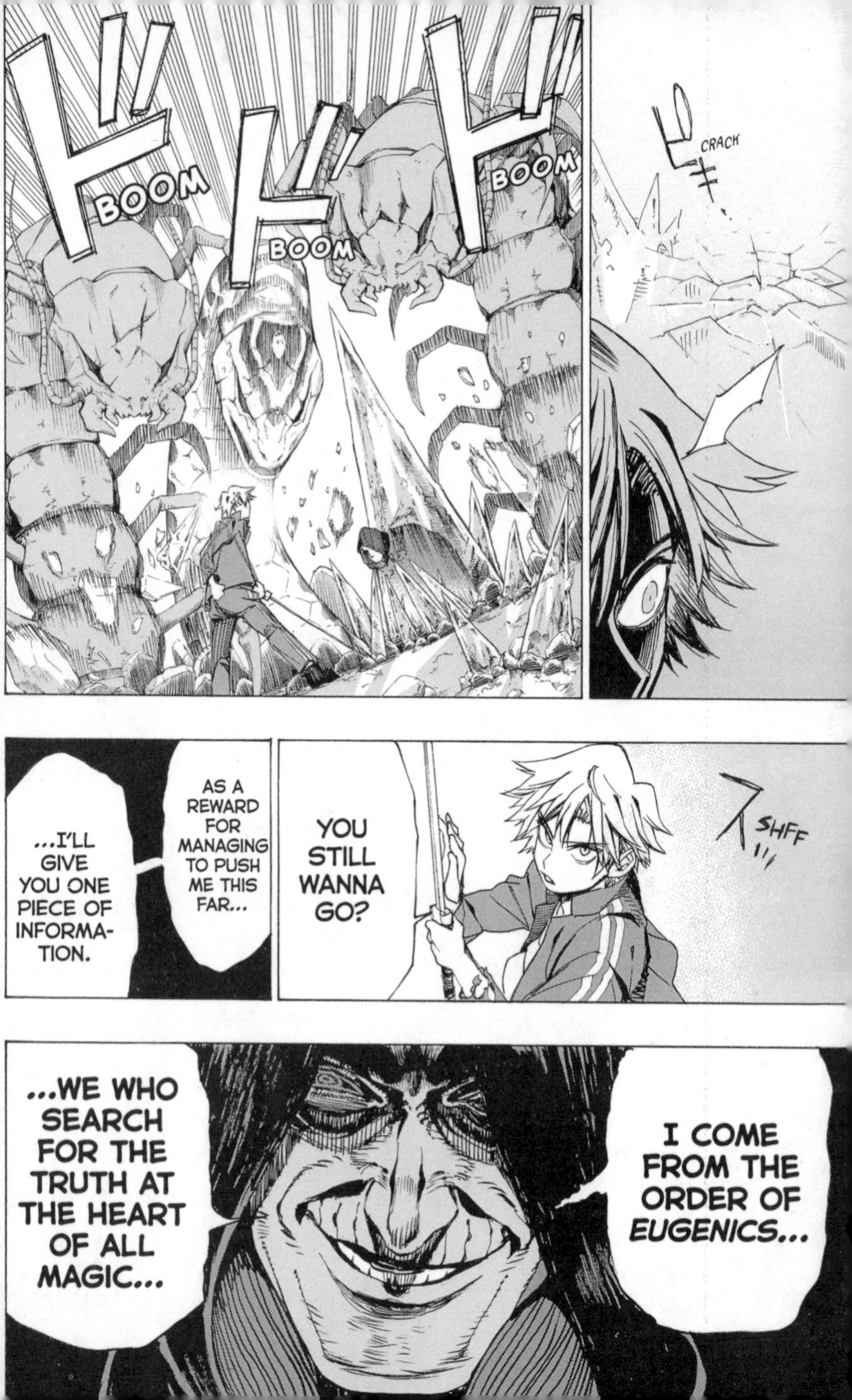
CRACK
BOOM
BOOM
BOOM
SHFF
YOU STILL WANNA GO?
AS A REWARD FOR MANAGING TO PUSH ME THIS FAR...
...I'LL GIVE YOU ONE PIECE OF INFORMA-TION.
I COME FROM THE ORDER OF EUGENICS...
...WE WHO SEARCH FOR THE TRUTH AT THE HEART OF ALL MAGIC...

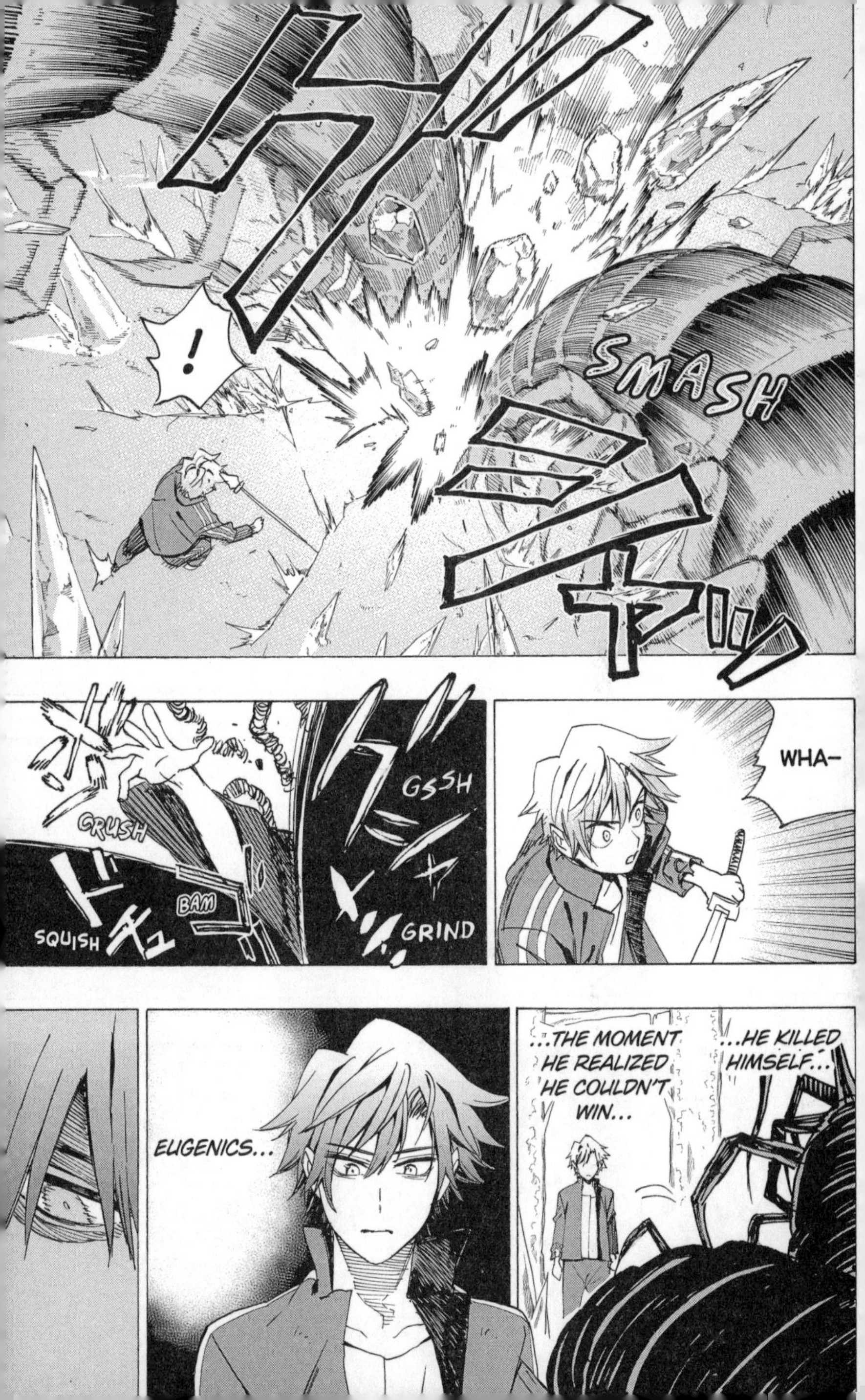
!
SMASH
WHA–
GSSH
GRIND
CRUSH
BAM
SQUISH
…THE MOMENT HE REALIZED HE COULDN'T WIN…
…HE KILLED HIMSELF…
EUGENICS…

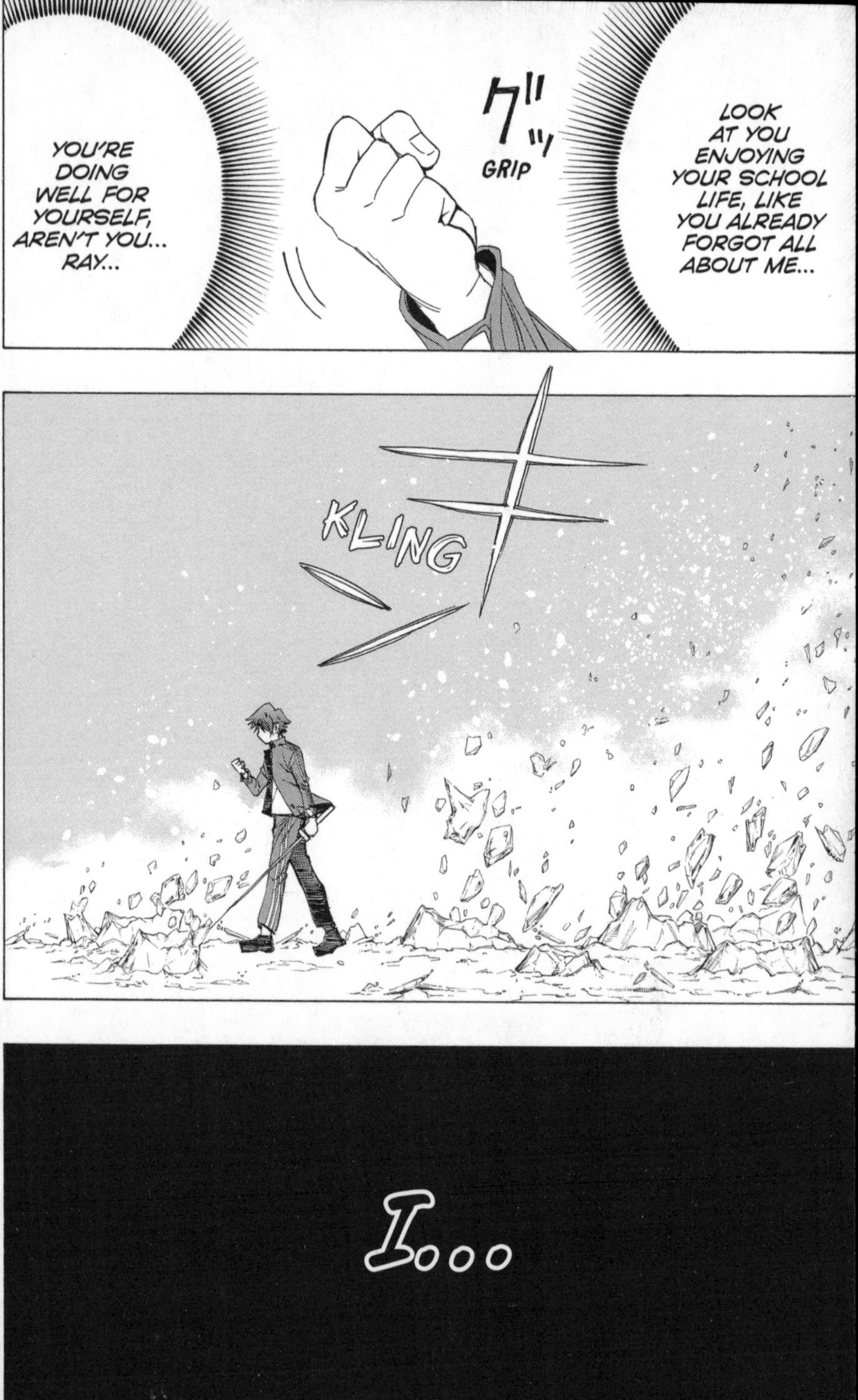
LOOK AT YOU ENJOYING YOUR SCHOOL LIFE, LIKE YOU ALREADY FORGOT ALL ABOUT ME...
グッ
GRIP
YOU'RE DOING WELL FOR YOURSELF, AREN'T YOU... RAY...
KLING
Iooo

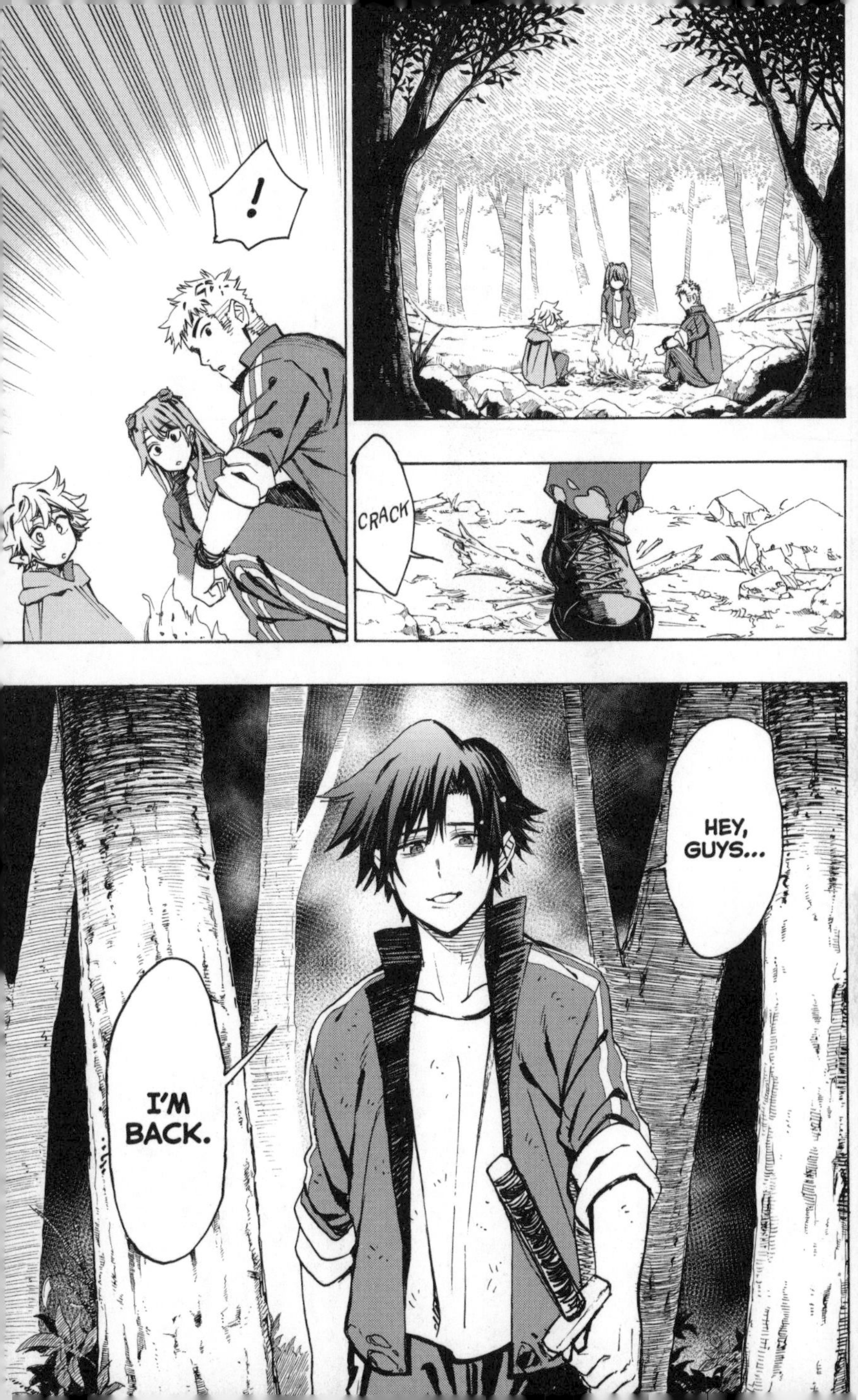
CRACK
!
HEY, GUYS...
I'M BACK.

The **ICEBLADE**
SORCERER
Shall RULE
the
WORLD

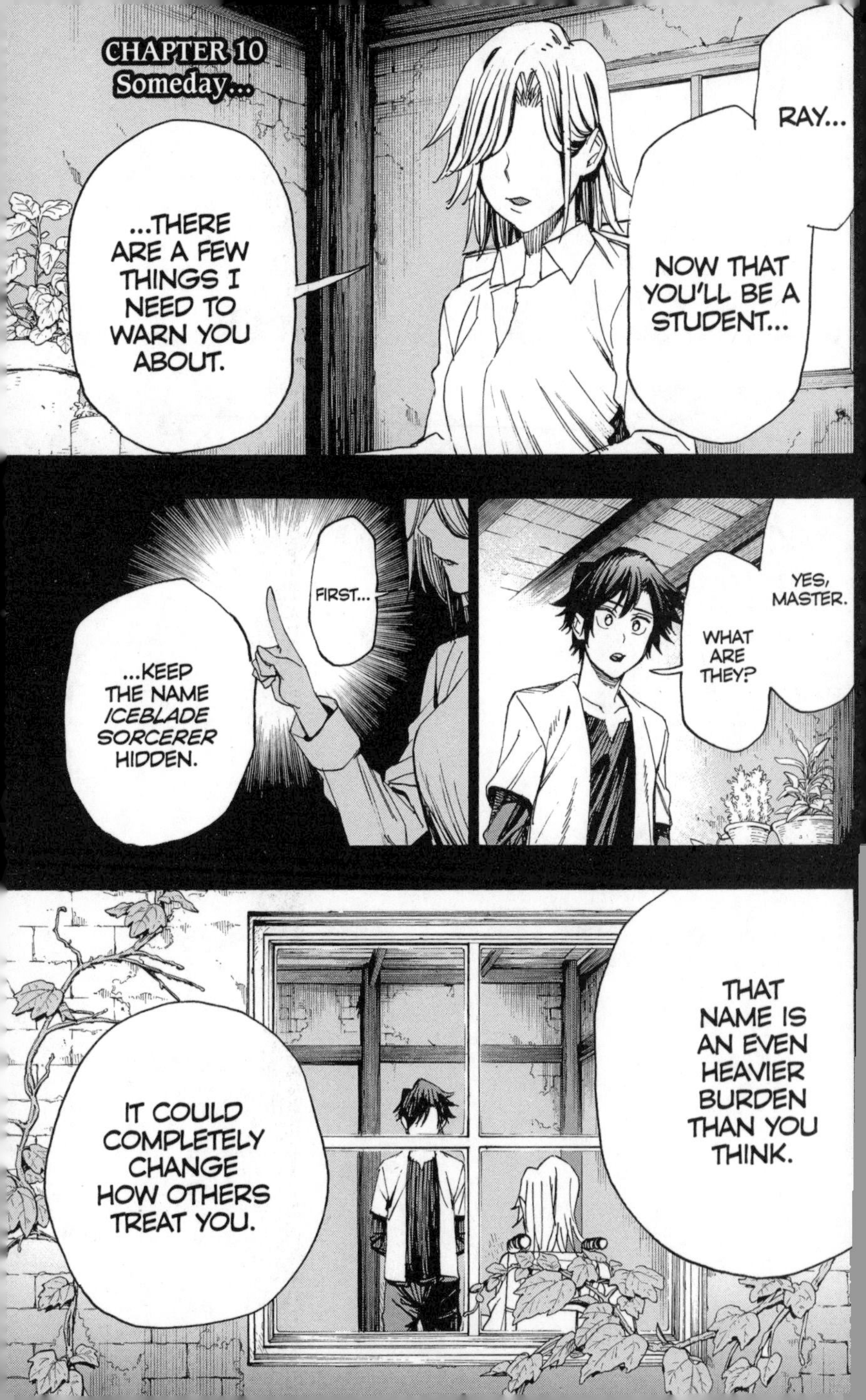
CHAPTER 10
Someday...
RAY...
NOW THAT YOU'LL BE A STUDENT...
...THERE ARE A FEW THINGS I NEED TO WARN YOU ABOUT.
YES, MASTER.
WHAT ARE THEY?
FIRST...
...KEEP THE NAME *ICEBLADE SORCERER* HIDDEN.
THAT NAME IS AN EVEN HEAVIER BURDEN THAN YOU THINK.
IT COULD COMPLETELY CHANGE HOW OTHERS TREAT YOU.

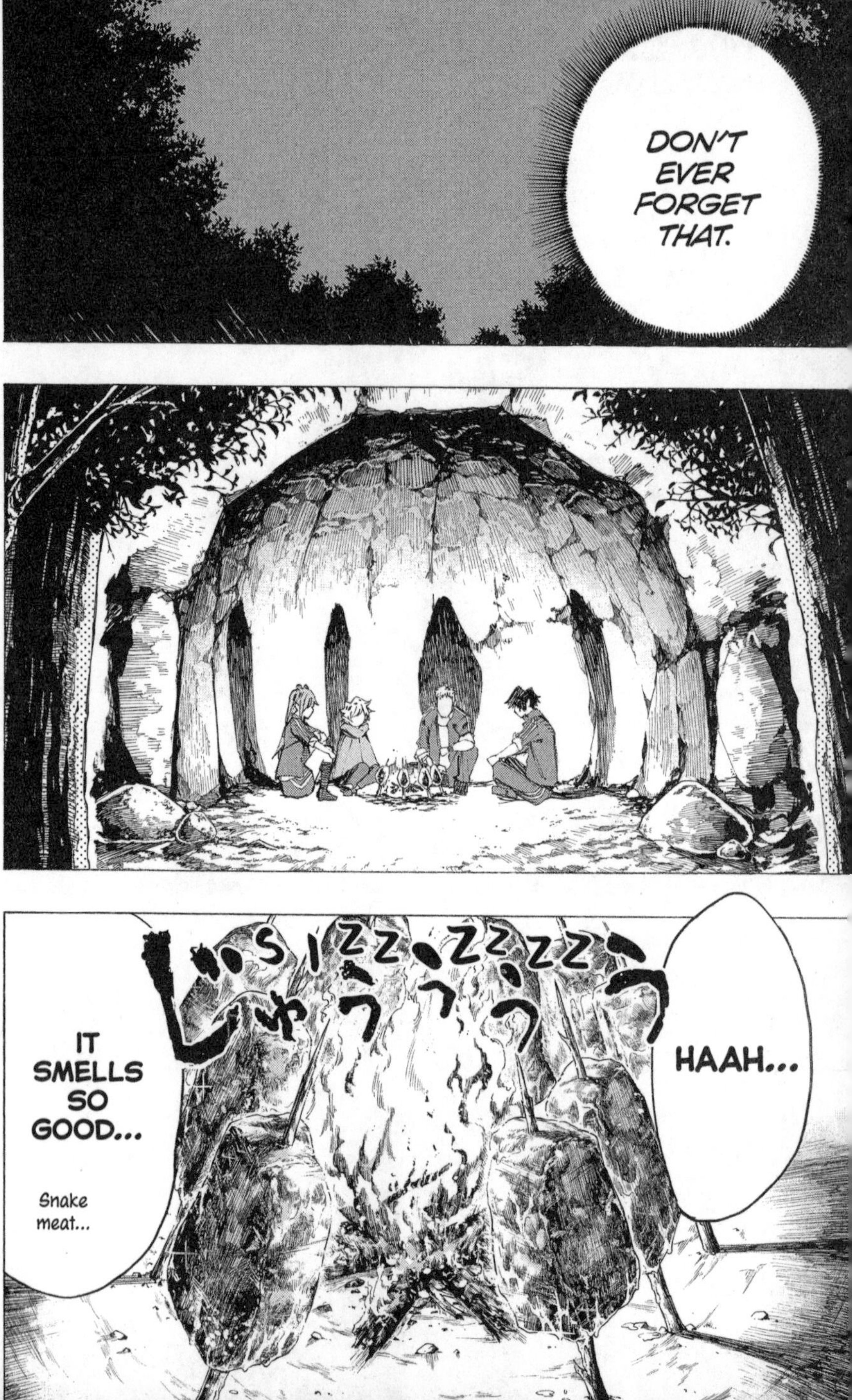
DON'T EVER FORGET THAT.
HAAH...
SIZZZZZZZ
IT SMELLS SO GOOD...
Snake meat...

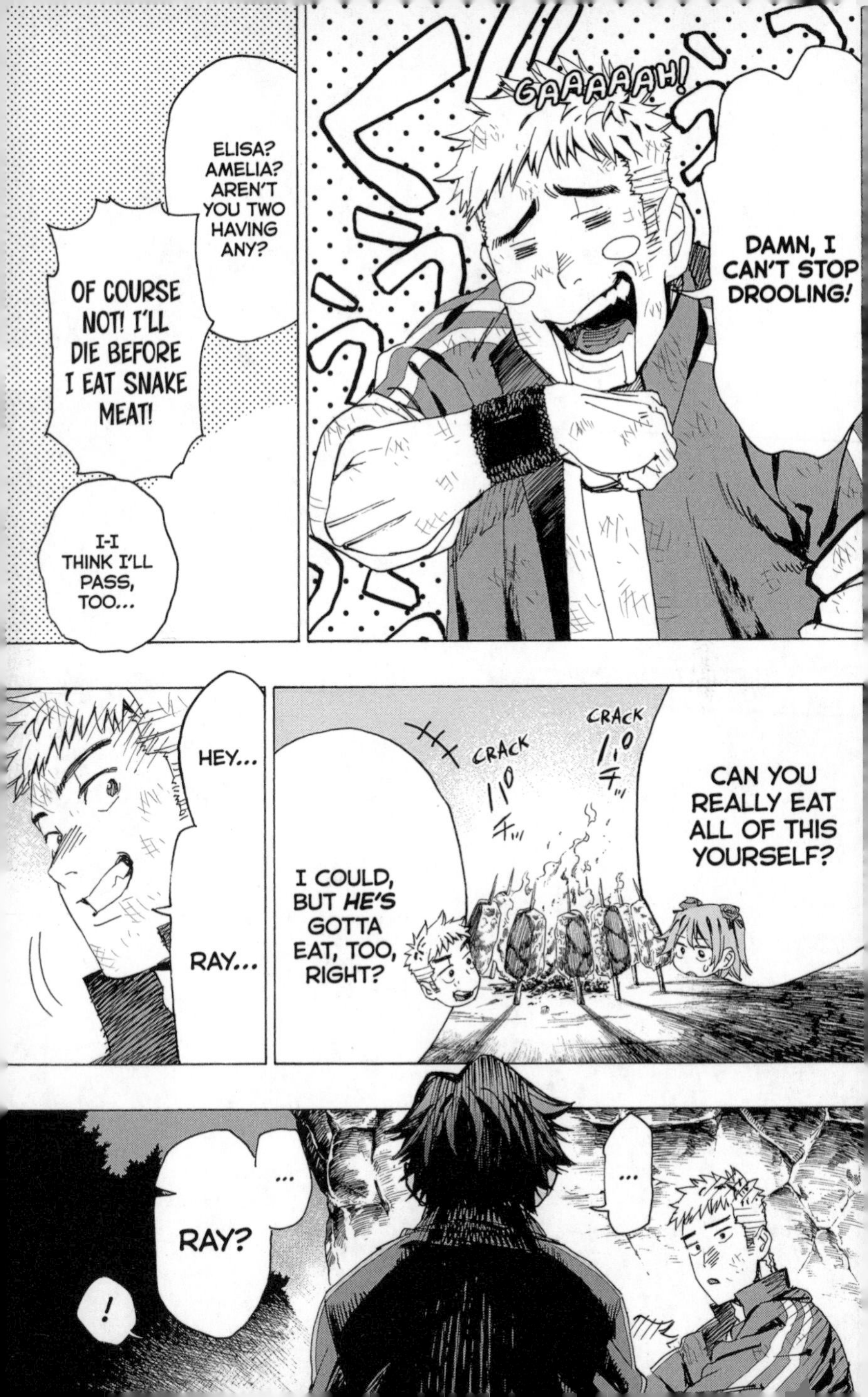
GAAAAAH!
DAMN, I CAN'T STOP DROOLING!
ELISA? AMELIA? AREN'T YOU TWO HAVING ANY?
OF COURSE NOT! I'LL DIE BEFORE I EAT SNAKE MEAT!
I-I THINK I'LL PASS, TOO...
CAN YOU REALLY EAT ALL OF THIS YOURSELF?
CRACK
CRACK
I COULD, BUT *HE'S* GOTTA EAT, TOO, RIGHT?
HEY...
RAY...
...
...
RAY?
!

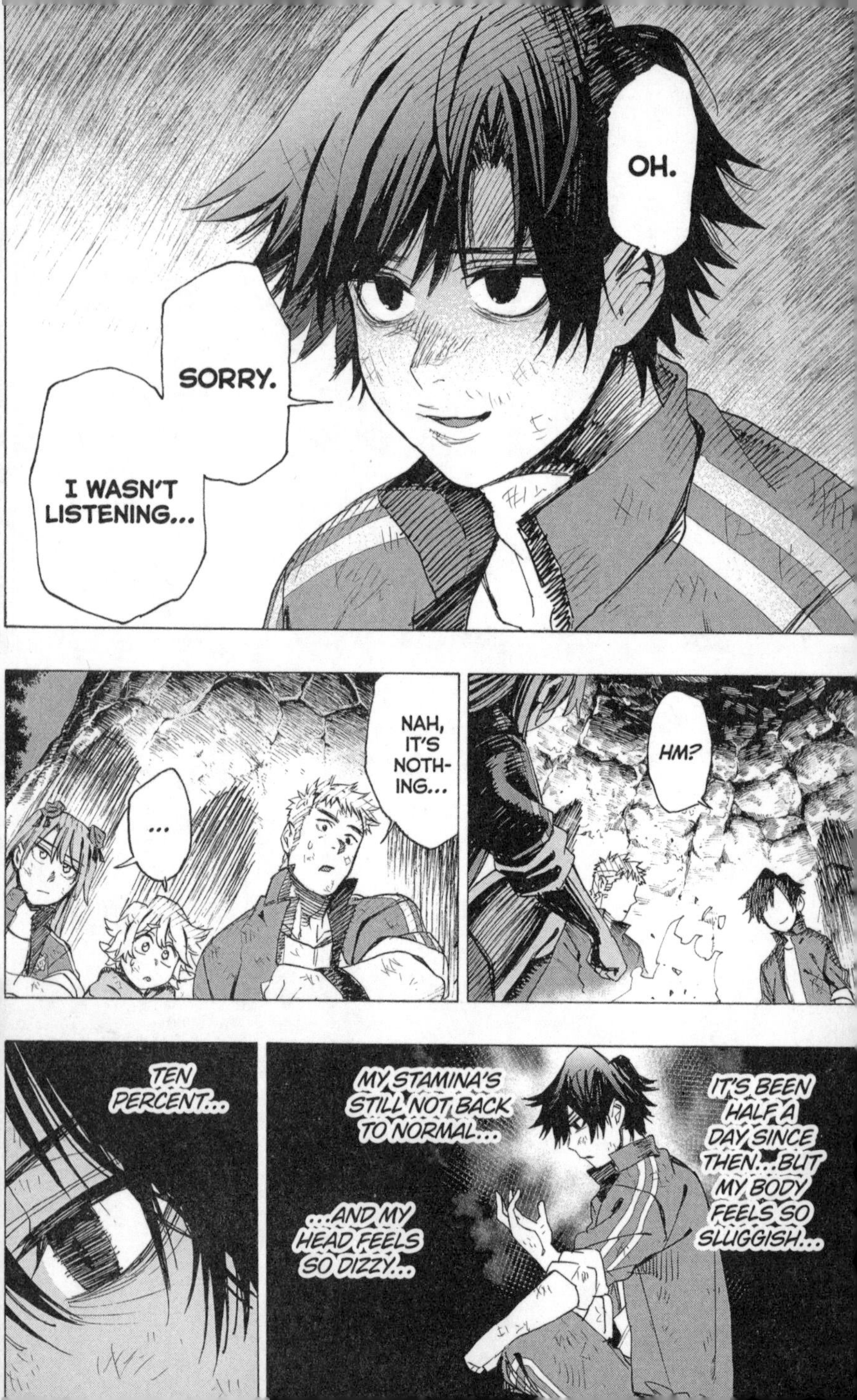
OH.
SORRY.
I WASN'T LISTENING...
HM?
NAH, IT'S NOTH-ING...
...
IT'S BEEN HALF A DAY SINCE THEN... BUT MY BODY FEELS SO SLUGGISH...
MY STAMINA'S STILL NOT BACK TO NORMAL...
...AND MY HEAD FEELS SO DIZZY...
TEN PERCENT...

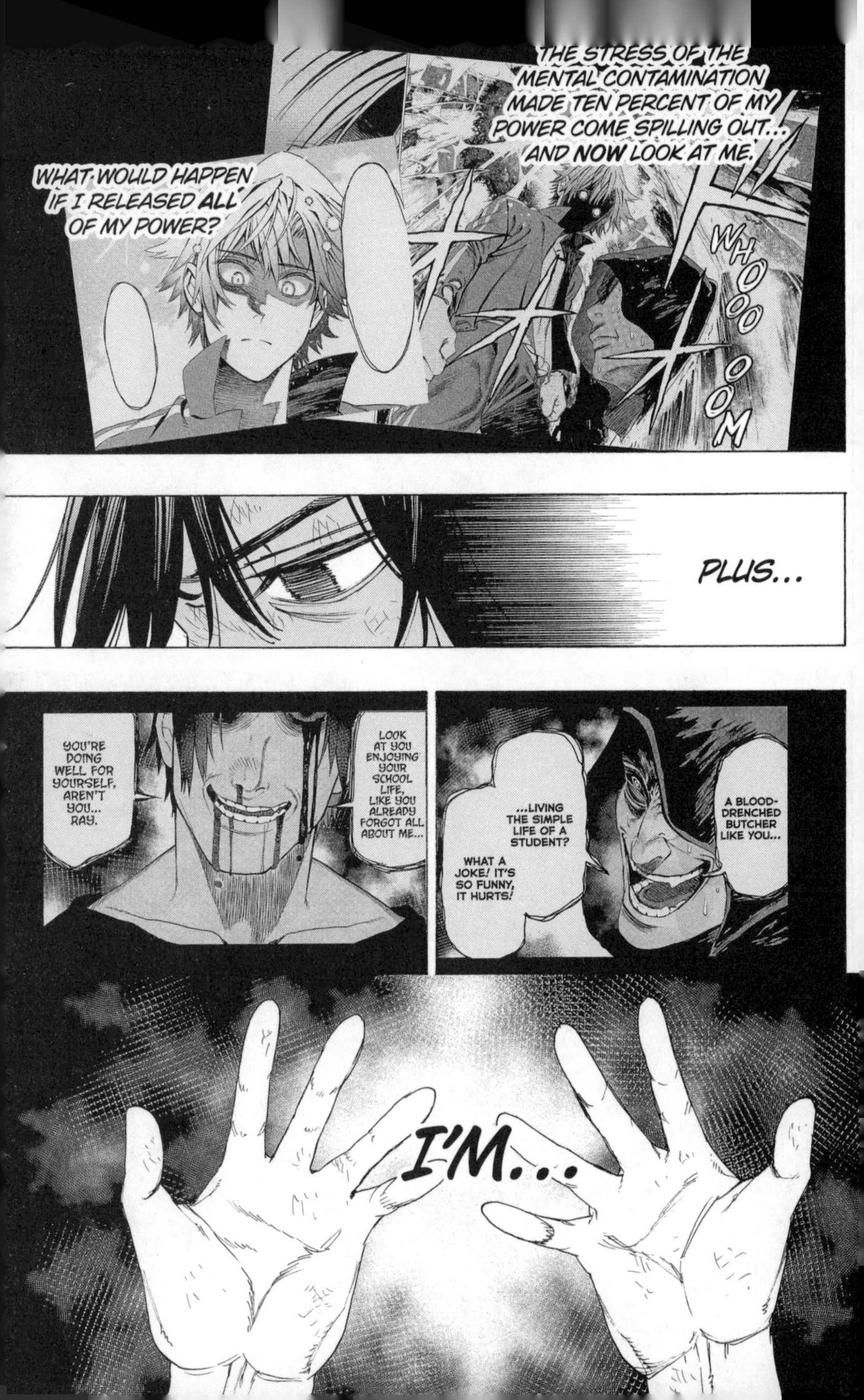
THE STRESS OF THE MENTAL CONTAMINATION MADE TEN PERCENT OF MY POWER COME SPILLING OUT... AND NOW LOOK AT ME.
WHOOOOOM
WHAT WOULD HAPPEN IF I RELEASED ALL OF MY POWER?
PLUS...
A BLOOD-DRENCHED BUTCHER LIKE YOU...
...LIVING THE SIMPLE LIFE OF A STUDENT?
WHAT A JOKE! IT'S SO FUNNY, IT HURTS!
LOOK AT YOU ENJOYING YOUR SCHOOL LIFE, LIKE YOU ALREADY FORGOT ALL ABOUT ME...
YOU'RE DOING WELL FOR YOURSELF, AREN'T YOU... RAY.
I'M...

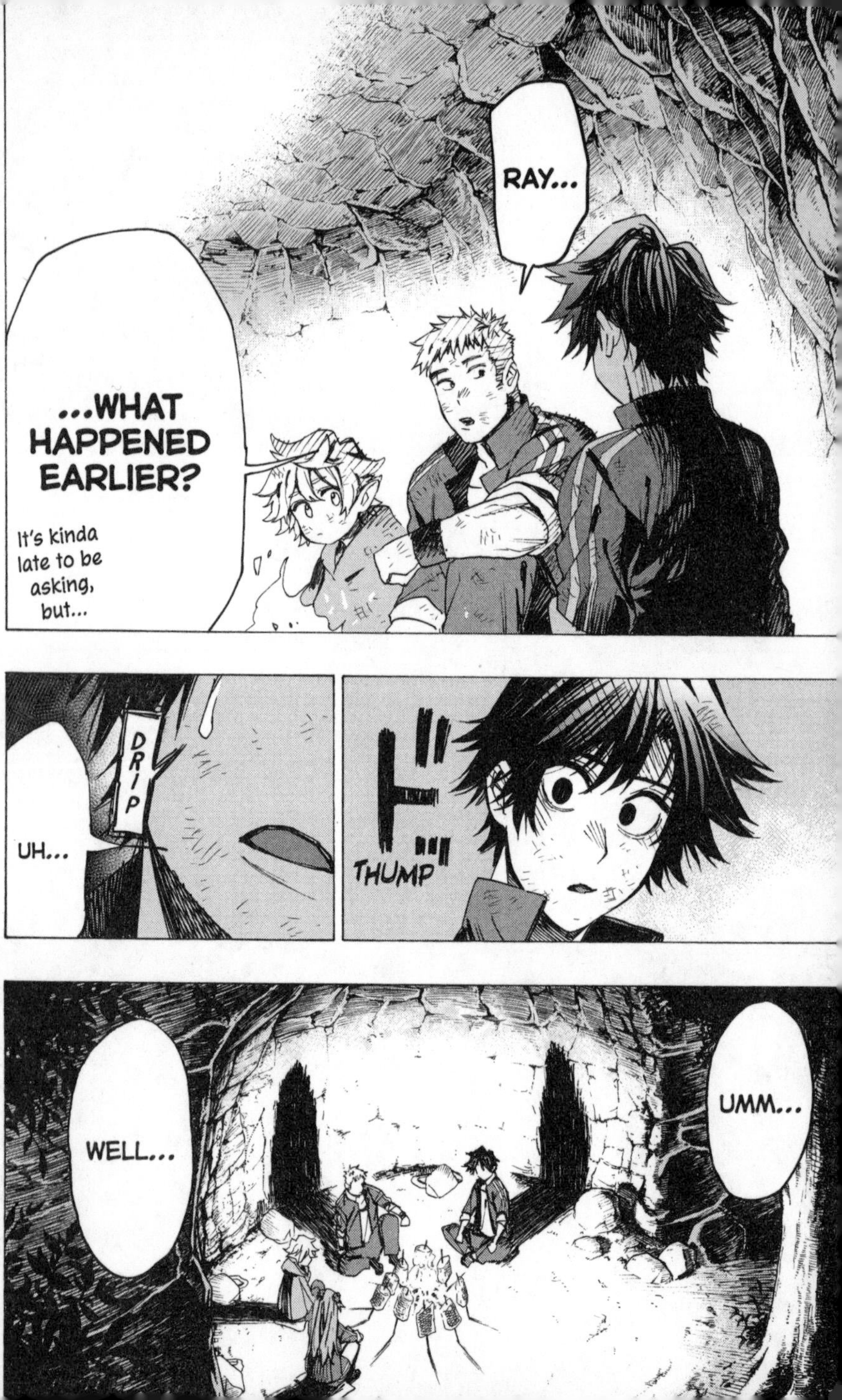
RAY...
...WHAT HAPPENED EARLIER?
It's kinda late to be asking, but...
THUMP
DRIP
UH...
UMM...
WELL...

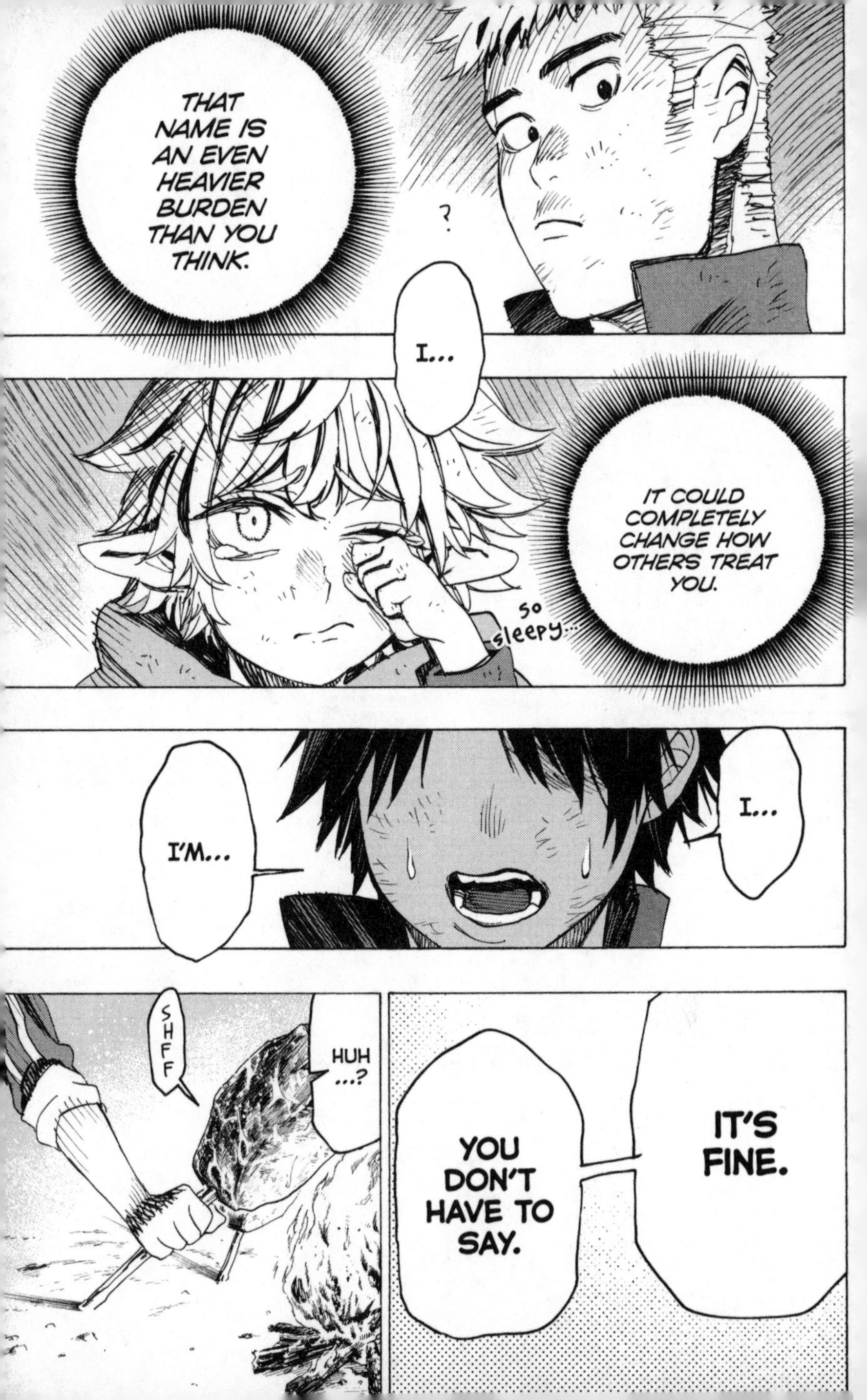
THAT NAME IS AN EVEN HEAVIER BURDEN THAN YOU THINK.
?
I...
IT COULD COMPLETELY CHANGE HOW OTHERS TREAT YOU.
so sleepy...
I...
I'M...
IT'S FINE.
YOU DON'T HAVE TO SAY.
HUH ...?
SHFF

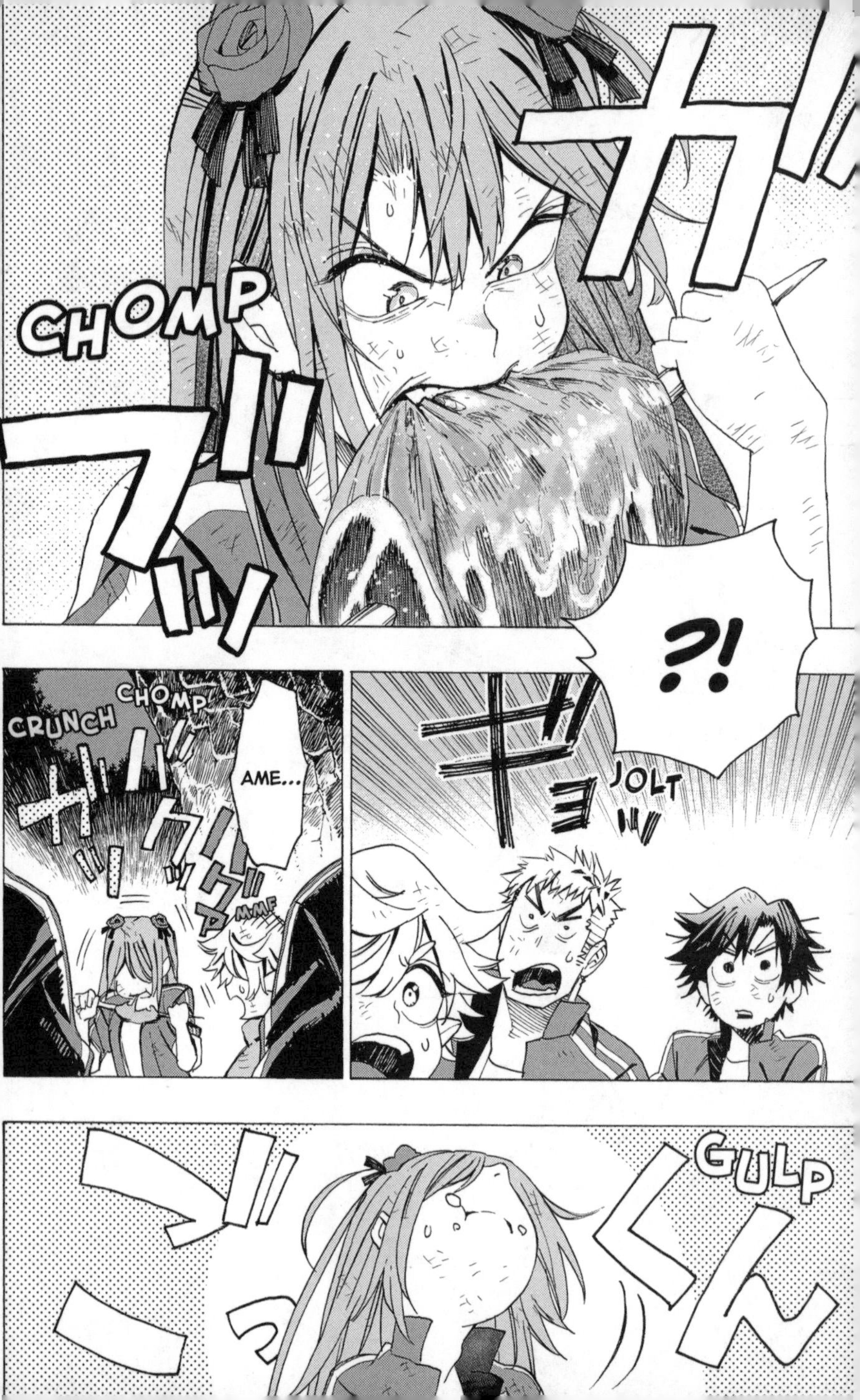
CHOMP
?!
JOLT
AME...
CHOMP
CRUNCH
MMF
GULP

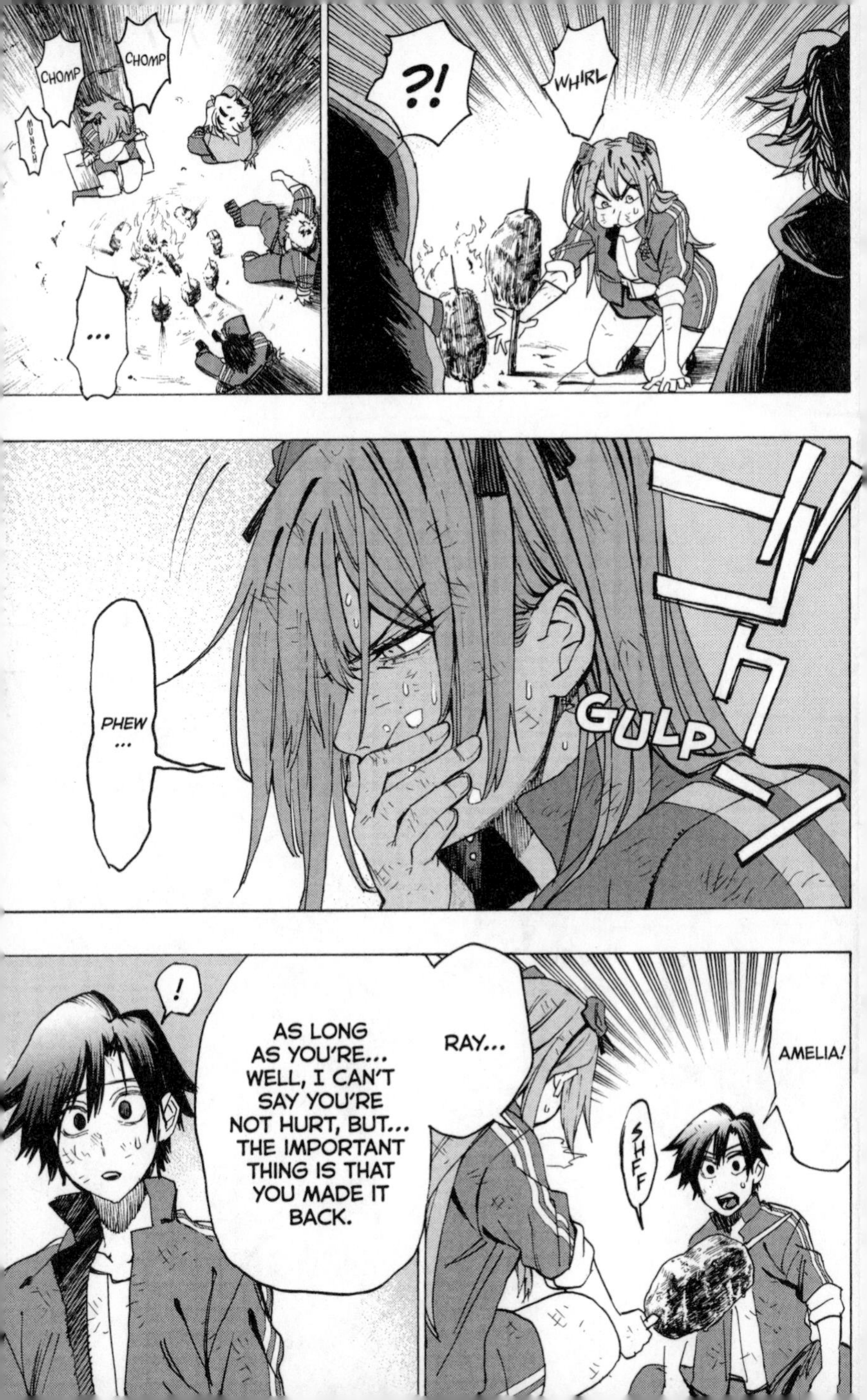
WHIRL
?!
CHOMP
CHOMP
MUNCH
...
GULP
PHEW...
AMELIA!
SHFF
RAY...
AS LONG AS YOU'RE... WELL, I CAN'T SAY YOU'RE NOT HURT, BUT... THE IMPORTANT THING IS THAT YOU MADE IT BACK.
!

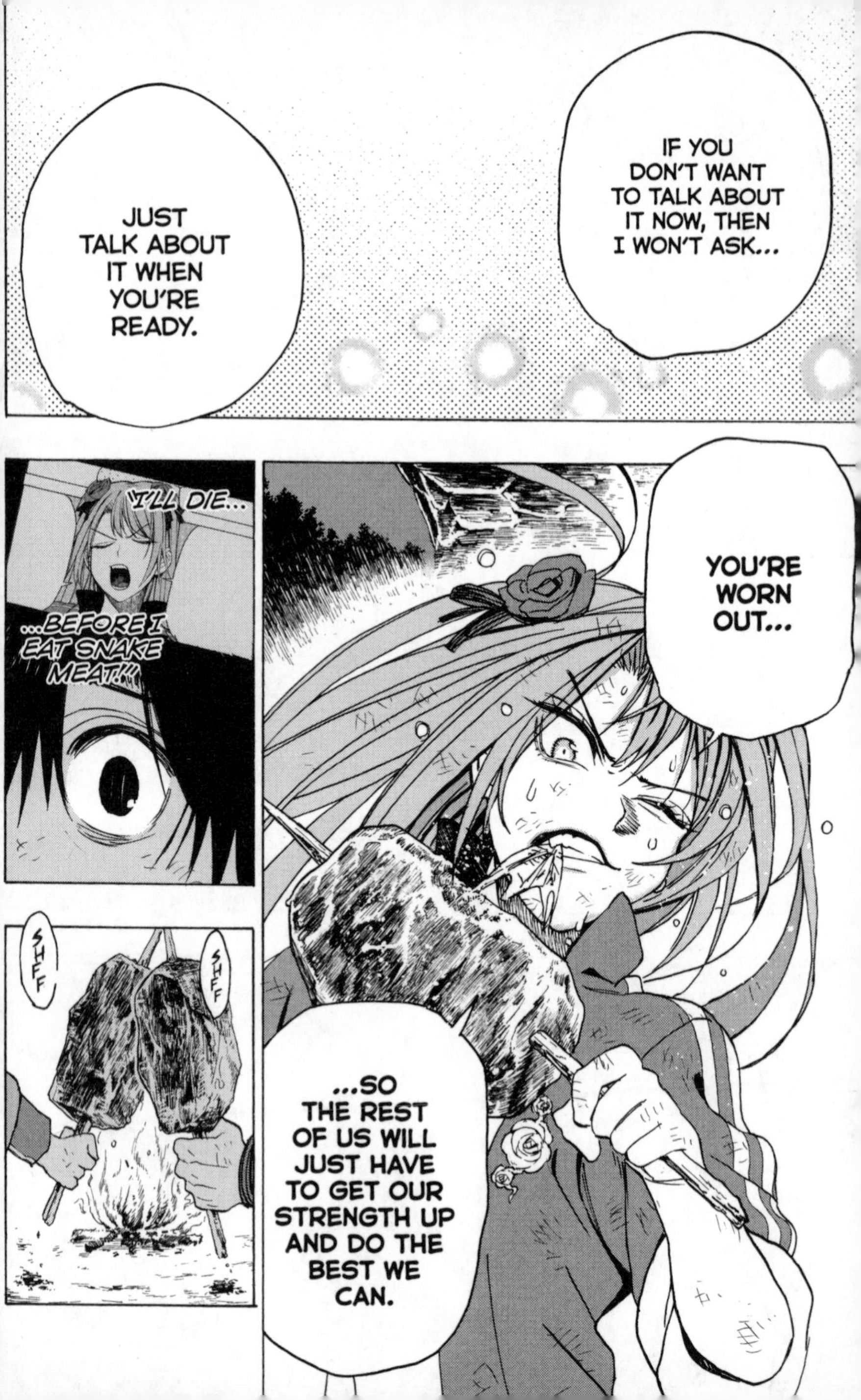
IF YOU DON'T WANT TO TALK ABOUT IT NOW, THEN I WON'T ASK...
JUST TALK ABOUT IT WHEN YOU'RE READY.
YOU'RE WORN OUT...
...SO THE REST OF US WILL JUST HAVE TO GET OUR STRENGTH UP AND DO THE BEST WE CAN.
"I'LL DIE...
...BEFORE I EAT SNAKE MEAT!!"
SHFF
SHFF

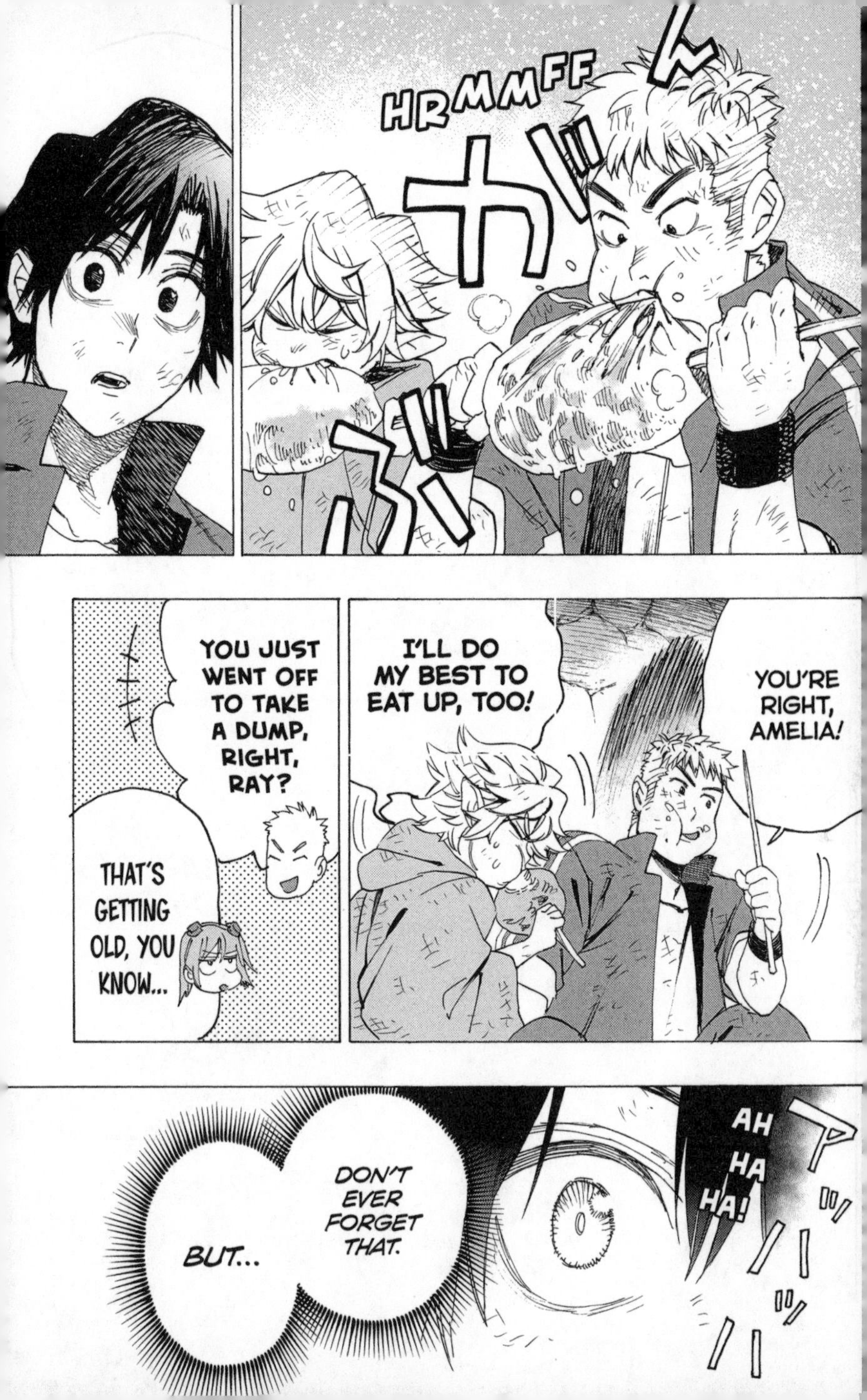
HRMMFF
YOU'RE RIGHT, AMELIA!
I'LL DO MY BEST TO EAT UP, TOO!
YOU JUST WENT OFF TO TAKE A DUMP, RIGHT, RAY?
THAT'S GETTING OLD, YOU KNOW...
AH HA HA!
DON'T EVER FORGET THAT.
BUT...

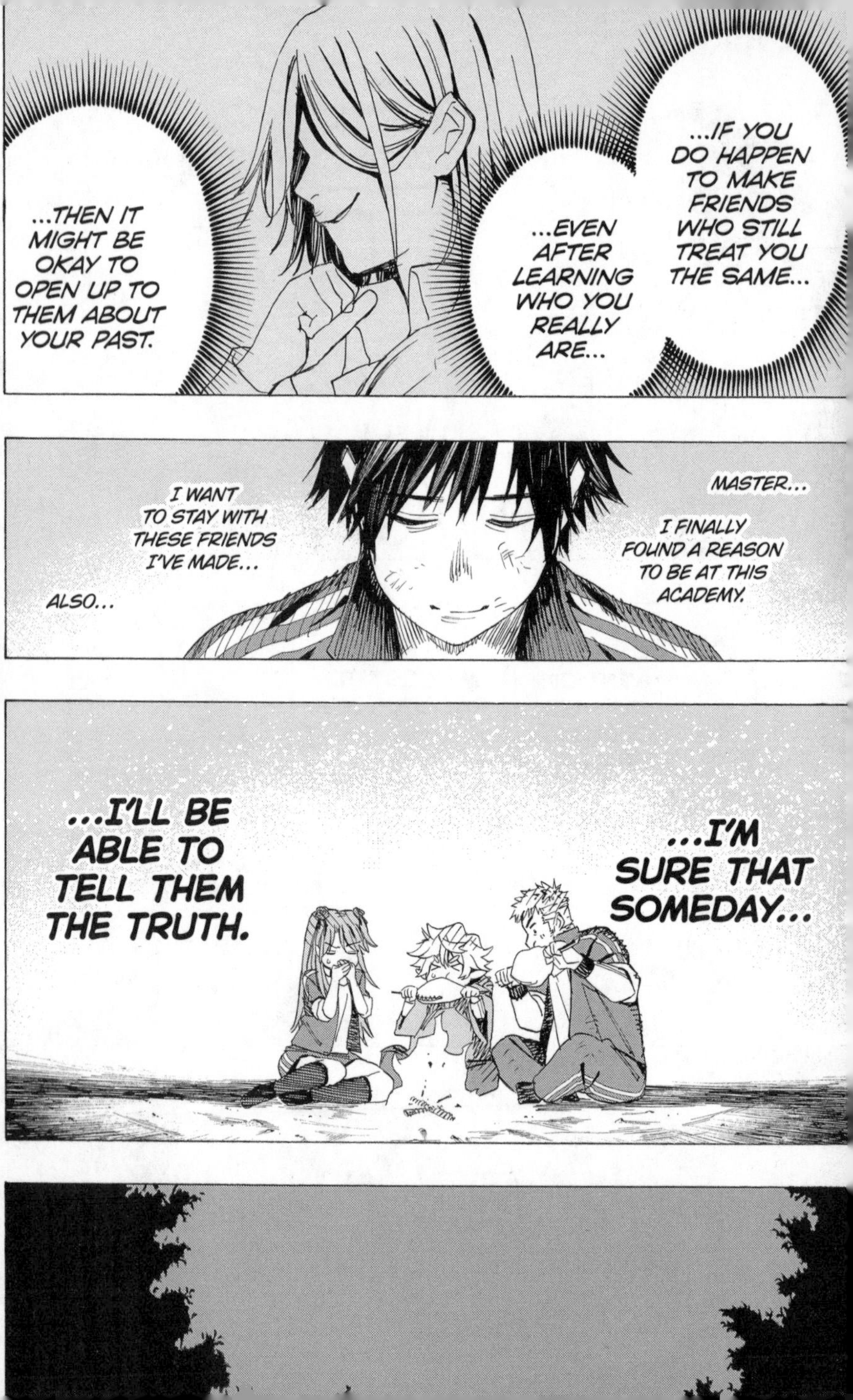
...IF YOU DO HAPPEN TO MAKE FRIENDS WHO STILL TREAT YOU THE SAME...
...EVEN AFTER LEARNING WHO YOU REALLY ARE...
...THEN IT MIGHT BE OKAY TO OPEN UP TO THEM ABOUT YOUR PAST.
MASTER...
I FINALLY FOUND A REASON TO BE AT THIS ACADEMY.
I WANT TO STAY WITH THESE FRIENDS I'VE MADE...
ALSO...
...I'M SURE THAT SOMEDAY...
...I'LL BE ABLE TO TELL THEM THE TRUTH.

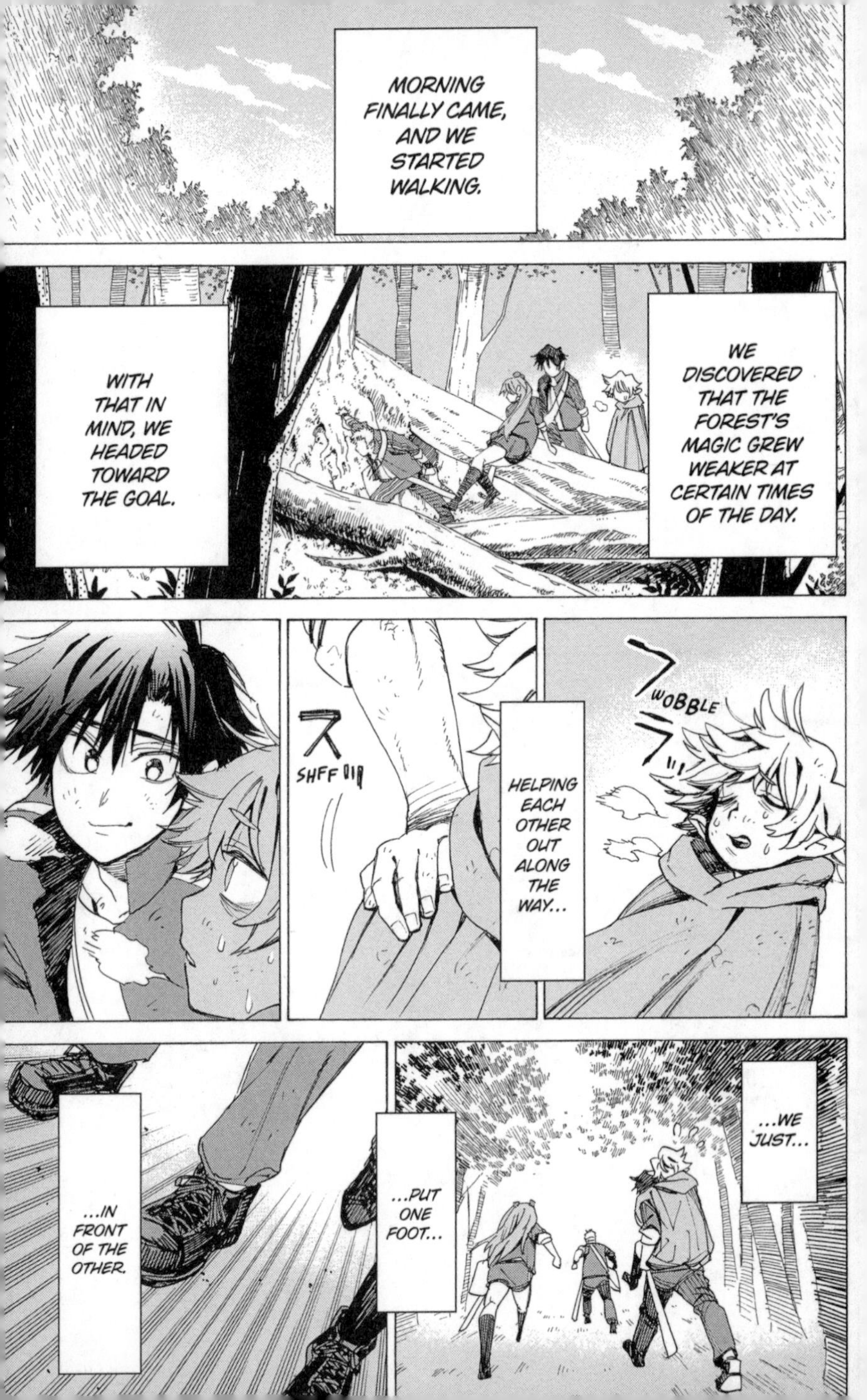
MORNING FINALLY CAME, AND WE STARTED WALKING.
WE DISCOVERED THAT THE FOREST'S MAGIC GREW WEAKER AT CERTAIN TIMES OF THE DAY.
WITH THAT IN MIND, WE HEADED TOWARD THE GOAL.
WOBBLE
SHFF
HELPING EACH OTHER OUT ALONG THE WAY...
...WE JUST...
...PUT ONE FOOT...
...IN FRONT OF THE OTHER.

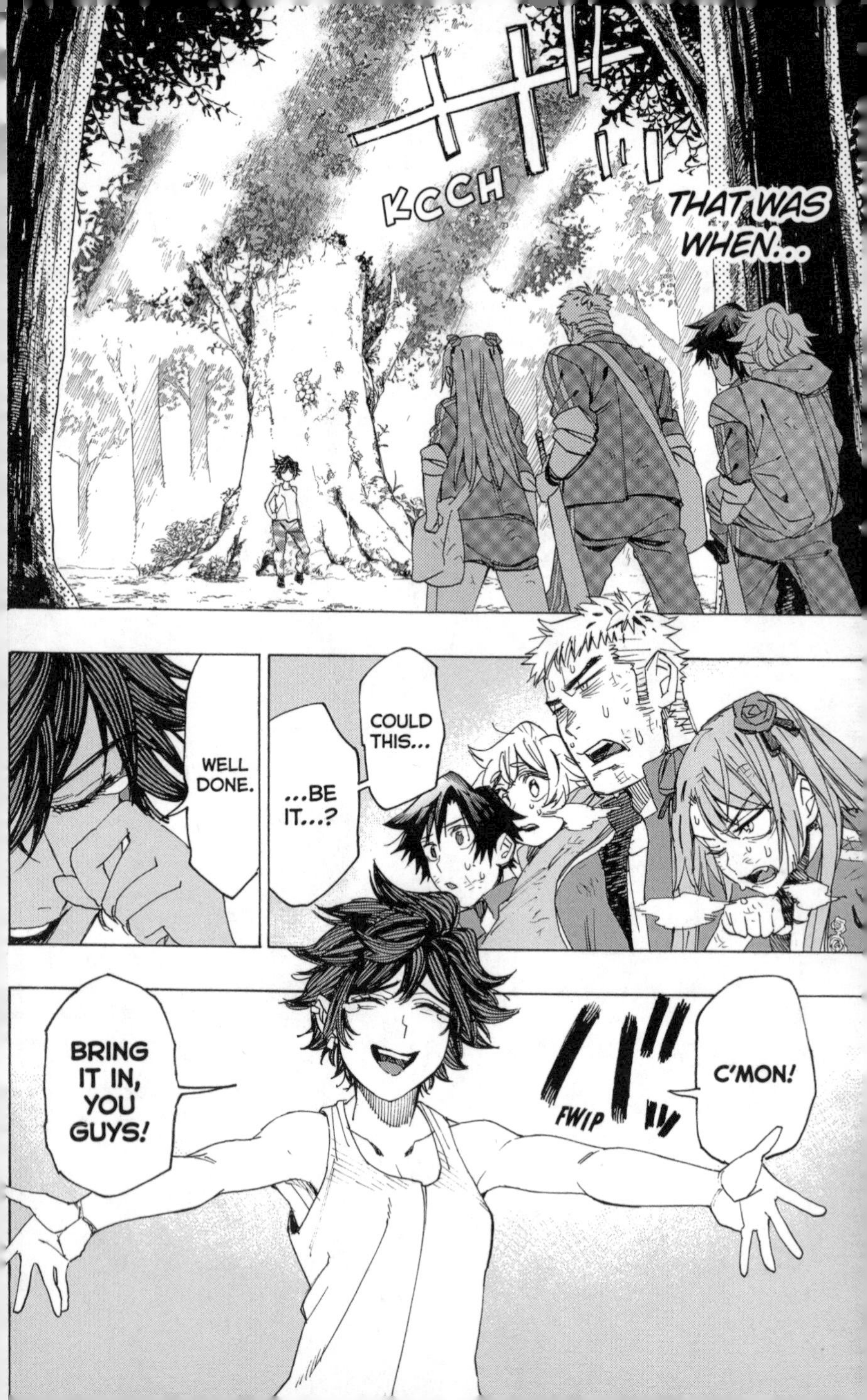
THAT WAS WHEN...
KCCH
COULD THIS...
...BE IT...?
WELL DONE.
C'MON!
FWIP
BRING IT IN, YOU GUYS!

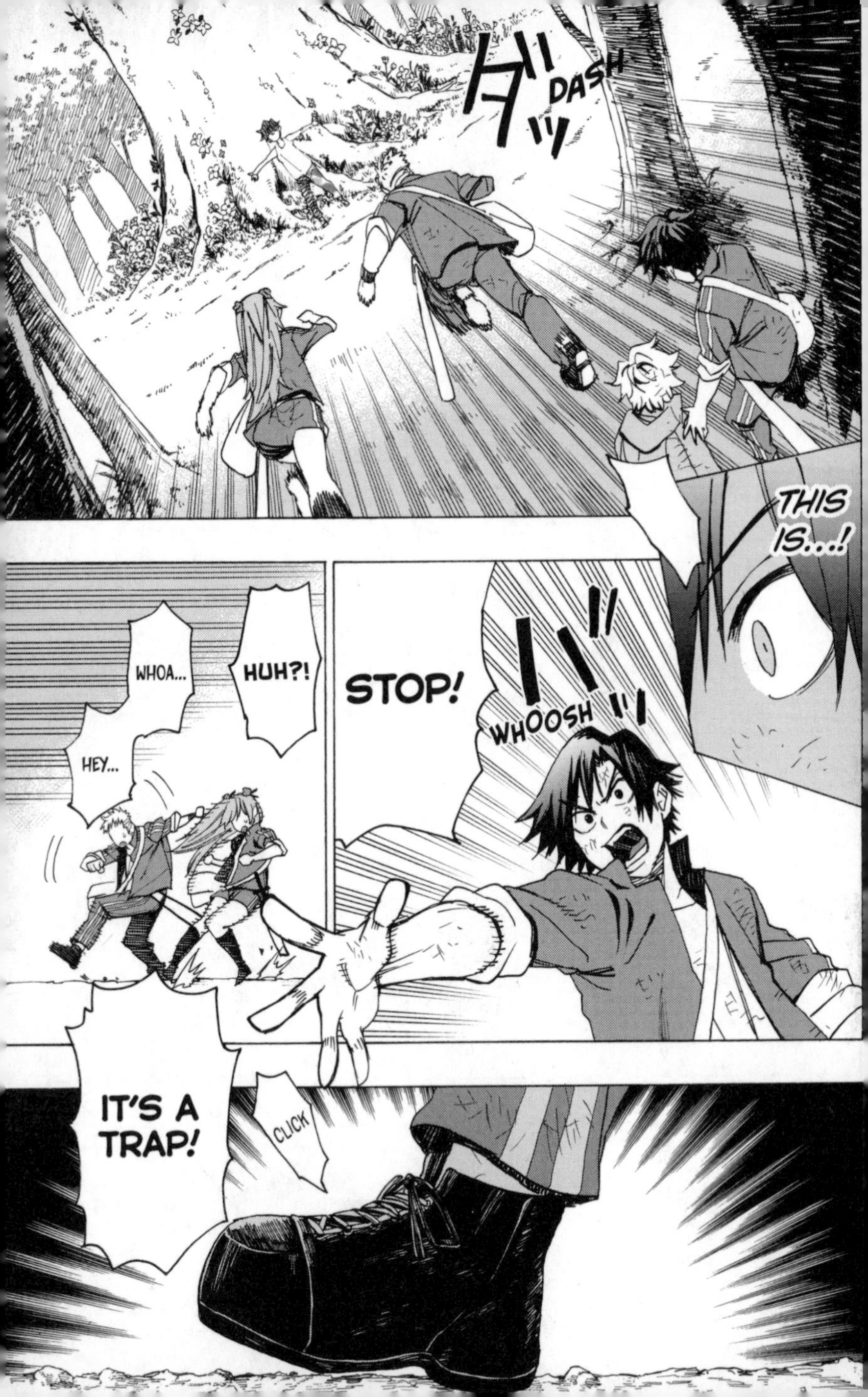
ダッ
DASH
THIS IS...!
WHOOSH
STOP!
HUH?!
WHOA...
HEY...
CLICK
IT'S A TRAP!

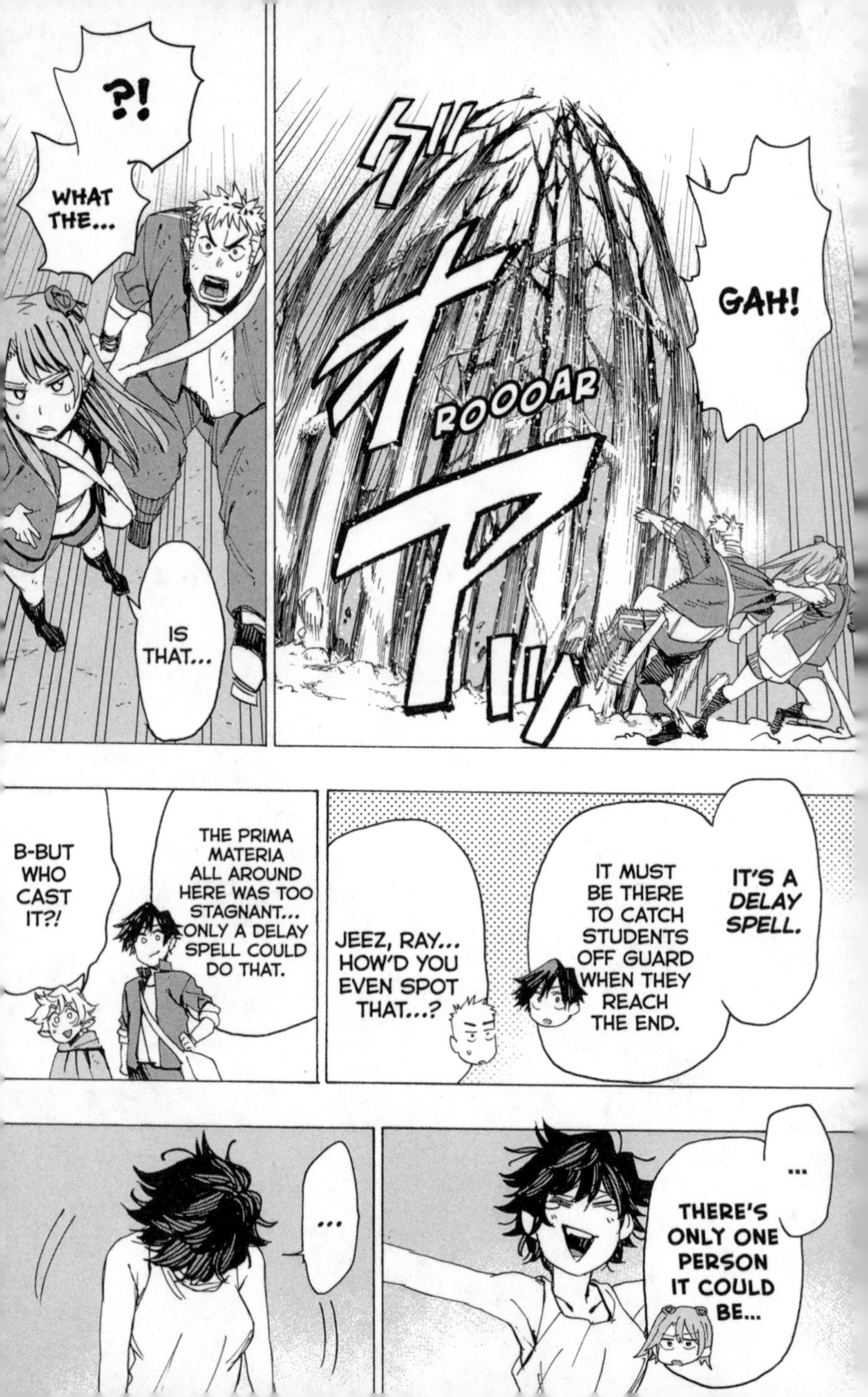
GAH!
ROOOAR
?!
WHAT THE...
IS THAT...
IT'S A *DELAY SPELL.*
IT MUST BE THERE TO CATCH STUDENTS OFF GUARD WHEN THEY REACH THE END.
JEEZ, RAY... HOW'D YOU EVEN SPOT THAT...?
THE PRIMA MATERIA ALL AROUND HERE WAS TOO STAGNANT... ONLY A DELAY SPELL COULD DO THAT.
B-BUT WHO CAST IT?!
... THERE'S ONLY ONE PERSON IT COULD BE...
...

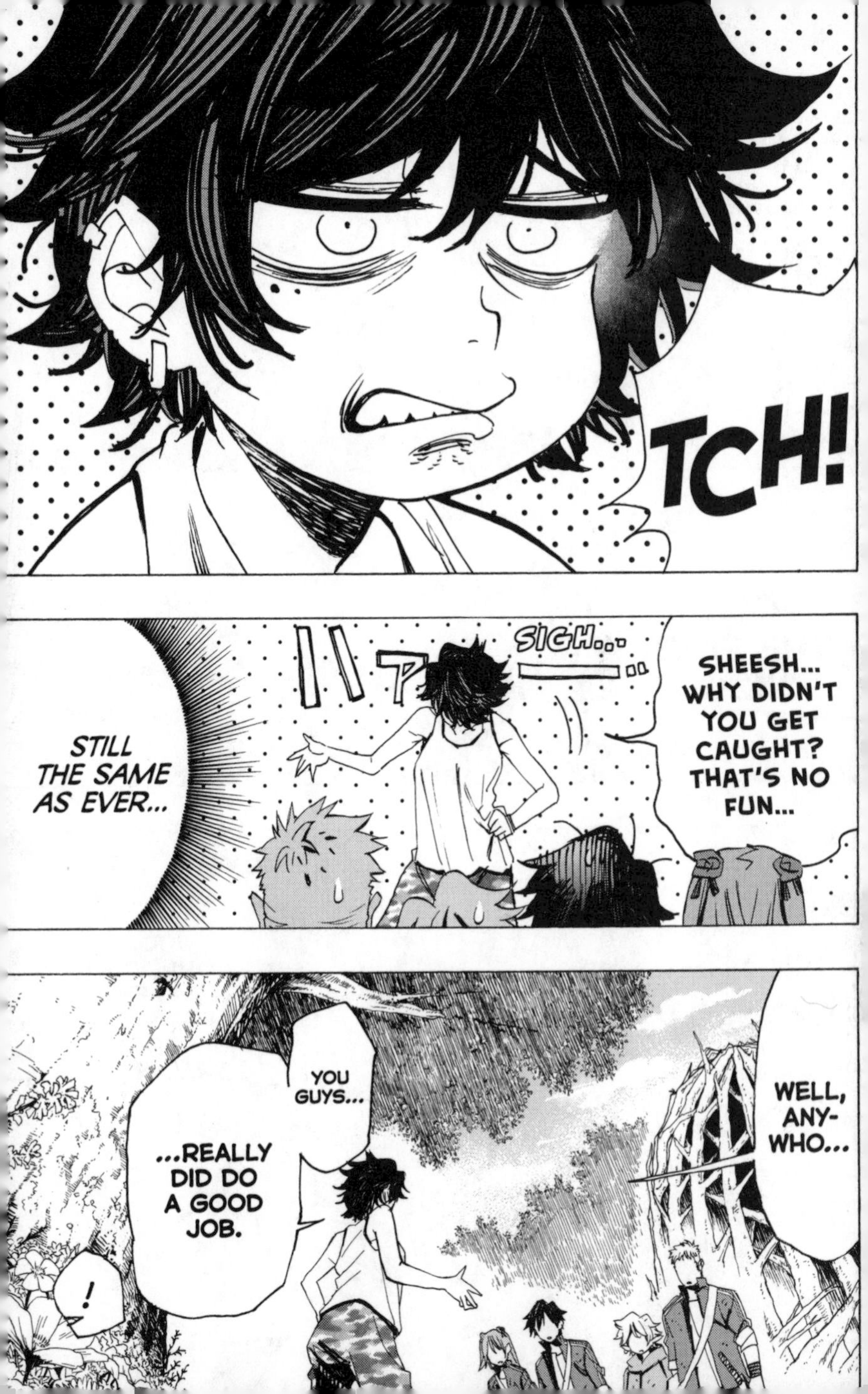
TCH!
SHEESH... WHY DIDN'T YOU GET CAUGHT? THAT'S NO FUN...
SIGH...
STILL THE SAME AS EVER...
WELL, ANY-WHO...
YOU GUYS...
...REALLY DID DO A GOOD JOB.
!

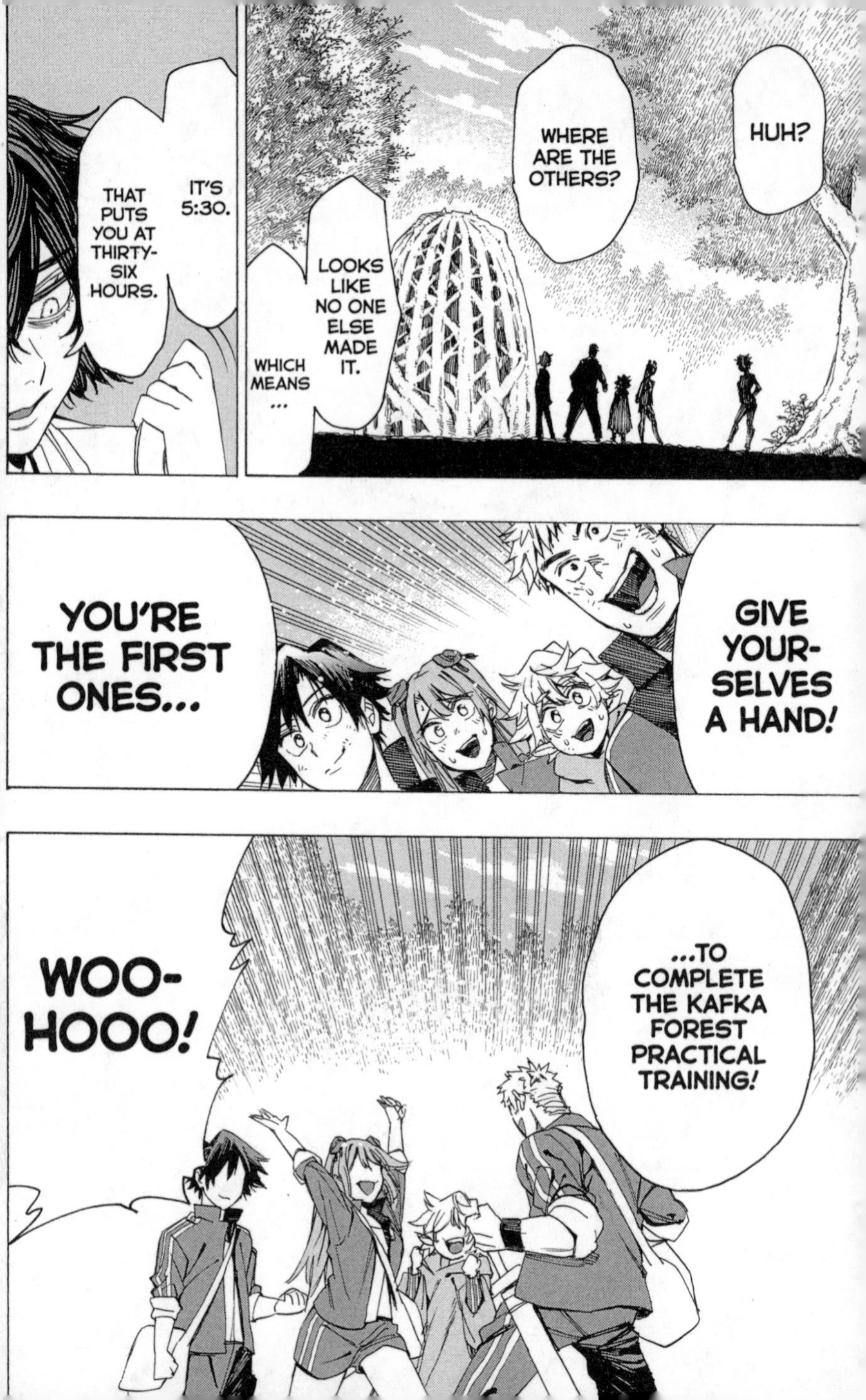
HUH?
WHERE ARE THE OTHERS?
LOOKS LIKE NO ONE ELSE MADE IT.
WHICH MEANS ...
IT'S 5:30.
THAT PUTS YOU AT THIRTY-SIX HOURS.
GIVE YOURSELVES A HAND!
YOU'RE THE FIRST ONES...
...TO COMPLETE THE KAFKA FOREST PRACTICAL TRAINING!
WOO-HOOO!

The ICEBLADE SORCERER Shall RULE the WORLD

CHAPTER 11
After the Training

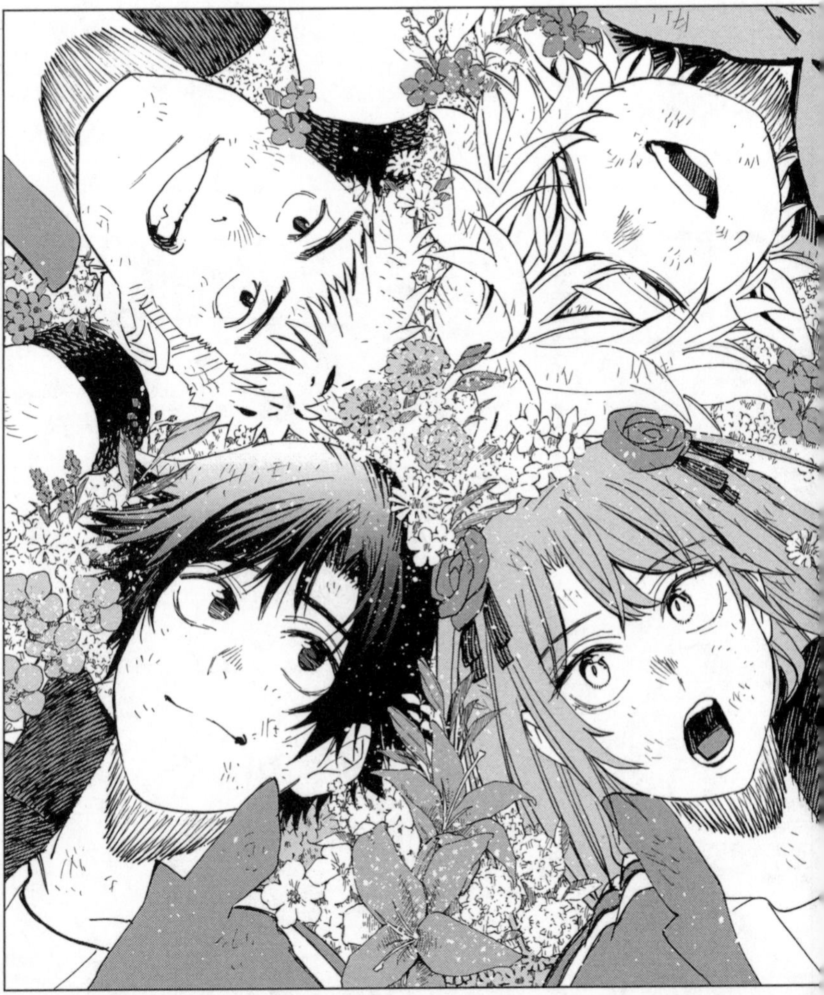

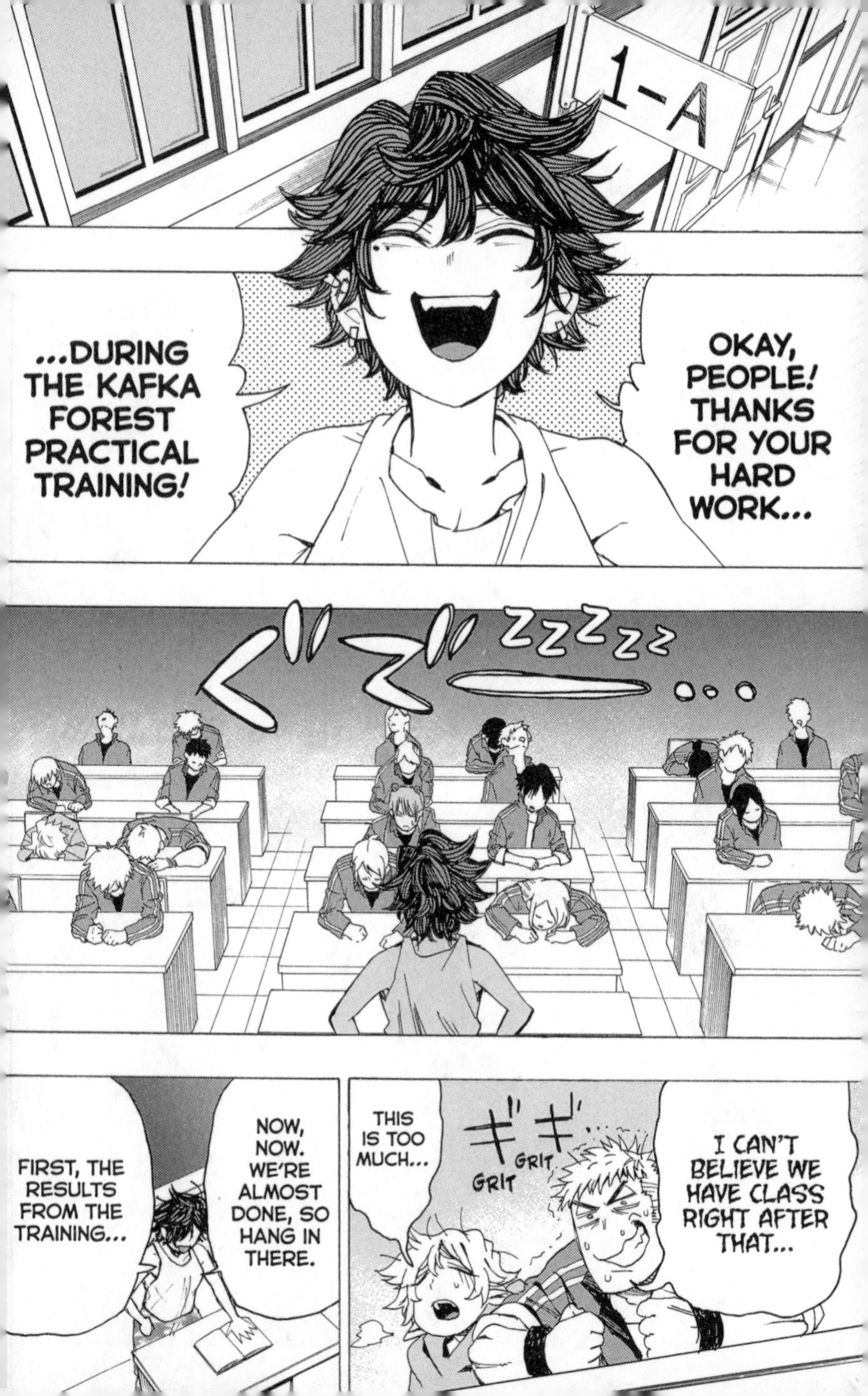1-A
OKAY, PEOPLE! THANKS FOR YOUR HARD WORK...
...DURING THE KAFKA FOREST PRACTICAL TRAINING!
ZZZZZZ
I CAN'T BELIEVE WE HAVE CLASS RIGHT AFTER THAT...
ギギ
GRIT GRIT
THIS IS TOO MUCH...
NOW, NOW. WE'RE ALMOST DONE, SO HANG IN THERE.
FIRST, THE RESULTS FROM THE TRAINING...

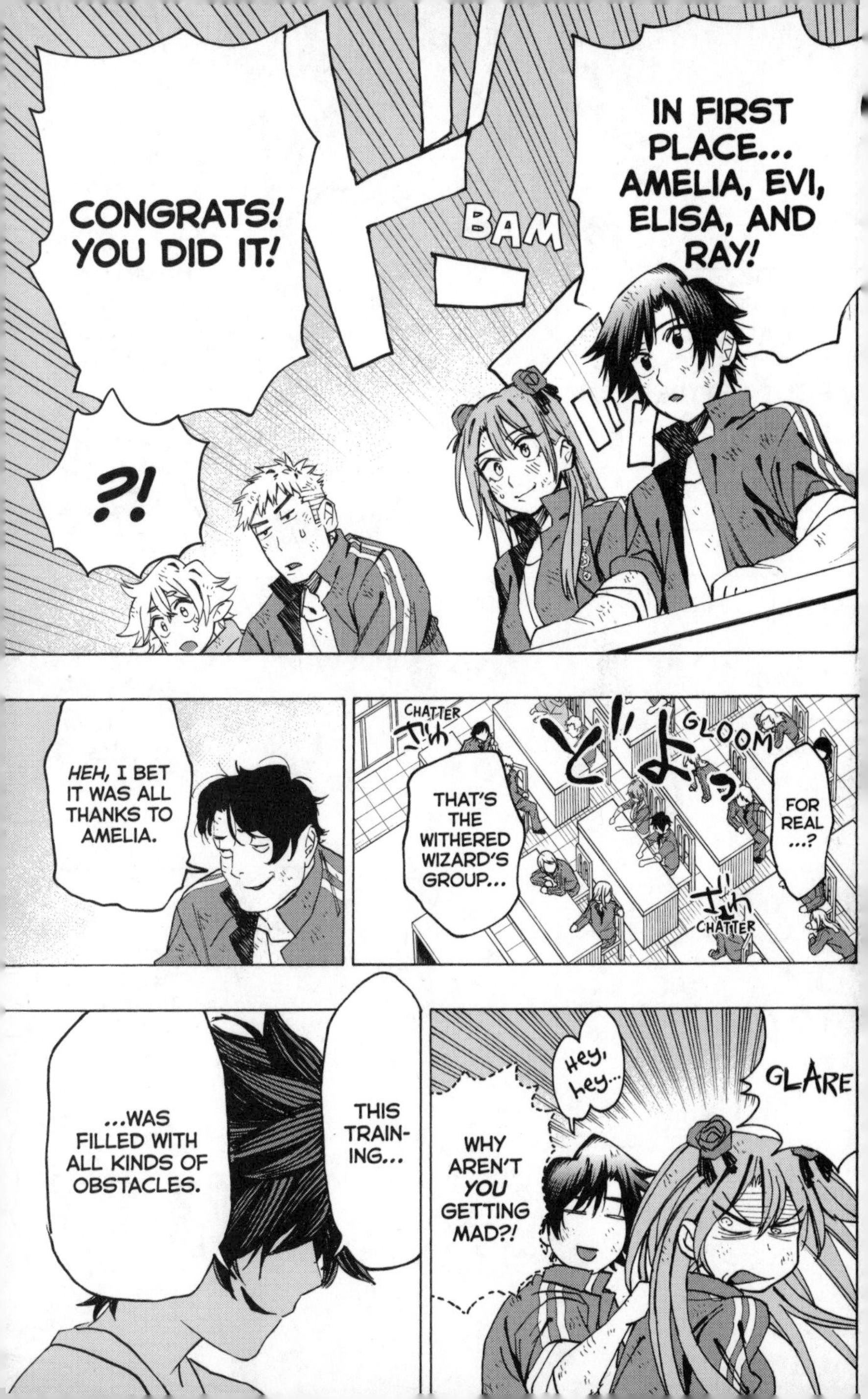
IN FIRST PLACE... AMELIA, EVI, ELISA, AND RAY!
BAM
CONGRATS! YOU DID IT!
?!
GLOOM
CHATTER
FOR REAL ...?
THAT'S THE WITHERED WIZARD'S GROUP...
CHATTER
HEH, I BET IT WAS ALL THANKS TO AMELIA.
GLARE
Hey, hey...
WHY AREN'T *YOU* GETTING MAD?!
THIS TRAIN-ING...
...WAS FILLED WITH ALL KINDS OF OBSTACLES.

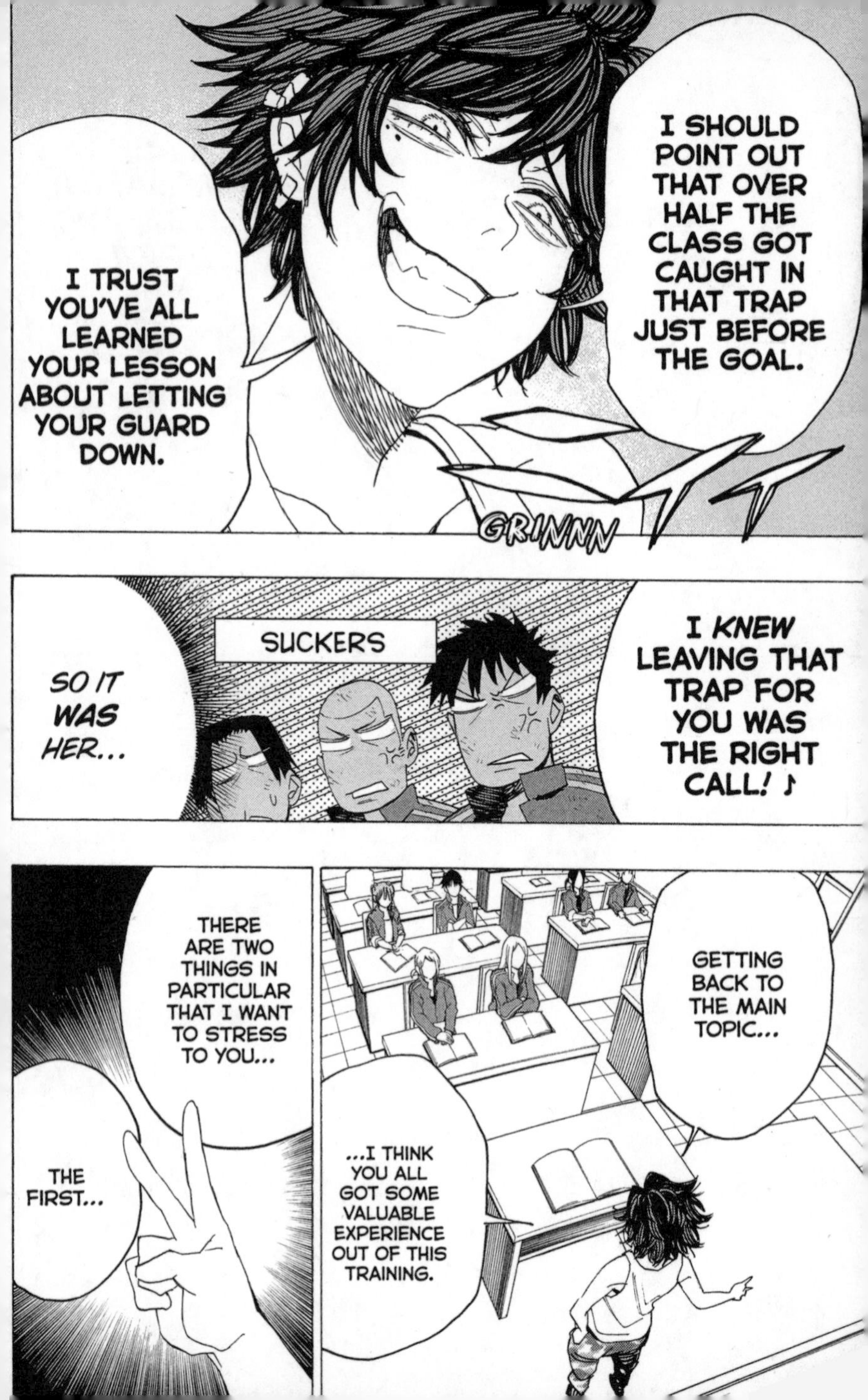
I SHOULD POINT OUT THAT OVER HALF THE CLASS GOT CAUGHT IN THAT TRAP JUST BEFORE THE GOAL.
I TRUST YOU'VE ALL LEARNED YOUR LESSON ABOUT LETTING YOUR GUARD DOWN.
GRINNN
I *KNEW* LEAVING THAT TRAP FOR YOU WAS THE RIGHT CALL! ♪
SUCKERS
SO IT WAS HER...
GETTING BACK TO THE MAIN TOPIC...
...I THINK YOU ALL GOT SOME VALUABLE EXPERIENCE OUT OF THIS TRAINING.
THERE ARE TWO THINGS IN PARTICULAR THAT I WANT TO STRESS TO YOU...
THE FIRST...

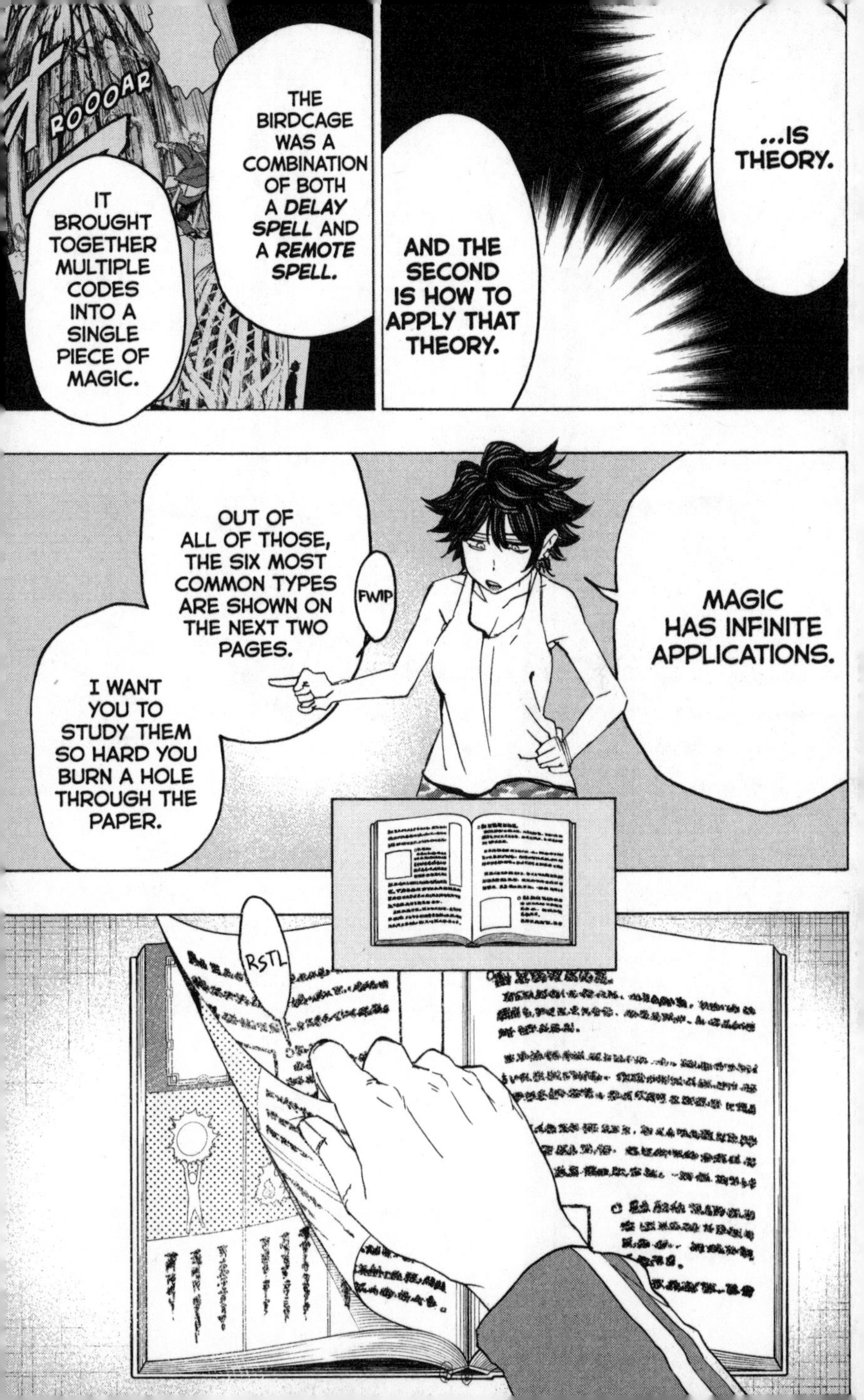
...IS THEORY.
AND THE SECOND IS HOW TO APPLY THAT THEORY.
THE BIRDCAGE WAS A COMBINATION OF BOTH A *DELAY SPELL* AND A *REMOTE SPELL.*
ROOOAR
IT BROUGHT TOGETHER MULTIPLE CODES INTO A SINGLE PIECE OF MAGIC.
MAGIC HAS INFINITE APPLICATIONS.
FWIP
OUT OF ALL OF THOSE, THE SIX MOST COMMON TYPES ARE SHOWN ON THE NEXT TWO PAGES.
I WANT YOU TO STUDY THEM SO HARD YOU BURN A HOLE THROUGH THE PAPER.
RSTL

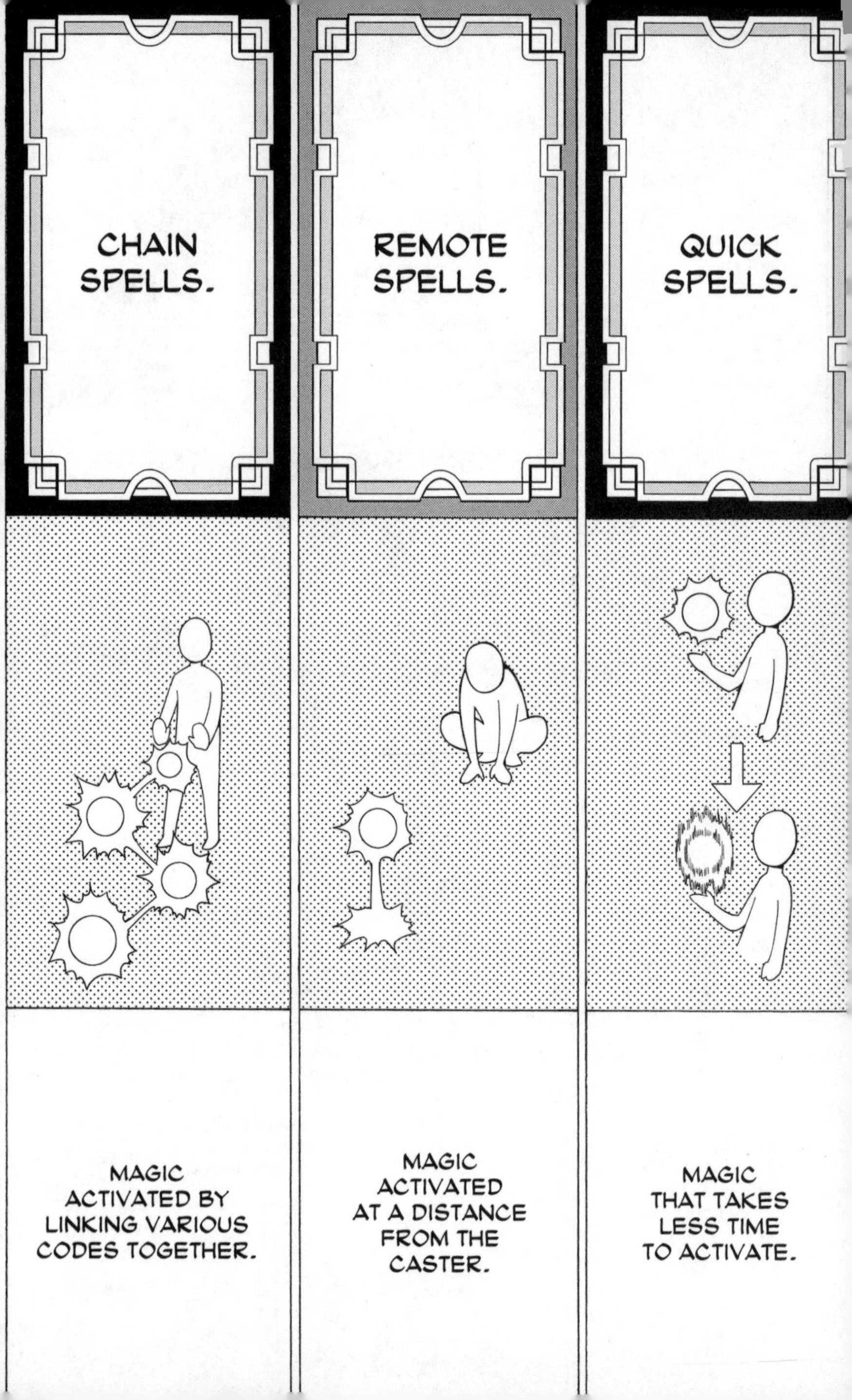
QUICK SPELLS.
MAGIC THAT TAKES LESS TIME TO ACTIVATE.
REMOTE SPELLS.
MAGIC ACTIVATED AT A DISTANCE FROM THE CASTER.
CHAIN SPELLS.
MAGIC ACTIVATED BY LINKING VARIOUS CODES TOGETHER.

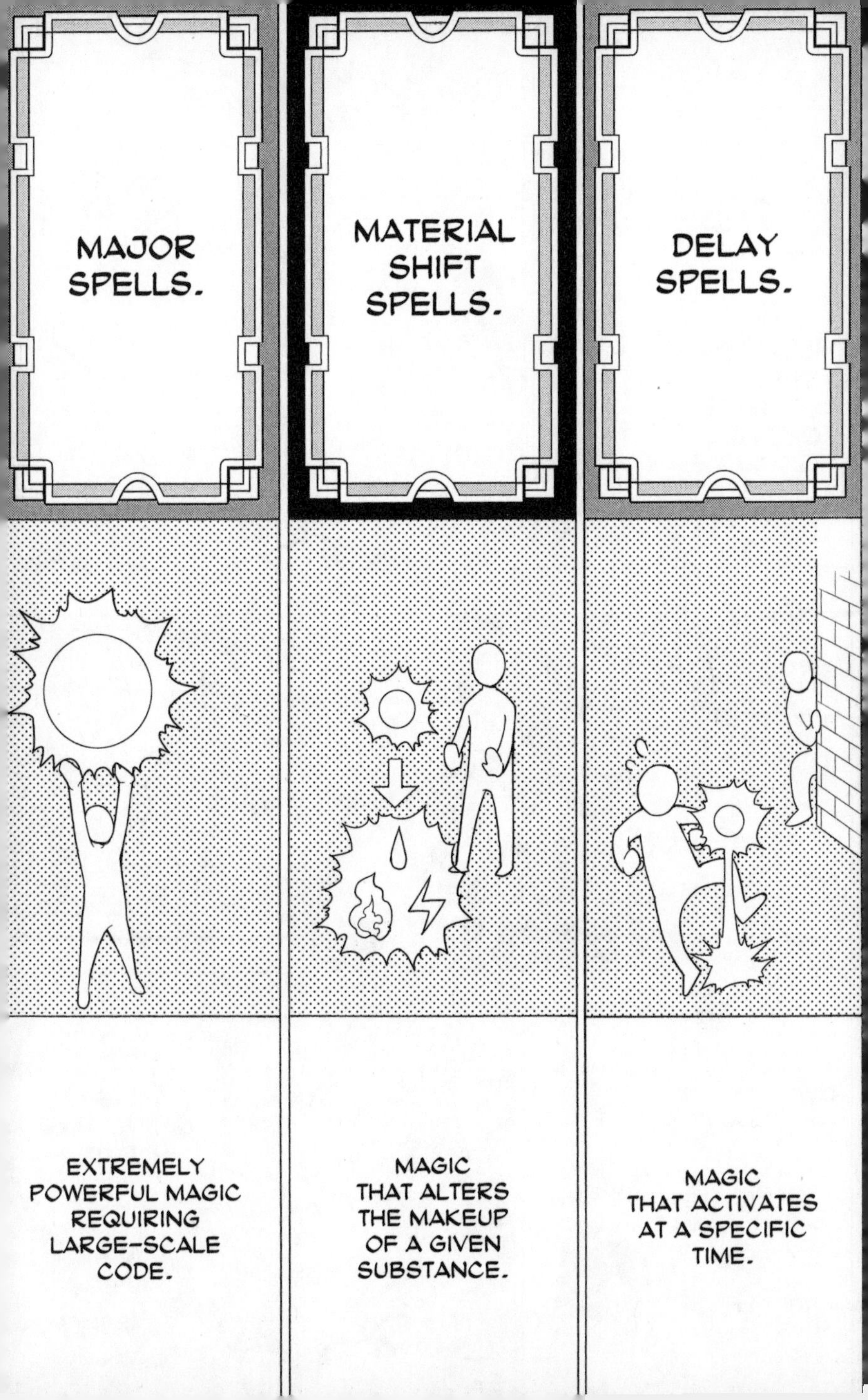
DELAY SPELLS.
MAGIC THAT ACTIVATES AT A SPECIFIC TIME.
MATERIAL SHIFT SPELLS.
MAGIC THAT ALTERS THE MAKEUP OF A GIVEN SUBSTANCE.
MAJOR SPELLS.
EXTREMELY POWERFUL MAGIC REQUIRING LARGE-SCALE CODE.

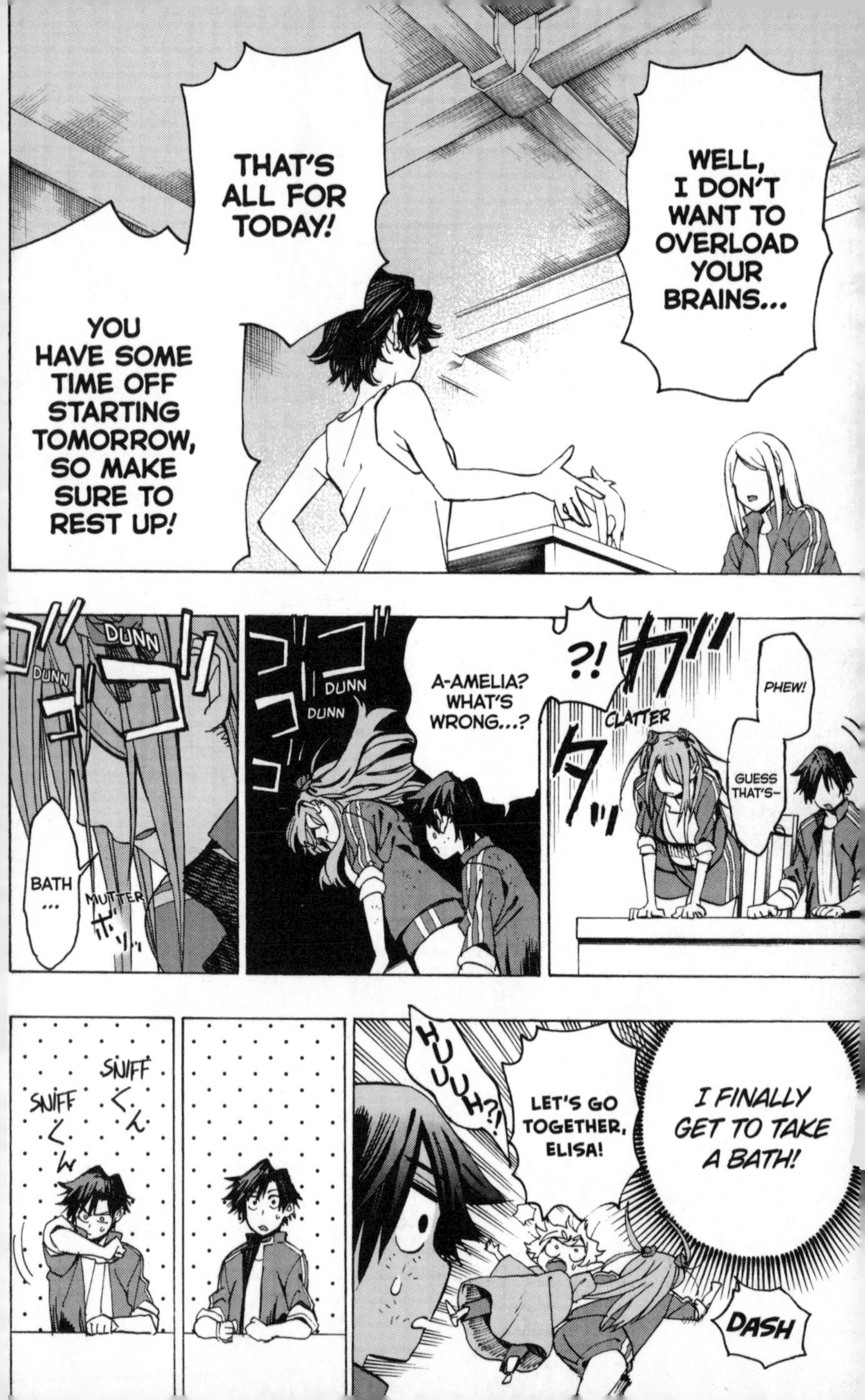
WELL, I DON'T WANT TO OVERLOAD YOUR BRAINS...
THAT'S ALL FOR TODAY!
YOU HAVE SOME TIME OFF STARTING TOMORROW, SO MAKE SURE TO REST UP!
PHEW!
GUESS THAT'S-
?!
CLATTER
A-AMELIA? WHAT'S WRONG...?
DUNN
DUNN
DUNN
DUNN
BATH...
MUTTER
I FINALLY GET TO TAKE A BATH!
LET'S GO TOGETHER, ELISA!
HUUUH?!
DASH
SNIFF
SNIFF

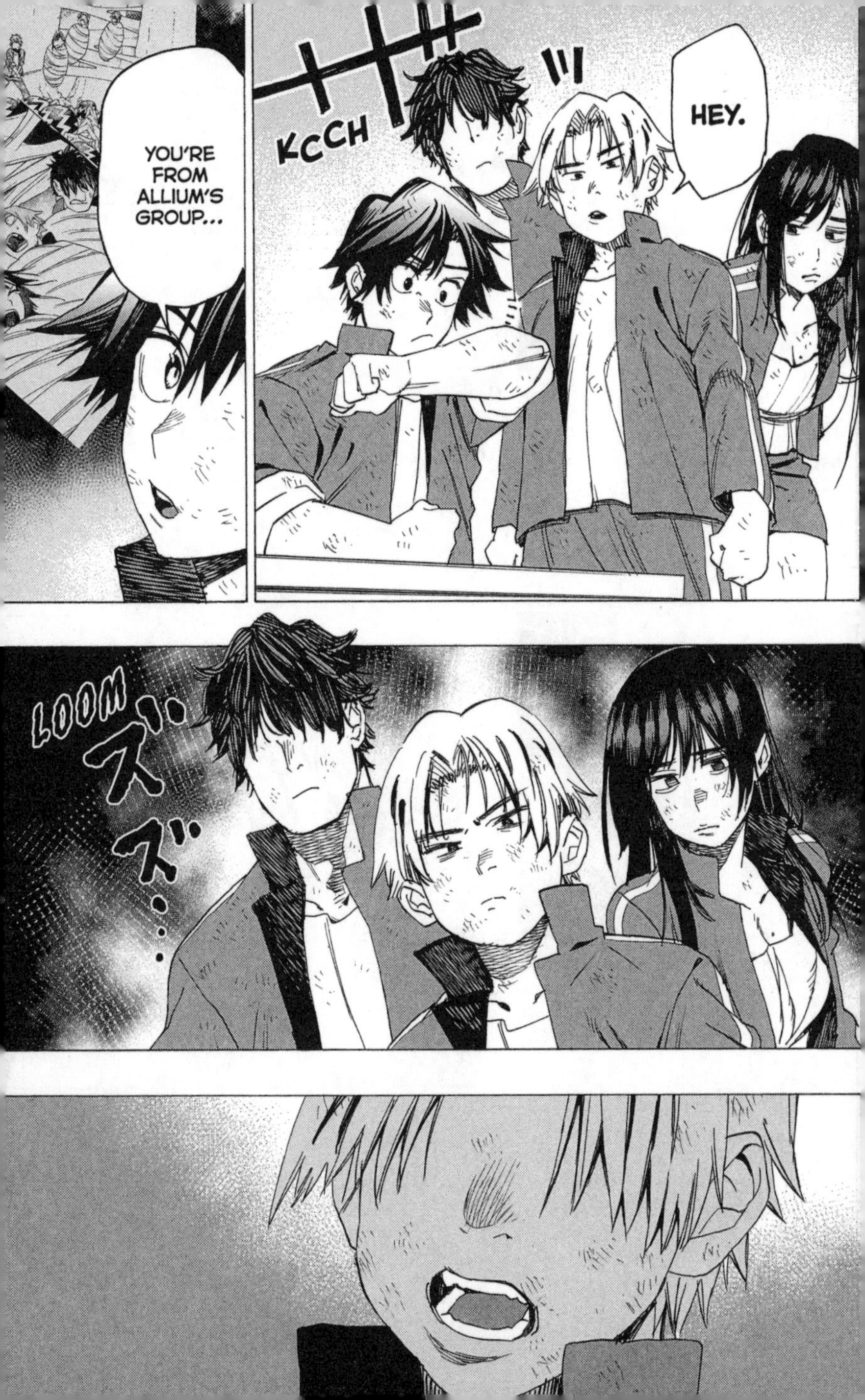
HEY.
ヅ
KCCH
YOU'RE FROM ALLIUM'S GROUP...
LOOM
ズズ…

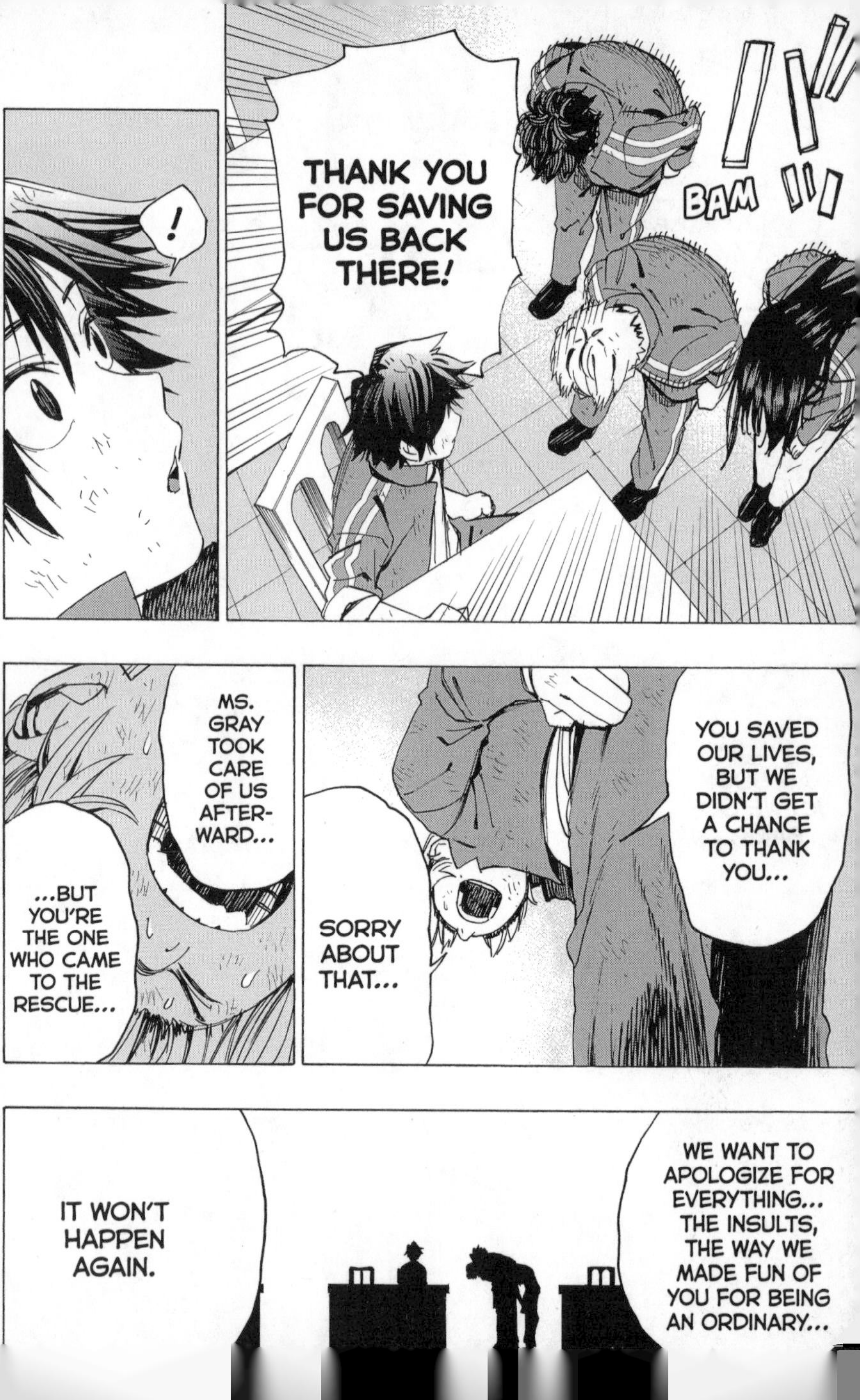
BAM
THANK YOU FOR SAVING US BACK THERE!
!
YOU SAVED OUR LIVES, BUT WE DIDN'T GET A CHANCE TO THANK YOU...
SORRY ABOUT THAT...
MS. GRAY TOOK CARE OF US AFTER-WARD...
...BUT YOU'RE THE ONE WHO CAME TO THE RESCUE...
WE WANT TO APOLOGIZE FOR EVERYTHING... THE INSULTS, THE WAY WE MADE FUN OF YOU FOR BEING AN ORDINARY...
IT WON'T HAPPEN AGAIN.

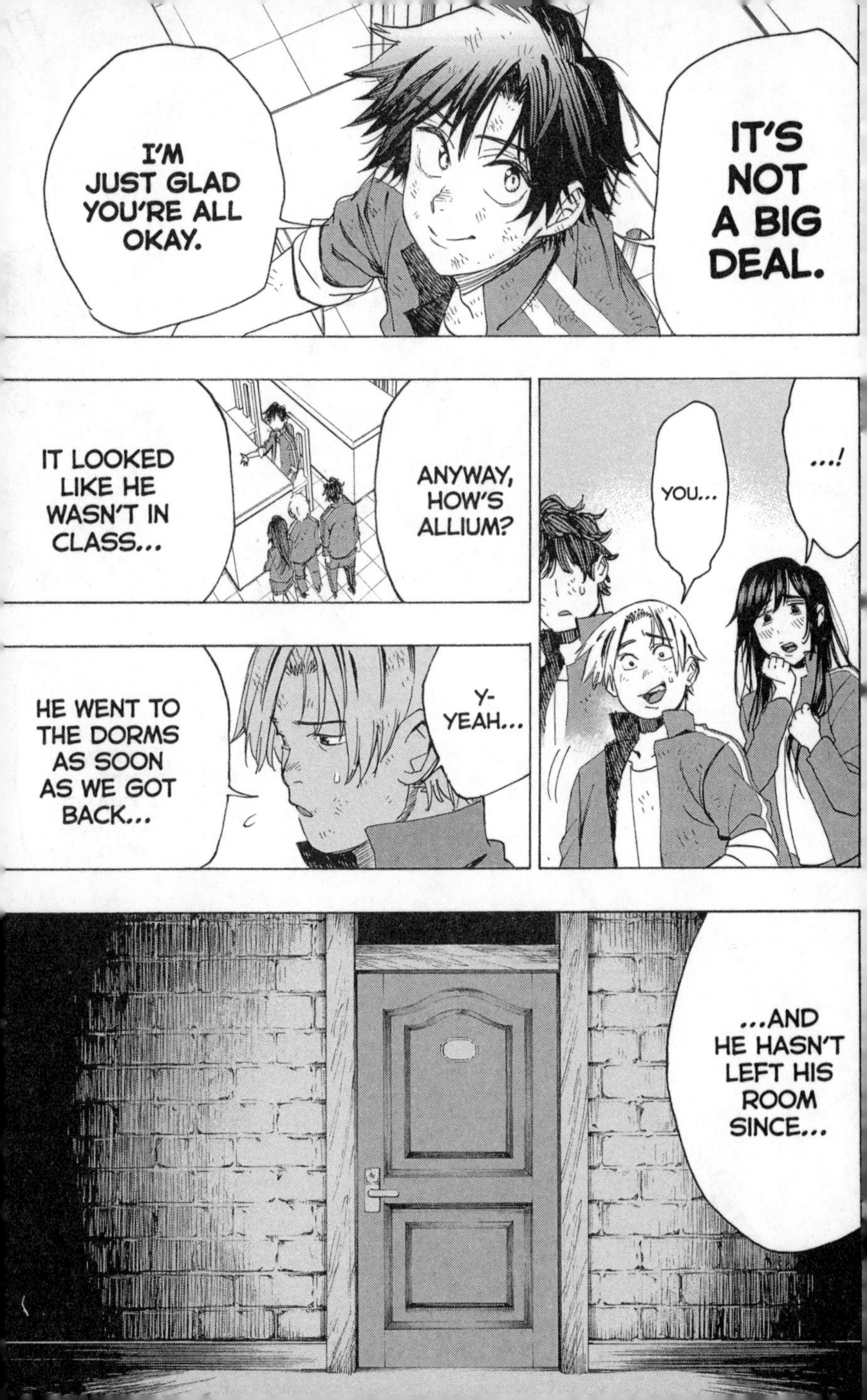
IT'S NOT A BIG DEAL.
I'M JUST GLAD YOU'RE ALL OKAY.
...!
YOU...
ANYWAY, HOW'S ALLIUM?
IT LOOKED LIKE HE WASN'T IN CLASS...
Y-YEAH...
HE WENT TO THE DORMS AS SOON AS WE GOT BACK...
...AND HE HASN'T LEFT HIS ROOM SINCE...

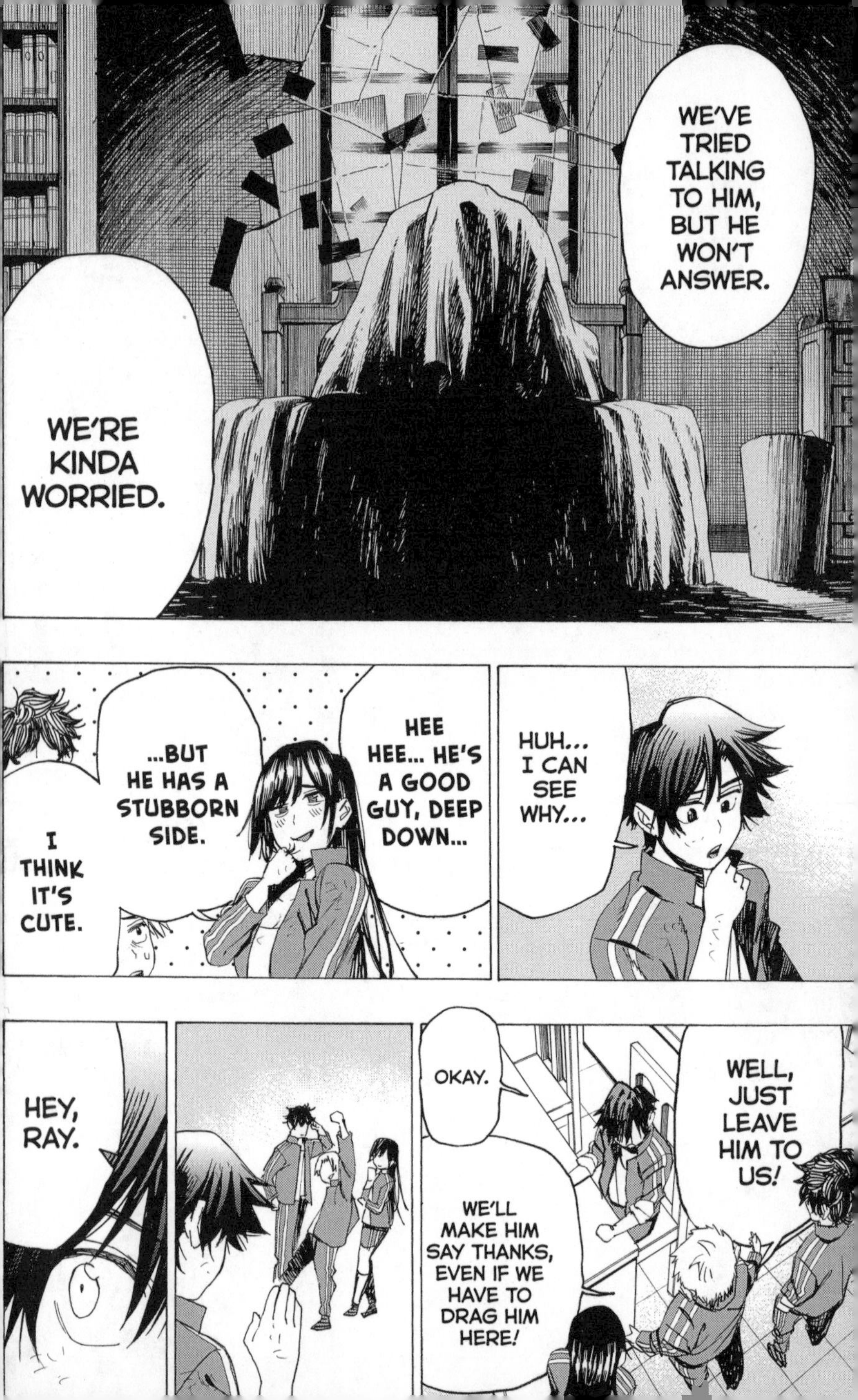
WE'VE TRIED TALKING TO HIM, BUT HE WON'T ANSWER.
WE'RE KINDA WORRIED.
HUH... I CAN SEE WHY...
HEE HEE... HE'S A GOOD GUY, DEEP DOWN...
...BUT HE HAS A STUBBORN SIDE.
I THINK IT'S CUTE.
WELL, JUST LEAVE HIM TO US!
WE'LL MAKE HIM SAY THANKS, EVEN IF WE HAVE TO DRAG HIM HERE!
OKAY.
HEY, RAY.

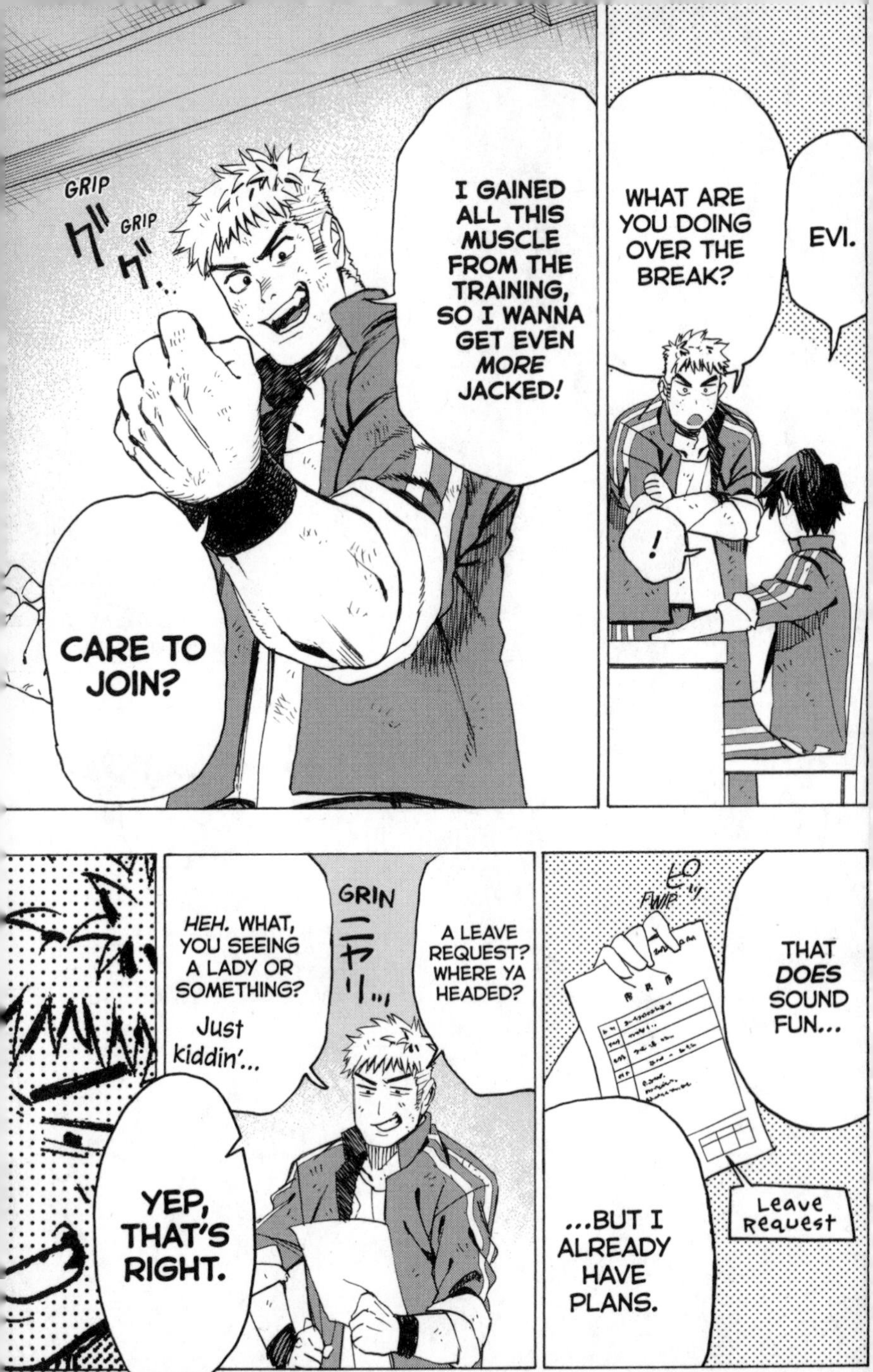
EVI.
WHAT ARE YOU DOING OVER THE BREAK?
!
I GAINED ALL THIS MUSCLE FROM THE TRAINING, SO I WANNA GET EVEN *MORE* JACKED!
GRIP
GRIP
CARE TO JOIN?
THAT *DOES* SOUND FUN...
FWIP
Leave Request
...BUT I ALREADY HAVE PLANS.
A LEAVE REQUEST? WHERE YA HEADED?
GRIN
HEH. WHAT, YOU SEEING A LADY OR SOMETHING?
Just kiddin'...
YEP, THAT'S RIGHT.

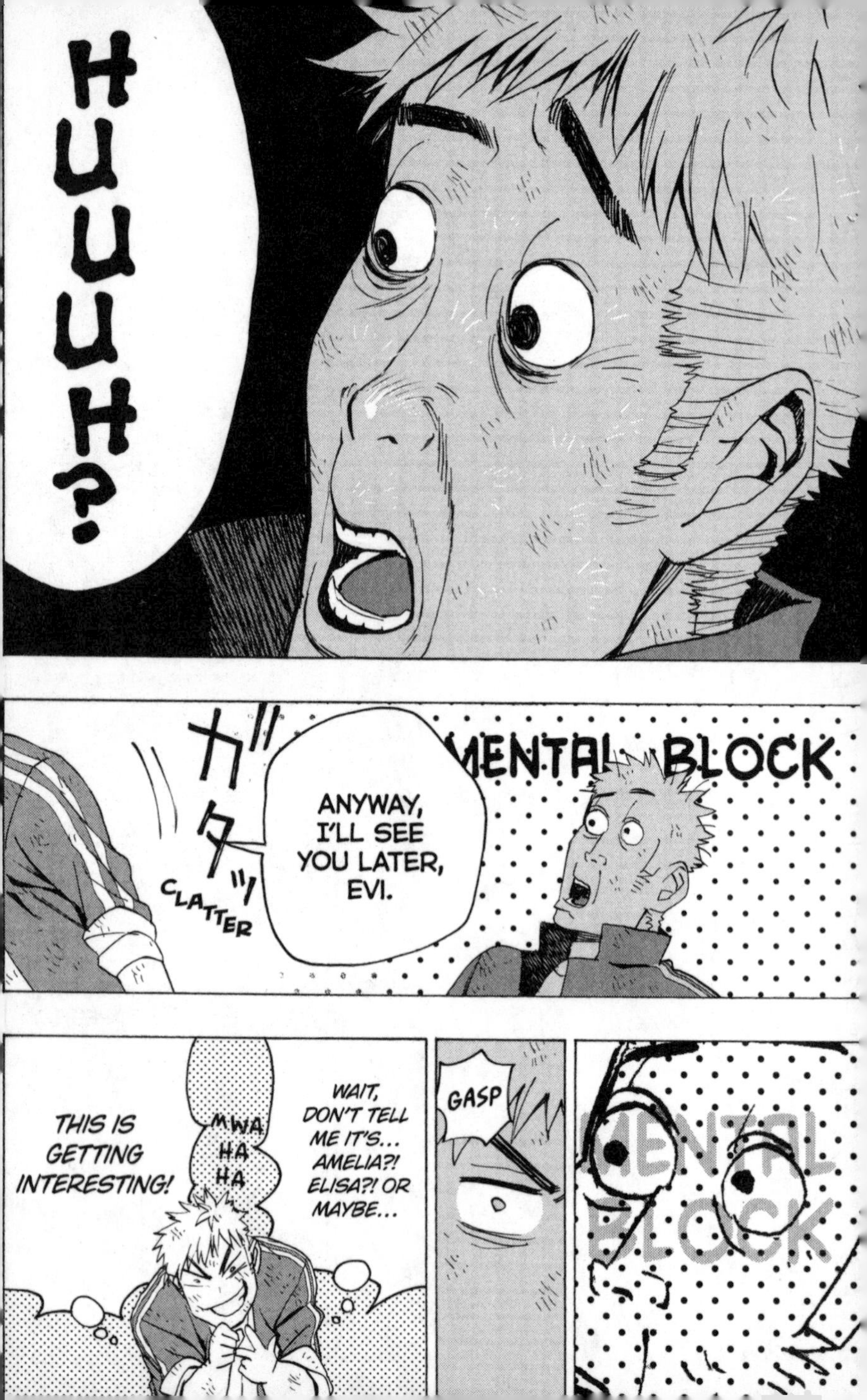
HUUUH?
MENTAL BLOCK
ANYWAY, I'LL SEE YOU LATER, EVI.
カタッ
CLATTER
MENTAL BLOCK
GASP
WAIT, DON'T TELL ME IT'S... AMELIA?! ELISA?! OR MAYBE...
MWA HA HA
THIS IS GETTING INTERESTING!

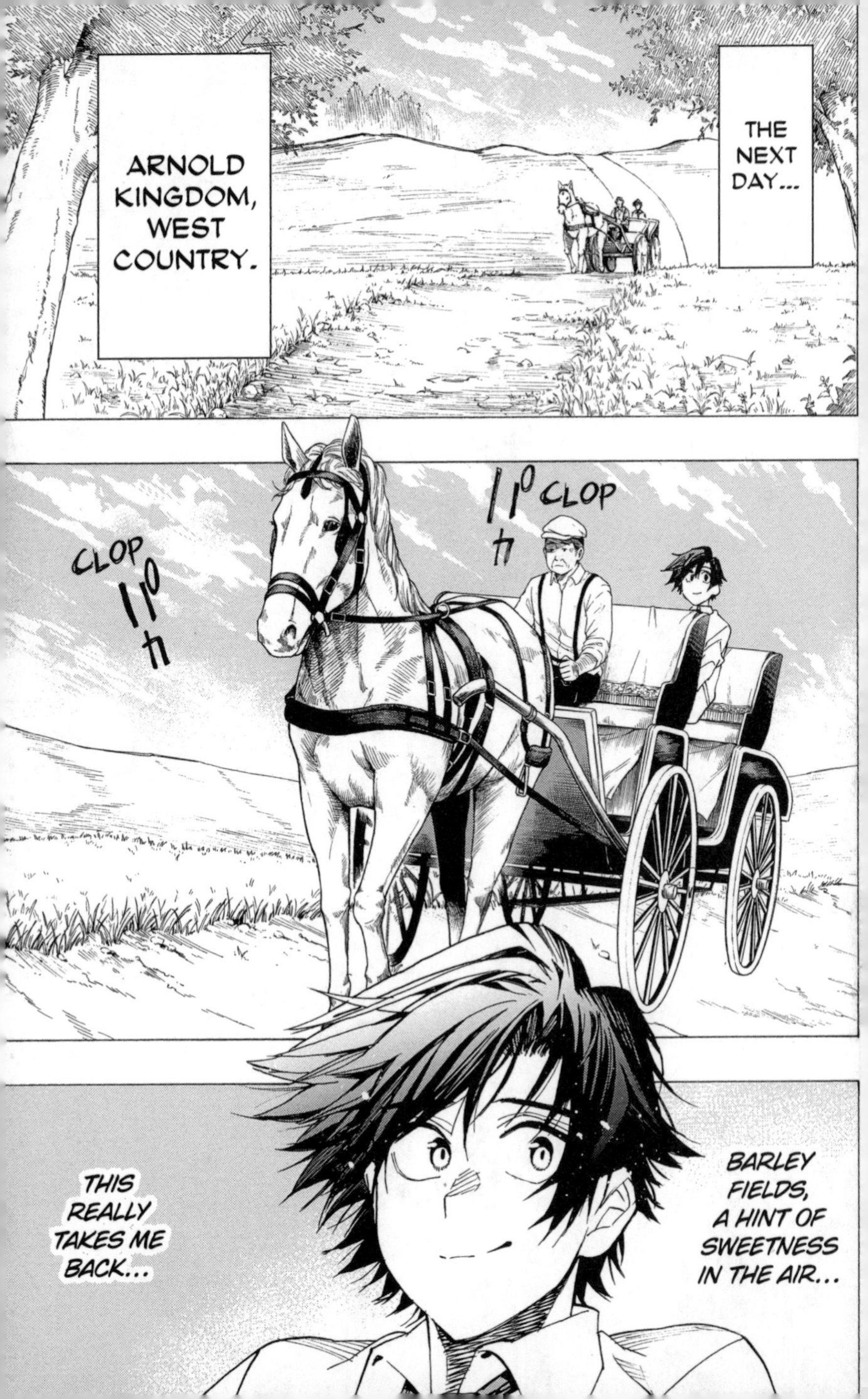
THE NEXT DAY...
ARNOLD KINGDOM, WEST COUNTRY.
CLOP
CLOP
BARLEY FIELDS, A HINT OF SWEETNESS IN THE AIR...
THIS REALLY TAKES ME BACK...

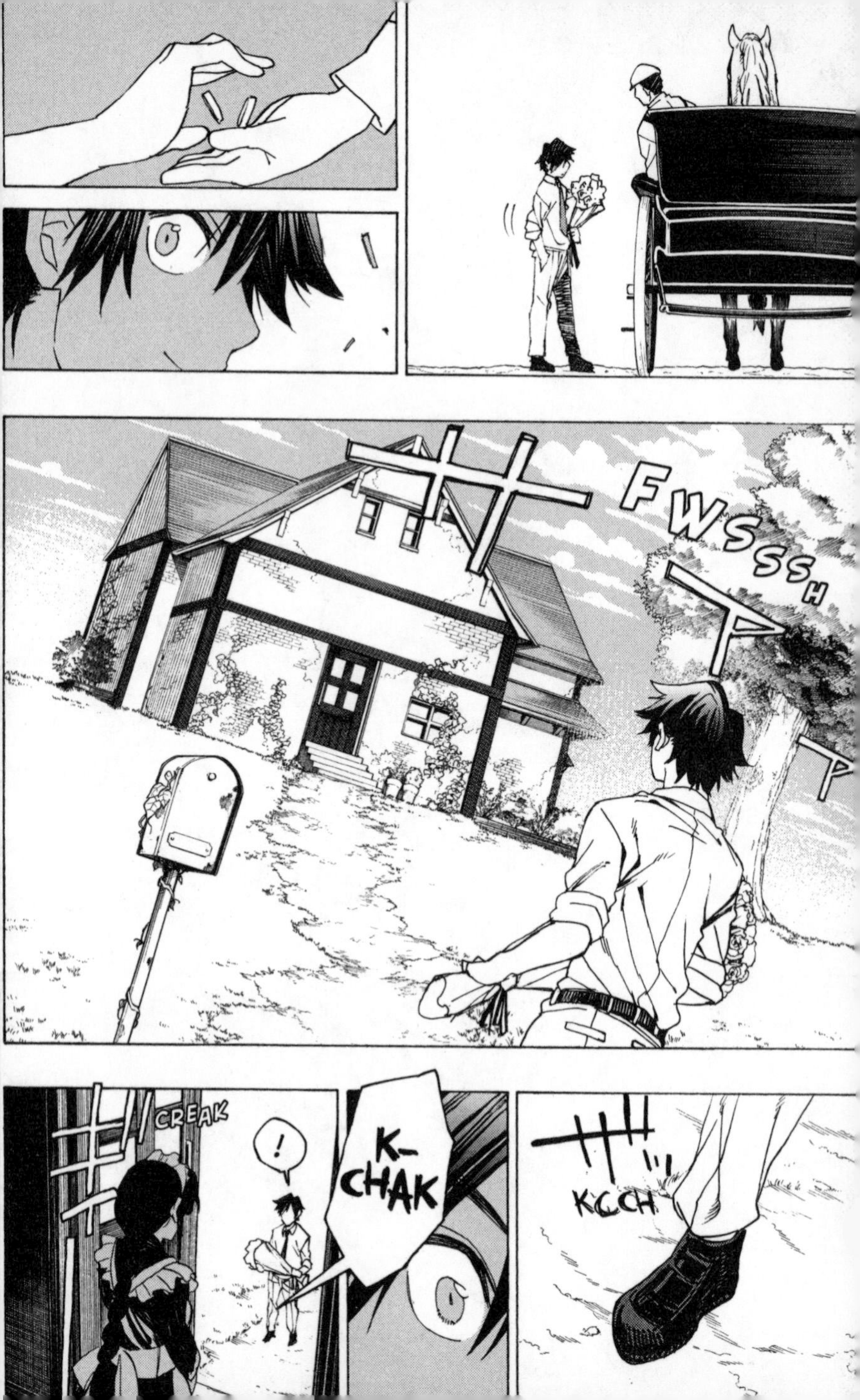
FWSSSH
CREAK
!
K-CHAK
KCCH

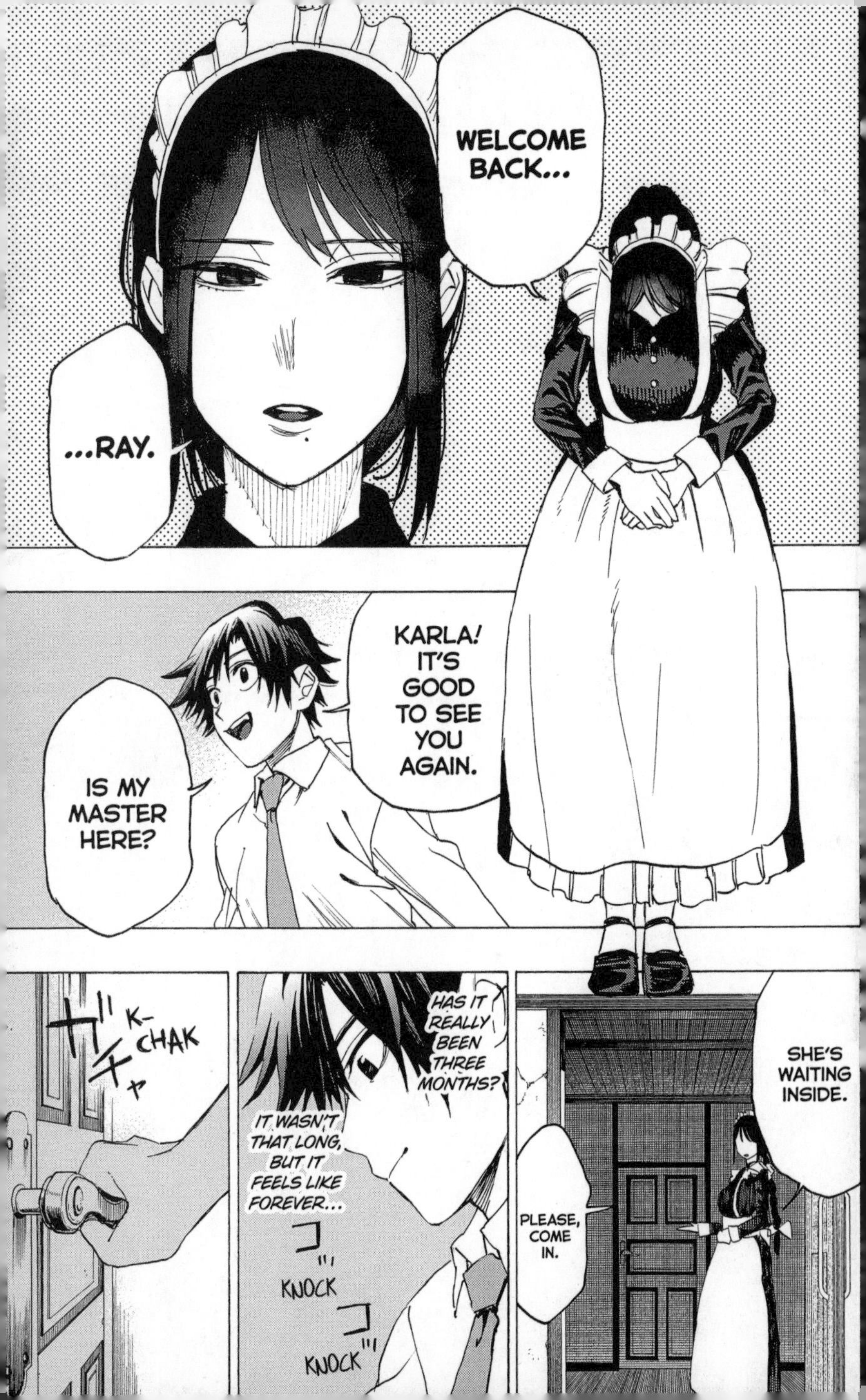
WELCOME BACK...
...RAY.
KARLA! IT'S GOOD TO SEE YOU AGAIN.
IS MY MASTER HERE?
SHE'S WAITING INSIDE.
PLEASE, COME IN.
HAS IT REALLY BEEN THREE MONTHS?
IT WASN'T THAT LONG, BUT IT FEELS LIKE FOREVER...
KNOCK
KNOCK
K-CHAK

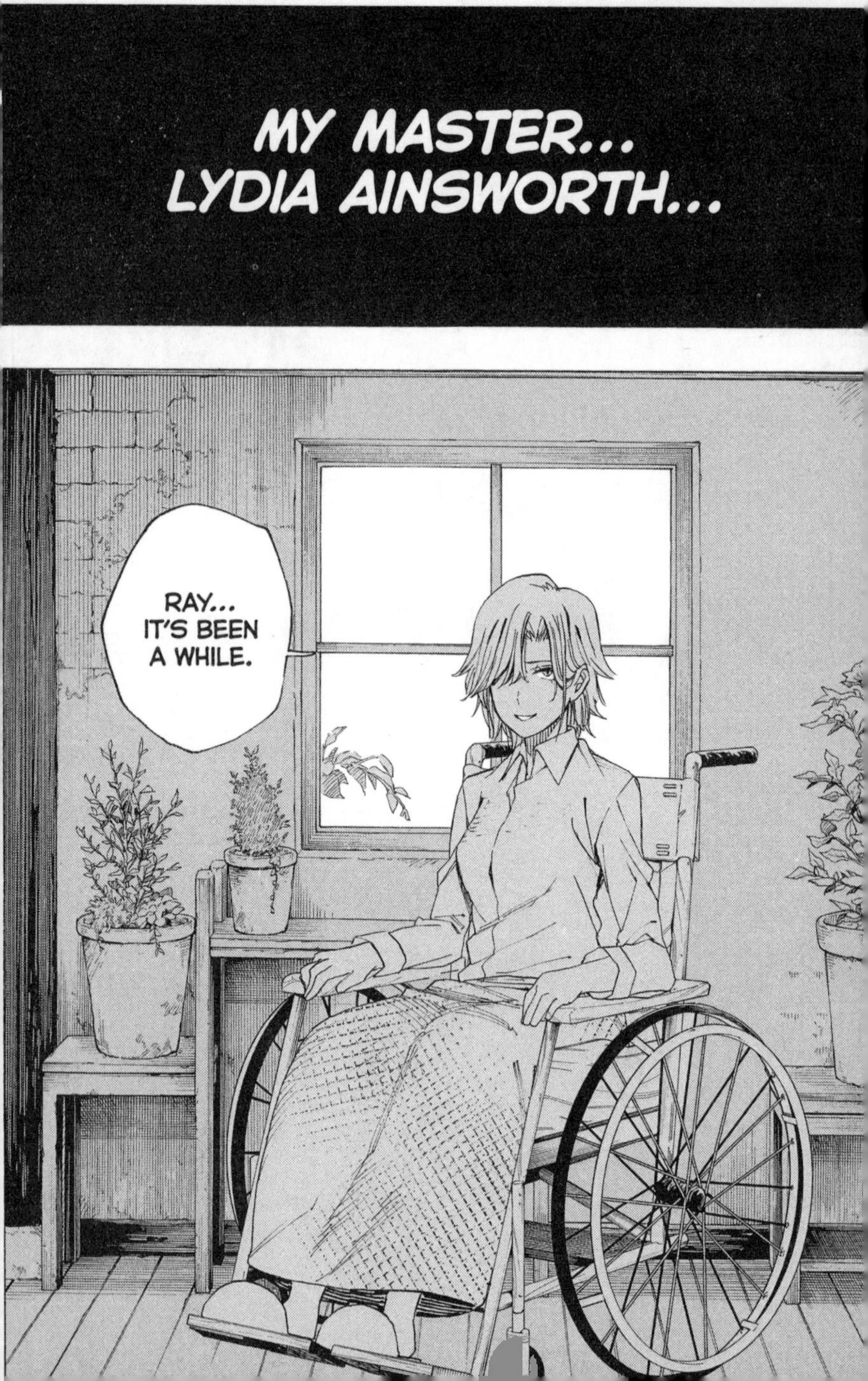
MY MASTER... LYDIA AINSWORTH...
RAY... IT'S BEEN A WHILE.

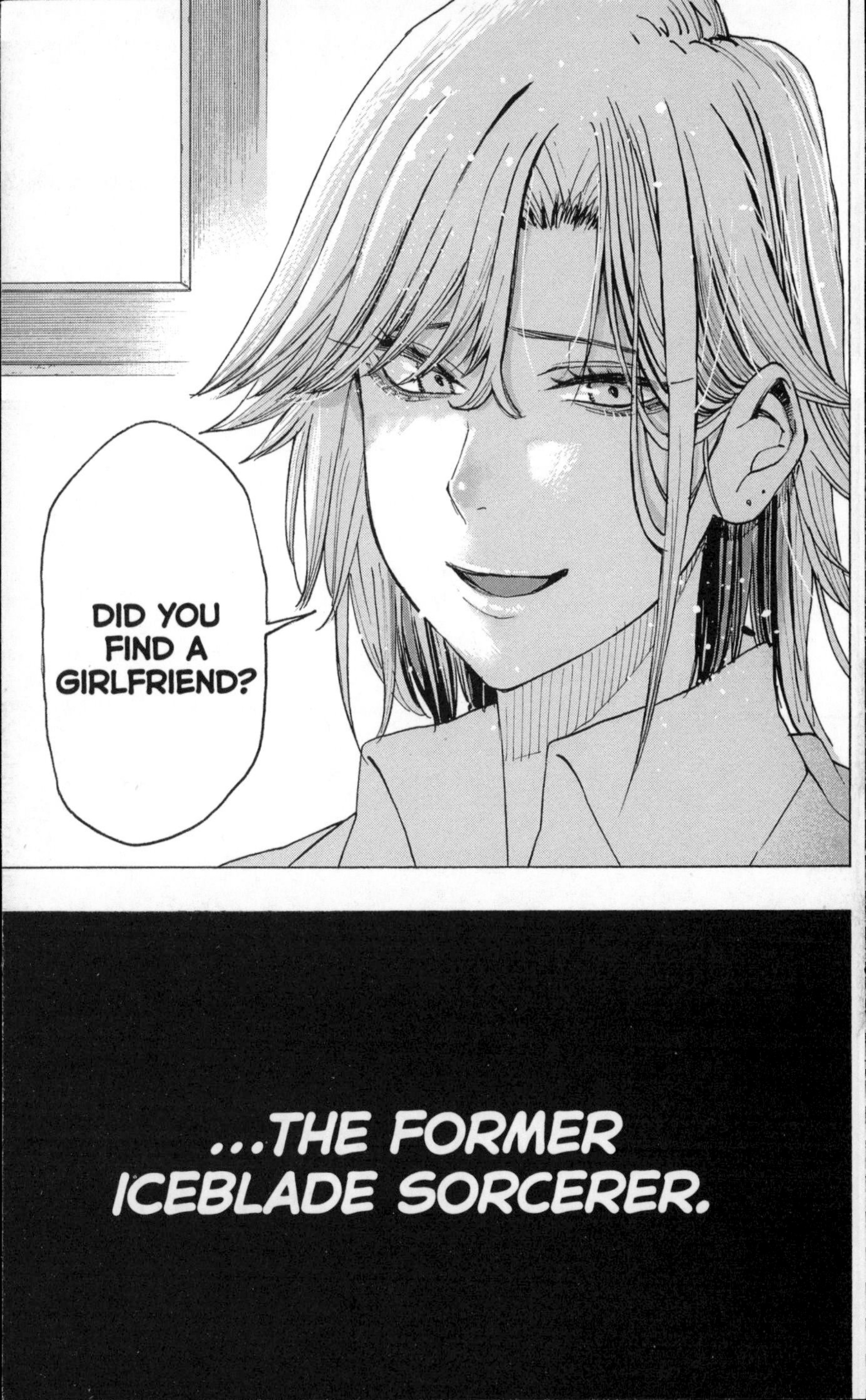
DID YOU FIND A GIRLFRIEND?
...THE FORMER ICEBLADE SORCERER.

The
**ICEBLADE
SORCERER
Shall RULE
the
WORLD**

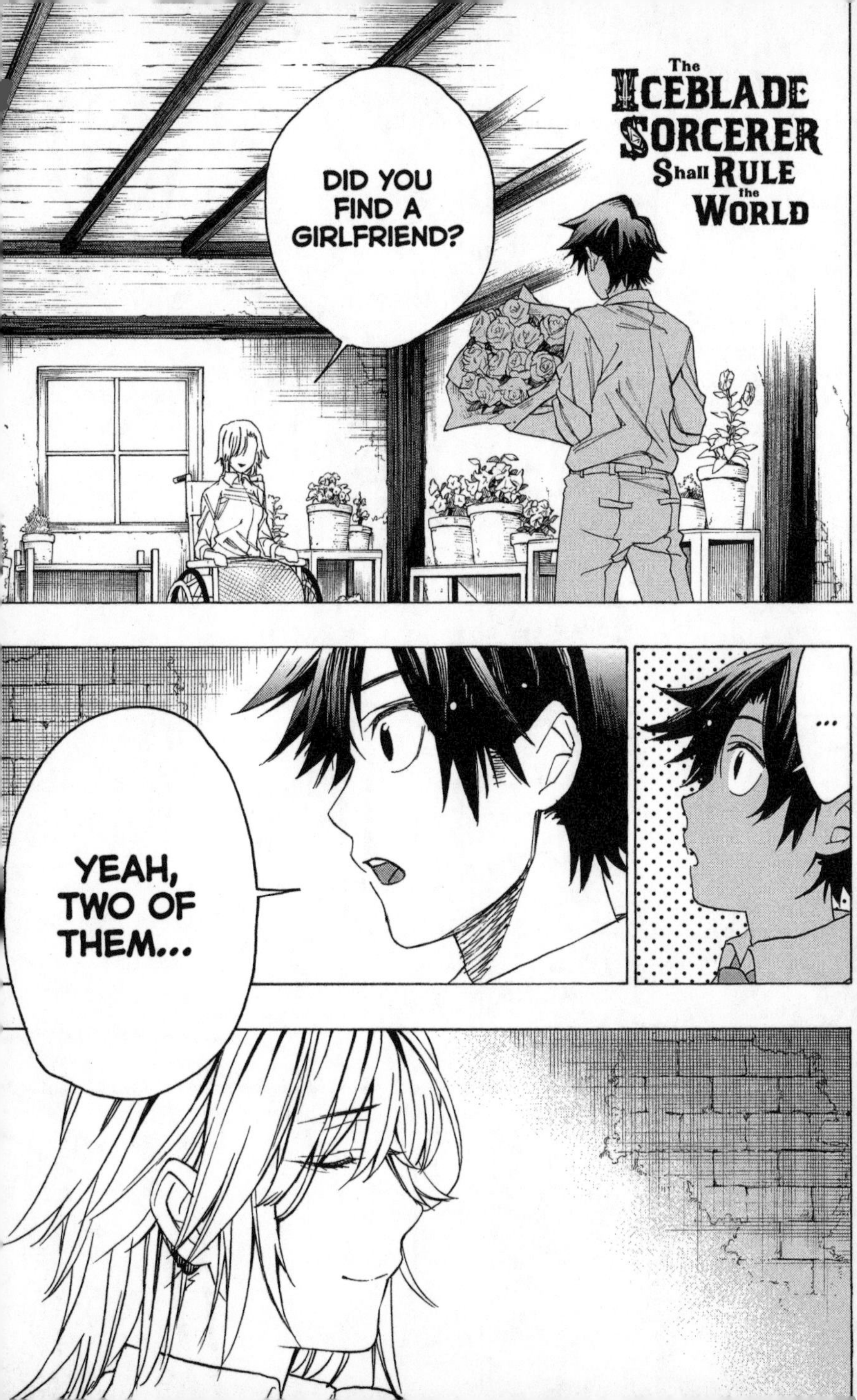
The ICEBLADE SORCERER Shall RULE the WORLD
DID YOU FIND A GIRLFRIEND?
...
YEAH, TWO OF THEM...

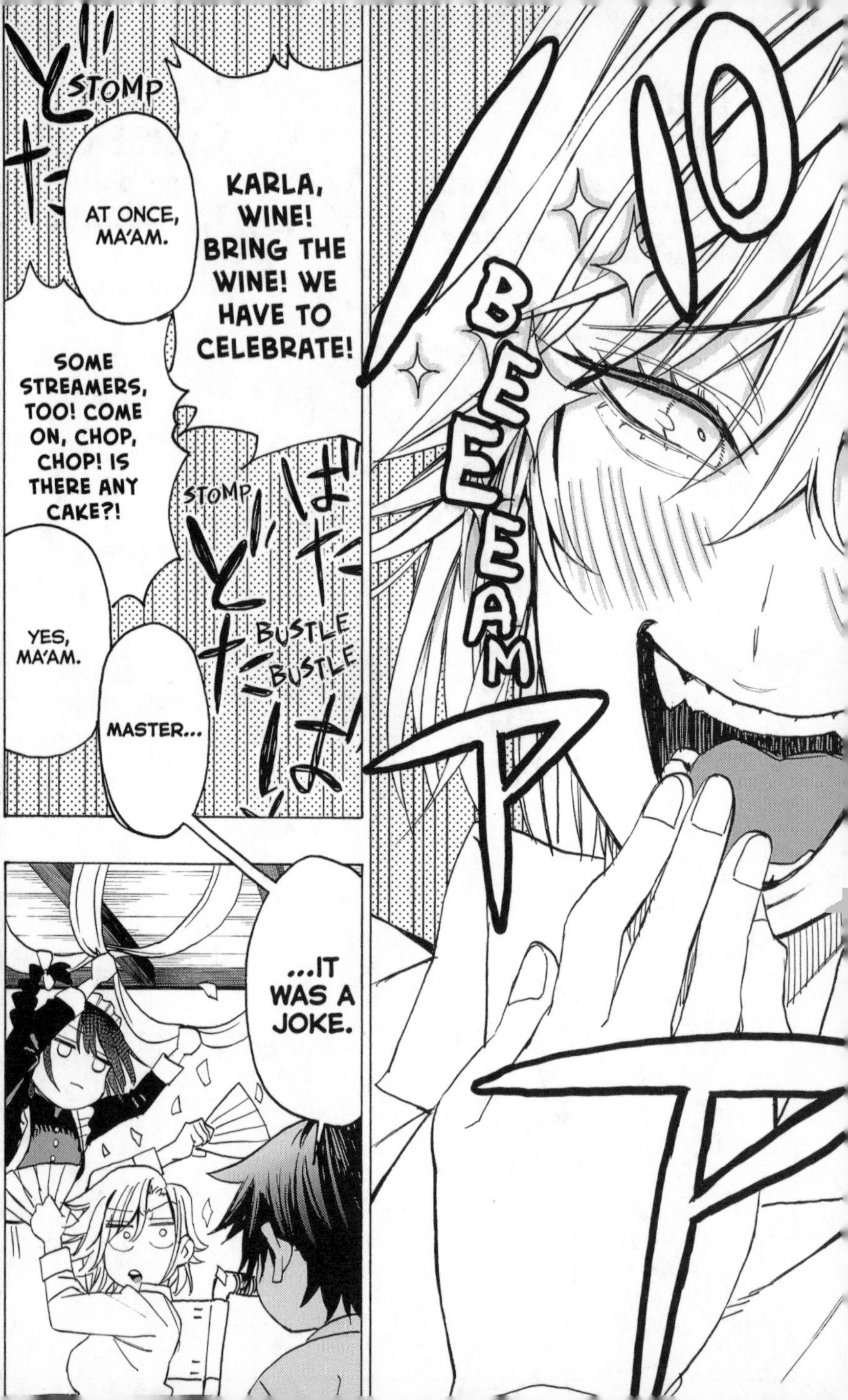
BEEEAM
KARLA, WINE! BRING THE WINE! WE HAVE TO CELEBRATE!
AT ONCE, MA'AM.
STOMP
SOME STREAMERS, TOO! COME ON, CHOP, CHOP! IS THERE ANY CAKE?!
YES, MA'AM.
STOMP
BUSTLE BUSTLE
MASTER...
...IT WAS A JOKE.

CHAPTER 12
Master

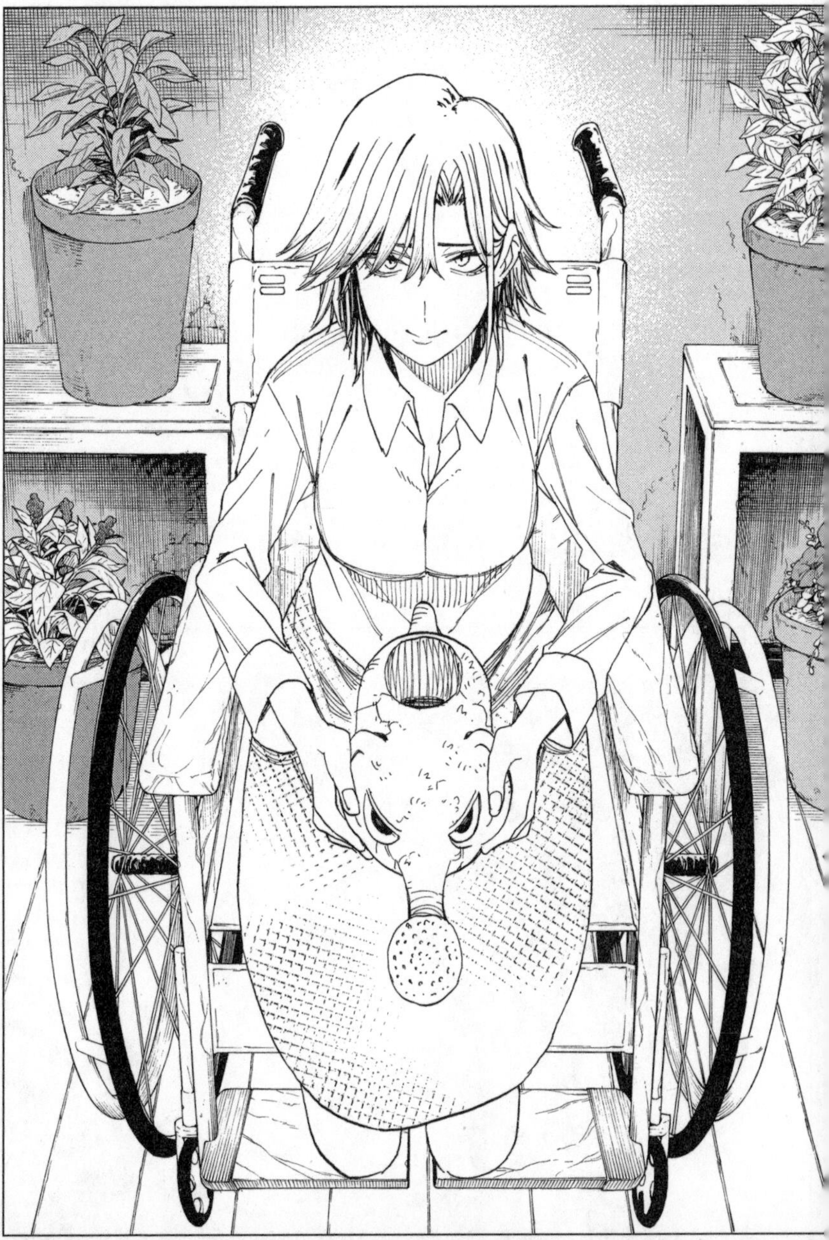

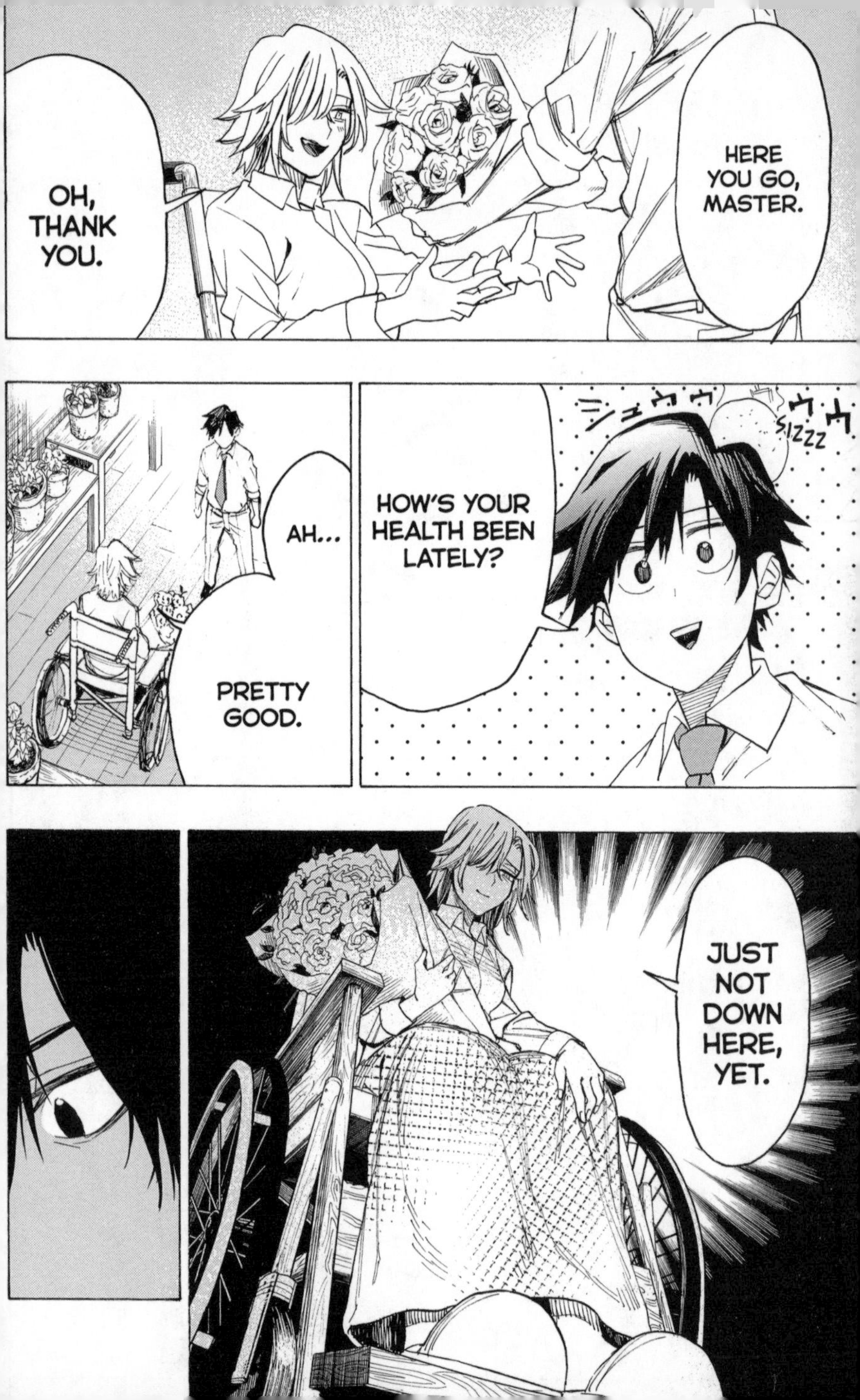
HERE YOU GO, MASTER.
OH, THANK YOU.
HOW'S YOUR HEALTH BEEN LATELY?
SIZZZ
AH...
PRETTY GOOD.
JUST NOT DOWN HERE, YET.

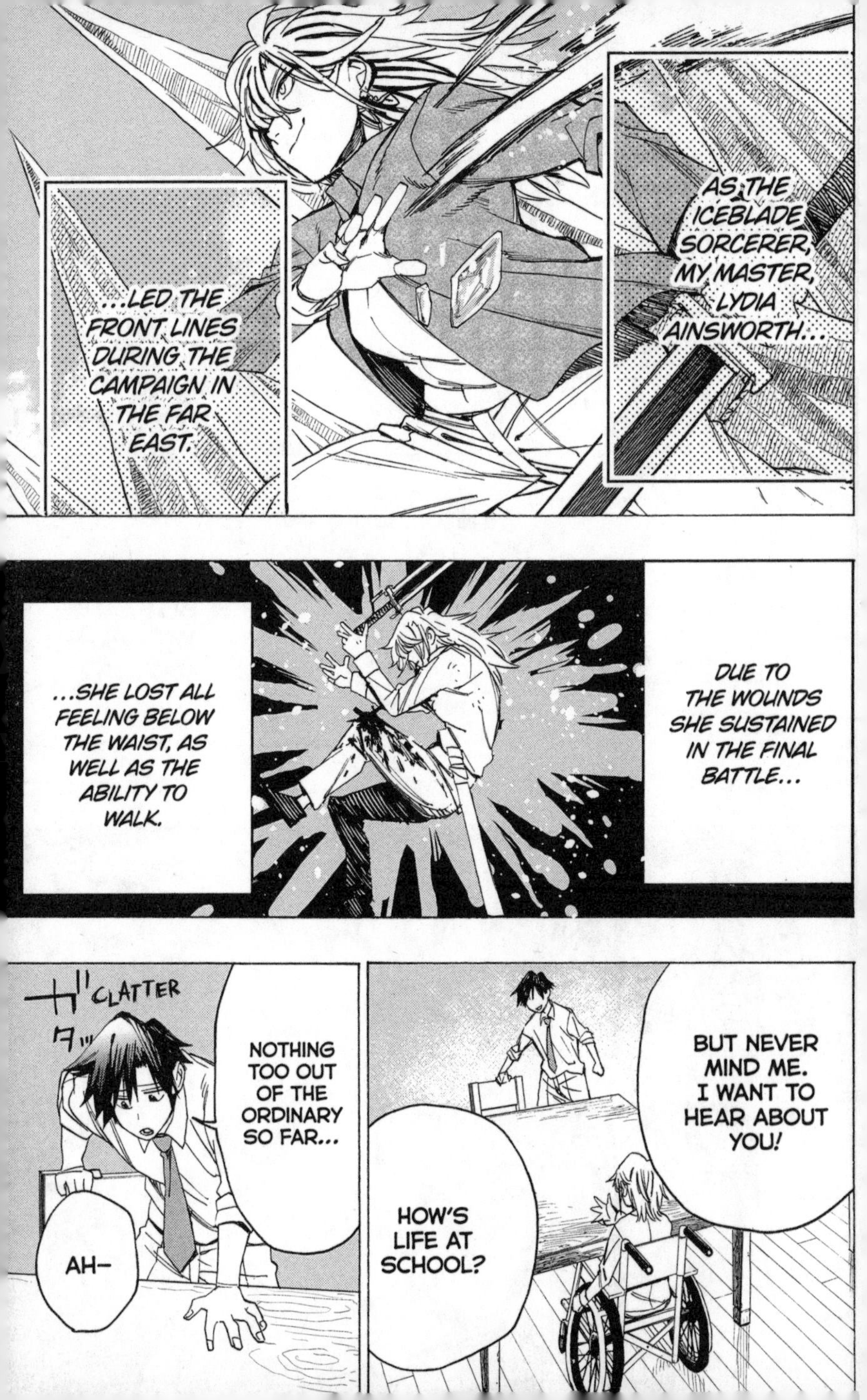
AS THE ICEBLADE SORCERER, MY MASTER, LYDIA AINSWORTH...
...LED THE FRONT LINES DURING THE CAMPAIGN IN THE FAR EAST.
DUE TO THE WOUNDS SHE SUSTAINED IN THE FINAL BATTLE...
...SHE LOST ALL FEELING BELOW THE WAIST, AS WELL AS THE ABILITY TO WALK.
BUT NEVER MIND ME. I WANT TO HEAR ABOUT YOU!
HOW'S LIFE AT SCHOOL?
NOTHING TOO OUT OF THE ORDINARY SO FAR...
CLATTER
AH–

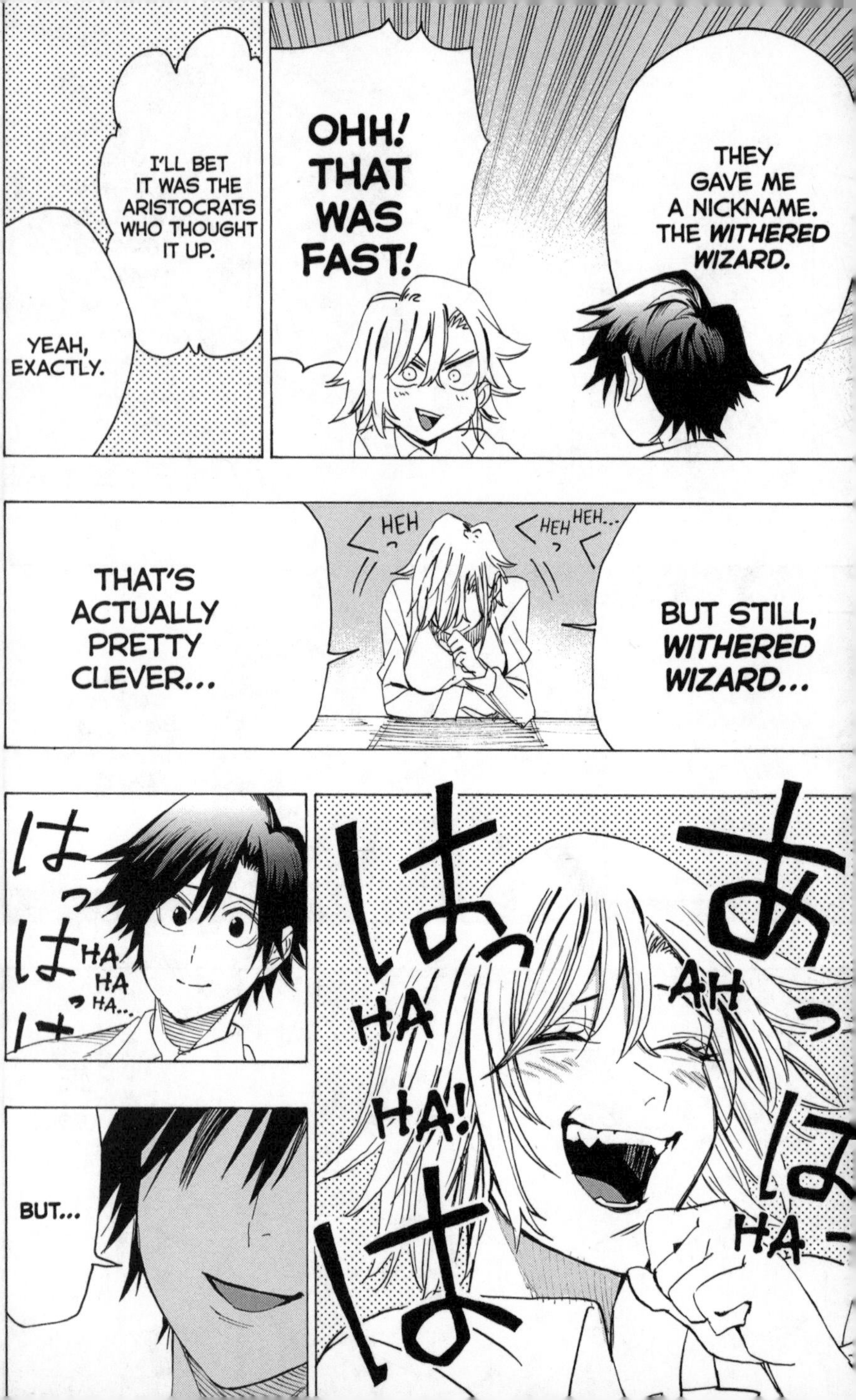

THEY GAVE ME A NICKNAME. THE *WITHERED WIZARD.*
OHH! THAT WAS FAST!
I'LL BET IT WAS THE ARISTOCRATS WHO THOUGHT IT UP.
YEAH, EXACTLY.
BUT STILL, *WITHERED WIZARD...*
HEH HEH HEH...
THAT'S ACTUALLY PRETTY CLEVER...
あっはー
AH HA-
はっは
HA HA!
はっはっは
HA HA HA...
BUT...

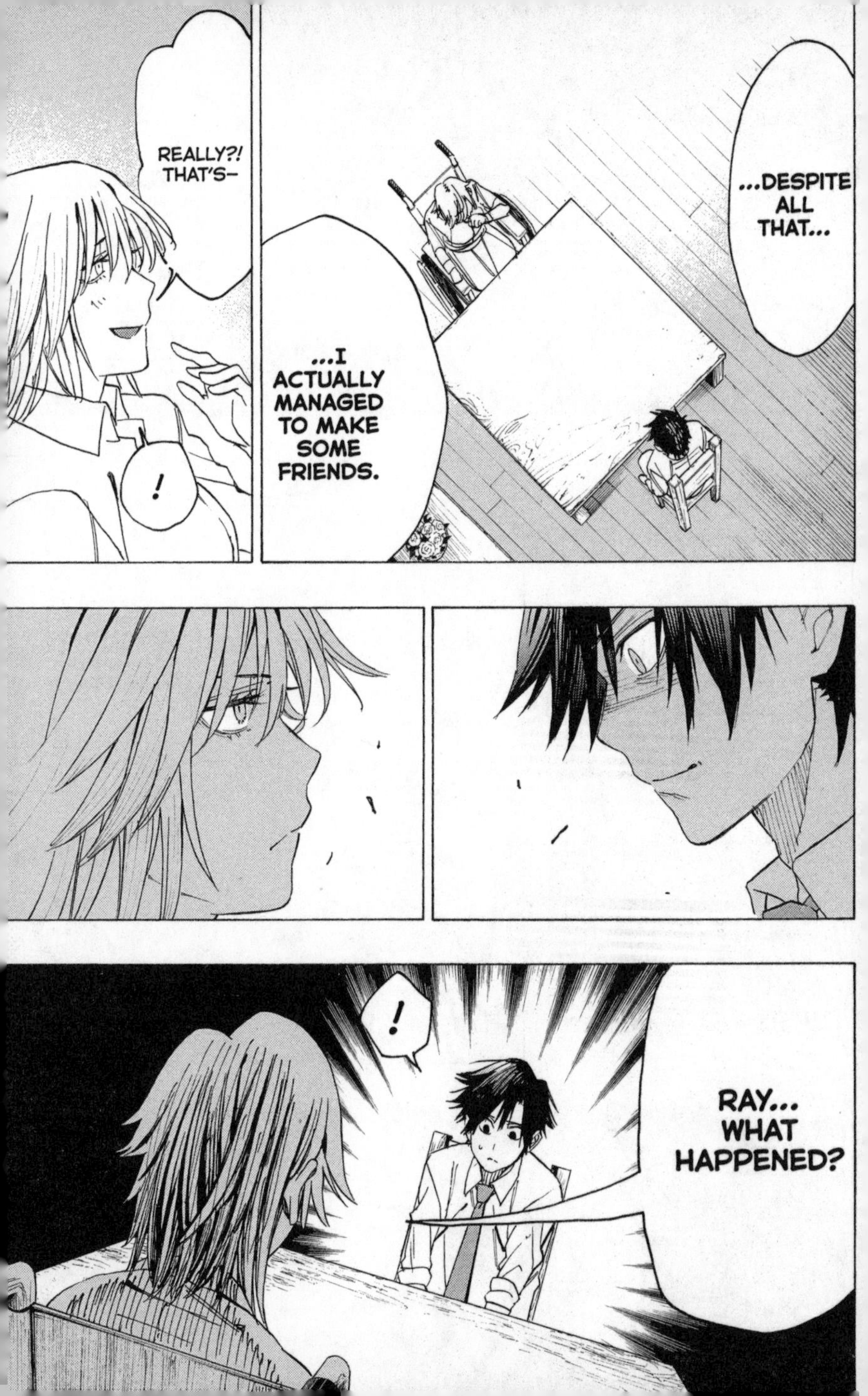
...DESPITE ALL THAT...
...I ACTUALLY MANAGED TO MAKE SOME FRIENDS.
REALLY?! THAT'S—
!
!
RAY... WHAT HAPPENED?

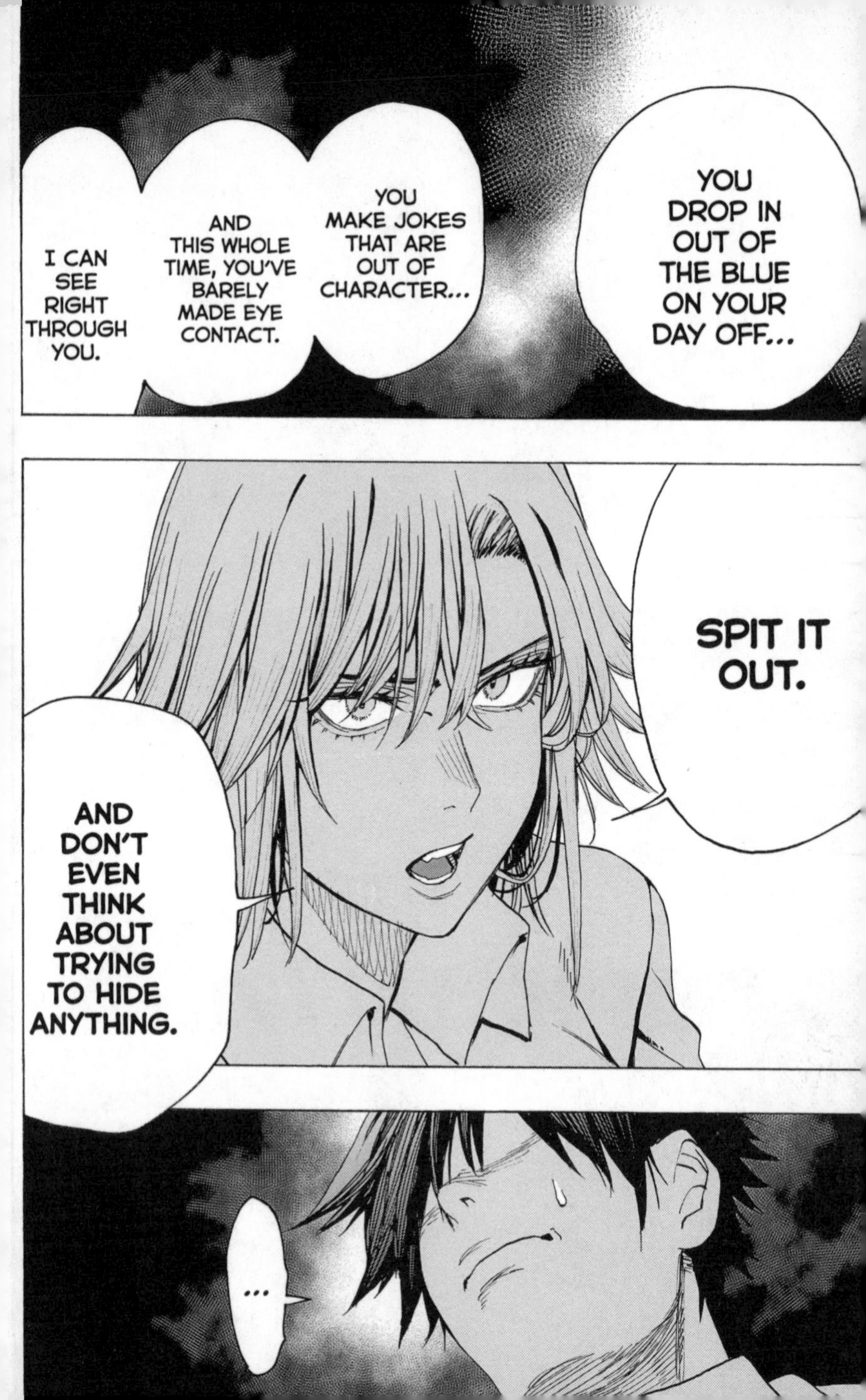
YOU DROP IN OUT OF THE BLUE ON YOUR DAY OFF...
YOU MAKE JOKES THAT ARE OUT OF CHARACTER...
AND THIS WHOLE TIME, YOU'VE BARELY MADE EYE CONTACT.
I CAN SEE RIGHT THROUGH YOU.
SPIT IT OUT.
AND DON'T EVEN THINK ABOUT TRYING TO HIDE ANYTHING.
...

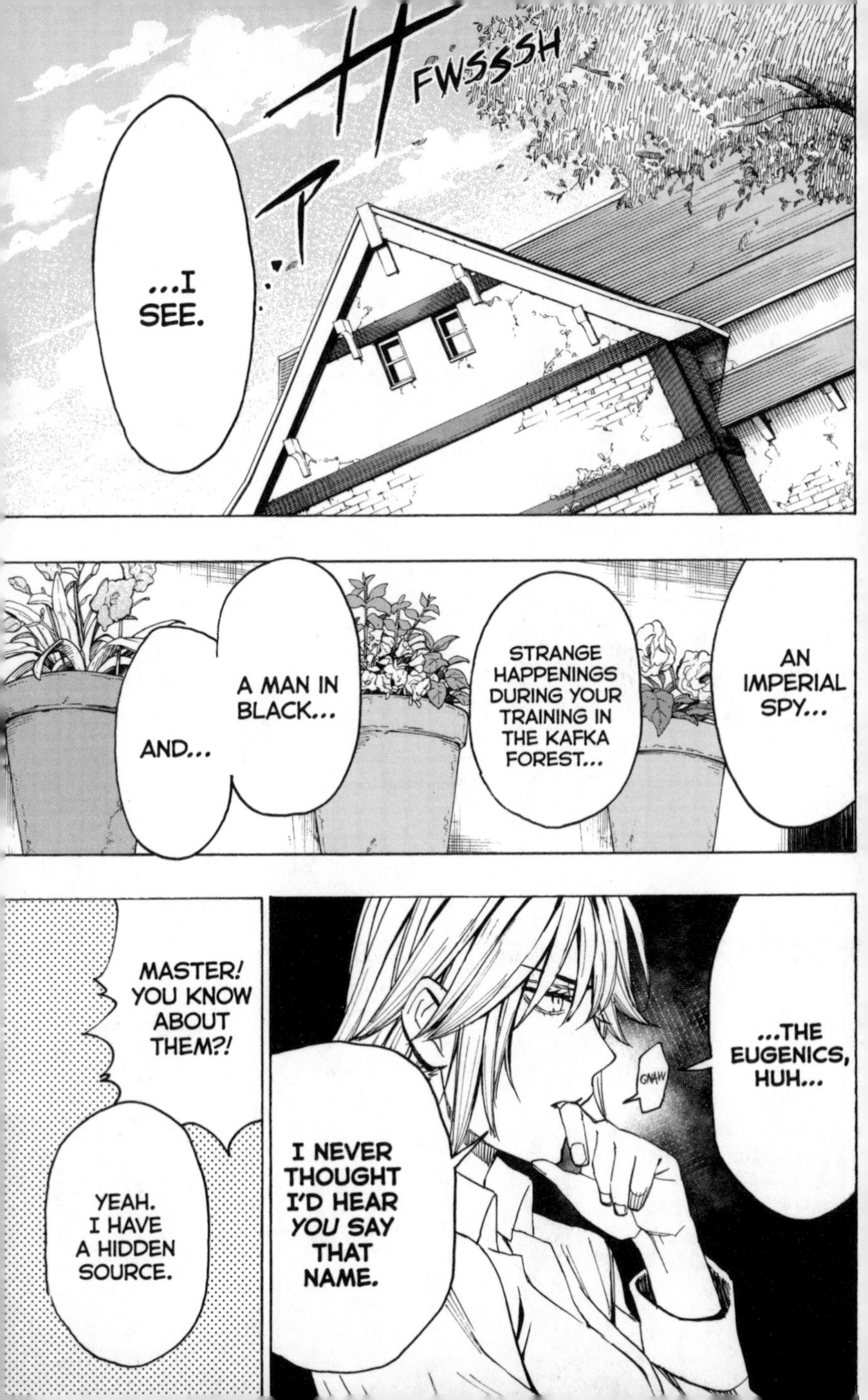
FWSSSH
...I SEE.
AN IMPERIAL SPY...
STRANGE HAPPENINGS DURING YOUR TRAINING IN THE KAFKA FOREST...
A MAN IN BLACK...
AND...
...THE EUGENICS, HUH...
GNAW
I NEVER THOUGHT I'D HEAR *YOU* SAY THAT NAME.
MASTER! YOU KNOW ABOUT THEM?!
YEAH. I HAVE A HIDDEN SOURCE.

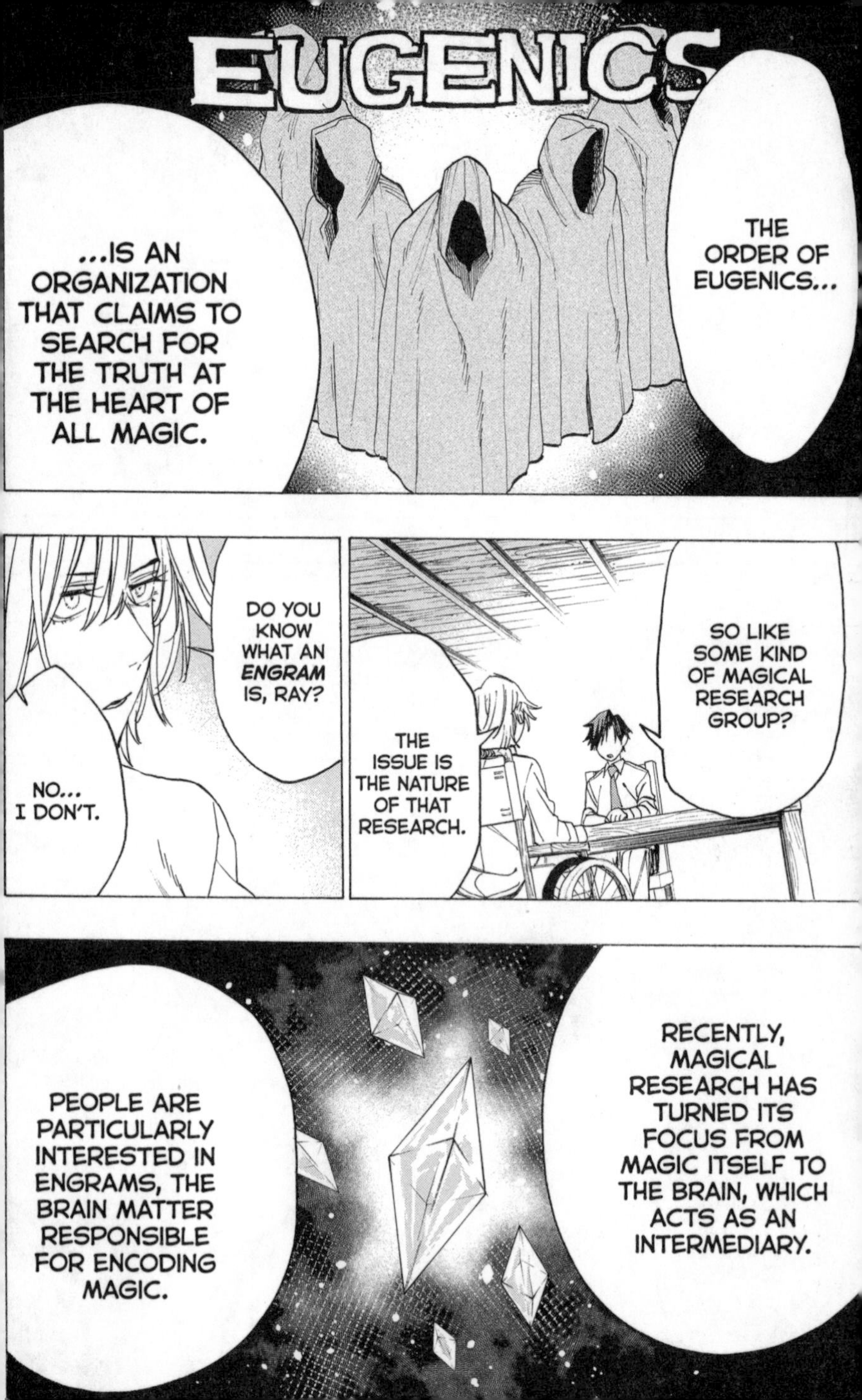
EUGENICS
THE ORDER OF EUGENICS...
...IS AN ORGANIZATION THAT CLAIMS TO SEARCH FOR THE TRUTH AT THE HEART OF ALL MAGIC.
SO LIKE SOME KIND OF MAGICAL RESEARCH GROUP?
THE ISSUE IS THE NATURE OF THAT RESEARCH.
DO YOU KNOW WHAT AN *ENGRAM* IS, RAY?
NO... I DON'T.
RECENTLY, MAGICAL RESEARCH HAS TURNED ITS FOCUS FROM MAGIC ITSELF TO THE BRAIN, WHICH ACTS AS AN INTERMEDIARY.
PEOPLE ARE PARTICULARLY INTERESTED IN ENGRAMS, THE BRAIN MATTER RESPONSIBLE FOR ENCODING MAGIC.

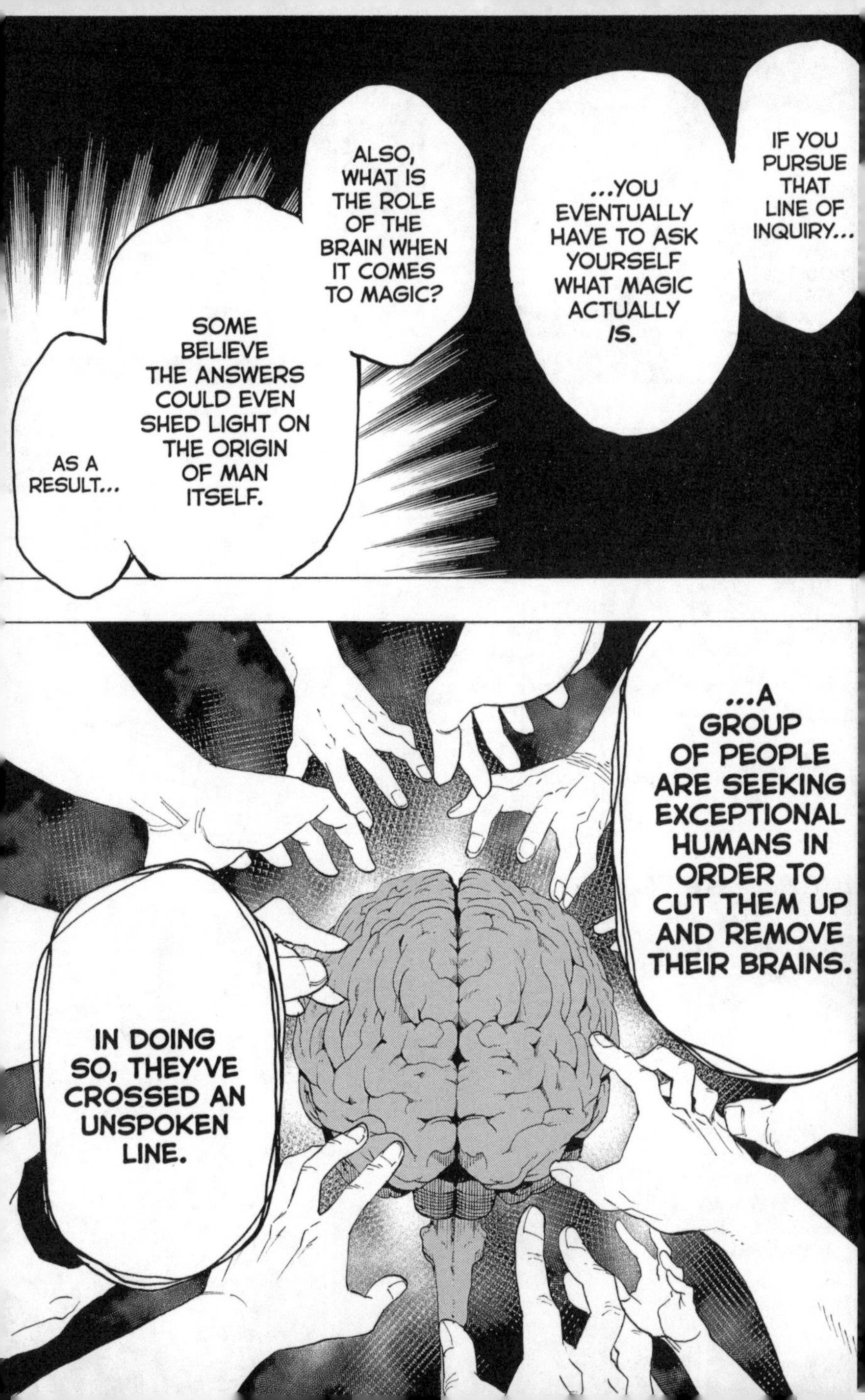
IF YOU PURSUE THAT LINE OF INQUIRY...
...YOU EVENTUALLY HAVE TO ASK YOURSELF WHAT MAGIC ACTUALLY *IS.*
ALSO, WHAT IS THE ROLE OF THE BRAIN WHEN IT COMES TO MAGIC?
SOME BELIEVE THE ANSWERS COULD EVEN SHED LIGHT ON THE ORIGIN OF MAN ITSELF.
AS A RESULT...
...A GROUP OF PEOPLE ARE SEEKING EXCEPTIONAL HUMANS IN ORDER TO CUT THEM UP AND REMOVE THEIR BRAINS.
IN DOING SO, THEY'VE CROSSED AN UNSPOKEN LINE.

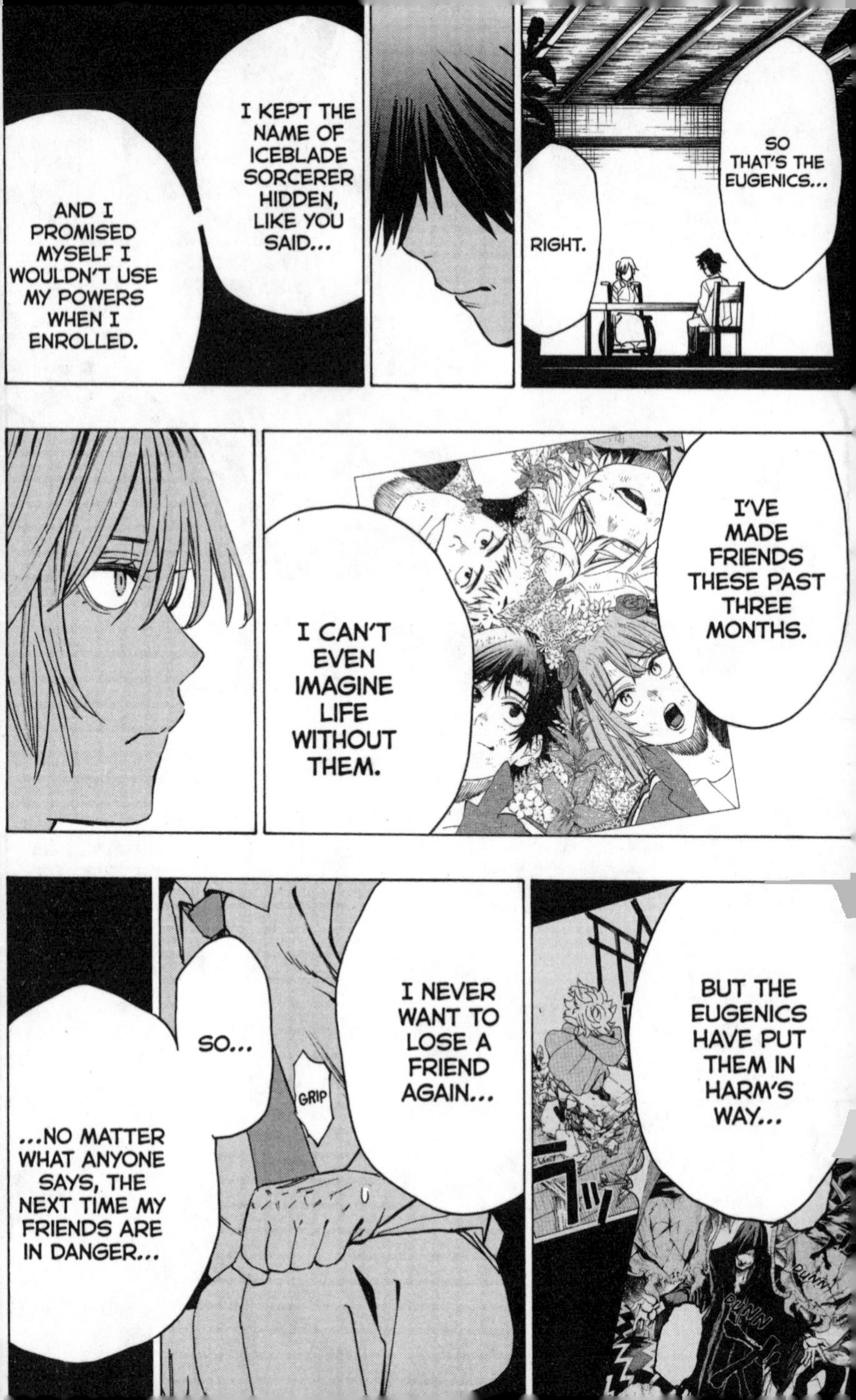
SO THAT'S THE EUGENICS...
RIGHT.
I KEPT THE NAME OF ICEBLADE SORCERER HIDDEN, LIKE YOU SAID...
AND I PROMISED MYSELF I WOULDN'T USE MY POWERS WHEN I ENROLLED.
I'VE MADE FRIENDS THESE PAST THREE MONTHS.
I CAN'T EVEN IMAGINE LIFE WITHOUT THEM.
BUT THE EUGENICS HAVE PUT THEM IN HARM'S WAY...
I NEVER WANT TO LOSE A FRIEND AGAIN...
SO...
GRIP
...NO MATTER WHAT ANYONE SAYS, THE NEXT TIME MY FRIENDS ARE IN DANGER...

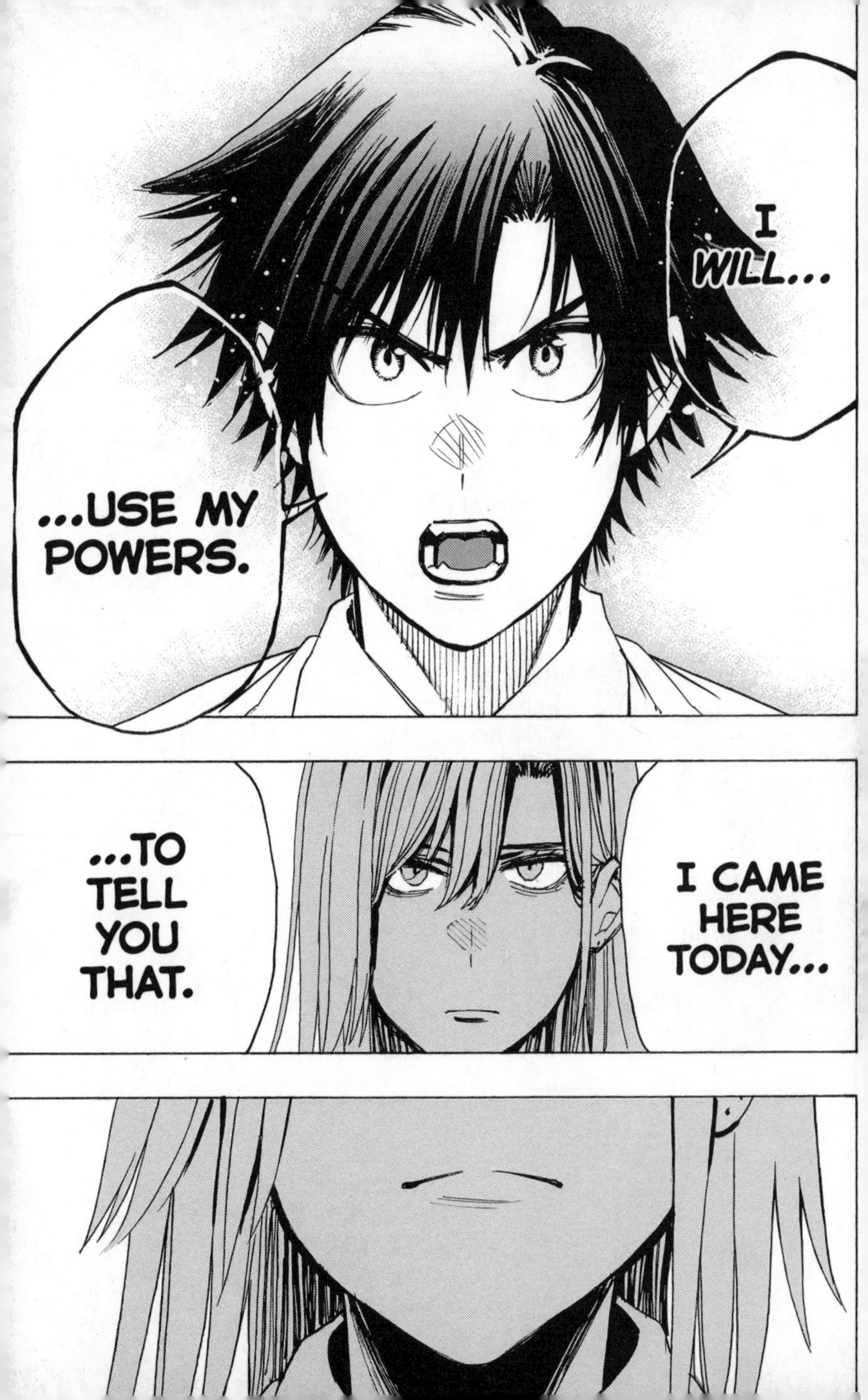
I WILL...
...USE MY POWERS.
I CAME HERE TODAY...
...TO TELL YOU THAT.

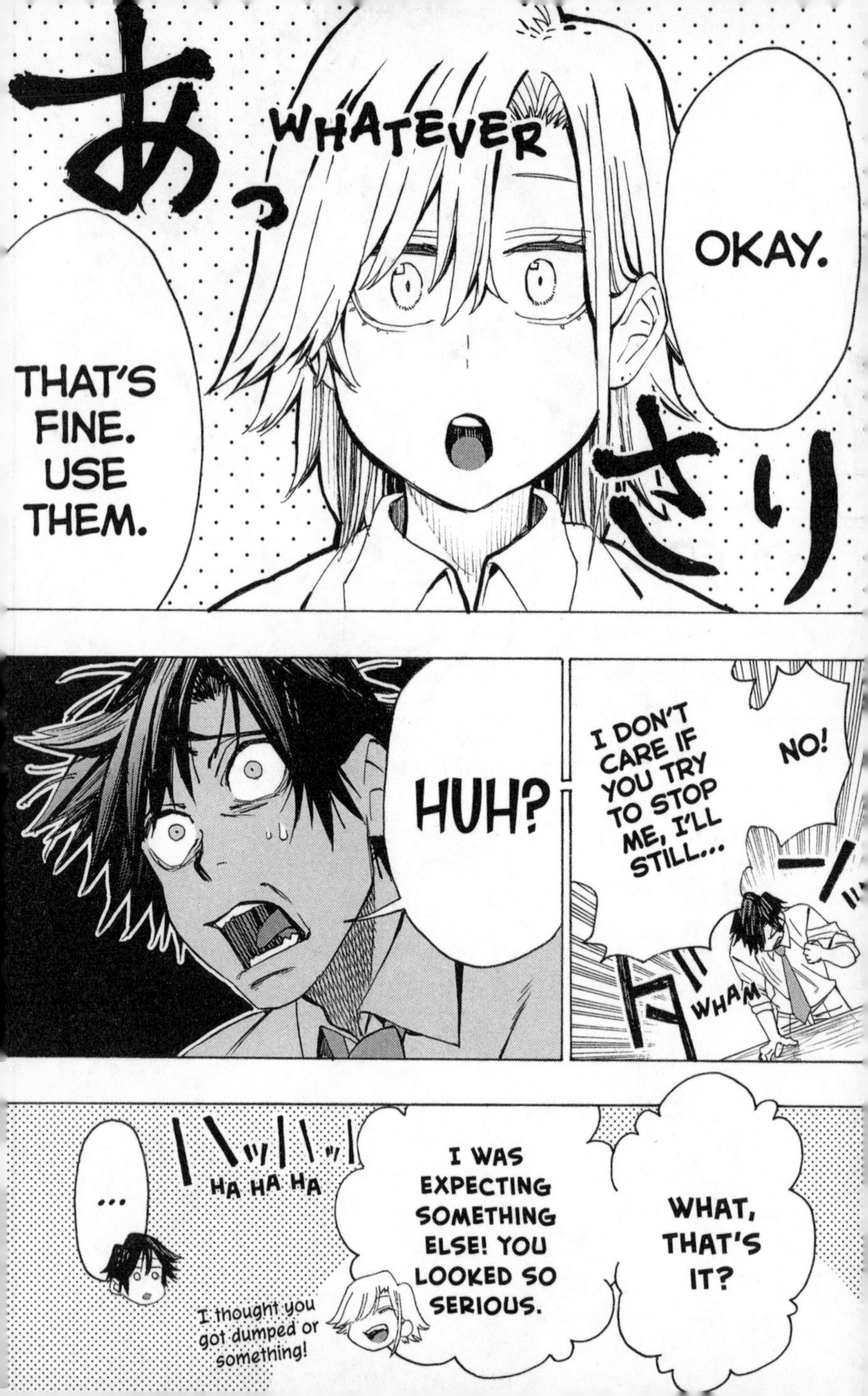
OKAY.
さり
WHATEVER
あっ
THAT'S FINE. USE THEM.
NO!
I DON'T CARE IF YOU TRY TO STOP ME, I'LL STILL...
WHAM
HUH?
WHAT, THAT'S IT?
I WAS EXPECTING SOMETHING ELSE! YOU LOOKED SO SERIOUS.
HA HA HA
I thought you got dumped or something!
...

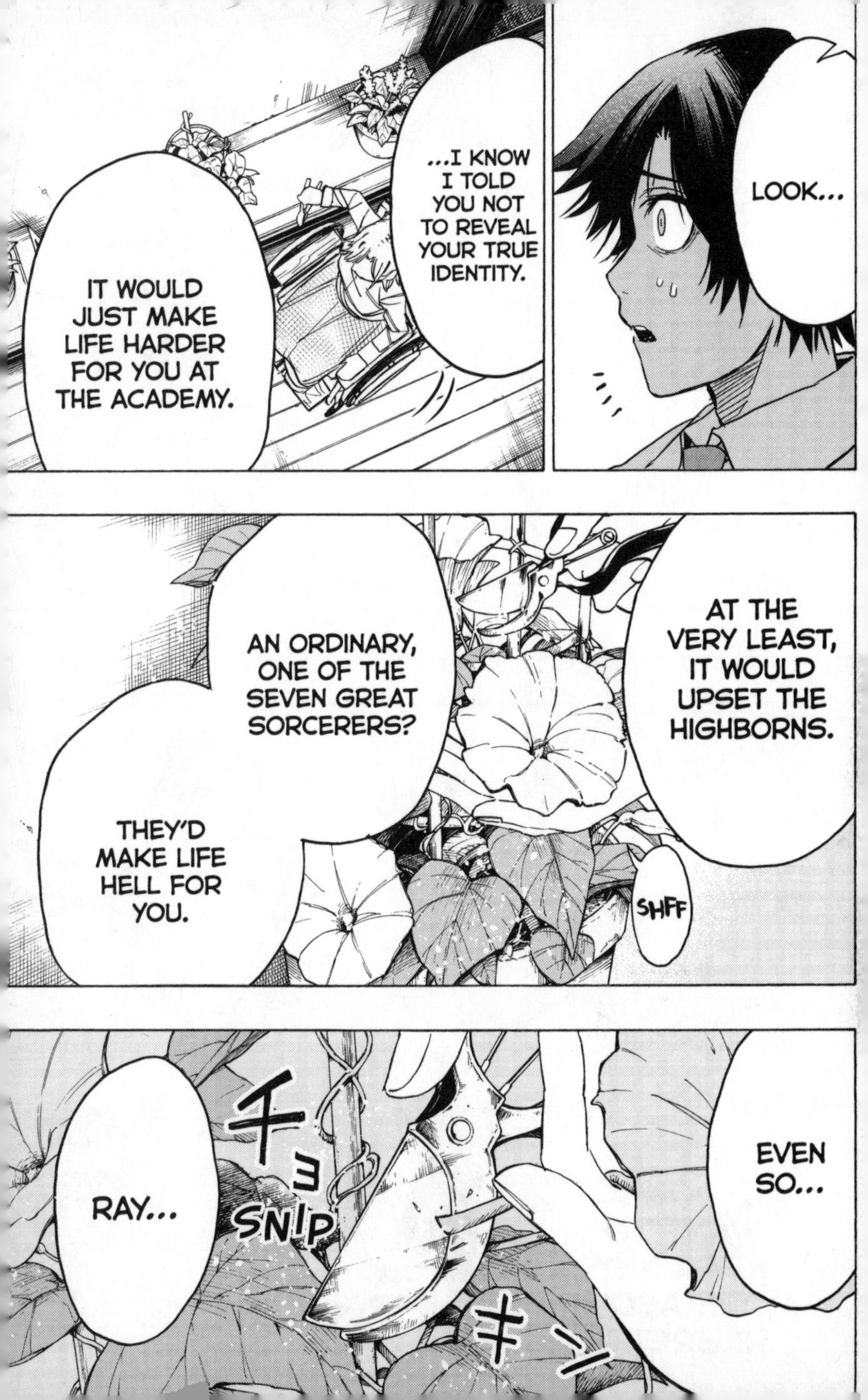
LOOK...
...I KNOW I TOLD YOU NOT TO REVEAL YOUR TRUE IDENTITY.
IT WOULD JUST MAKE LIFE HARDER FOR YOU AT THE ACADEMY.
AT THE VERY LEAST, IT WOULD UPSET THE HIGHBORNS.
SHFF
AN ORDINARY, ONE OF THE SEVEN GREAT SORCERERS?
THEY'D MAKE LIFE HELL FOR YOU.
EVEN SO...
チョキン
SNIP
RAY...

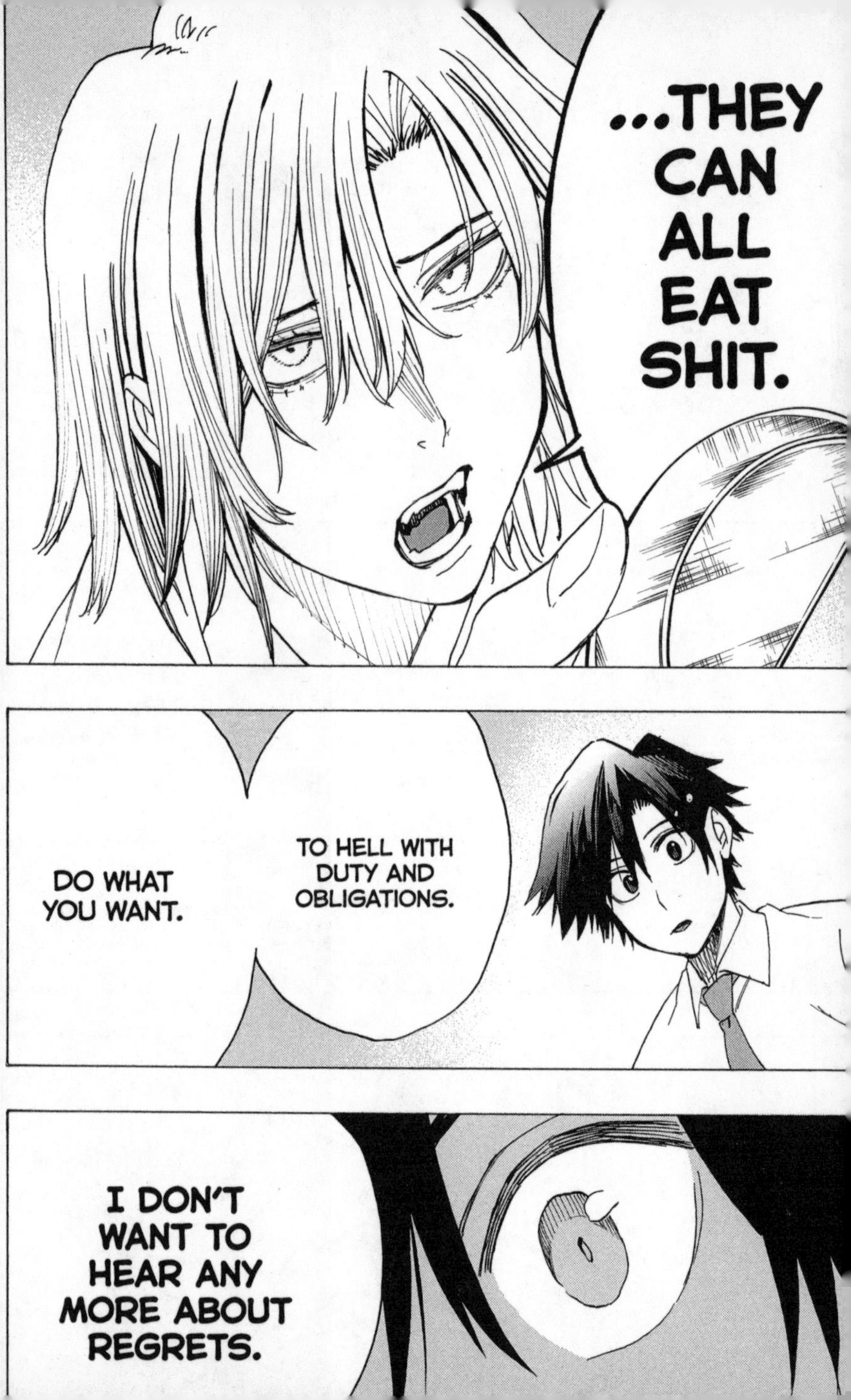
...THEY CAN ALL EAT SHIT.
TO HELL WITH DUTY AND OBLIGATIONS.
DO WHAT YOU WANT.
I DON'T WANT TO HEAR ANY MORE ABOUT REGRETS.

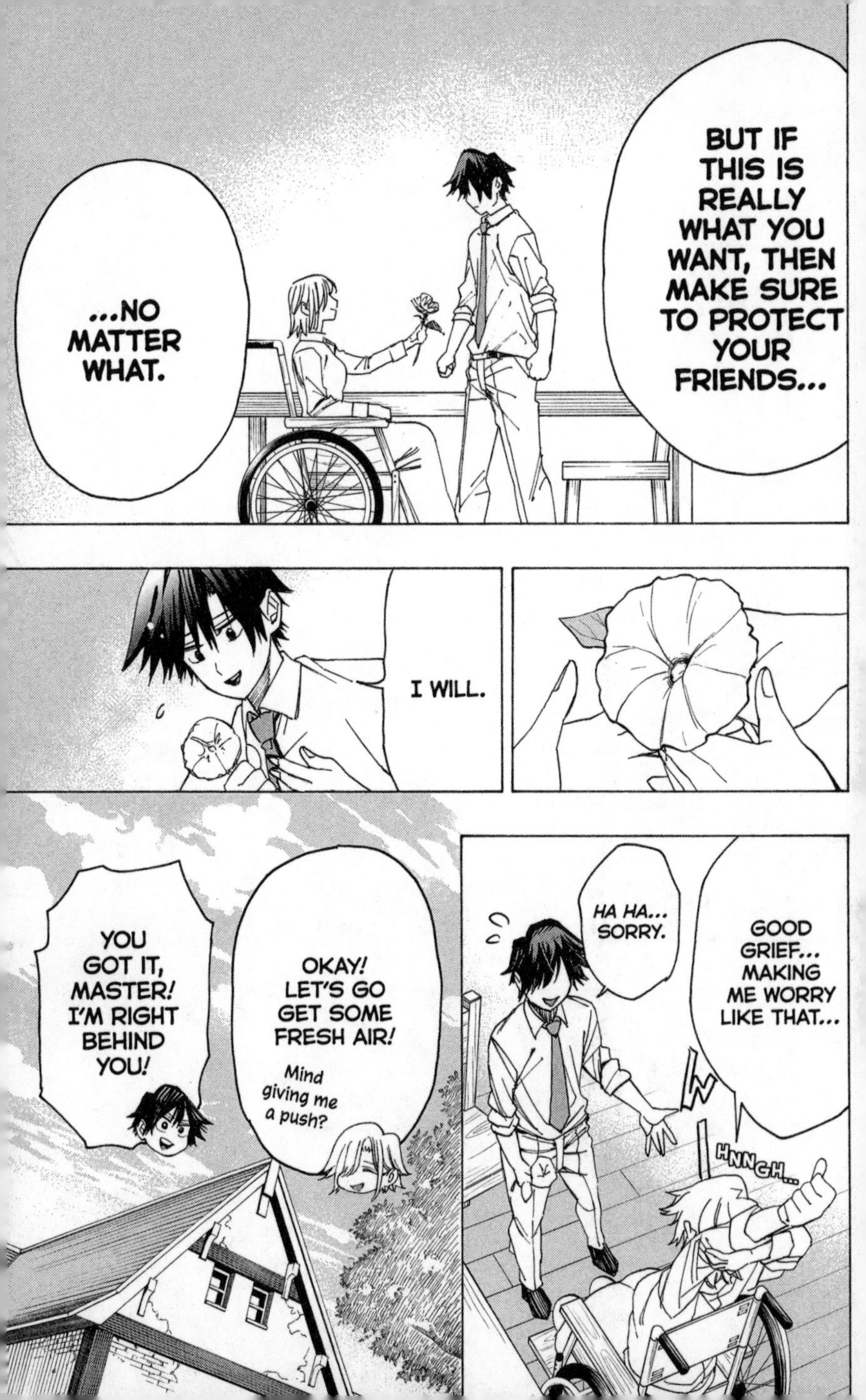
BUT IF THIS IS REALLY WHAT YOU WANT, THEN MAKE SURE TO PROTECT YOUR FRIENDS...
...NO MATTER WHAT.
I WILL.
GOOD GRIEF... MAKING ME WORRY LIKE THAT...
HA HA... SORRY.
HNNGH...
OKAY! LET'S GO GET SOME FRESH AIR!
Mind giving me a push?
YOU GOT IT, MASTER! I'M RIGHT BEHIND YOU!

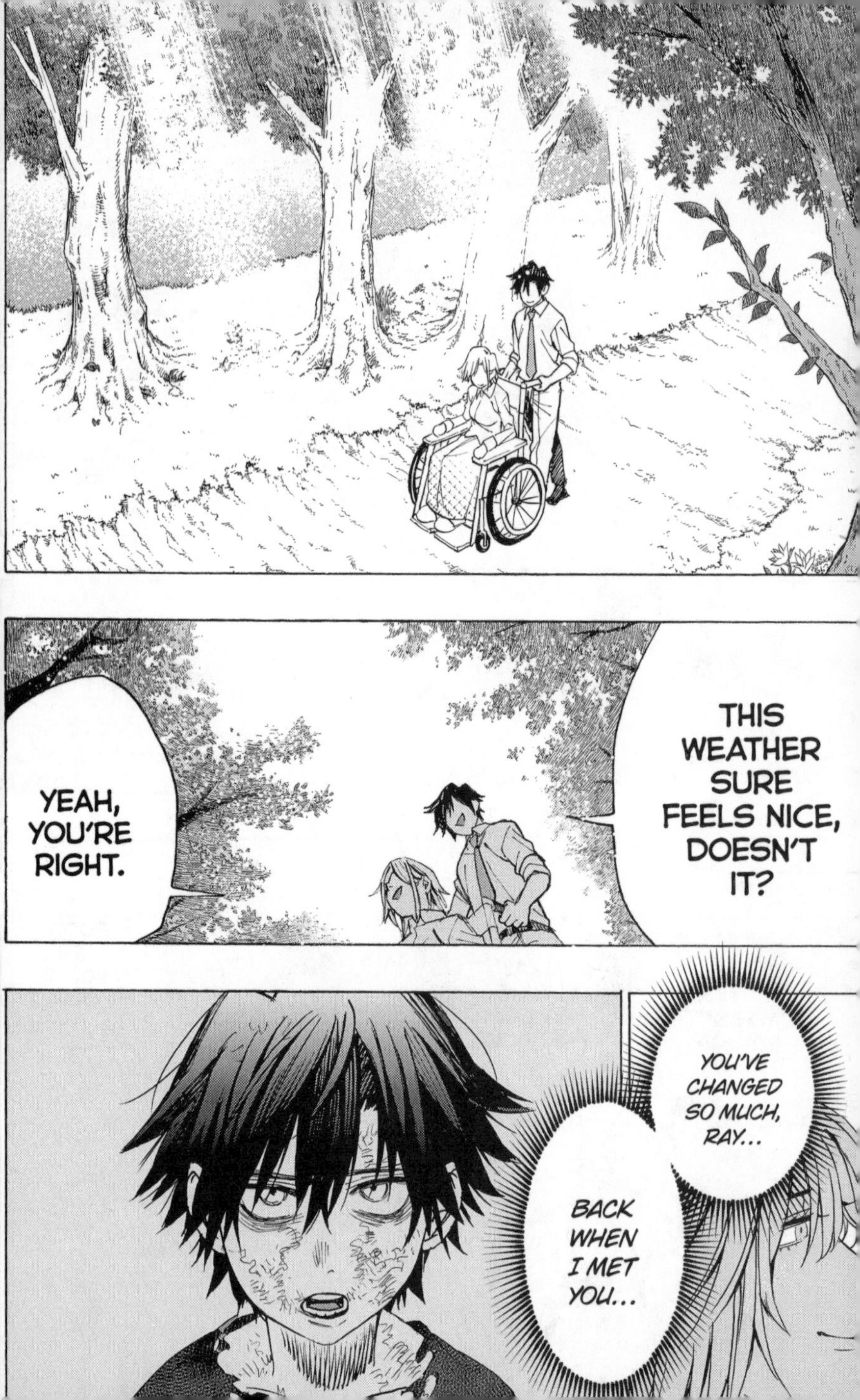
THIS WEATHER SURE FEELS NICE, DOESN'T IT?
YEAH, YOU'RE RIGHT.
YOU'VE CHANGED SO MUCH, RAY...
BACK WHEN I MET YOU...

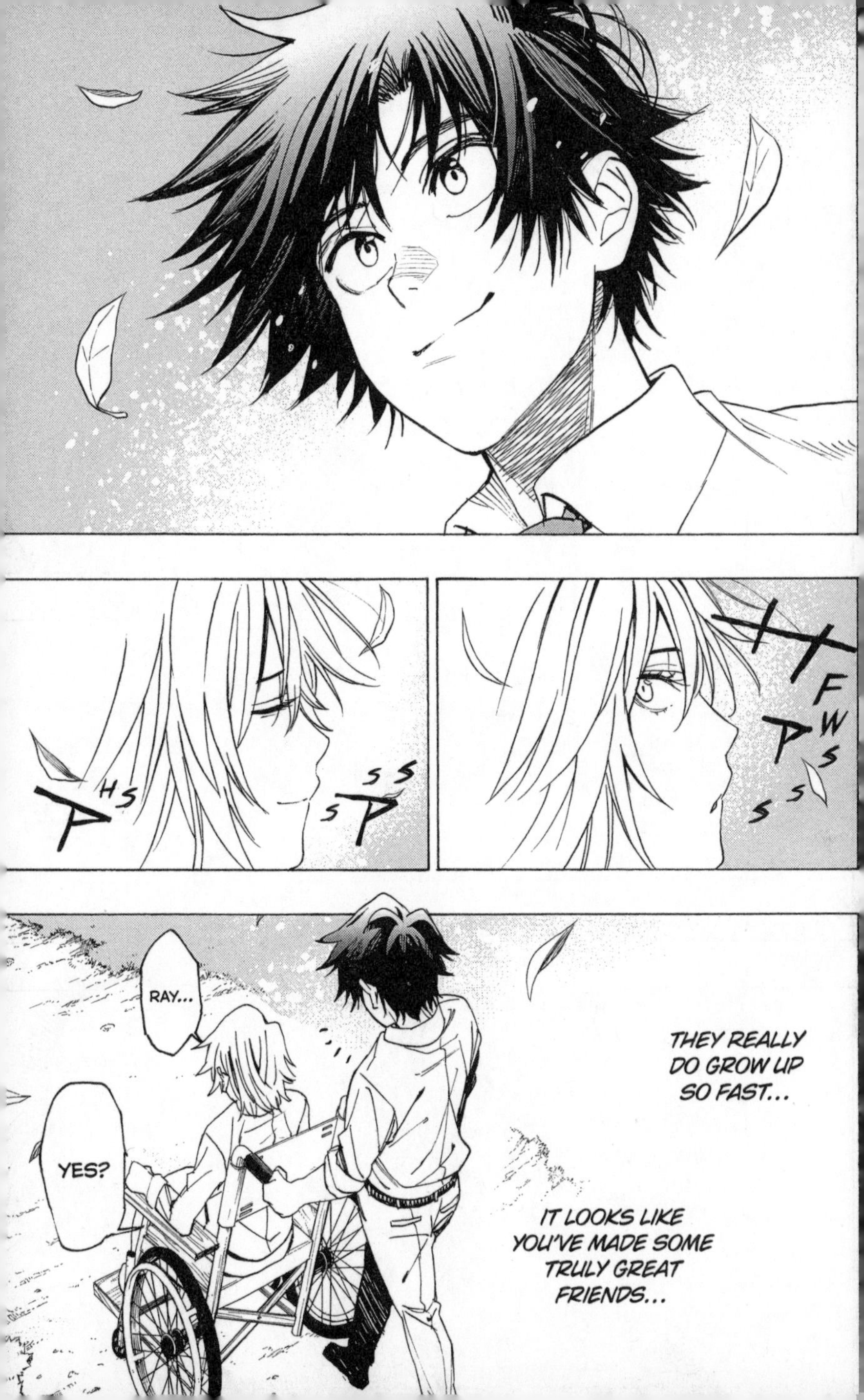
THEY REALLY DO GROW UP SO FAST...
IT LOOKS LIKE YOU'VE MADE SOME TRULY GREAT FRIENDS...
RAY...
YES?

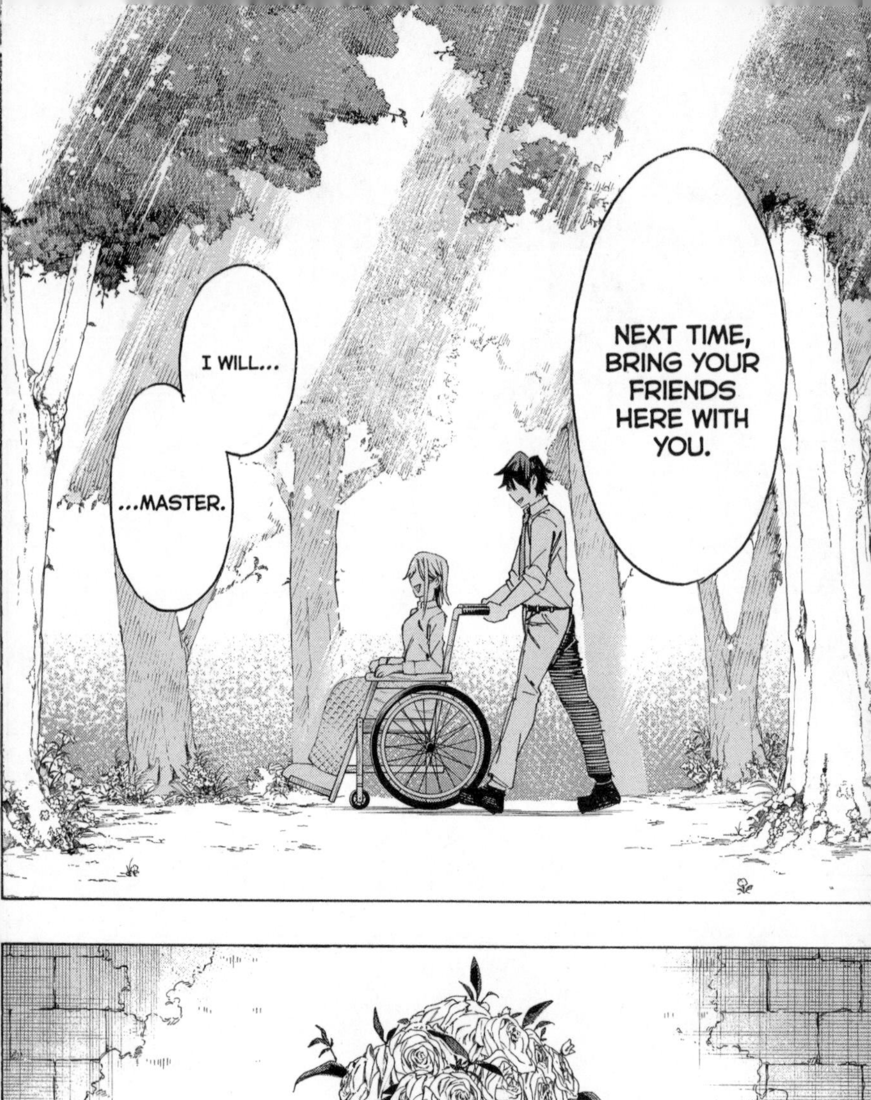
NEXT TIME, BRING YOUR FRIENDS HERE WITH YOU.
I WILL...
...MASTER.
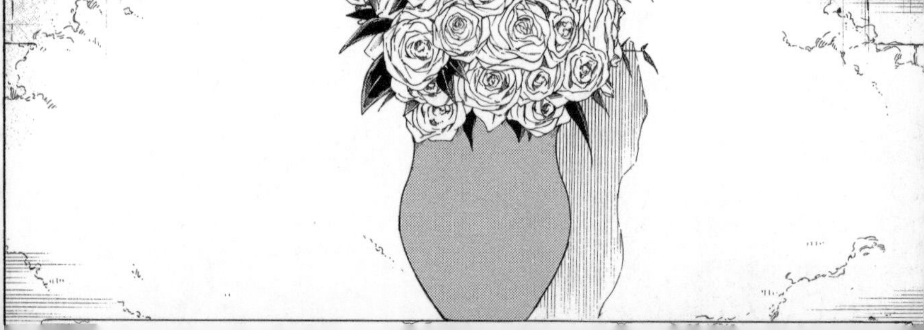

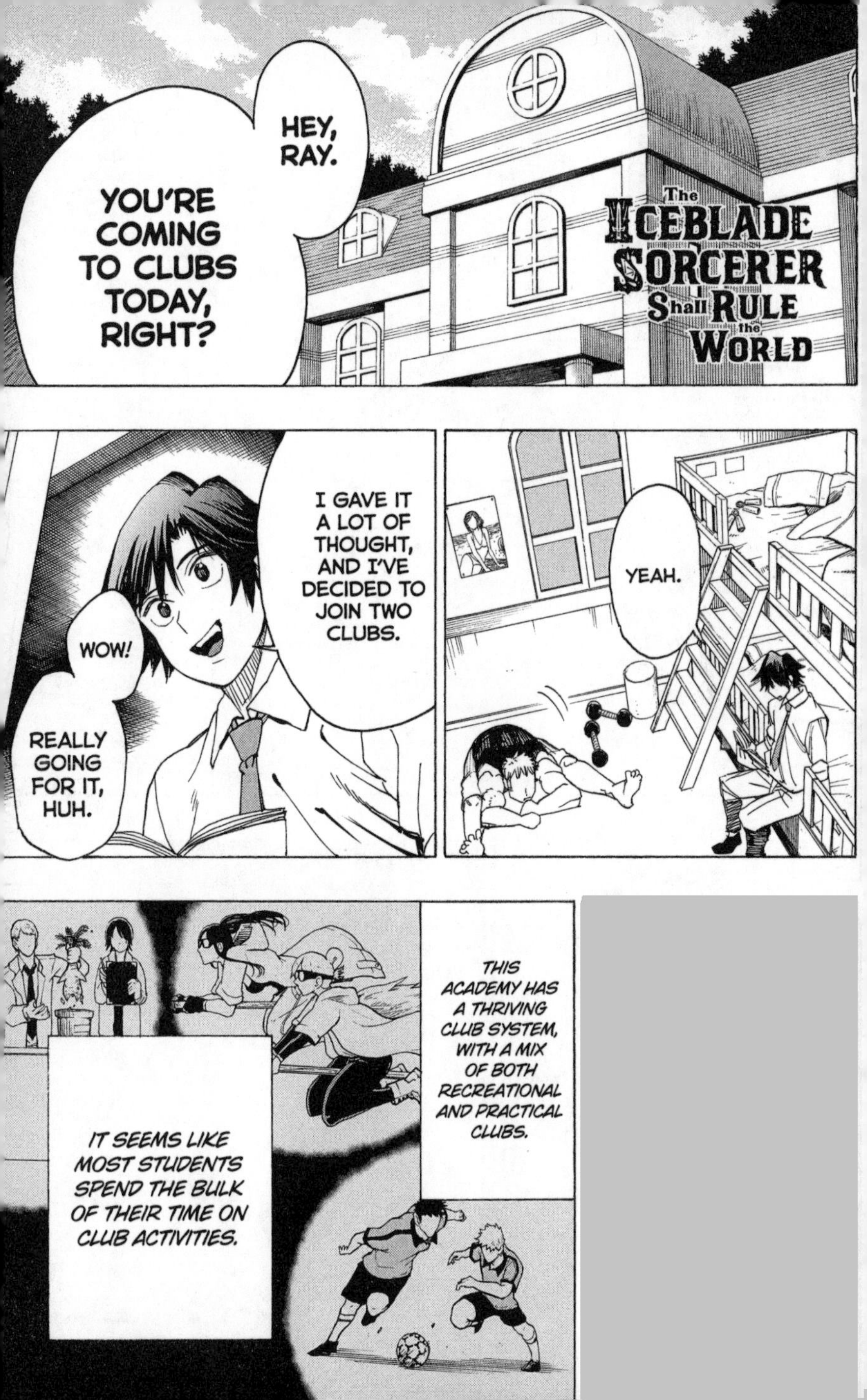
The ICEBLADE SORCERER Shall RULE the WORLD
HEY, RAY.
YOU'RE COMING TO CLUBS TODAY, RIGHT?
YEAH.
I GAVE IT A LOT OF THOUGHT, AND I'VE DECIDED TO JOIN TWO CLUBS.
WOW!
REALLY GOING FOR IT, HUH.
THIS ACADEMY HAS A THRIVING CLUB SYSTEM, WITH A MIX OF BOTH RECREATIONAL AND PRACTICAL CLUBS.
IT SEEMS LIKE MOST STUDENTS SPEND THE BULK OF THEIR TIME ON CLUB ACTIVITIES.

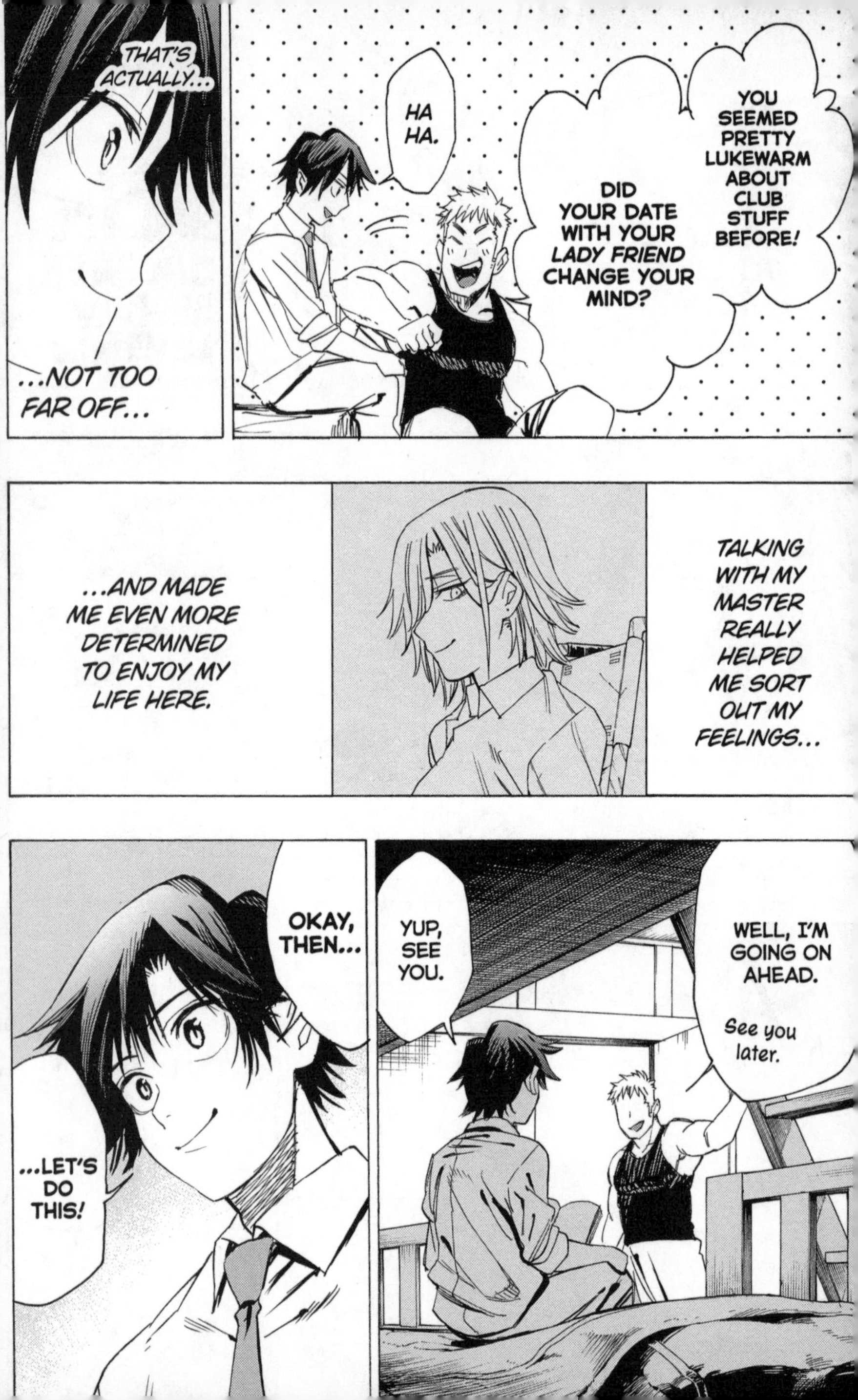
YOU SEEMED PRETTY LUKEWARM ABOUT CLUB STUFF BEFORE!
DID YOUR DATE WITH YOUR LADY FRIEND CHANGE YOUR MIND?
HA HA.
THAT'S ACTUALLY...
...NOT TOO FAR OFF...
TALKING WITH MY MASTER REALLY HELPED ME SORT OUT MY FEELINGS...
...AND MADE ME EVEN MORE DETERMINED TO ENJOY MY LIFE HERE.
WELL, I'M GOING ON AHEAD.
See you later.
YUP, SEE YOU.
OKAY, THEN...
...LET'S DO THIS!

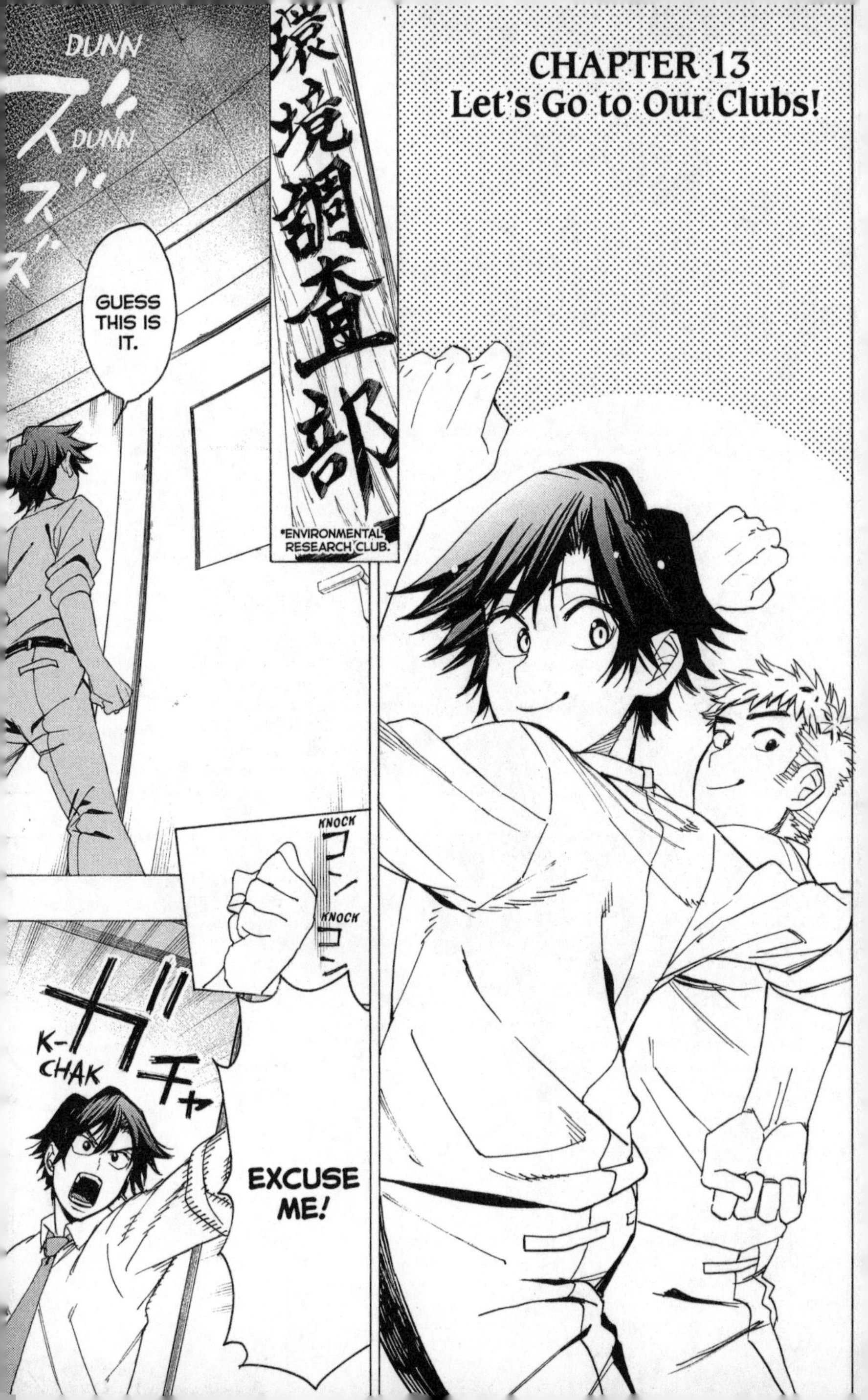
CHAPTER 13
Let's Go to Our Clubs!
DUNN
DUNN
環境調査部
*ENVIRONMENTAL RESEARCH CLUB.
GUESS THIS IS IT.
KNOCK
KNOCK
K-CHAK
EXCUSE ME!

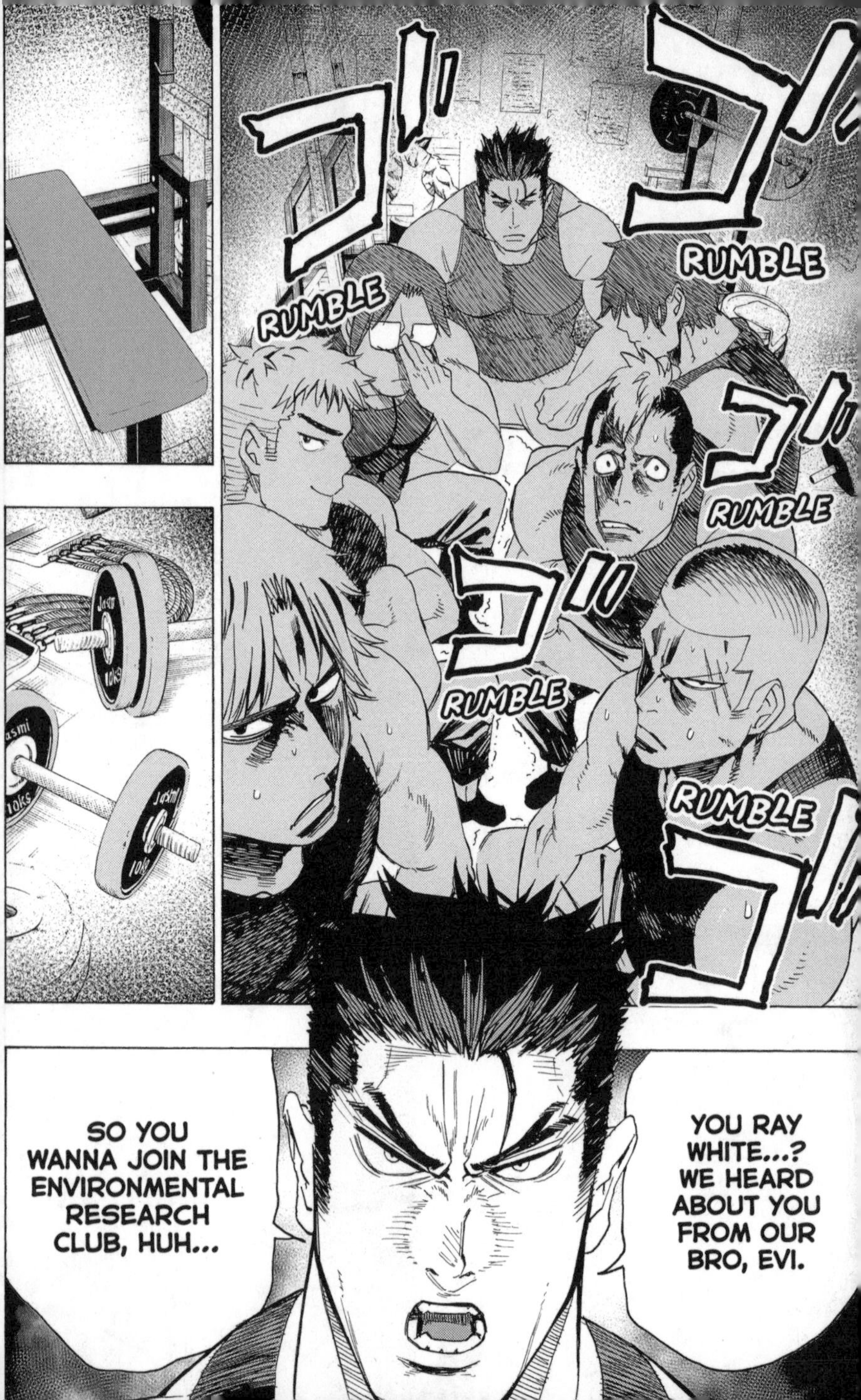
RUMBLE
RUMBLE
RUMBLE
RUMBLE
RUMBLE
YOU RAY WHITE...? WE HEARD ABOUT YOU FROM OUR BRO, EVI.
SO YOU WANNA JOIN THE ENVIRONMENTAL RESEARCH CLUB, HUH...

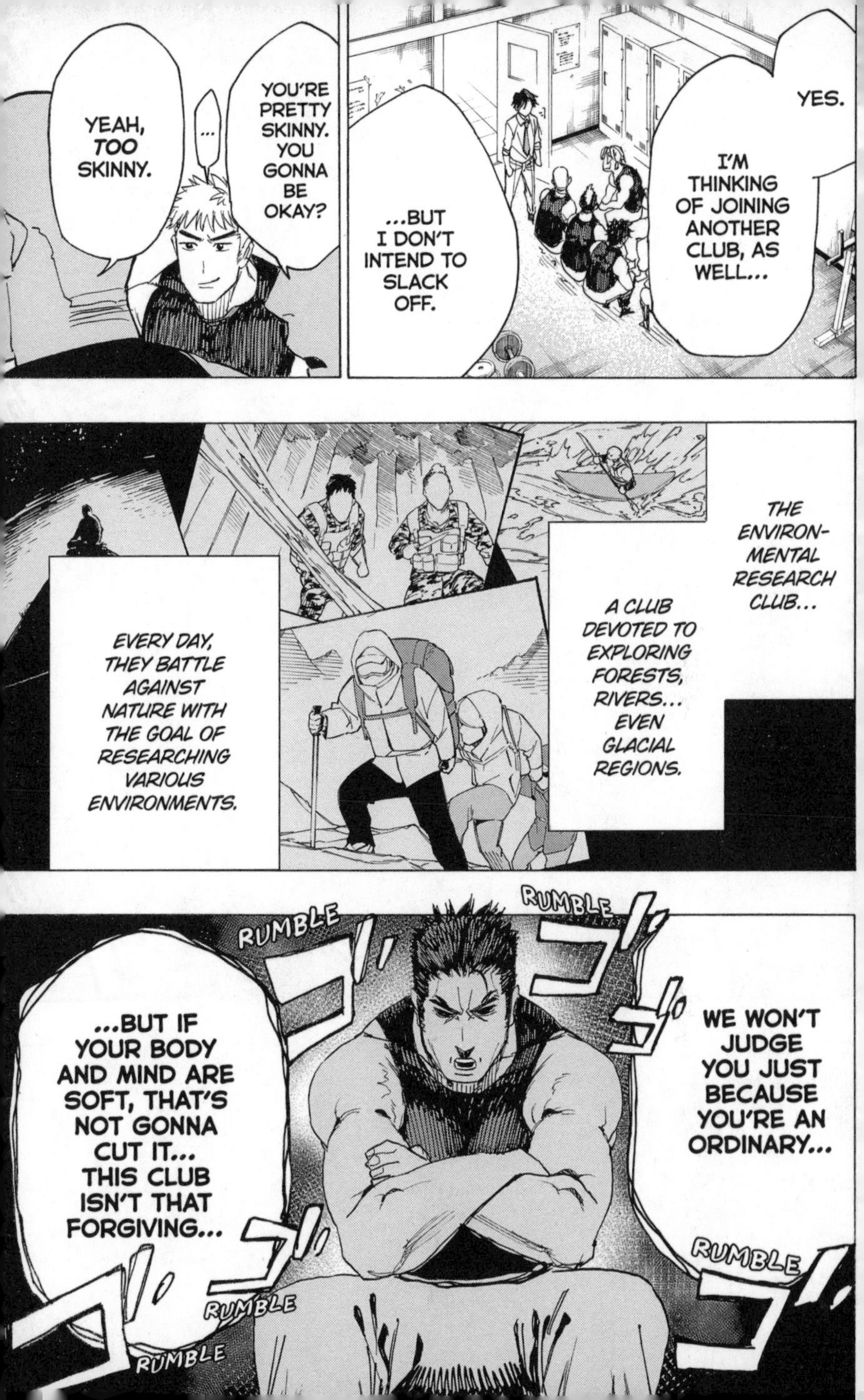
YES.
I'M THINKING OF JOINING ANOTHER CLUB, AS WELL...
...BUT I DON'T INTEND TO SLACK OFF.
YOU'RE PRETTY SKINNY. YOU GONNA BE OKAY?
...
YEAH, *TOO* SKINNY.
THE ENVIRONMENTAL RESEARCH CLUB...
A CLUB DEVOTED TO EXPLORING FORESTS, RIVERS... EVEN GLACIAL REGIONS.
EVERY DAY, THEY BATTLE AGAINST NATURE WITH THE GOAL OF RESEARCHING VARIOUS ENVIRONMENTS.
RUMBLE
RUMBLE
WE WON'T JUDGE YOU JUST BECAUSE YOU'RE AN ORDINARY...
...BUT IF YOUR BODY AND MIND ARE SOFT, THAT'S NOT GONNA CUT IT... THIS CLUB ISN'T THAT FORGIVING...
RUMBLE
RUMBLE
RUMBLE

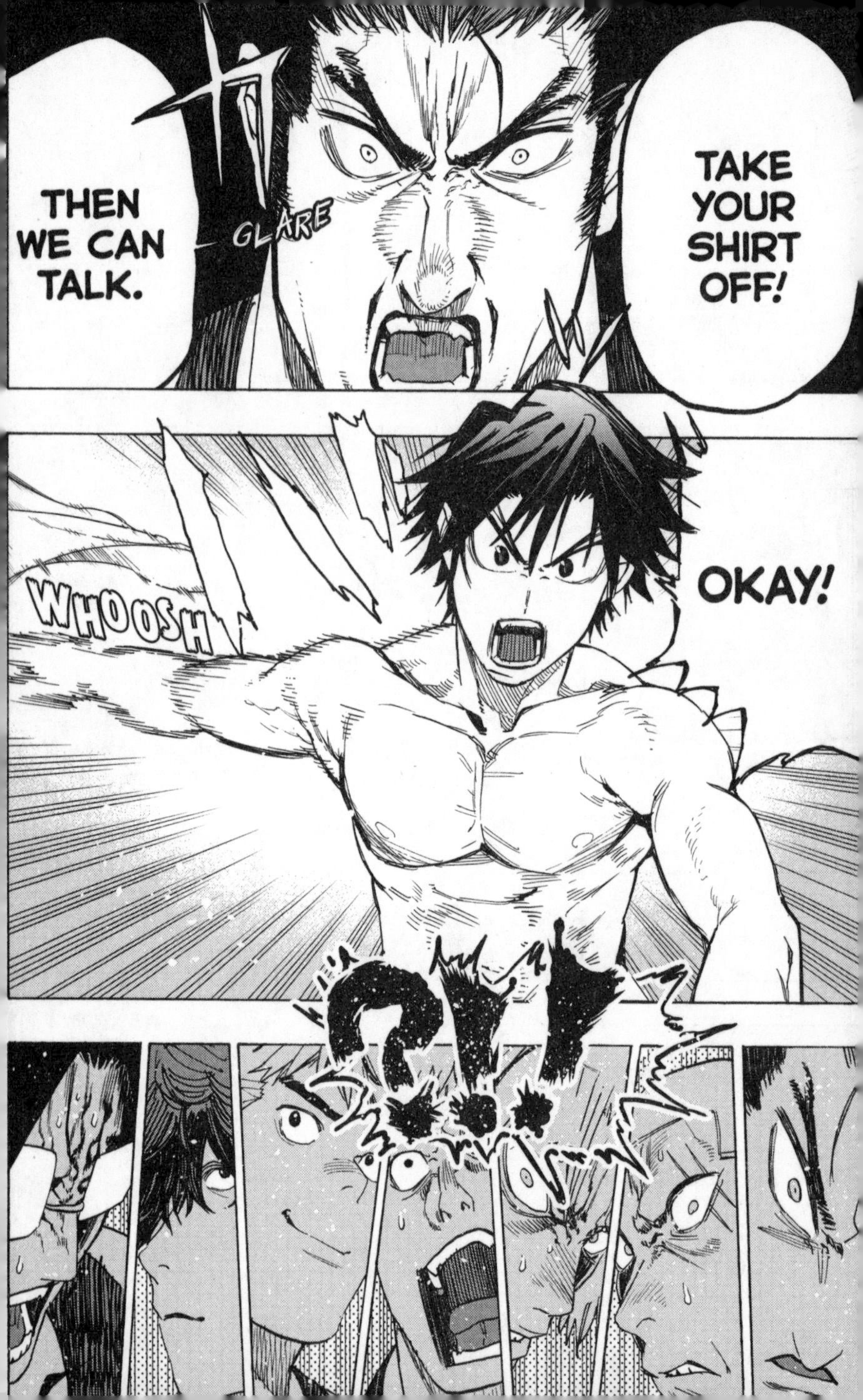
TAKE YOUR SHIRT OFF!
GLARE
THEN WE CAN TALK.
OKAY!
WHOOSH
?!!

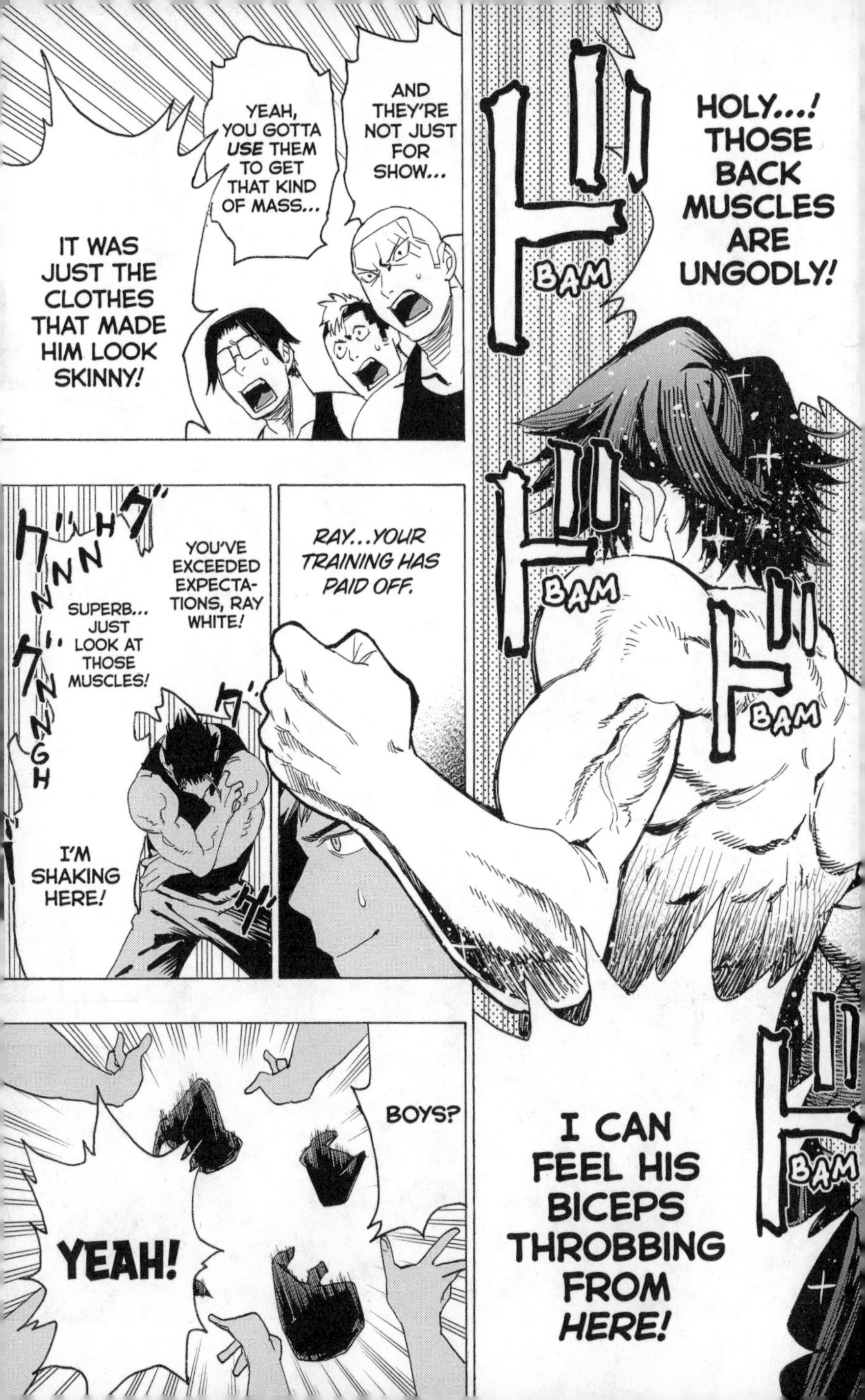

BAM
HOLY...! THOSE BACK MUSCLES ARE UNGODLY!
BAM
BAM
BAM
I CAN FEEL HIS BICEPS THROBBING FROM HERE!
AND THEY'RE NOT JUST FOR SHOW...
YEAH, YOU GOTTA USE THEM TO GET THAT KIND OF MASS...
IT WAS JUST THE CLOTHES THAT MADE HIM LOOK SKINNY!
RAY...YOUR TRAINING HAS PAID OFF.
YOU'VE EXCEEDED EXPECTA-TIONS, RAY WHITE!
GNNNNNNGH
SUPERB... JUST LOOK AT THOSE MUSCLES!
I'M SHAKING HERE!
BOYS?
YEAH!

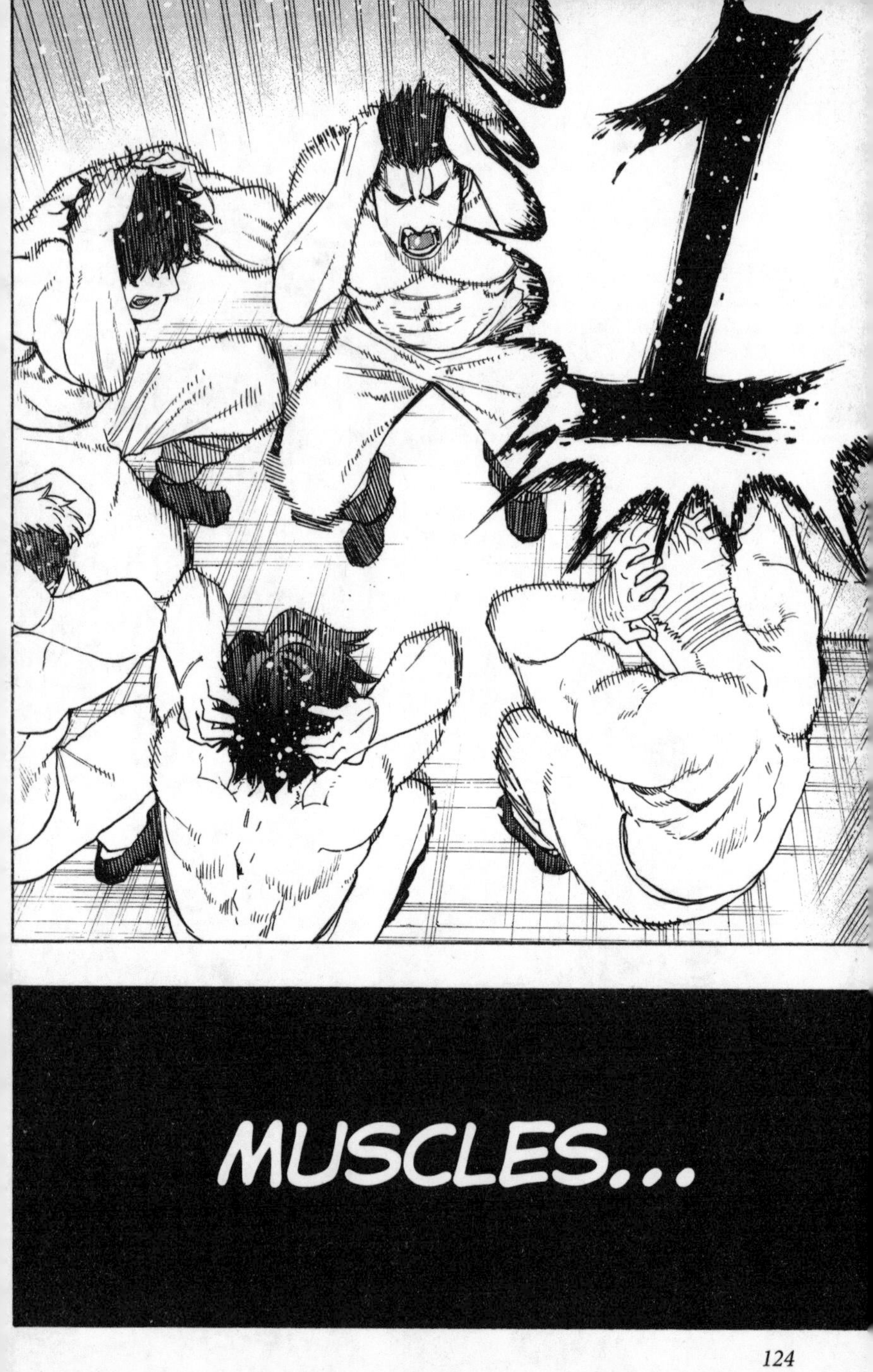

MUSCLES...

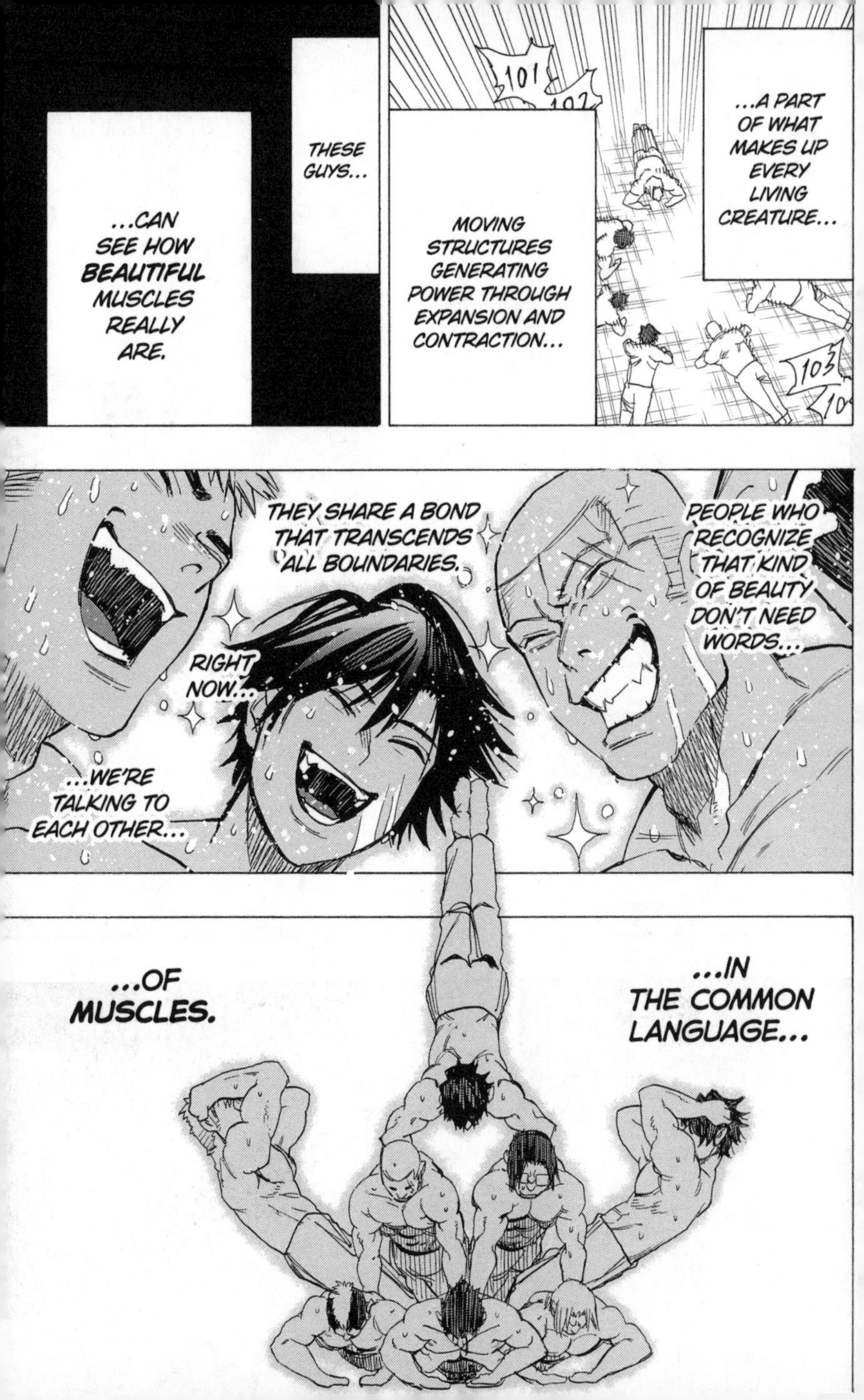
...A PART OF WHAT MAKES UP EVERY LIVING CREATURE...
101
MOVING STRUCTURES GENERATING POWER THROUGH EXPANSION AND CONTRACTION...
103
THESE GUYS...
...CAN SEE HOW BEAUTIFUL MUSCLES REALLY ARE.
PEOPLE WHO RECOGNIZE THAT KIND OF BEAUTY DON'T NEED WORDS...
THEY SHARE A BOND THAT TRANSCENDS ALL BOUNDARIES.
RIGHT NOW...
...WE'RE TALKING TO EACH OTHER...
...IN THE COMMON LANGUAGE...
...OF MUSCLES.

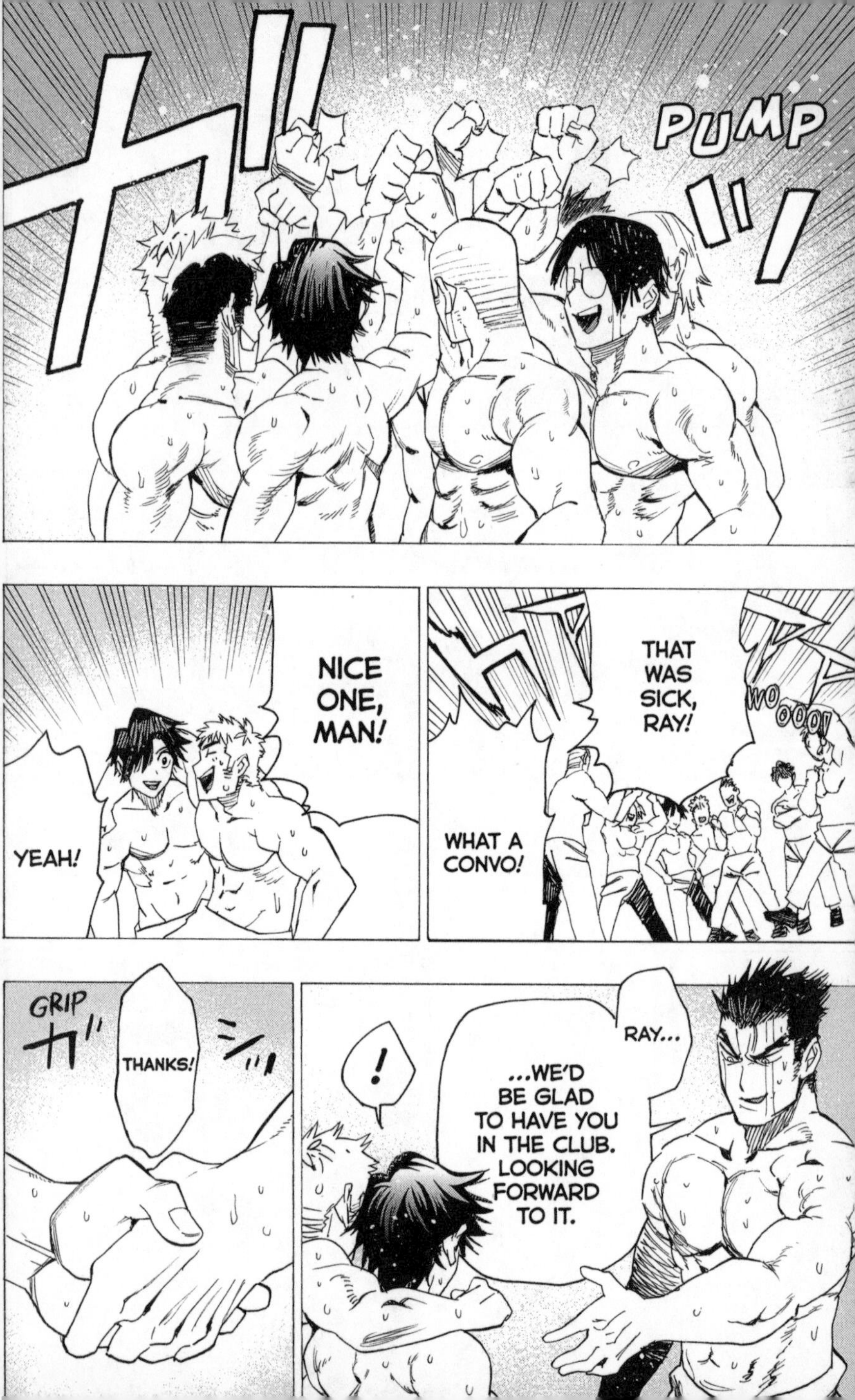
PUMP
THAT WAS SICK, RAY!
WOOOOO!
WHAT A CONVO!
NICE ONE, MAN!
YEAH!
!
RAY...
...WE'D BE GLAD TO HAVE YOU IN THE CLUB. LOOKING FORWARD TO IT.
GRIP
THANKS!

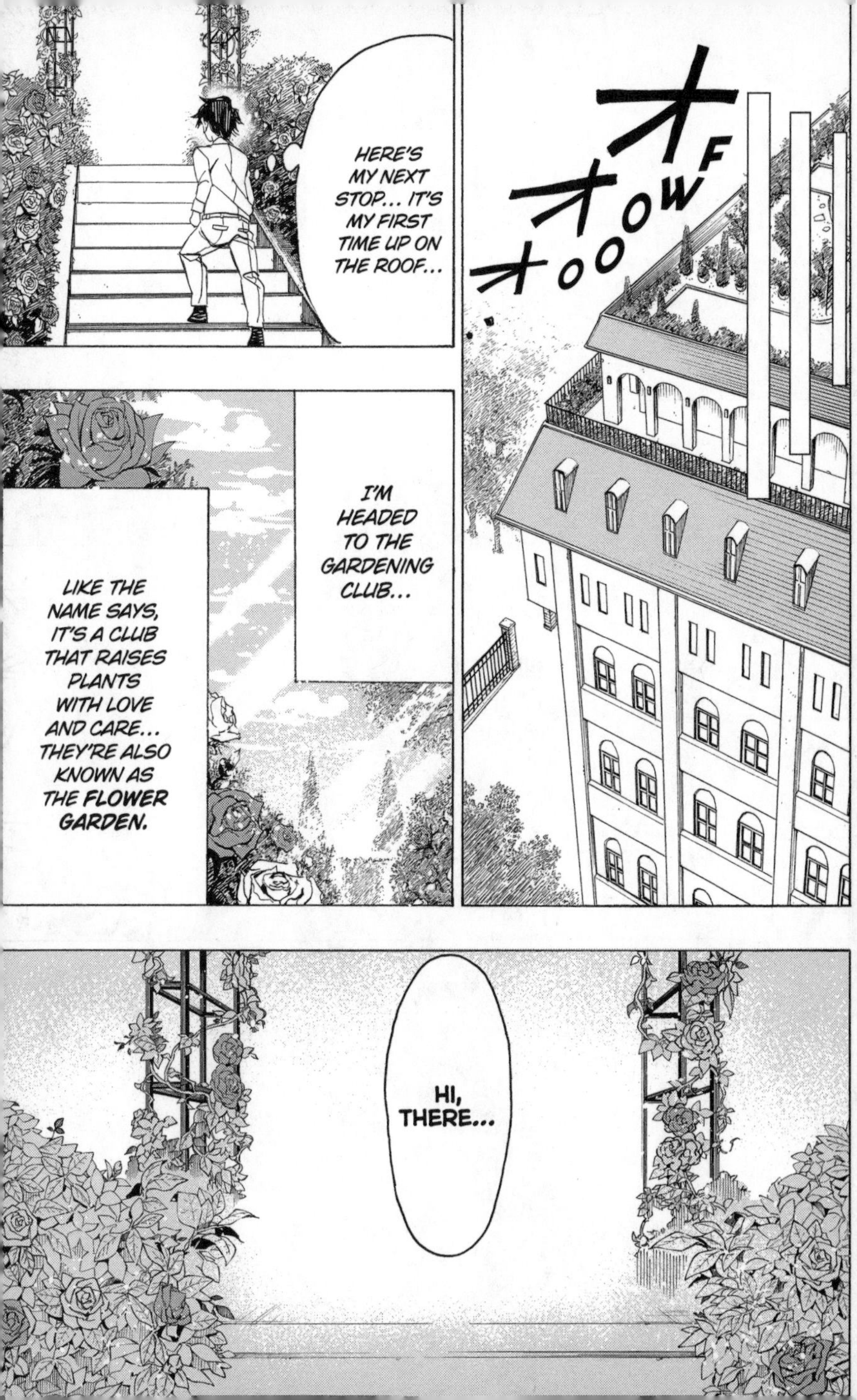
OOOOWF
HERE'S MY NEXT STOP... IT'S MY FIRST TIME UP ON THE ROOF...
I'M HEADED TO THE GARDENING CLUB...
LIKE THE NAME SAYS, IT'S A CLUB THAT RAISES PLANTS WITH LOVE AND CARE... THEY'RE ALSO KNOWN AS THE FLOWER GARDEN.
HI, THERE...

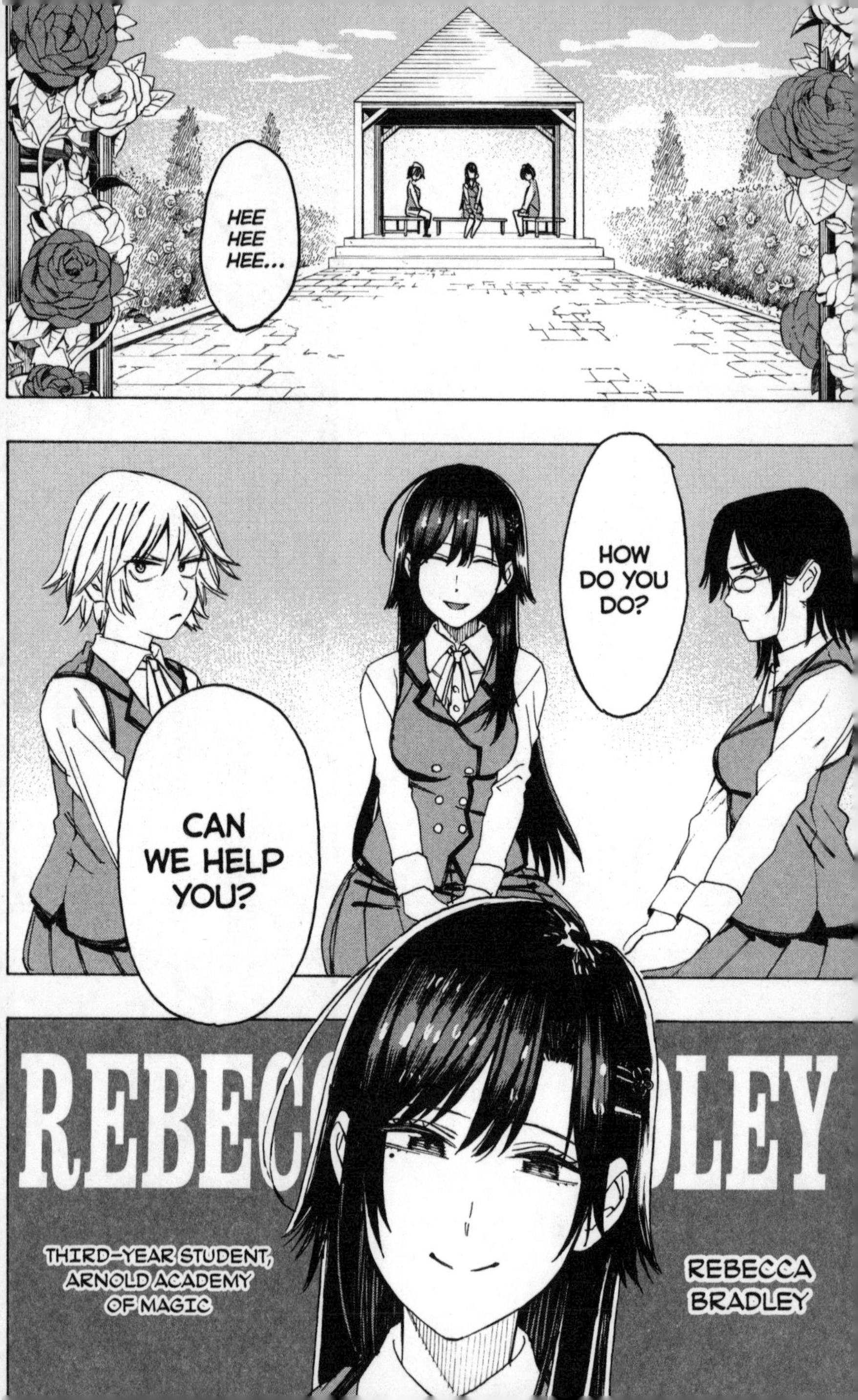
HEE HEE HEE...
HOW DO YOU DO?
CAN WE HELP YOU?
REBECCA BRADLEY
THIRD-YEAR STUDENT, ARNOLD ACADEMY OF MAGIC

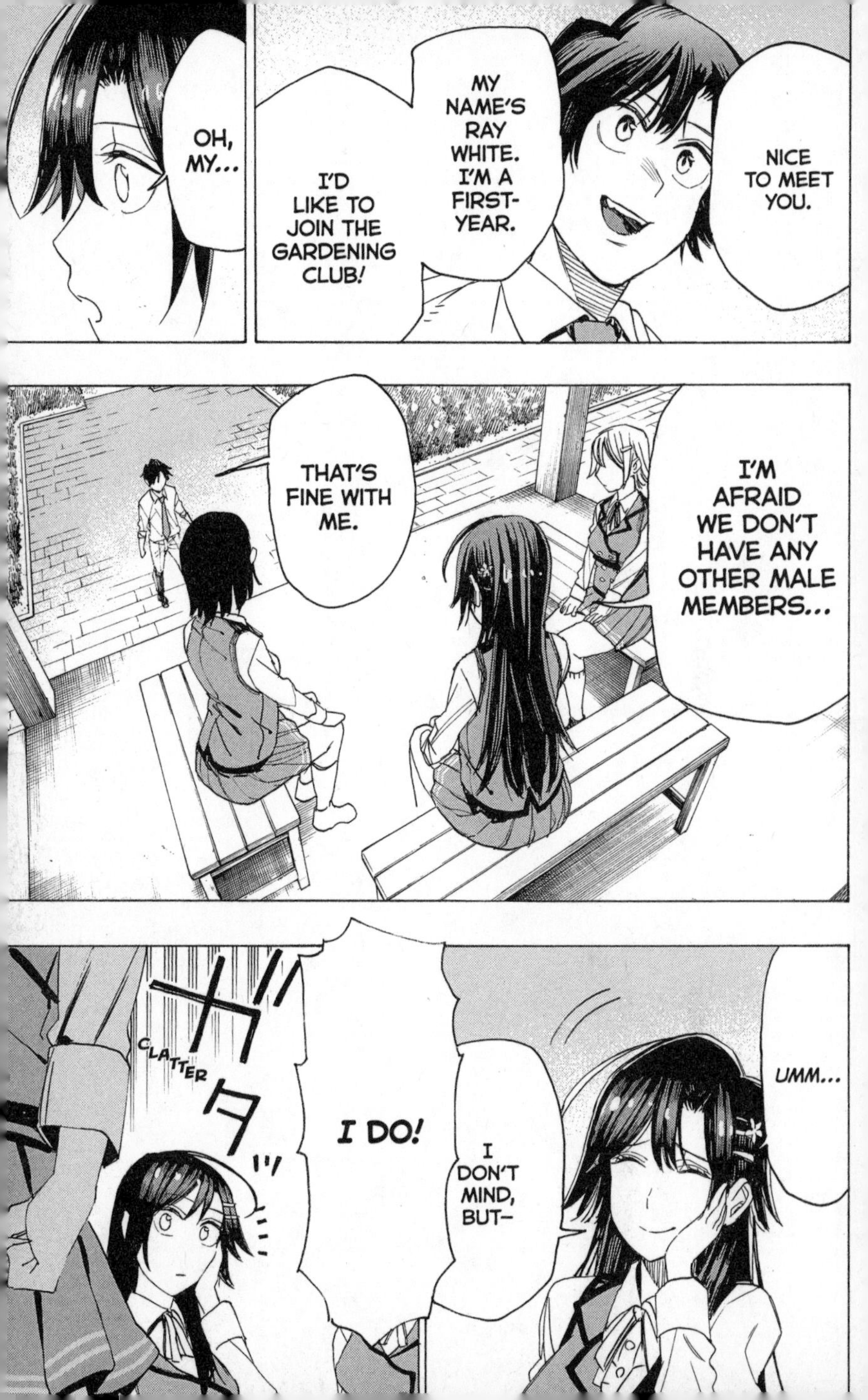
NICE TO MEET YOU.
MY NAME'S RAY WHITE. I'M A FIRST-YEAR.
I'D LIKE TO JOIN THE GARDENING CLUB!
OH, MY...
I'M AFRAID WE DON'T HAVE ANY OTHER MALE MEMBERS...
THAT'S FINE WITH ME.
UMM...
I DON'T MIND, BUT–
I DO!
CLATTER

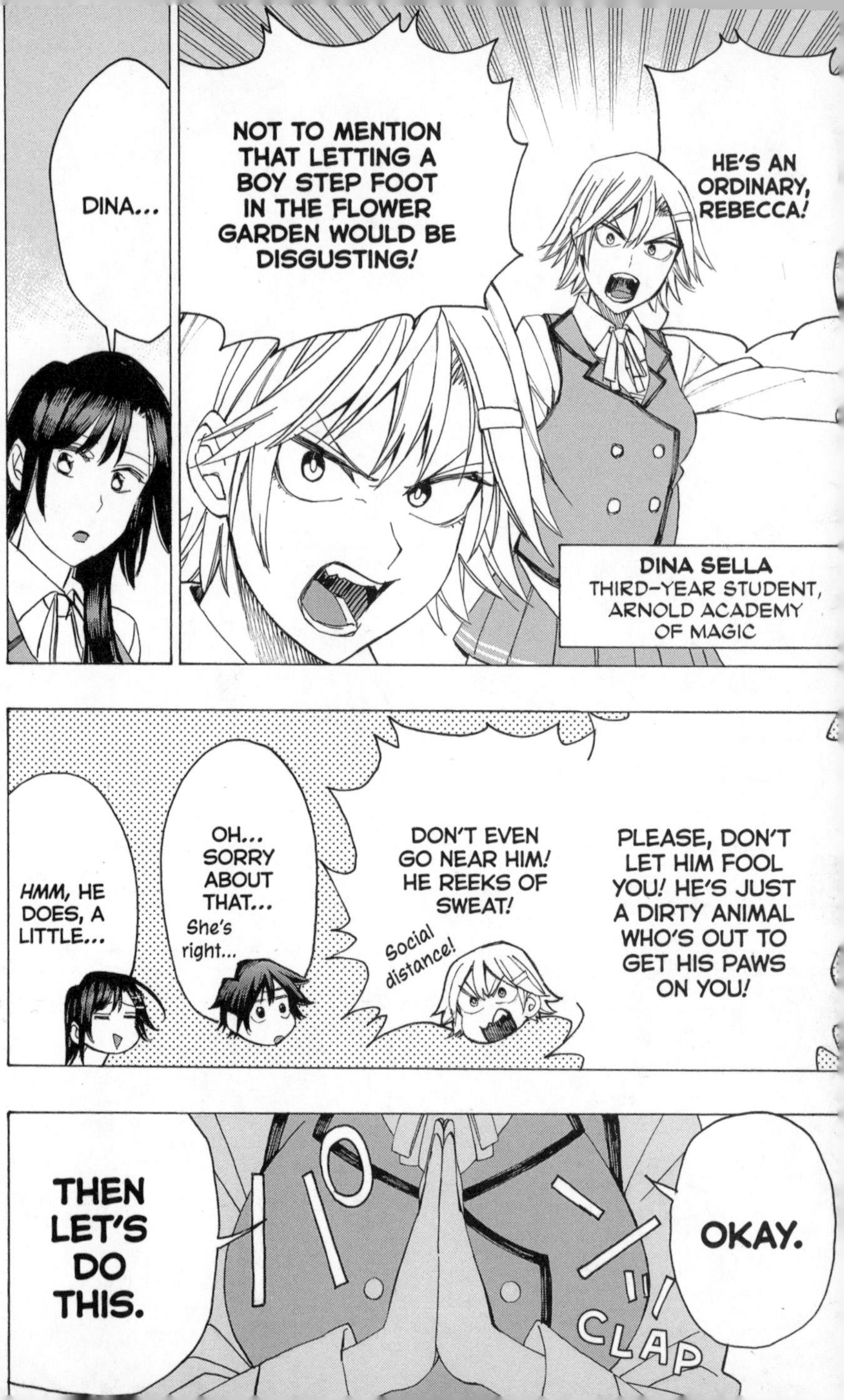
HE'S AN ORDINARY, REBECCA!
NOT TO MENTION THAT LETTING A BOY STEP FOOT IN THE FLOWER GARDEN WOULD BE DISGUSTING!
DINA SELLA
THIRD-YEAR STUDENT, ARNOLD ACADEMY OF MAGIC
DINA...
PLEASE, DON'T LET HIM FOOL YOU! HE'S JUST A DIRTY ANIMAL WHO'S OUT TO GET HIS PAWS ON YOU!
DON'T EVEN GO NEAR HIM! HE REEKS OF SWEAT!
Social distance!
OH... SORRY ABOUT THAT...
She's right...
HMM, HE DOES, A LITTLE...
OKAY.
CLAP
THEN LET'S DO THIS.

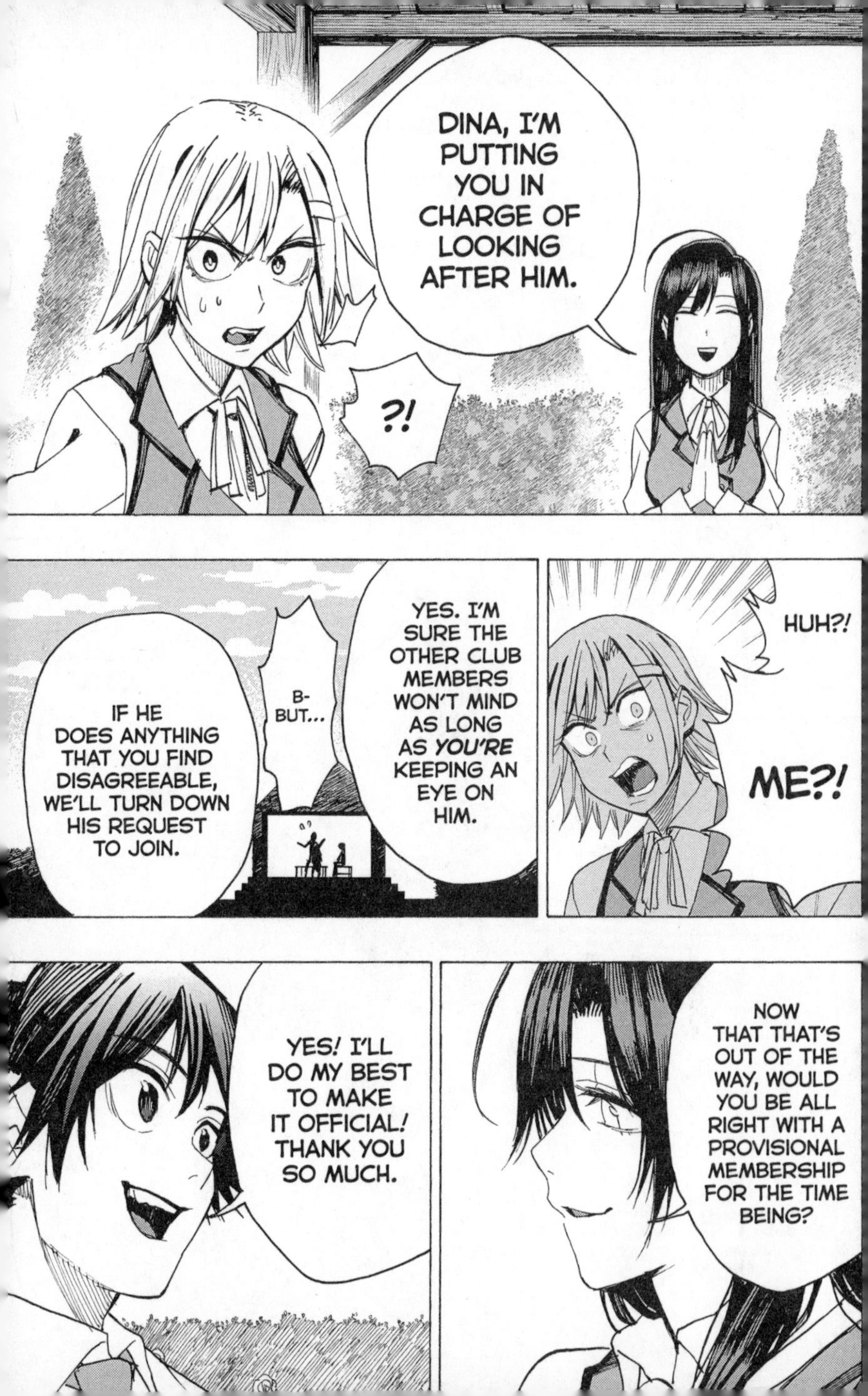
DINA, I'M PUTTING YOU IN CHARGE OF LOOKING AFTER HIM.
?!
HUH?!
ME?!
YES. I'M SURE THE OTHER CLUB MEMBERS WON'T MIND AS LONG AS *YOU'RE* KEEPING AN EYE ON HIM.
B-BUT...
IF HE DOES ANYTHING THAT YOU FIND DISAGREEABLE, WE'LL TURN DOWN HIS REQUEST TO JOIN.
NOW THAT THAT'S OUT OF THE WAY, WOULD YOU BE ALL RIGHT WITH A PROVISIONAL MEMBERSHIP FOR THE TIME BEING?
YES! I'LL DO MY BEST TO MAKE IT OFFICIAL! THANK YOU SO MUCH.

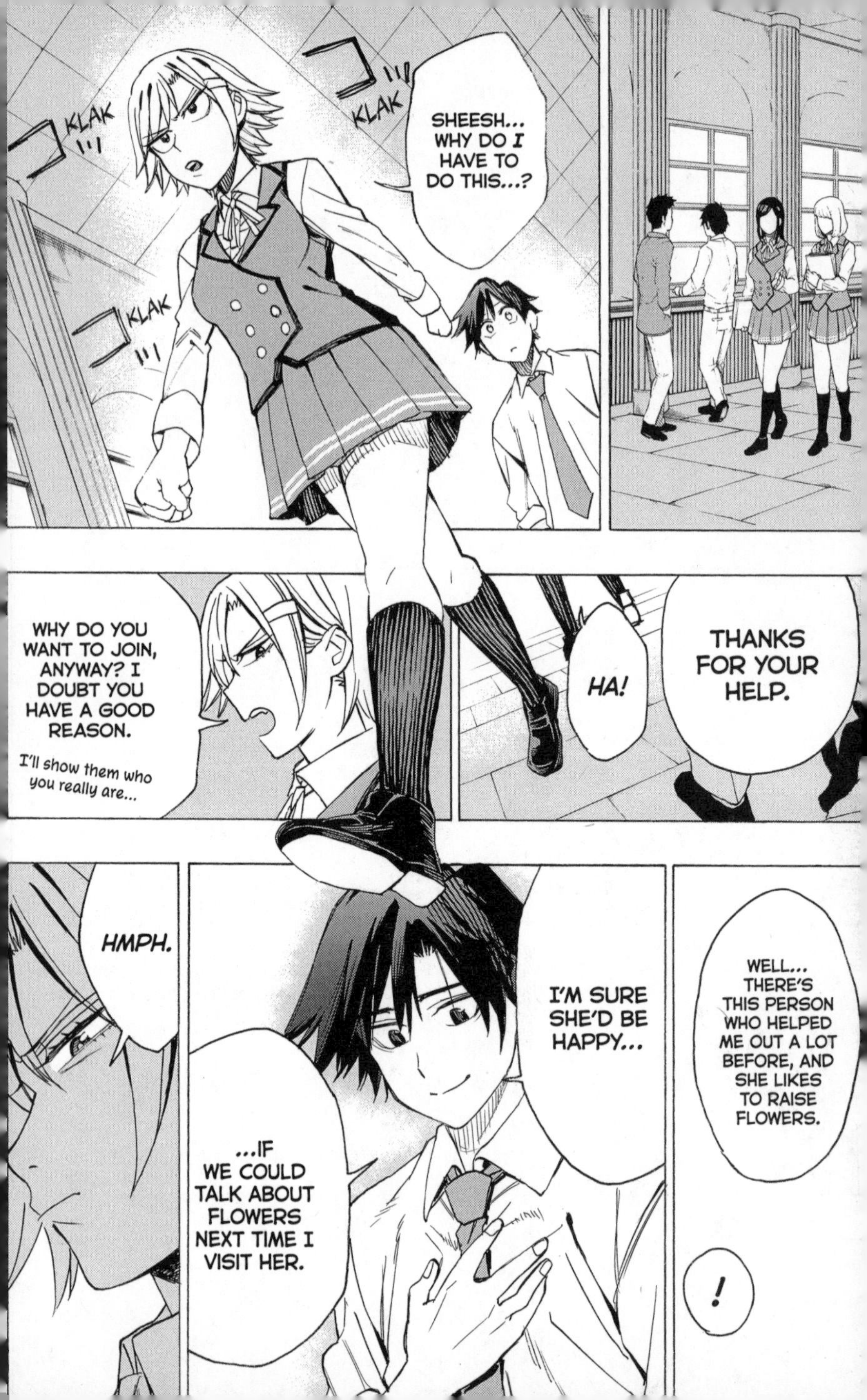
KLAK
SHEESH... WHY DO *I* HAVE TO DO THIS...?
KLAK
KLAK
THANKS FOR YOUR HELP.
HA!
WHY DO YOU WANT TO JOIN, ANYWAY? I DOUBT YOU HAVE A GOOD REASON.
I'll show them who you really are...
WELL... THERE'S THIS PERSON WHO HELPED ME OUT A LOT BEFORE, AND SHE LIKES TO RAISE FLOWERS.
!
I'M SURE SHE'D BE HAPPY...
...IF WE COULD TALK ABOUT FLOWERS NEXT TIME I VISIT HER.
HMPH.

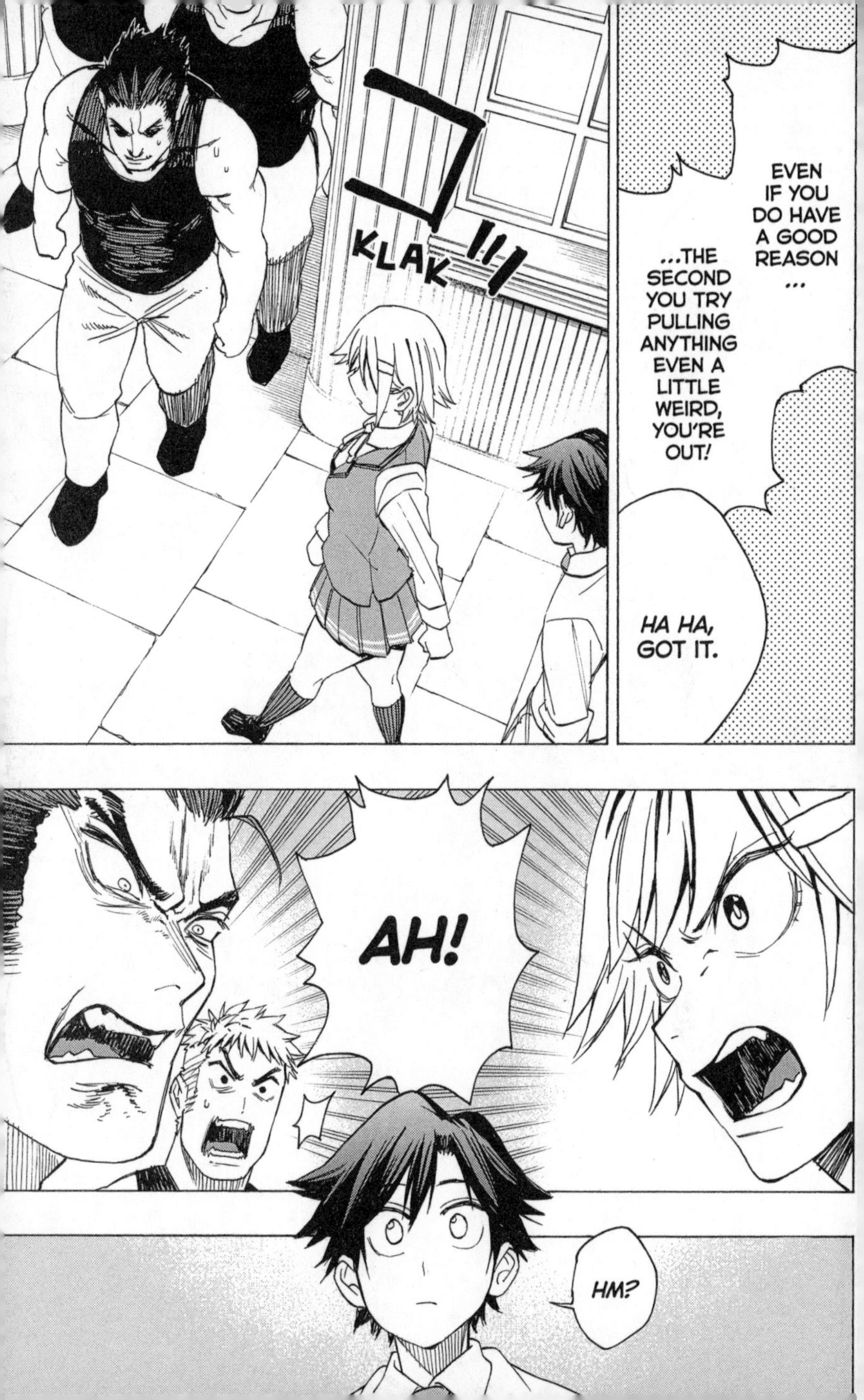
EVEN IF YOU DO HAVE A GOOD REASON ...
...THE SECOND YOU TRY PULLING ANYTHING EVEN A LITTLE WEIRD, YOU'RE OUT!
HA HA, GOT IT.
KLAK
AH!
HM?

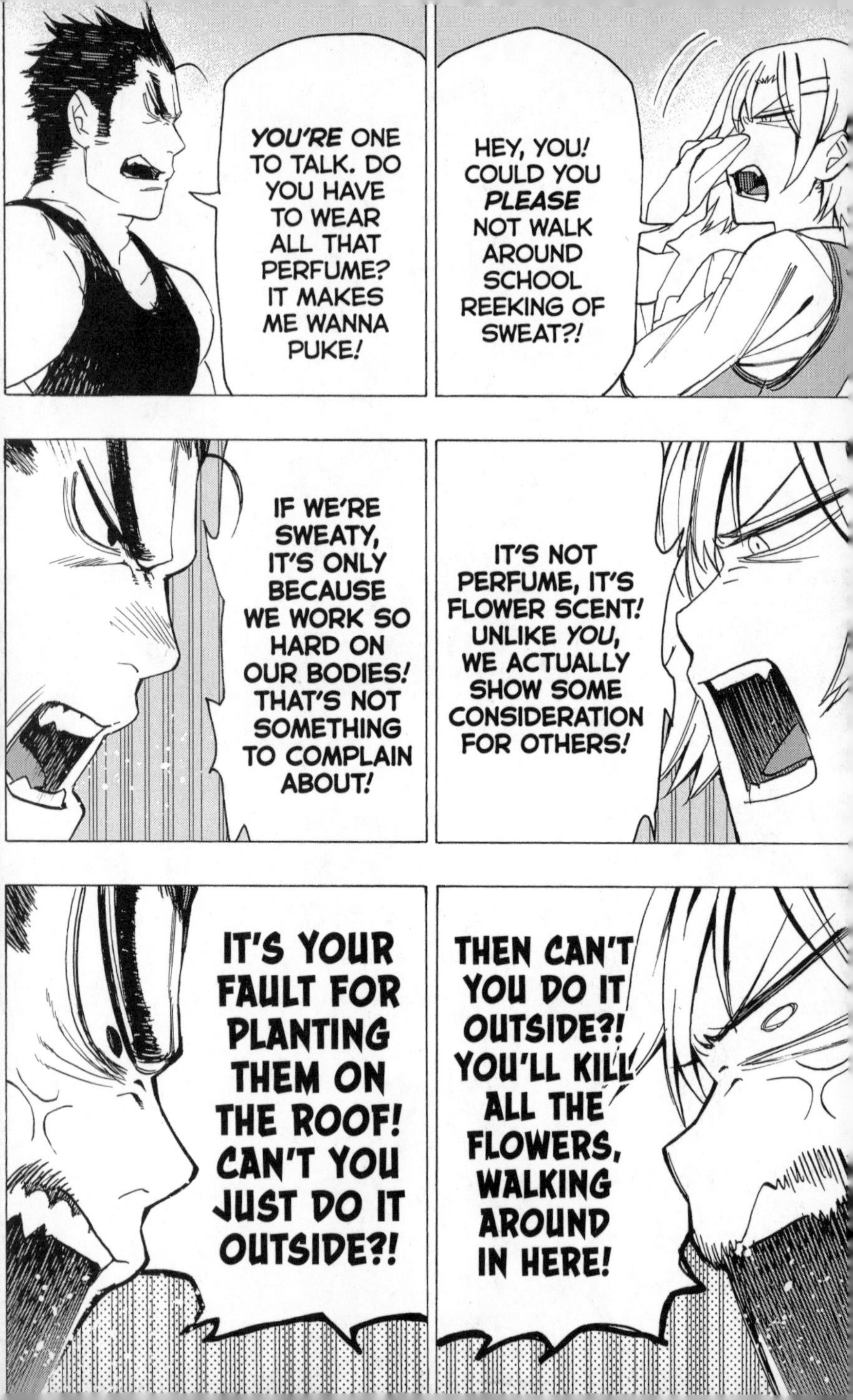
HEY, YOU! COULD YOU *PLEASE* NOT WALK AROUND SCHOOL REEKING OF SWEAT?!
YOU'RE ONE TO TALK. DO YOU HAVE TO WEAR ALL THAT PERFUME? IT MAKES ME WANNA PUKE!
IT'S NOT PERFUME, IT'S FLOWER SCENT! UNLIKE *YOU*, WE ACTUALLY SHOW SOME CONSIDERATION FOR OTHERS!
IF WE'RE SWEATY, IT'S ONLY BECAUSE WE WORK SO HARD ON OUR BODIES! THAT'S NOT SOMETHING TO COMPLAIN ABOUT!
THEN CAN'T YOU DO IT OUTSIDE?! YOU'LL KILL ALL THE FLOWERS, WALKING AROUND IN HERE!
IT'S YOUR FAULT FOR PLANTING THEM ON THE ROOF! CAN'T YOU JUST DO IT OUTSIDE?!

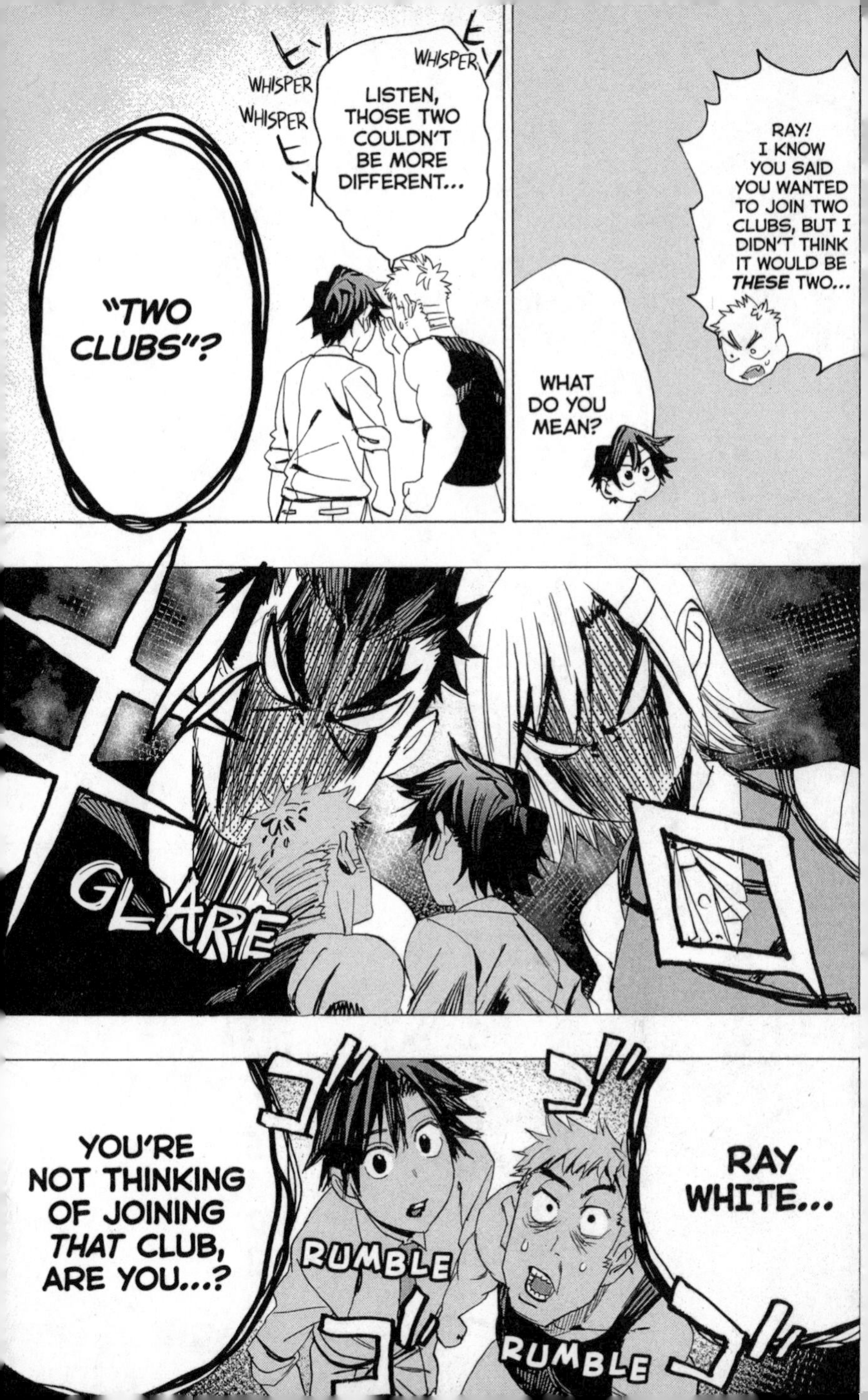
RAY! I KNOW YOU SAID YOU WANTED TO JOIN TWO CLUBS, BUT I DIDN'T THINK IT WOULD BE *THESE* TWO...
WHAT DO YOU MEAN?
WHISPER
WHISPER
WHISPER
LISTEN, THOSE TWO COULDN'T BE MORE DIFFERENT...
"TWO CLUBS"?
GLARE
RAY WHITE...
YOU'RE NOT THINKING OF JOINING *THAT* CLUB, ARE YOU...?
RUMBLE
RUMBLE

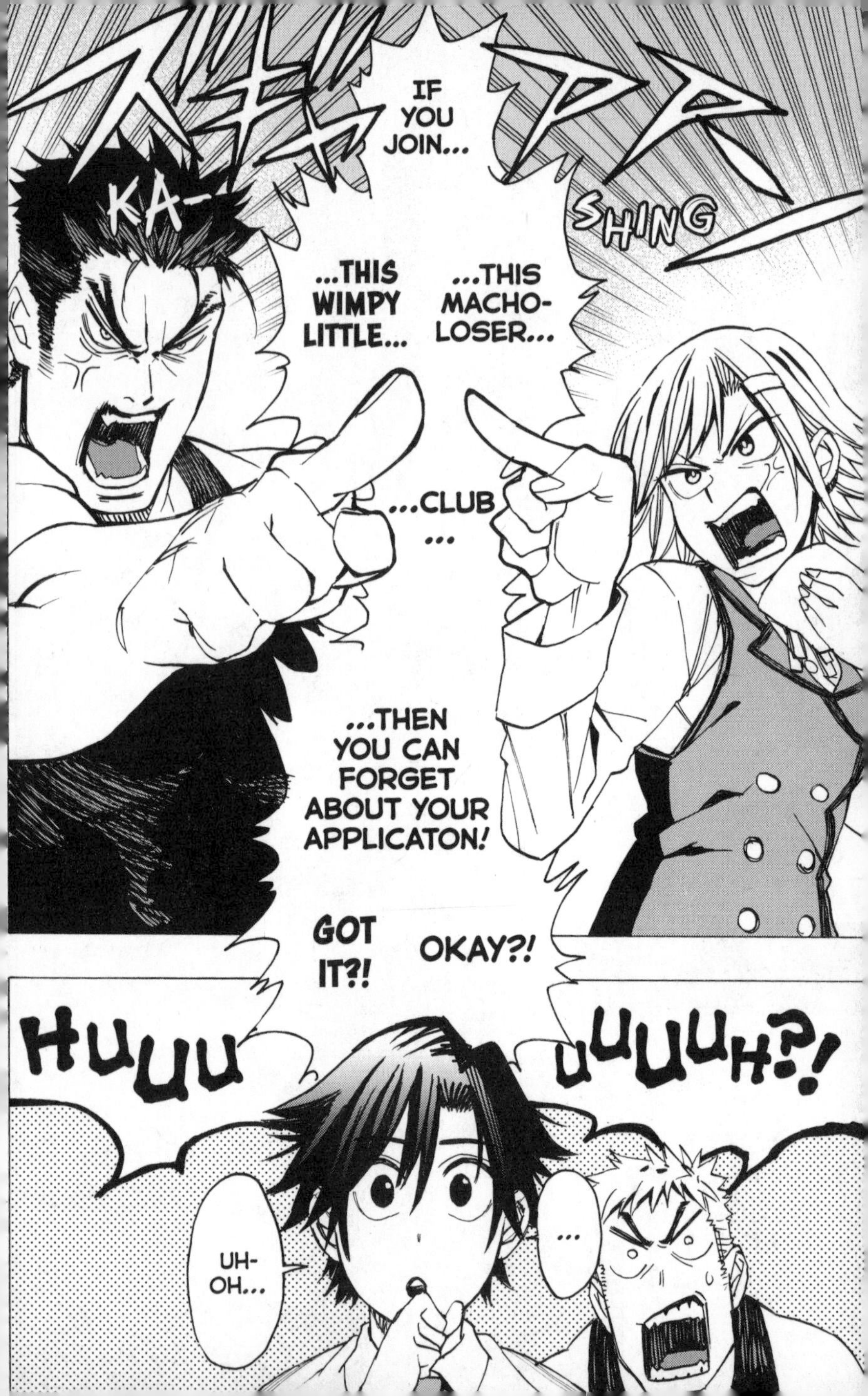
SHING
KA-
IF YOU JOIN...
...THIS MACHO-LOSER...
...THIS WIMPY LITTLE...
...CLUB...
...THEN YOU CAN FORGET ABOUT YOUR APPLICATON!
OKAY?!
GOT IT?!
HUUU UUUUH?!
...
UH-OH...

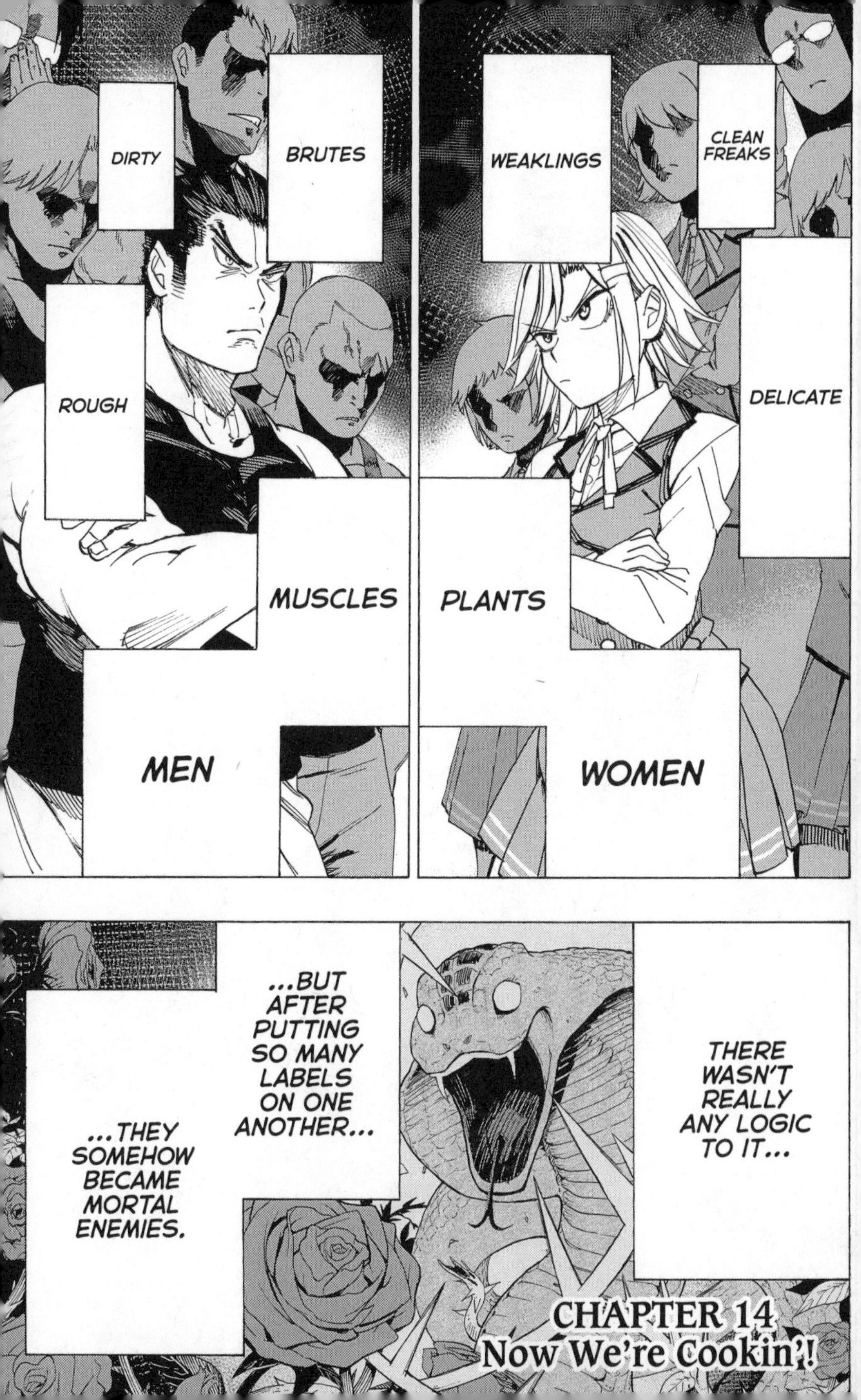
CLEAN FREAKS
WEAKLINGS
DELICATE
PLANTS
WOMEN
BRUTES
DIRTY
ROUGH
MUSCLES
MEN
THERE WASN'T REALLY ANY LOGIC TO IT...
...BUT AFTER PUTTING SO MANY LABELS ON ONE ANOTHER...
...THEY SOMEHOW BECAME MORTAL ENEMIES.

CHAPTER 14
Now We're Cookin'!

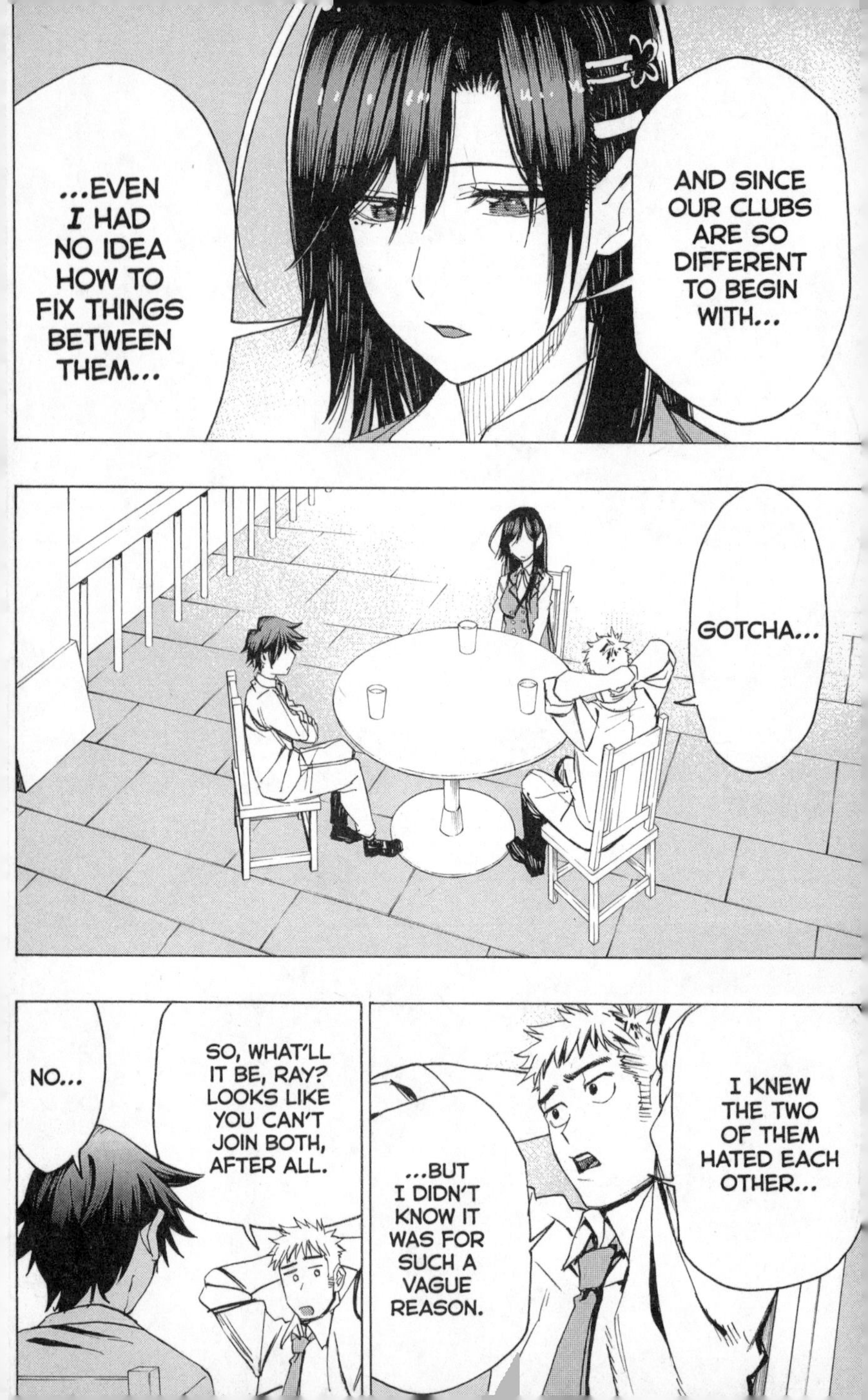
AND SINCE OUR CLUBS ARE SO DIFFERENT TO BEGIN WITH...
...EVEN I HAD NO IDEA HOW TO FIX THINGS BETWEEN THEM...
GOTCHA...
I KNEW THE TWO OF THEM HATED EACH OTHER...
...BUT I DIDN'T KNOW IT WAS FOR SUCH A VAGUE REASON.
SO, WHAT'LL IT BE, RAY? LOOKS LIKE YOU CAN'T JOIN BOTH, AFTER ALL.
NO...

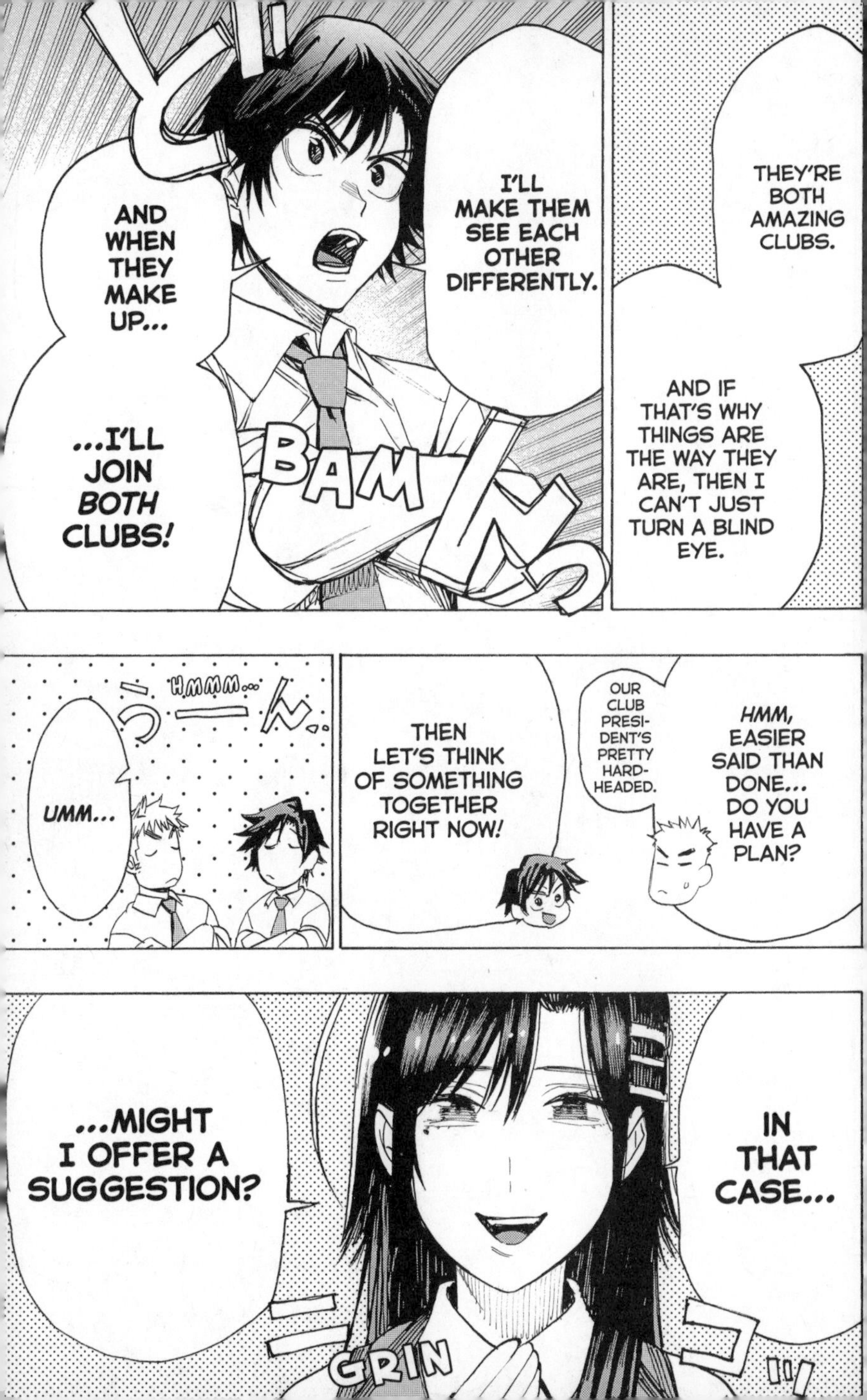
THEY'RE BOTH AMAZING CLUBS.
AND IF THAT'S WHY THINGS ARE THE WAY THEY ARE, THEN I CAN'T JUST TURN A BLIND EYE.
I'LL MAKE THEM SEE EACH OTHER DIFFERENTLY.
BAM
AND WHEN THEY MAKE UP...
...I'LL JOIN *BOTH* CLUBS!
HMM, EASIER SAID THAN DONE... DO YOU HAVE A PLAN?
OUR CLUB PRESIDENT'S PRETTY HARD-HEADED.
THEN LET'S THINK OF SOMETHING TOGETHER RIGHT NOW!
HMMM...
UMM...
IN THAT CASE...
...MIGHT I OFFER A SUGGESTION?
GRIN

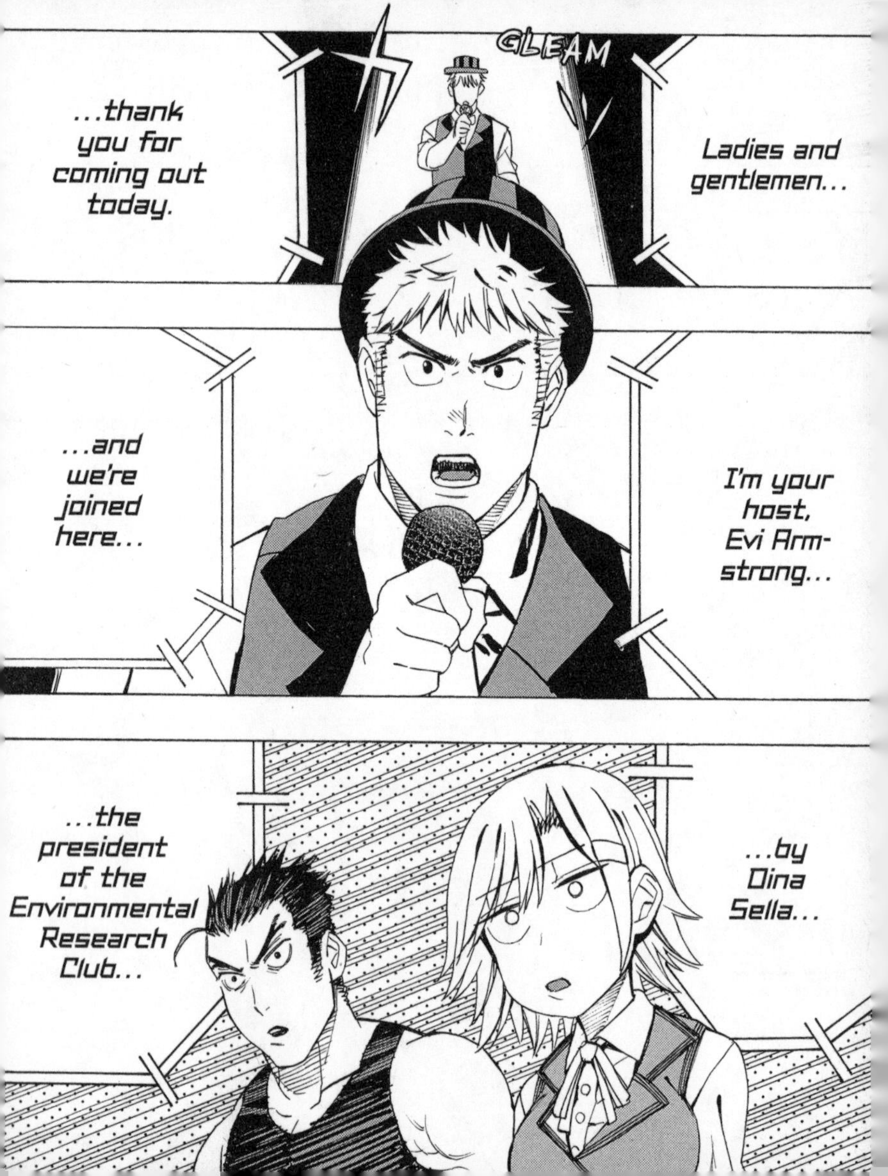
GLEAM
Ladies and gentlemen...
...thank you for coming out today.
I'm your host, Evi Armstrong...
...and we're joined here...
...by Dina Sella...
...the president of the Environmental Research Club...

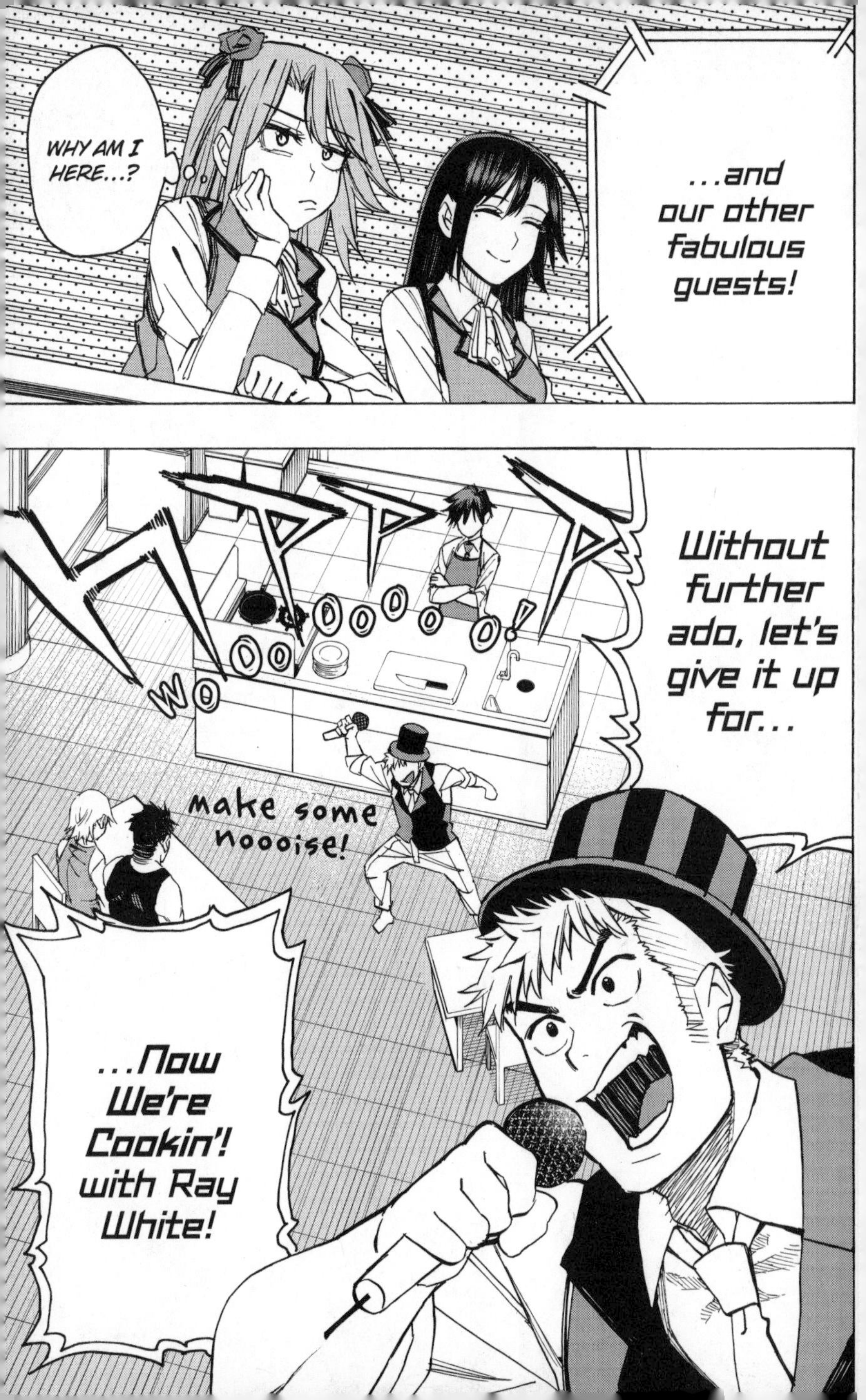
...and our other fabulous guests!
WHY AM I HERE...?
Without further ado, let's give it up for...
WOOOOOOOOOO!
make some noooise!
...Now We're Cookin'! with Ray White!

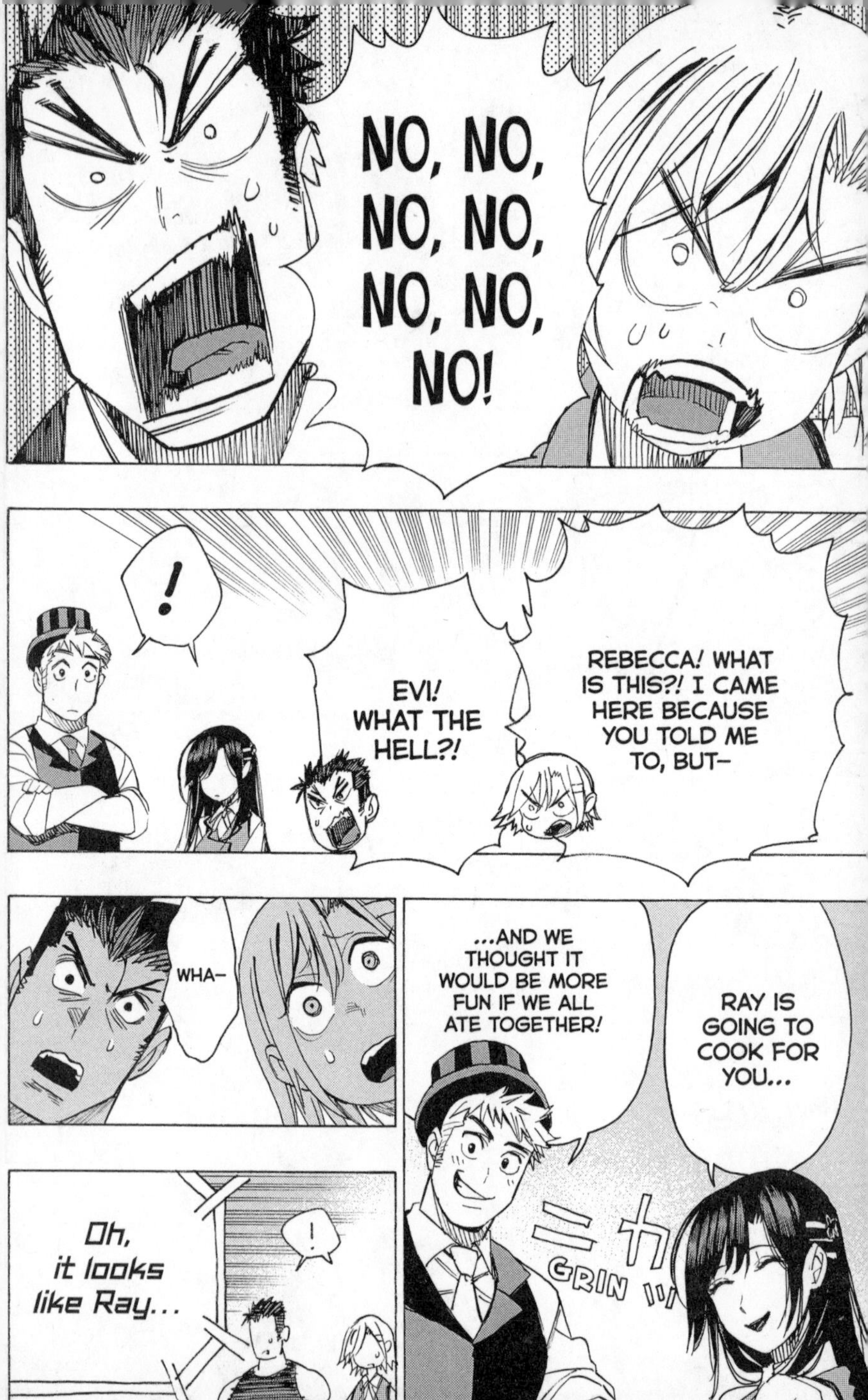

NO, NO, NO, NO, NO, NO, NO!
REBECCA! WHAT IS THIS?! I CAME HERE BECAUSE YOU TOLD ME TO, BUT–
EVI! WHAT THE HELL?!
!
RAY IS GOING TO COOK FOR YOU...
...AND WE THOUGHT IT WOULD BE MORE FUN IF WE ALL ATE TOGETHER!
GRIN
WHA–
!
Oh, it looks like Ray...

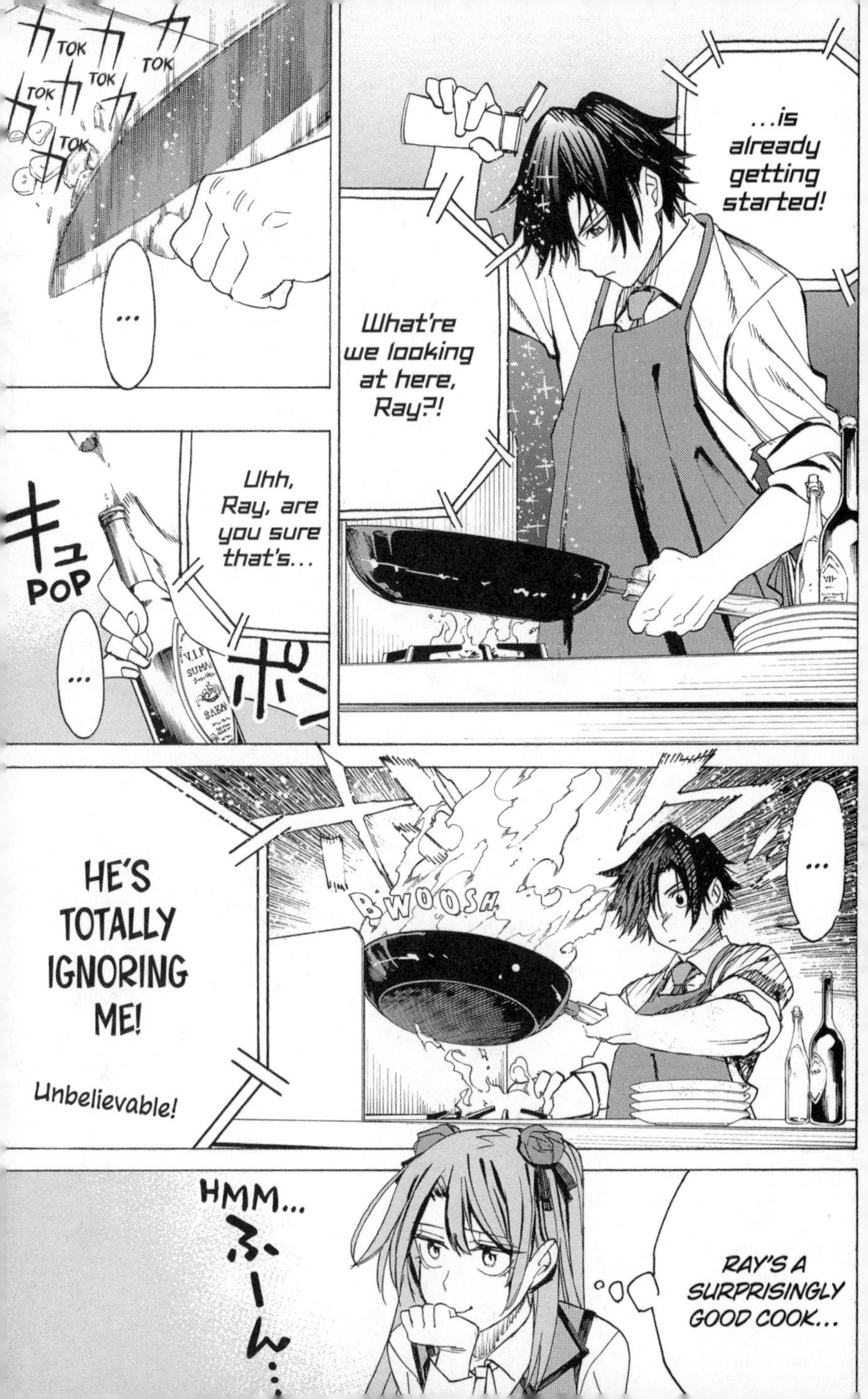
...is already getting started!
What're we looking at here, Ray?!
TOK TOK TOK TOK TOK
カカカカカ
...
Uhh, Ray, are you sure that's...
ポン
キュ
POP
...
...
BWOOSH
HE'S TOTALLY IGNORING ME!
Unbelievable!
RAY'S A SURPRISINGLY GOOD COOK...
HMM...
ふーん...

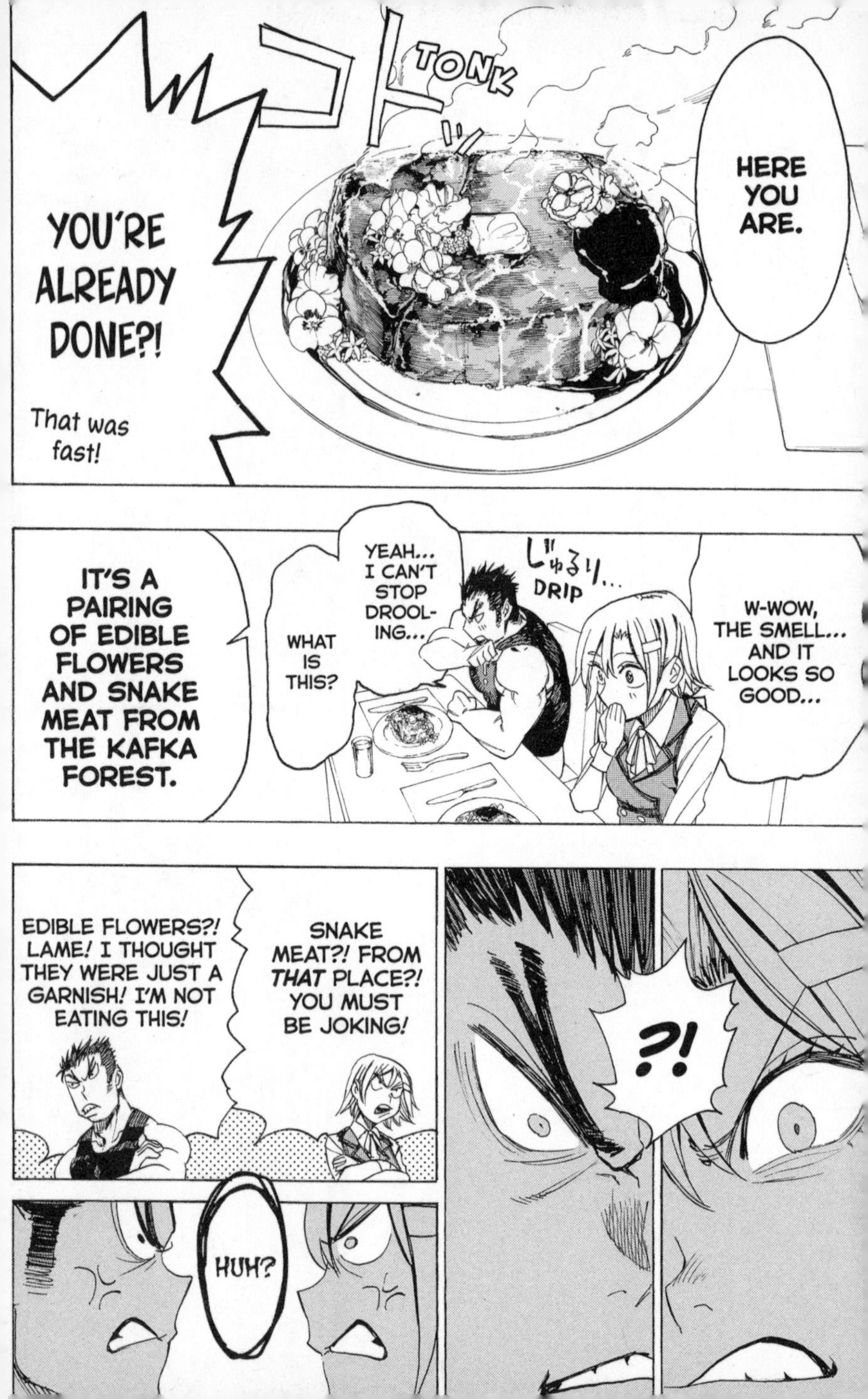
HERE YOU ARE.
コト
TONK
YOU'RE ALREADY DONE?!
That was fast!
W-WOW, THE SMELL... AND IT LOOKS SO GOOD...
じゅるり…
DRIP
YEAH... I CAN'T STOP DROOL-ING...
WHAT IS THIS?
IT'S A PAIRING OF EDIBLE FLOWERS AND SNAKE MEAT FROM THE KAFKA FOREST.
?!
SNAKE MEAT?! FROM THAT PLACE?! YOU MUST BE JOKING!
EDIBLE FLOWERS?! LAME! I THOUGHT THEY WERE JUST A GARNISH! I'M NOT EATING THIS!
HUH?

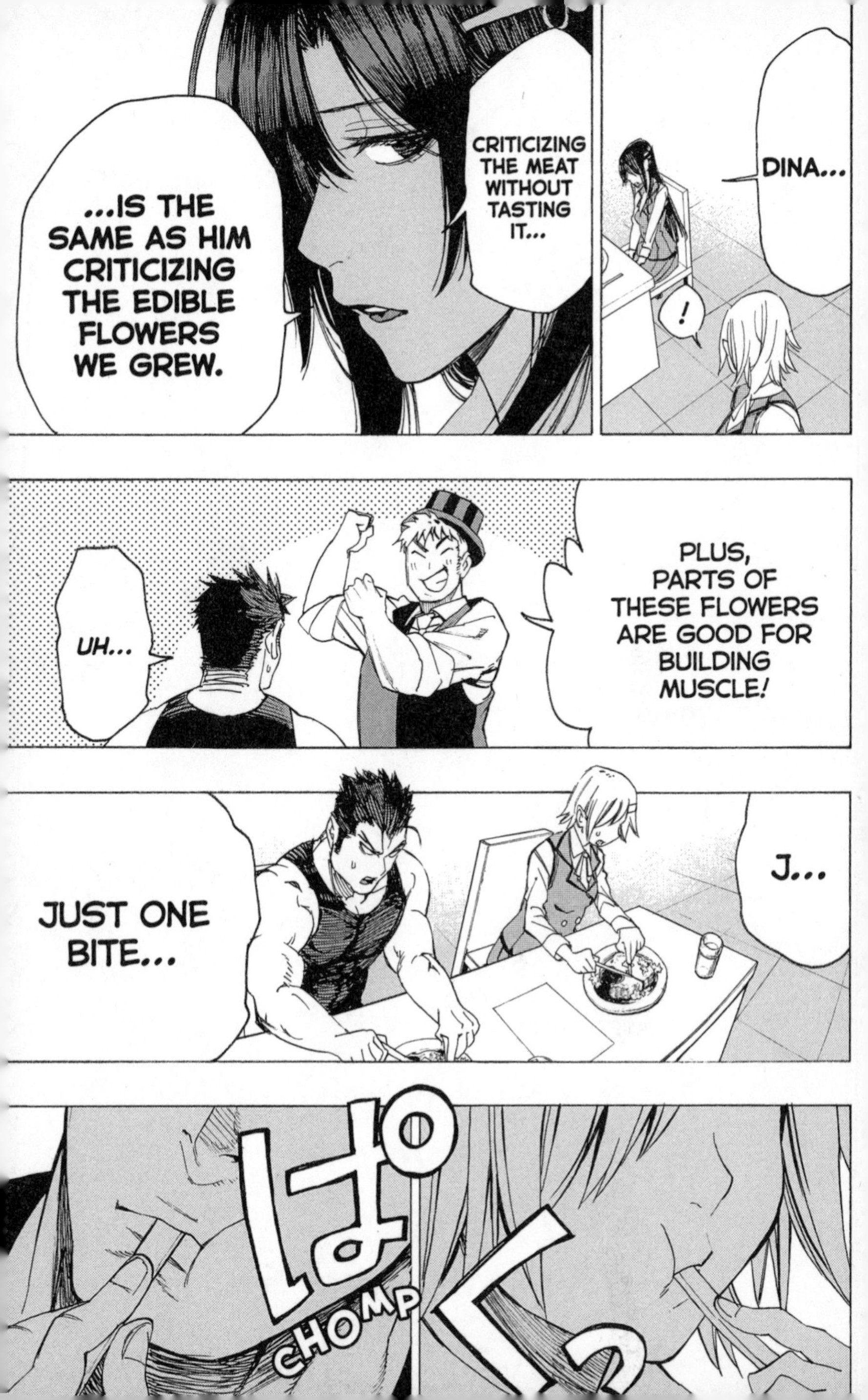
DINA...
!
CRITICIZING THE MEAT WITHOUT TASTING IT...
...IS THE SAME AS HIM CRITICIZING THE EDIBLE FLOWERS WE GREW.
PLUS, PARTS OF THESE FLOWERS ARE GOOD FOR BUILDING MUSCLE!
UH...
J...
JUST ONE BITE...
ぱくっ
CHOMP

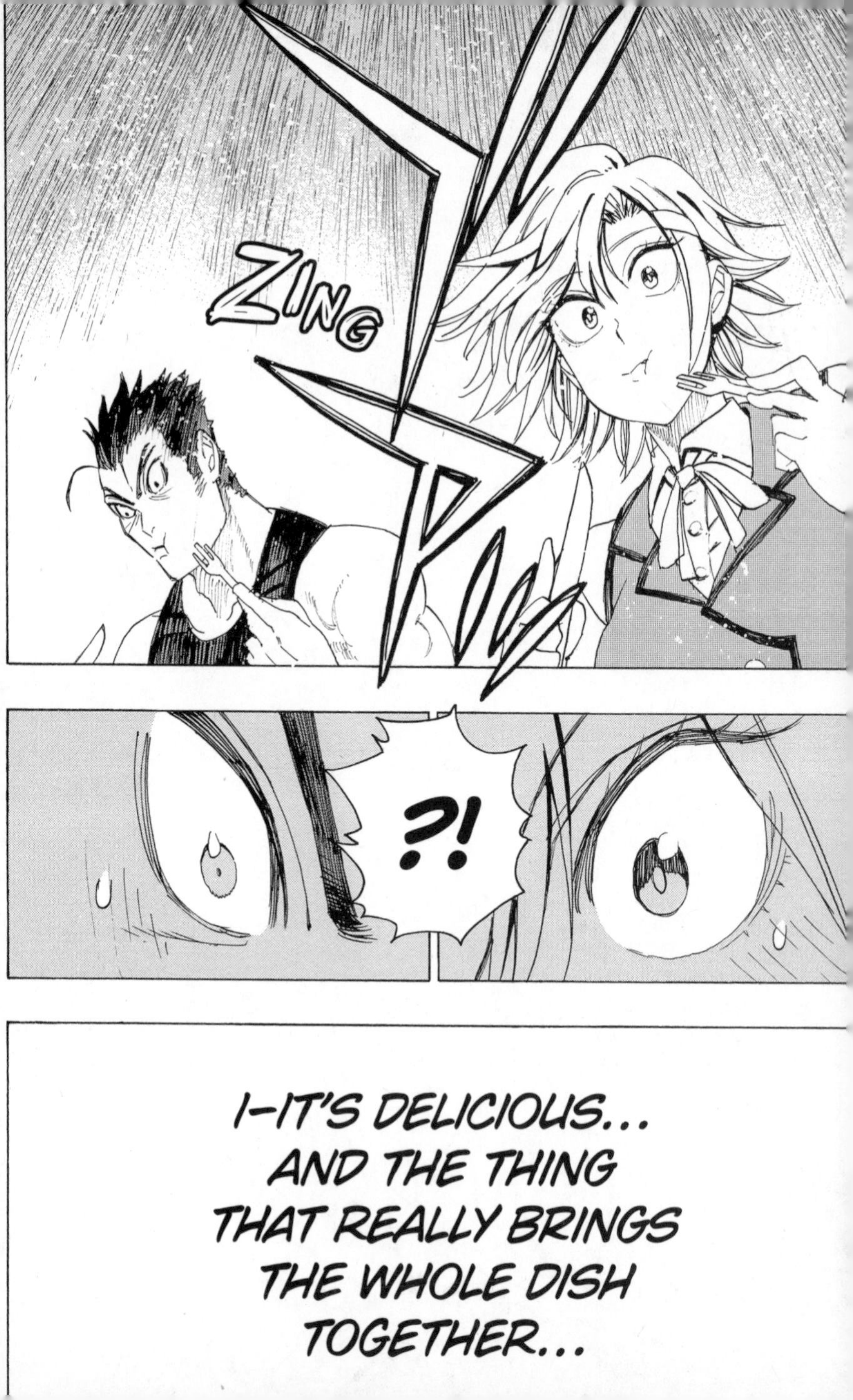
ZING
?!
I-IT'S DELICIOUS... AND THE THING THAT REALLY BRINGS THE WHOLE DISH TOGETHER...

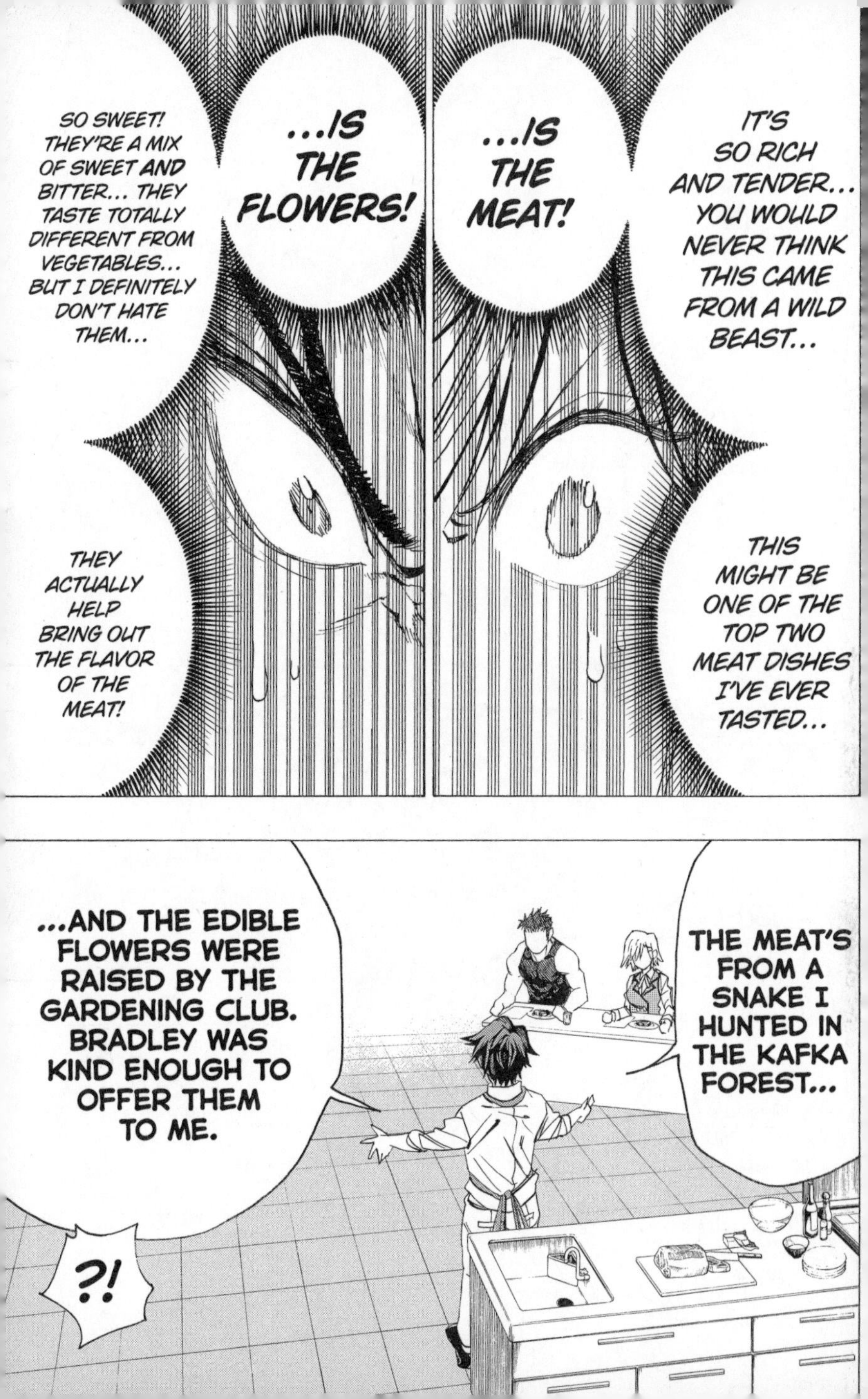

...IS THE MEAT!
IT'S SO RICH AND TENDER... YOU WOULD NEVER THINK THIS CAME FROM A WILD BEAST...
THIS MIGHT BE ONE OF THE TOP TWO MEAT DISHES I'VE EVER TASTED...
...IS THE FLOWERS!
SO SWEET! THEY'RE A MIX OF SWEET AND BITTER... THEY TASTE TOTALLY DIFFERENT FROM VEGETABLES... BUT I DEFINITELY DON'T HATE THEM...
THEY ACTUALLY HELP BRING OUT THE FLAVOR OF THE MEAT!
THE MEAT'S FROM A SNAKE I HUNTED IN THE KAFKA FOREST...
...AND THE EDIBLE FLOWERS WERE RAISED BY THE GARDENING CLUB. BRADLEY WAS KIND ENOUGH TO OFFER THEM TO ME.
?!

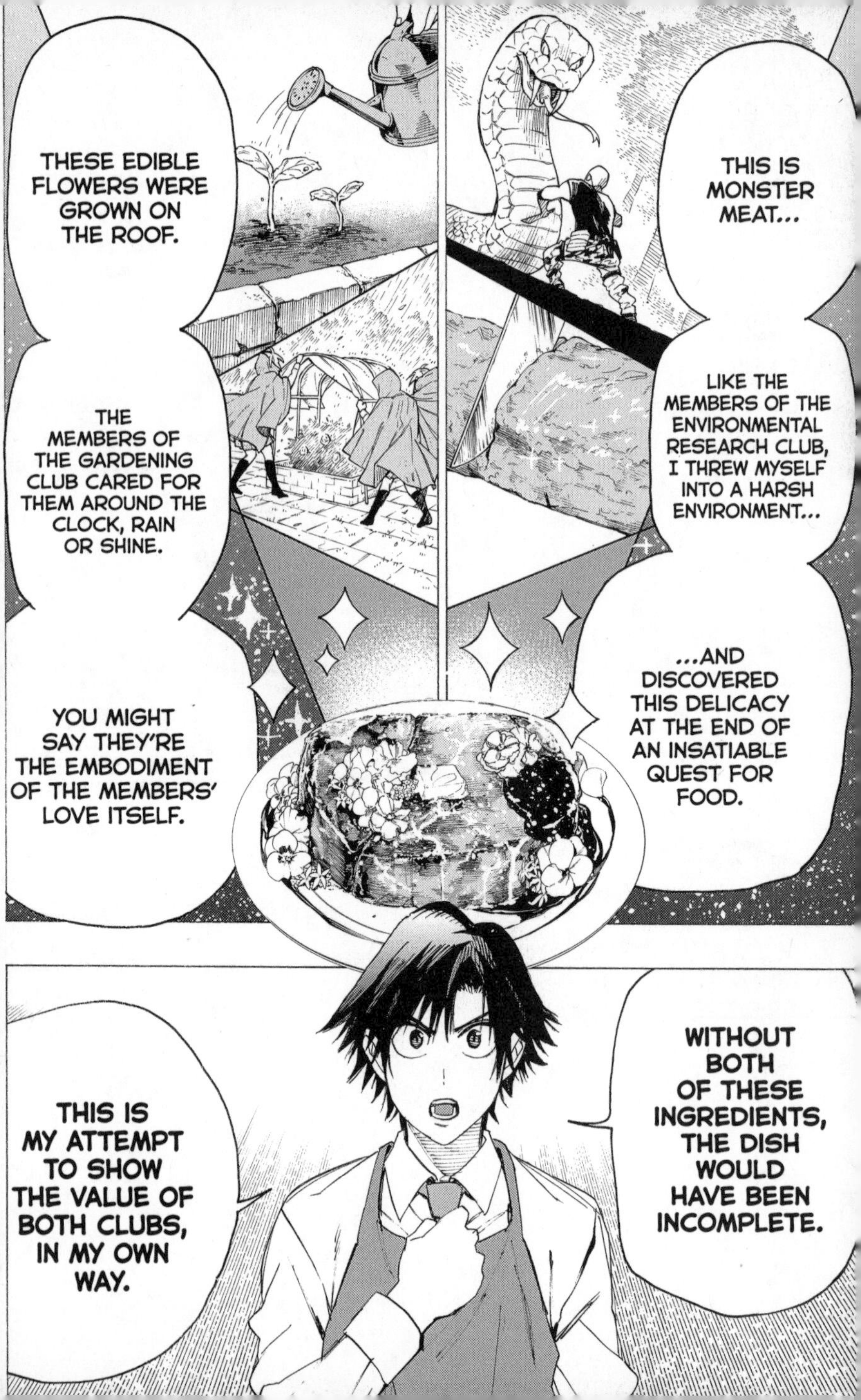
THIS IS MONSTER MEAT...
LIKE THE MEMBERS OF THE ENVIRONMENTAL RESEARCH CLUB, I THREW MYSELF INTO A HARSH ENVIRONMENT...
...AND DISCOVERED THIS DELICACY AT THE END OF AN INSATIABLE QUEST FOR FOOD.
THESE EDIBLE FLOWERS WERE GROWN ON THE ROOF.
THE MEMBERS OF THE GARDENING CLUB CARED FOR THEM AROUND THE CLOCK, RAIN OR SHINE.
YOU MIGHT SAY THEY'RE THE EMBODIMENT OF THE MEMBERS' LOVE ITSELF.
WITHOUT BOTH OF THESE INGREDIENTS, THE DISH WOULD HAVE BEEN INCOMPLETE.
THIS IS MY ATTEMPT TO SHOW THE VALUE OF BOTH CLUBS, IN MY OWN WAY.

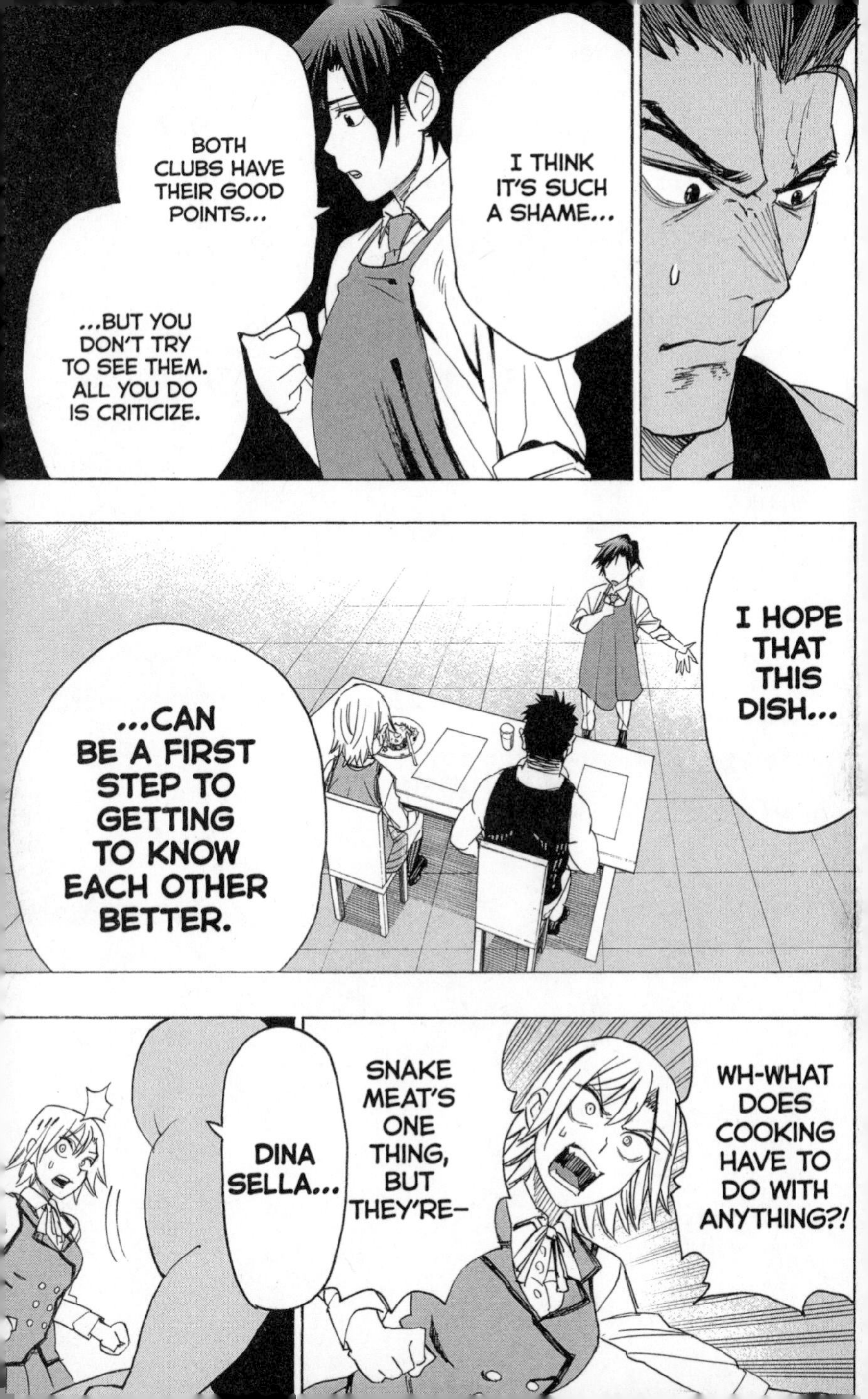
I THINK IT'S SUCH A SHAME...
BOTH CLUBS HAVE THEIR GOOD POINTS...
...BUT YOU DON'T TRY TO SEE THEM. ALL YOU DO IS CRITICIZE.
I HOPE THAT THIS DISH...
...CAN BE A FIRST STEP TO GETTING TO KNOW EACH OTHER BETTER.
WH-WHAT DOES COOKING HAVE TO DO WITH ANYTHING?!
SNAKE MEAT'S ONE THING, BUT THEY'RE–
DINA SELLA...

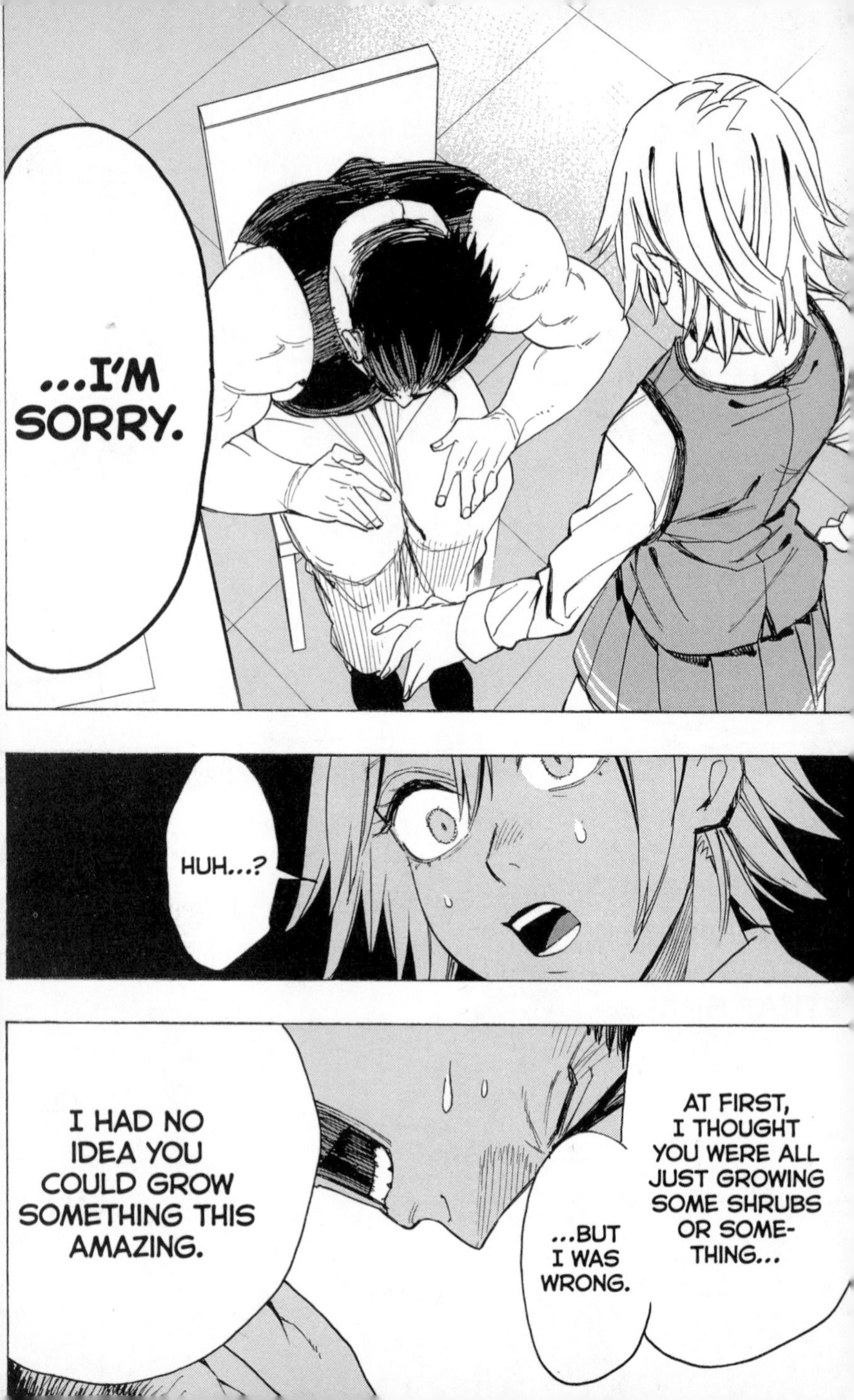
...I'M SORRY.
HUH...?
AT FIRST, I THOUGHT YOU WERE ALL JUST GROWING SOME SHRUBS OR SOME-THING...
...BUT I WAS WRONG.
I HAD NO IDEA YOU COULD GROW SOMETHING THIS AMAZING.

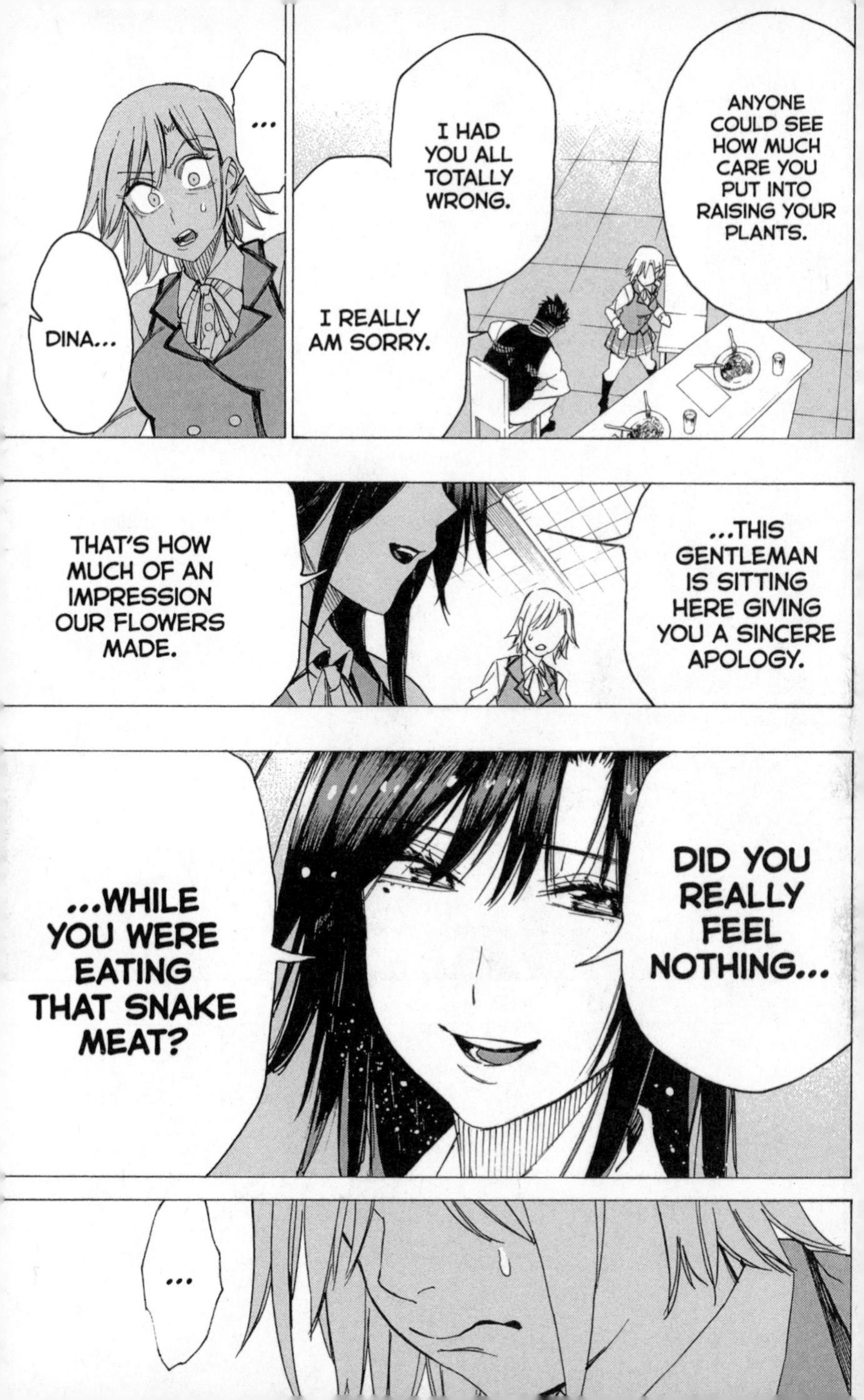
ANYONE COULD SEE HOW MUCH CARE YOU PUT INTO RAISING YOUR PLANTS.
I HAD YOU ALL TOTALLY WRONG.
I REALLY AM SORRY.
...
DINA...
...THIS GENTLEMAN IS SITTING HERE GIVING YOU A SINCERE APOLOGY.
THAT'S HOW MUCH OF AN IMPRESSION OUR FLOWERS MADE.
DID YOU REALLY FEEL NOTHING...
...WHILE YOU WERE EATING THAT SNAKE MEAT?
...

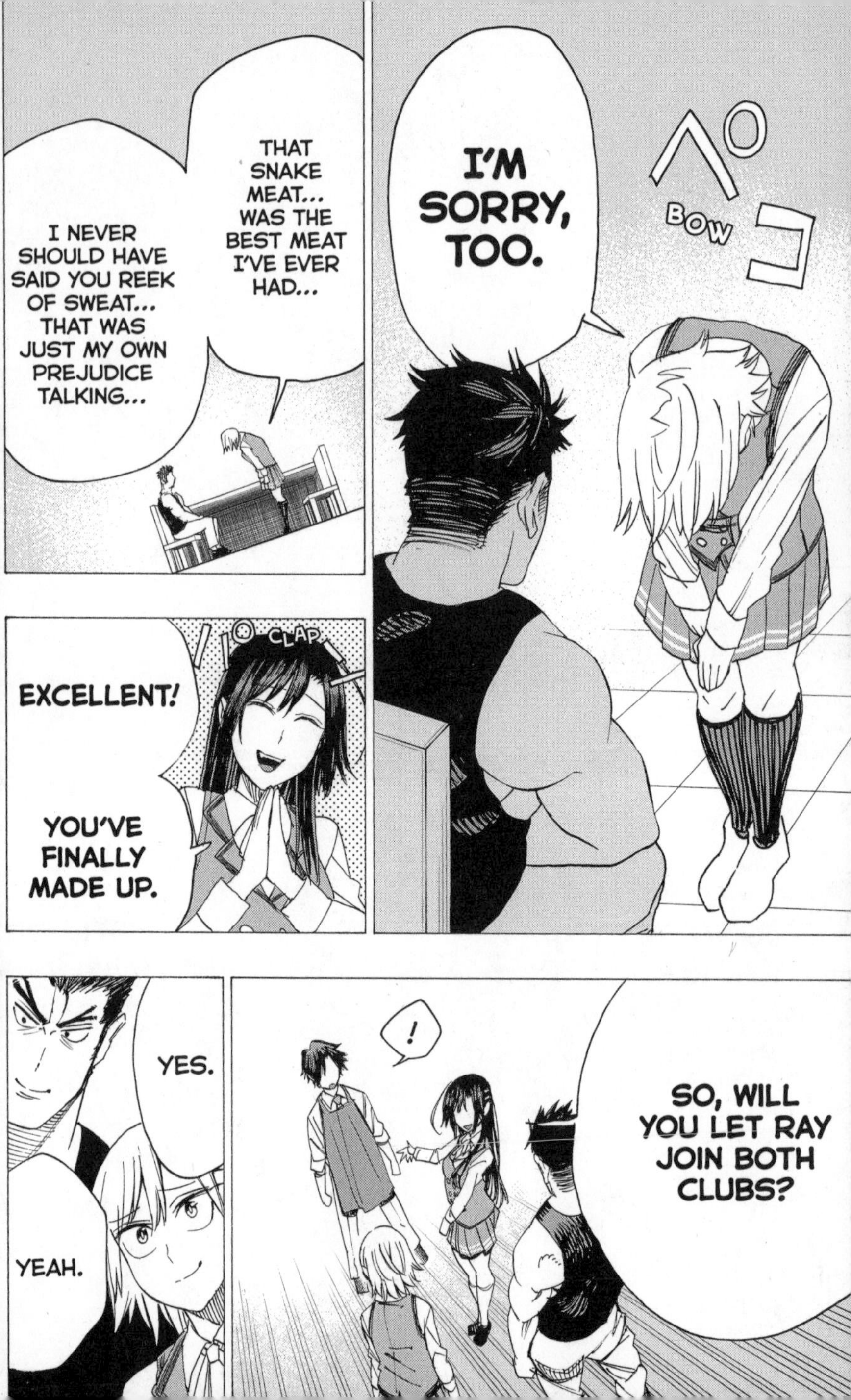
I'M SORRY, TOO.
BOW
THAT SNAKE MEAT... WAS THE BEST MEAT I'VE EVER HAD...
I NEVER SHOULD HAVE SAID YOU REEK OF SWEAT... THAT WAS JUST MY OWN PREJUDICE TALKING...
CLAP
EXCELLENT!
YOU'VE FINALLY MADE UP.
SO, WILL YOU LET RAY JOIN BOTH CLUBS?
!
YES.
YEAH.

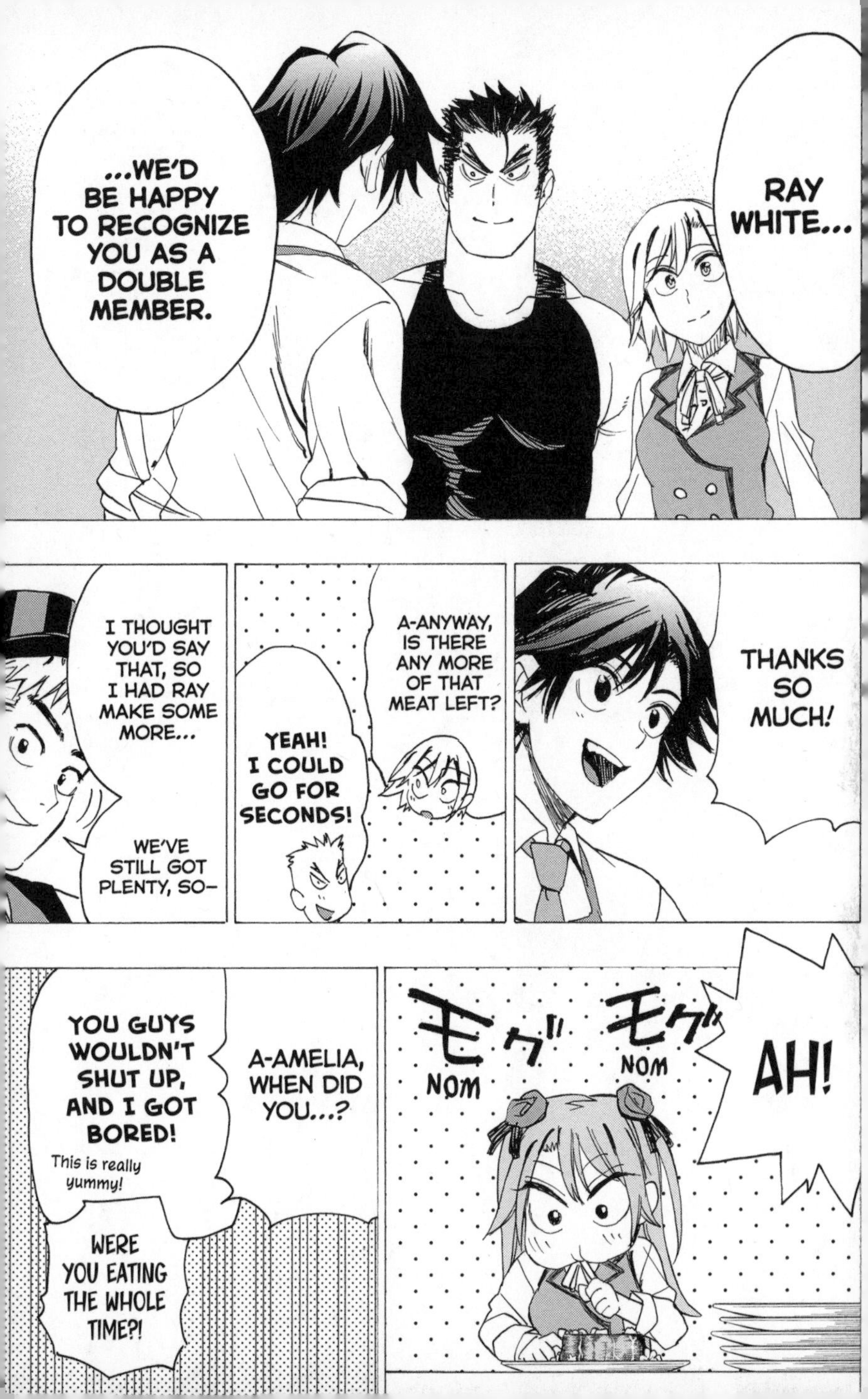
RAY WHITE...
...WE'D BE HAPPY TO RECOGNIZE YOU AS A DOUBLE MEMBER.
THANKS SO MUCH!
A-ANYWAY, IS THERE ANY MORE OF THAT MEAT LEFT?
YEAH! I COULD GO FOR SECONDS!
I THOUGHT YOU'D SAY THAT, SO I HAD RAY MAKE SOME MORE...
WE'VE STILL GOT PLENTY, SO–
AH!
モグ NOM
モグ NOM
A-AMELIA, WHEN DID YOU...?
YOU GUYS WOULDN'T SHUT UP, AND I GOT BORED!
This is really yummy!
WERE YOU EATING THE WHOLE TIME?!

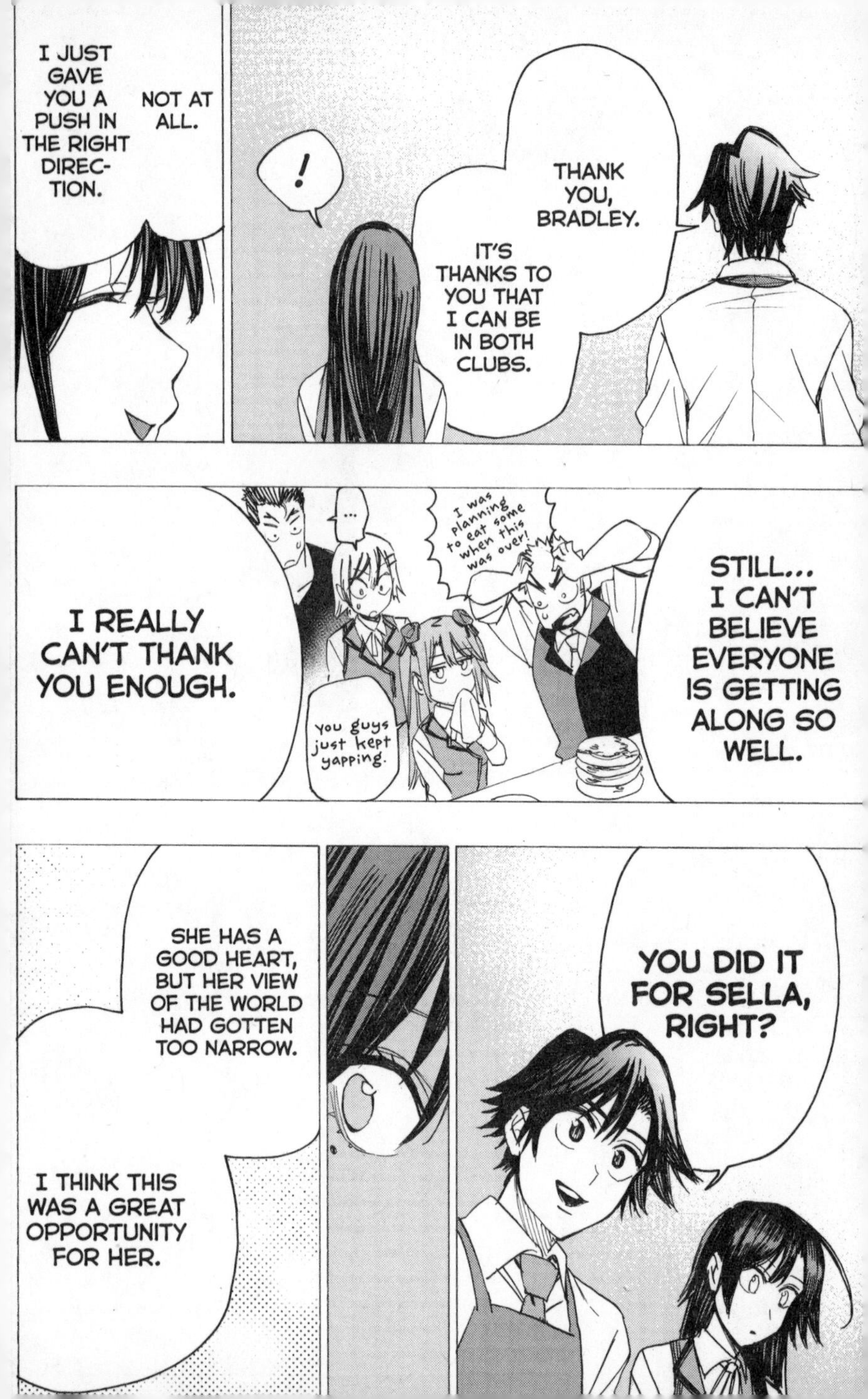
THANK YOU, BRADLEY.
IT'S THANKS TO YOU THAT I CAN BE IN BOTH CLUBS.
!
NOT AT ALL.
I JUST GAVE YOU A PUSH IN THE RIGHT DIREC-TION.
STILL... I CAN'T BELIEVE EVERYONE IS GETTING ALONG SO WELL.
I was planning to eat some when this was over!
...
I REALLY CAN'T THANK YOU ENOUGH.
you guys just kept yapping.
YOU DID IT FOR SELLA, RIGHT?
SHE HAS A GOOD HEART, BUT HER VIEW OF THE WORLD HAD GOTTEN TOO NARROW.
I THINK THIS WAS A GREAT OPPORTUNITY FOR HER.

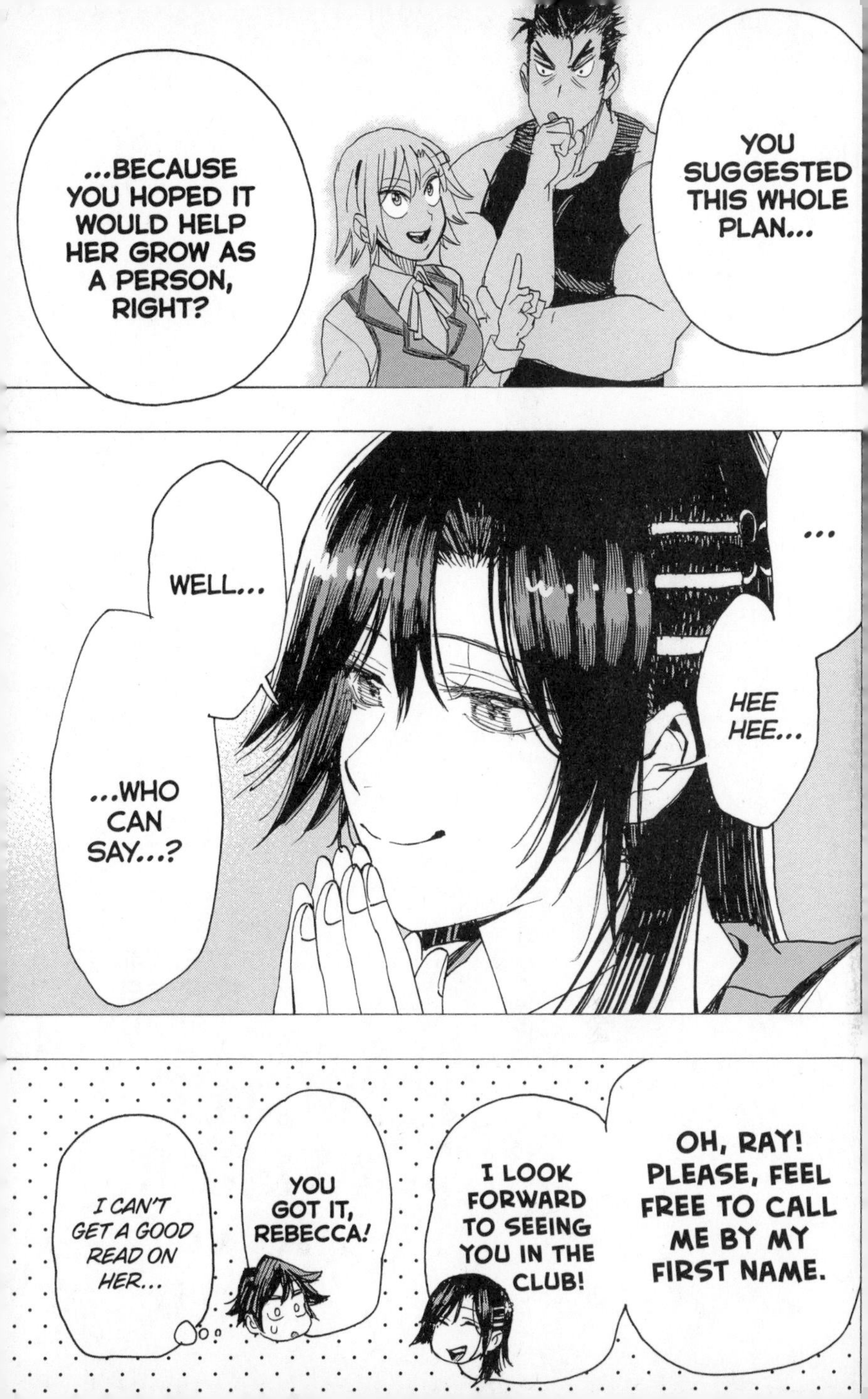
YOU SUGGESTED THIS WHOLE PLAN...
...BECAUSE YOU HOPED IT WOULD HELP HER GROW AS A PERSON, RIGHT?
...
HEE HEE...
WELL...
...WHO CAN SAY...?
OH, RAY! PLEASE, FEEL FREE TO CALL ME BY MY FIRST NAME.
I LOOK FORWARD TO SEEING YOU IN THE CLUB!
YOU GOT IT, REBECCA!
I CAN'T GET A GOOD READ ON HER...

The
ICEBLADE
SORCERER
Shall RULE
the
WORLD

CHAPTER 15
Moonlight Drinks

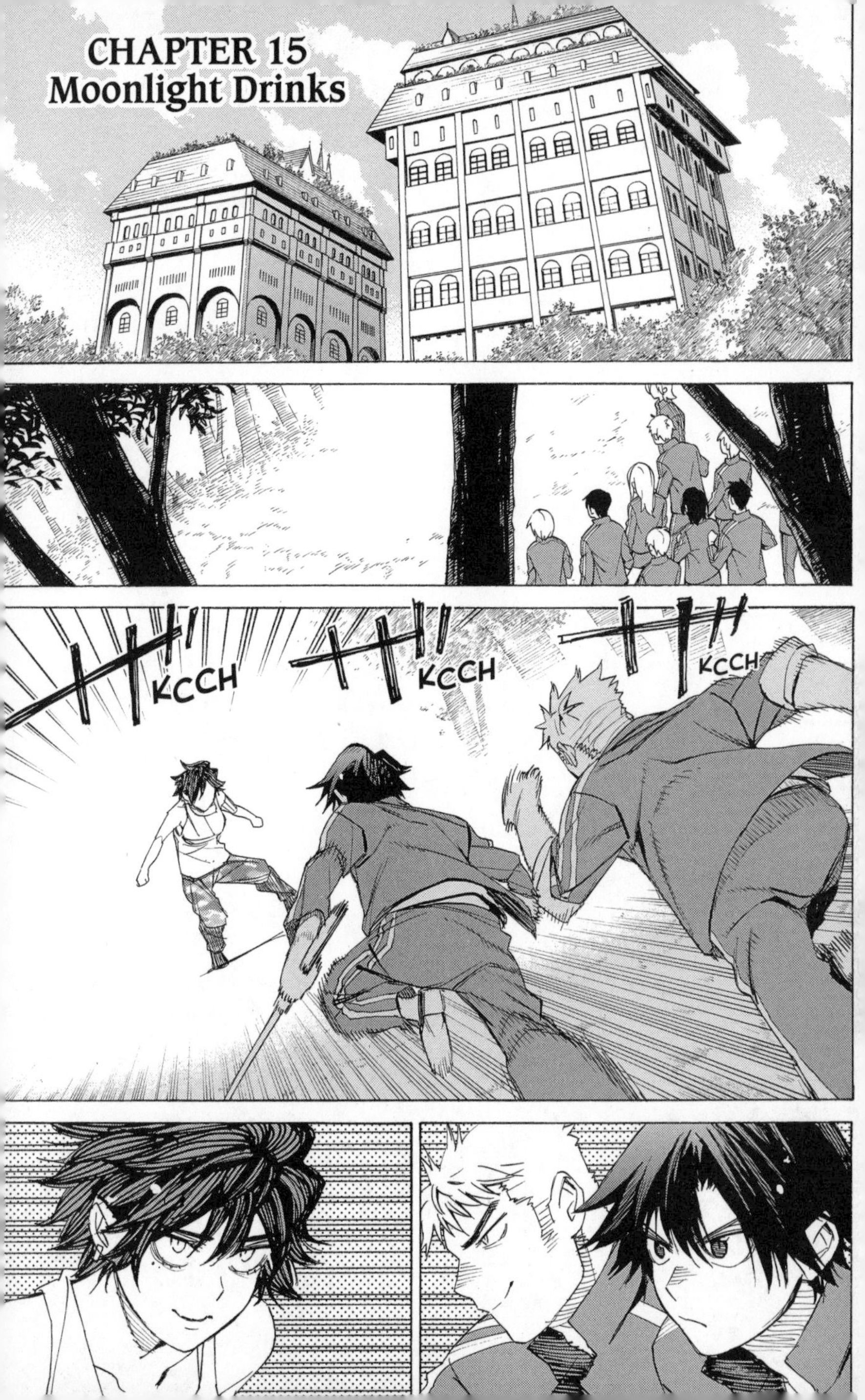
KCCH
KCCH
KCCH

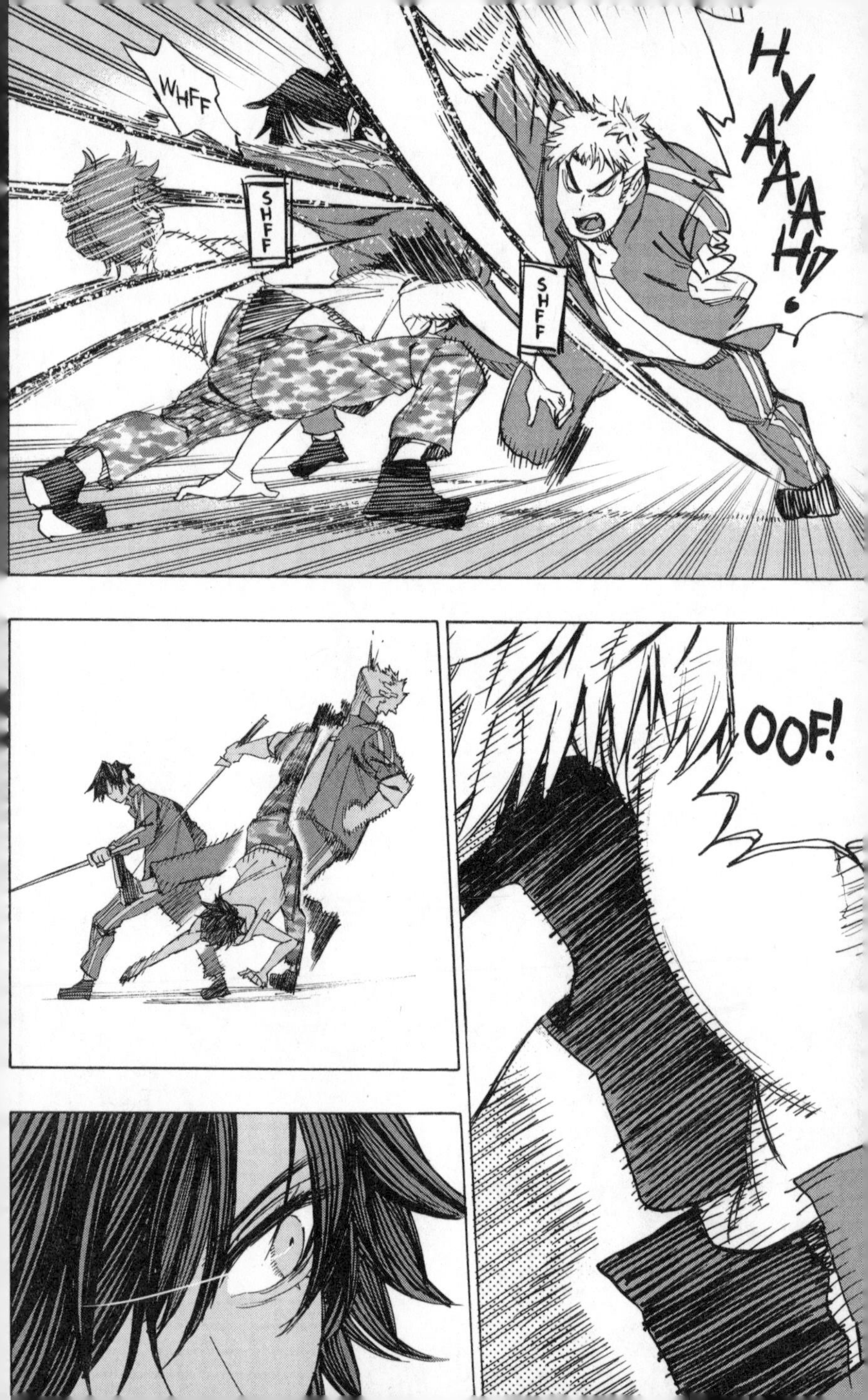
HYAAAAH!!
SHFF
SHFF
WHFF
OOF!

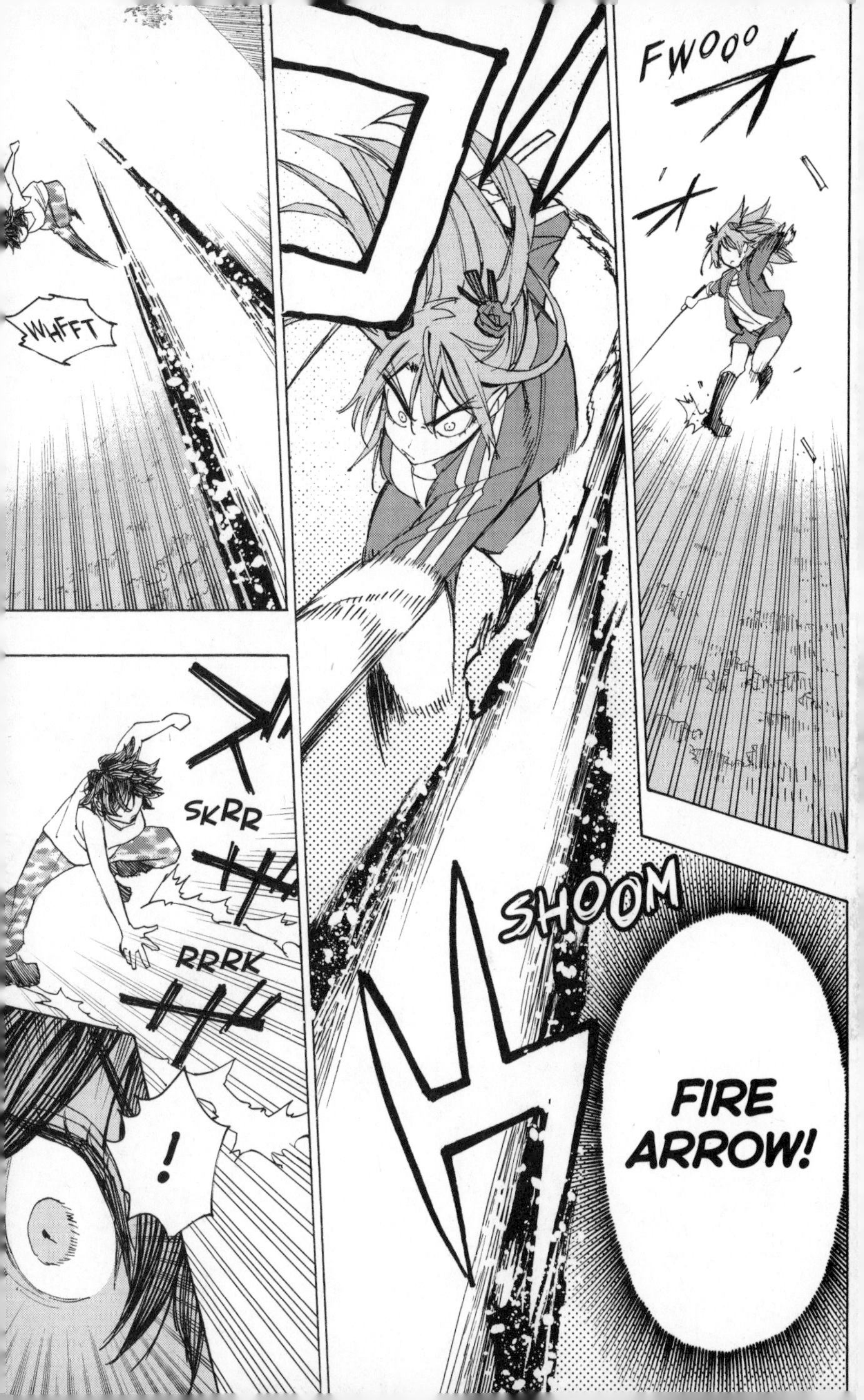
FWOOO
SHOOM
FIRE ARROW!
WHFFT
SKRR
RRRK
!

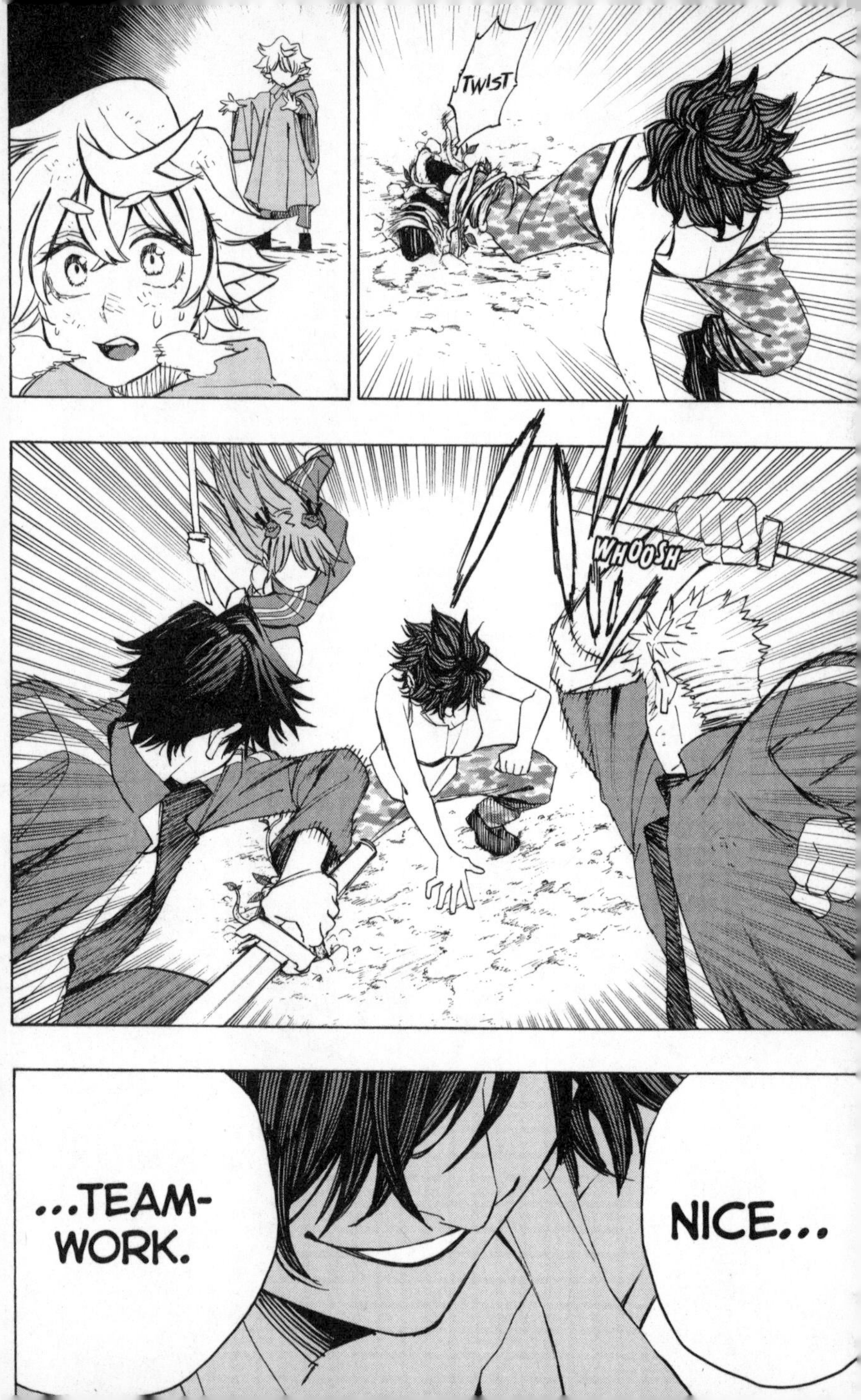
TWIST
WHOOSH
NICE...
...TEAM-WORK.

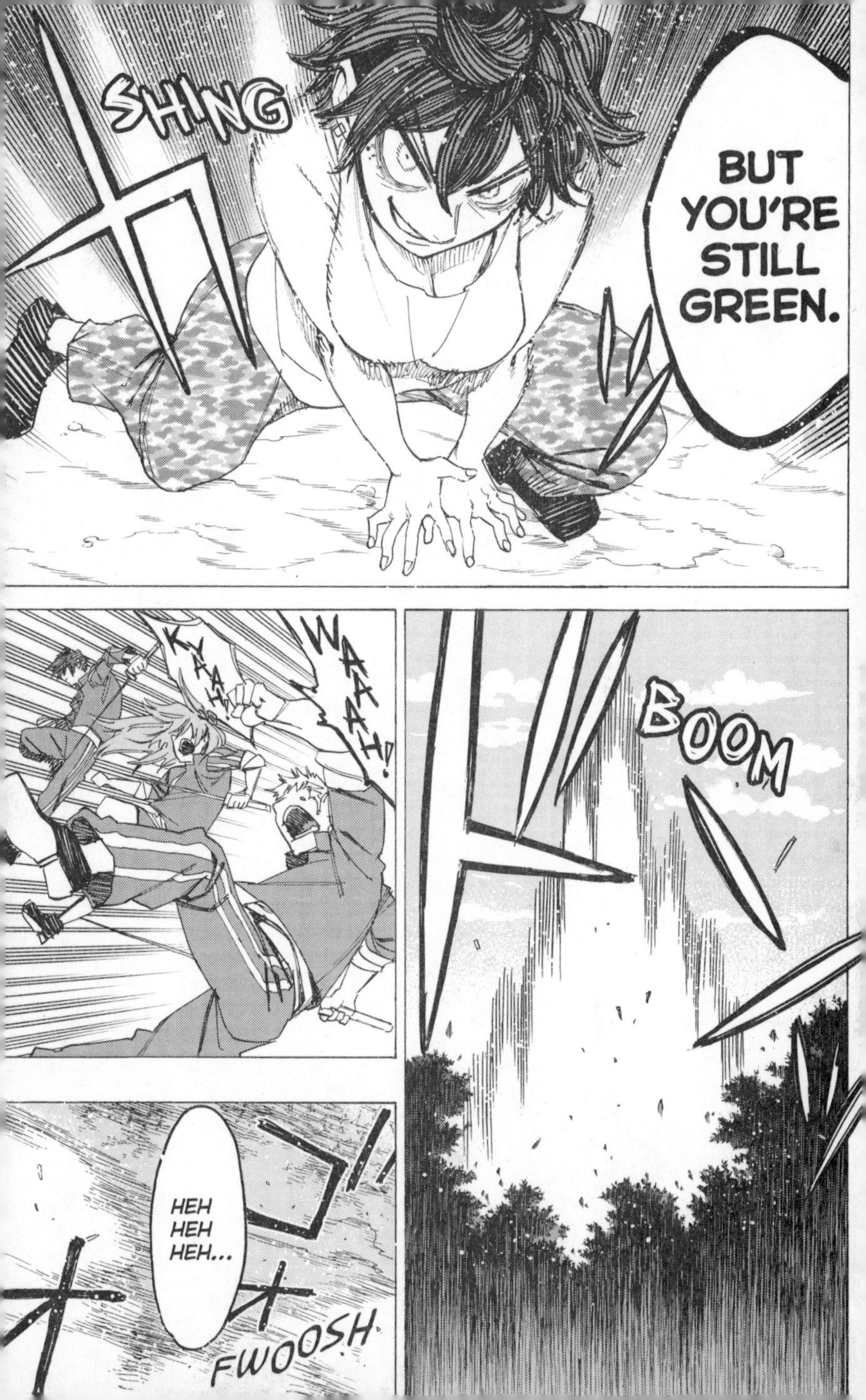
BUT YOU'RE STILL GREEN.
SHING
BOOM
WAAAAH!
KYAAAH!
HEH HEH HEH...
FWOOSH

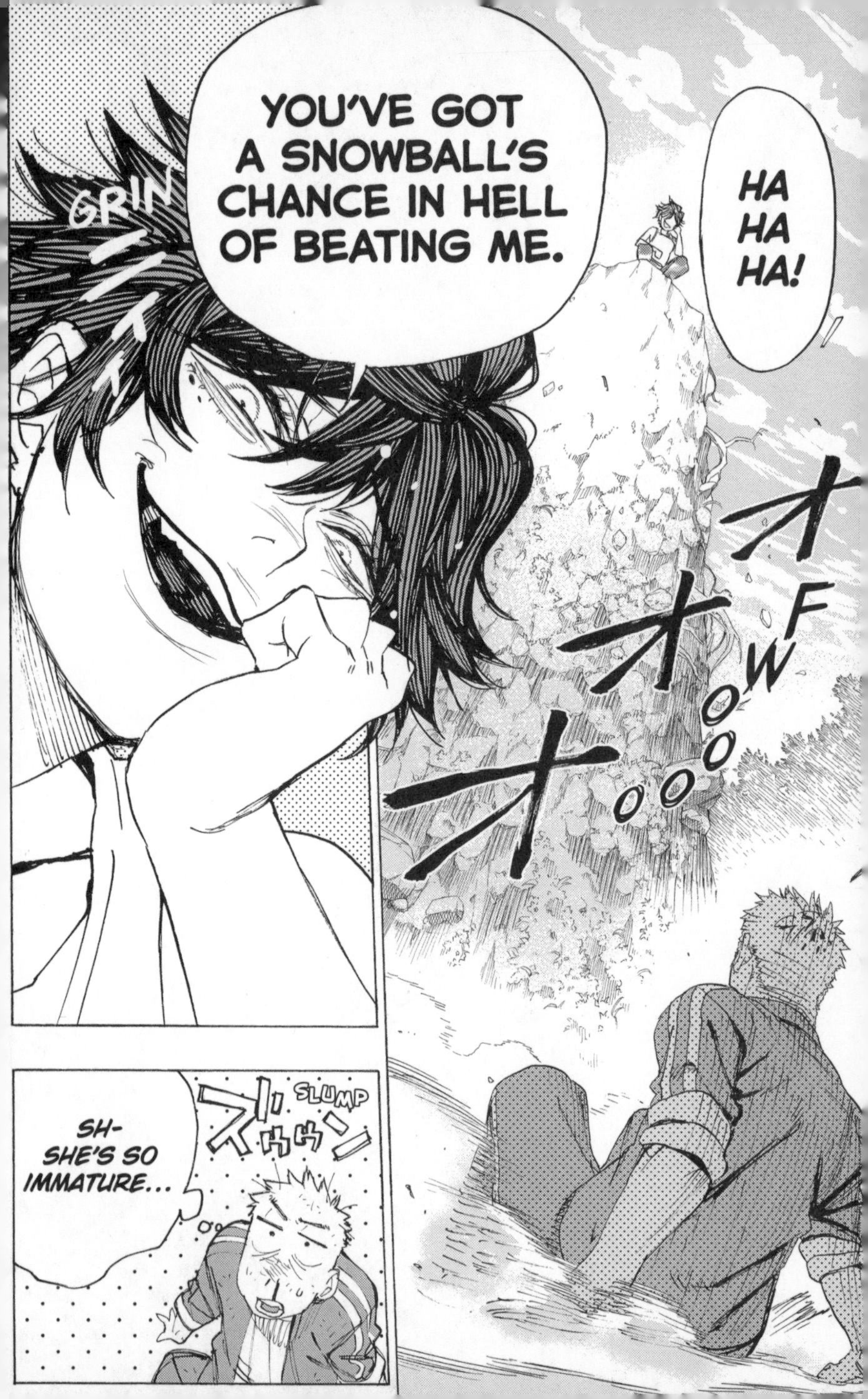
HA HA HA!
FWOOOO
YOU'VE GOT A SNOWBALL'S CHANCE IN HELL OF BEATING ME.
GRIN
SLUMP
SH- SHE'S SO IMMATURE...

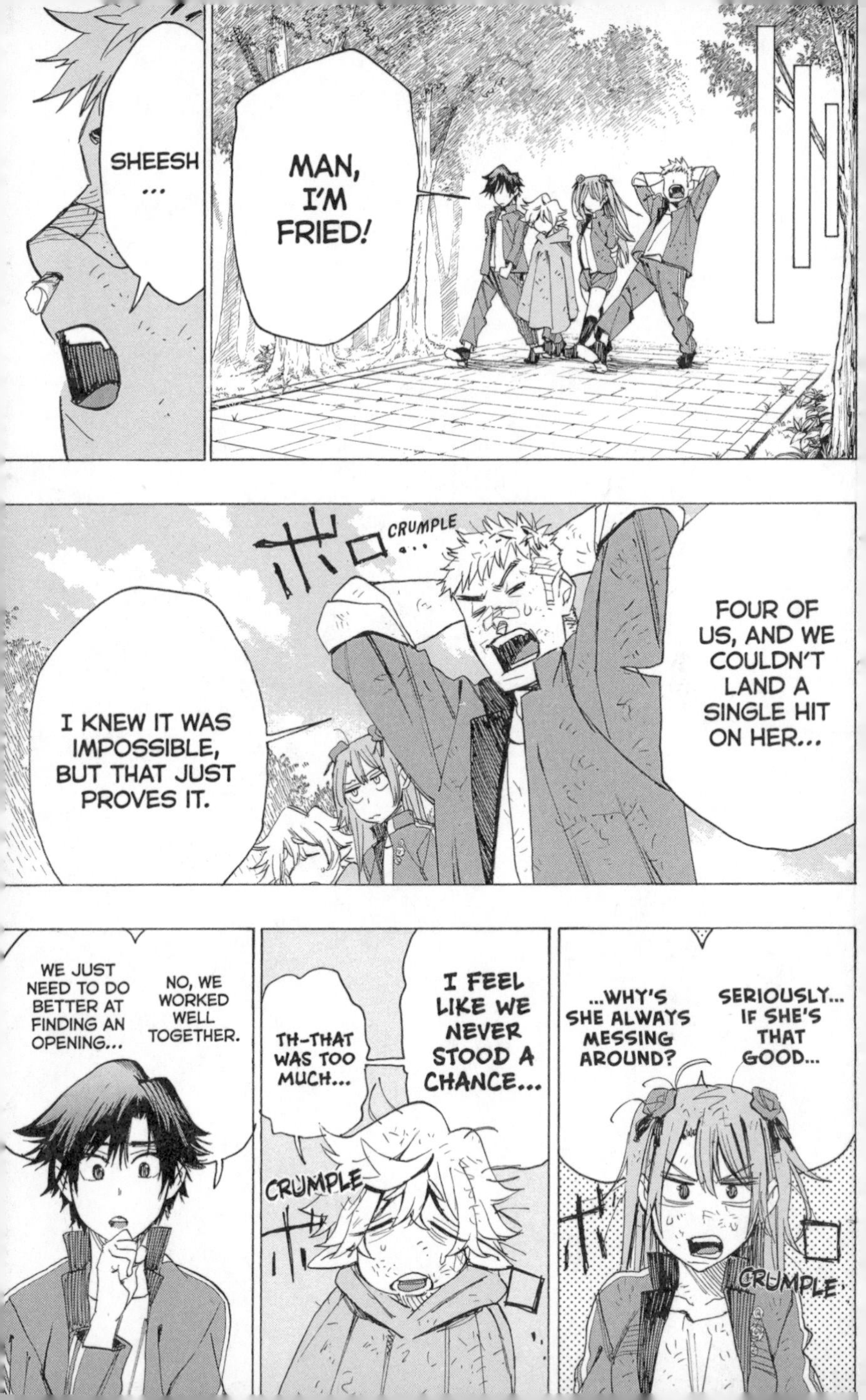
MAN, I'M FRIED!
SHEESH ...
ボロ
CRUMPLE...
FOUR OF US, AND WE COULDN'T LAND A SINGLE HIT ON HER...
I KNEW IT WAS IMPOSSIBLE, BUT THAT JUST PROVES IT.
SERIOUSLY... IF SHE'S THAT GOOD...
...WHY'S SHE ALWAYS MESSING AROUND?
CRUMPLE
I FEEL LIKE WE NEVER STOOD A CHANCE...
TH-THAT WAS TOO MUCH...
CRUMPLE
NO, WE WORKED WELL TOGETHER.
WE JUST NEED TO DO BETTER AT FINDING AN OPENING...

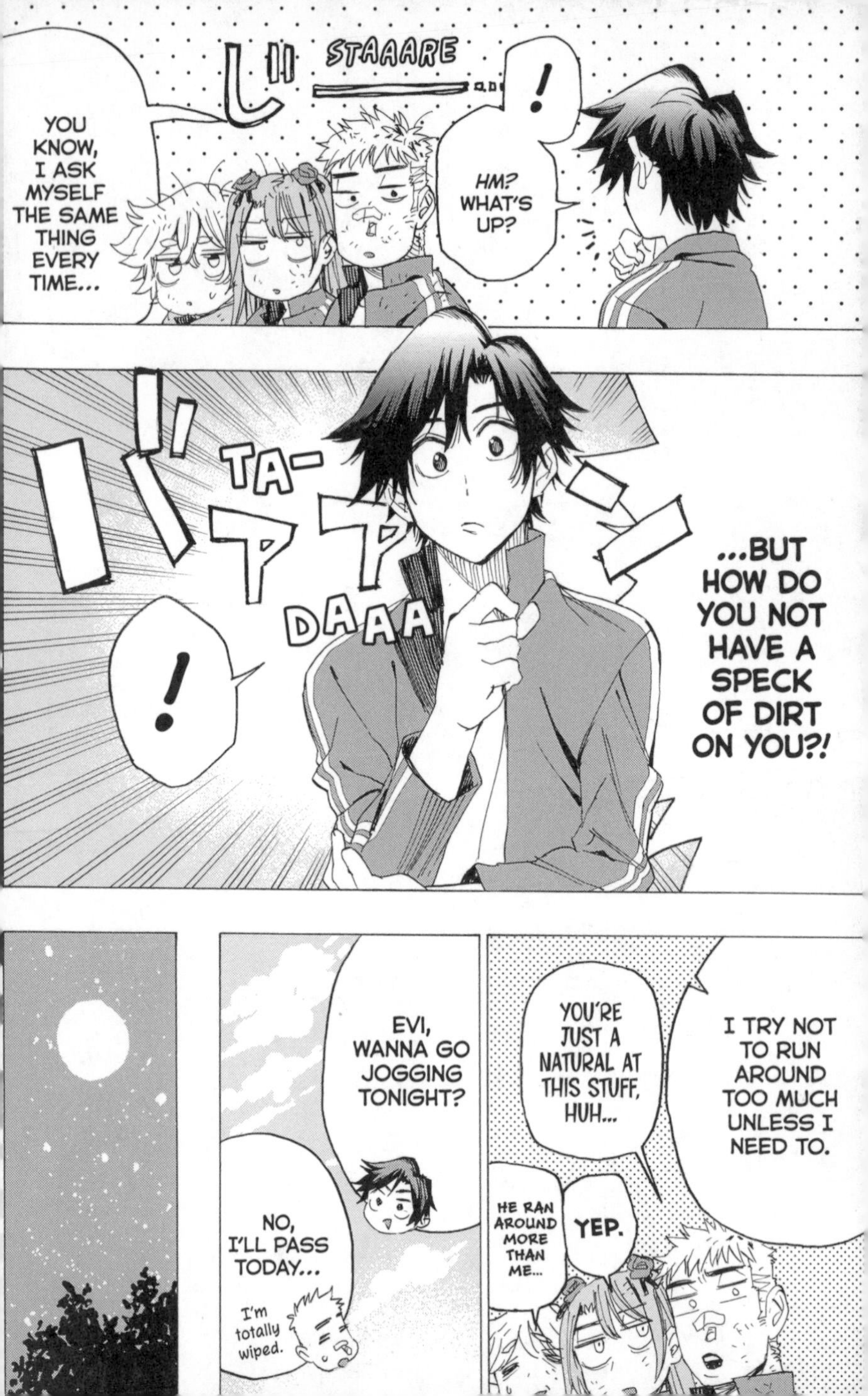
!
STAAARE
HM? WHAT'S UP?
YOU KNOW, I ASK MYSELF THE SAME THING EVERY TIME...
...BUT HOW DO YOU NOT HAVE A SPECK OF DIRT ON YOU?!
TA-
DAAA
!
I TRY NOT TO RUN AROUND TOO MUCH UNLESS I NEED TO.
YOU'RE JUST A NATURAL AT THIS STUFF, HUH...
YEP.
HE RAN AROUND MORE THAN ME...
EVI, WANNA GO JOGGING TONIGHT?
NO, I'LL PASS TODAY...
I'm totally wiped.

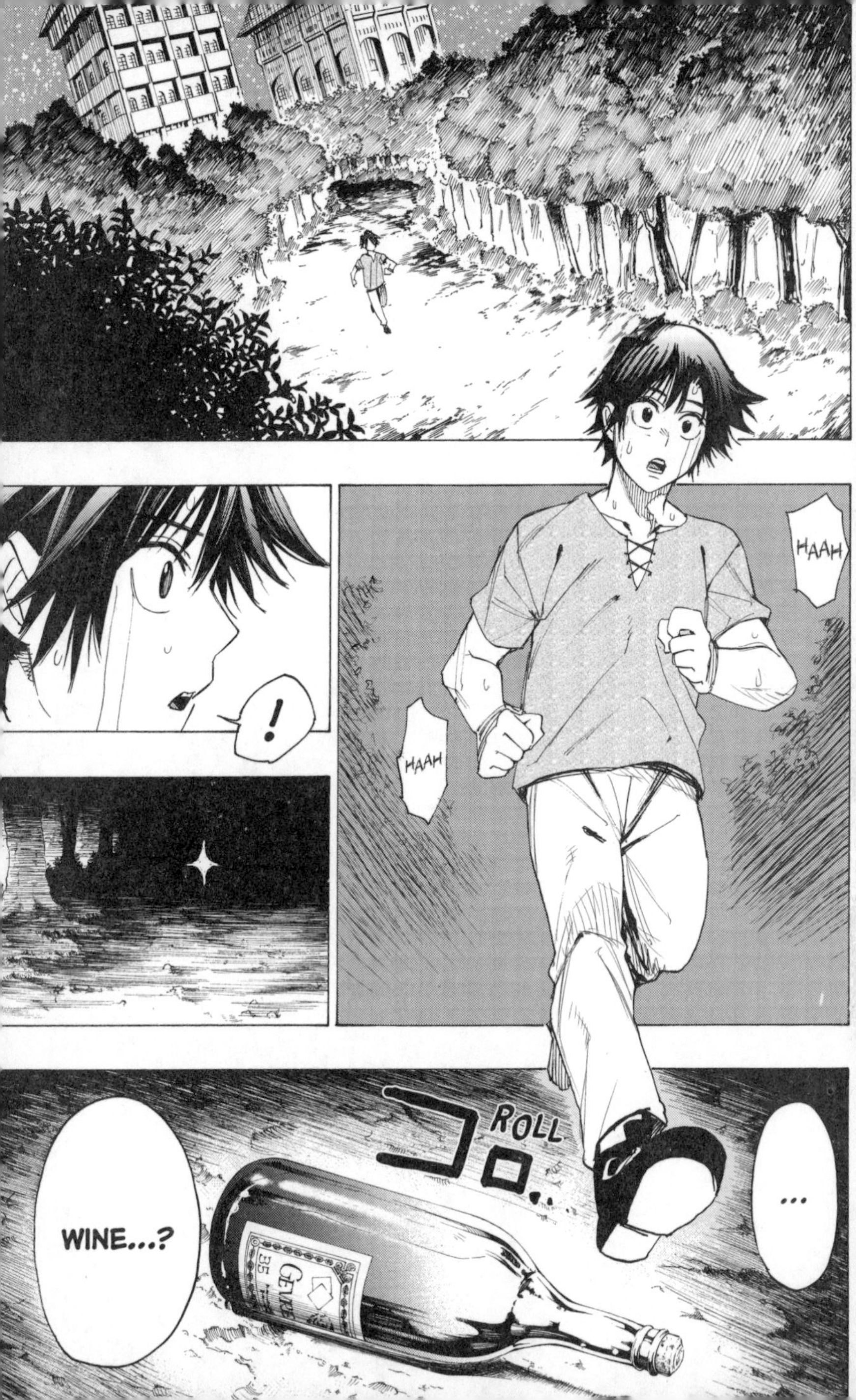
HAAH
HAAH
!
...
コロ...
ROLL
WINE...?

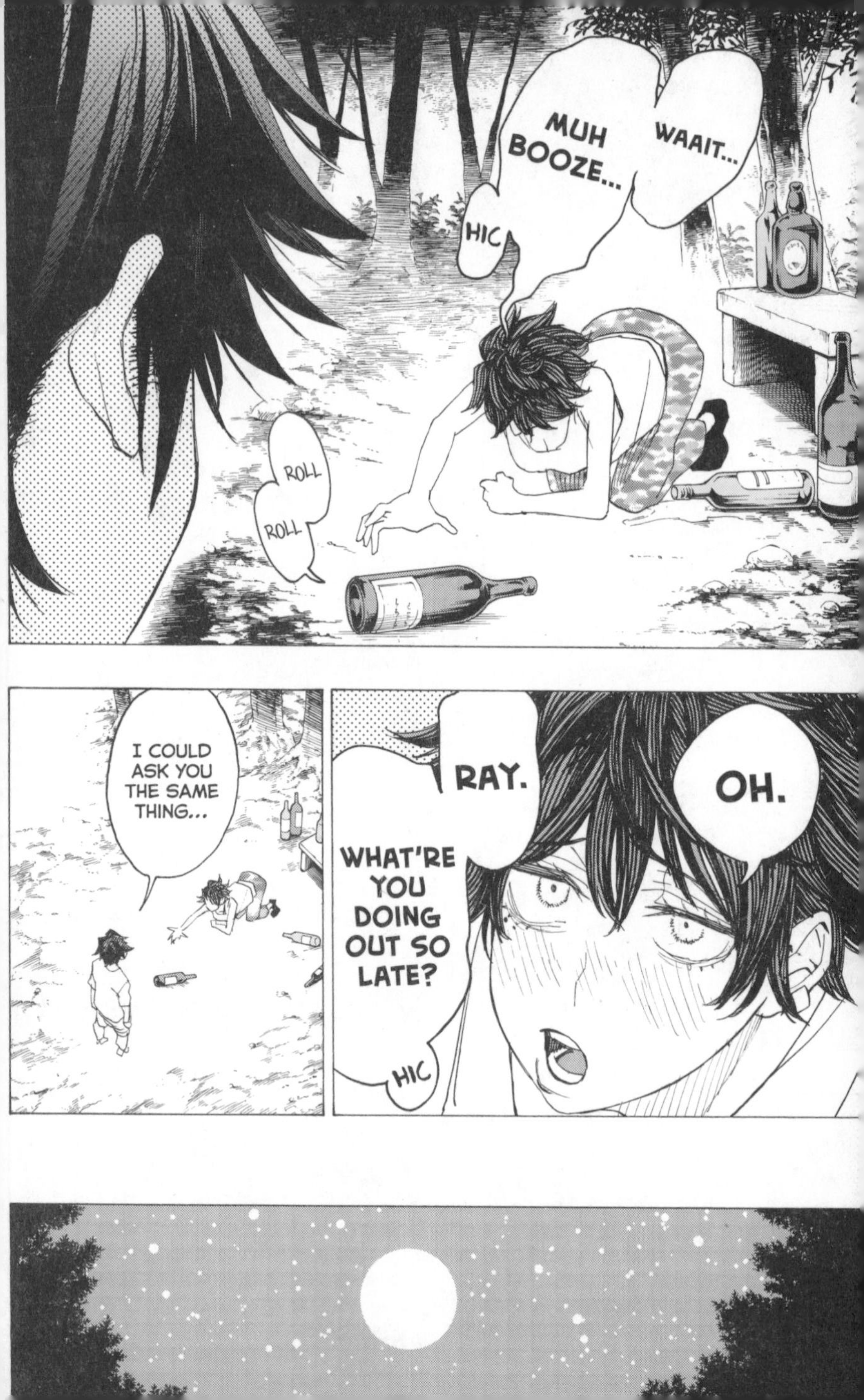
WAAIT...
MUH BOOZE...
HIC
ROLL ROLL
OH.
RAY.
WHAT'RE YOU DOING OUT SO LATE?
HIC
I COULD ASK YOU THE SAME THING...

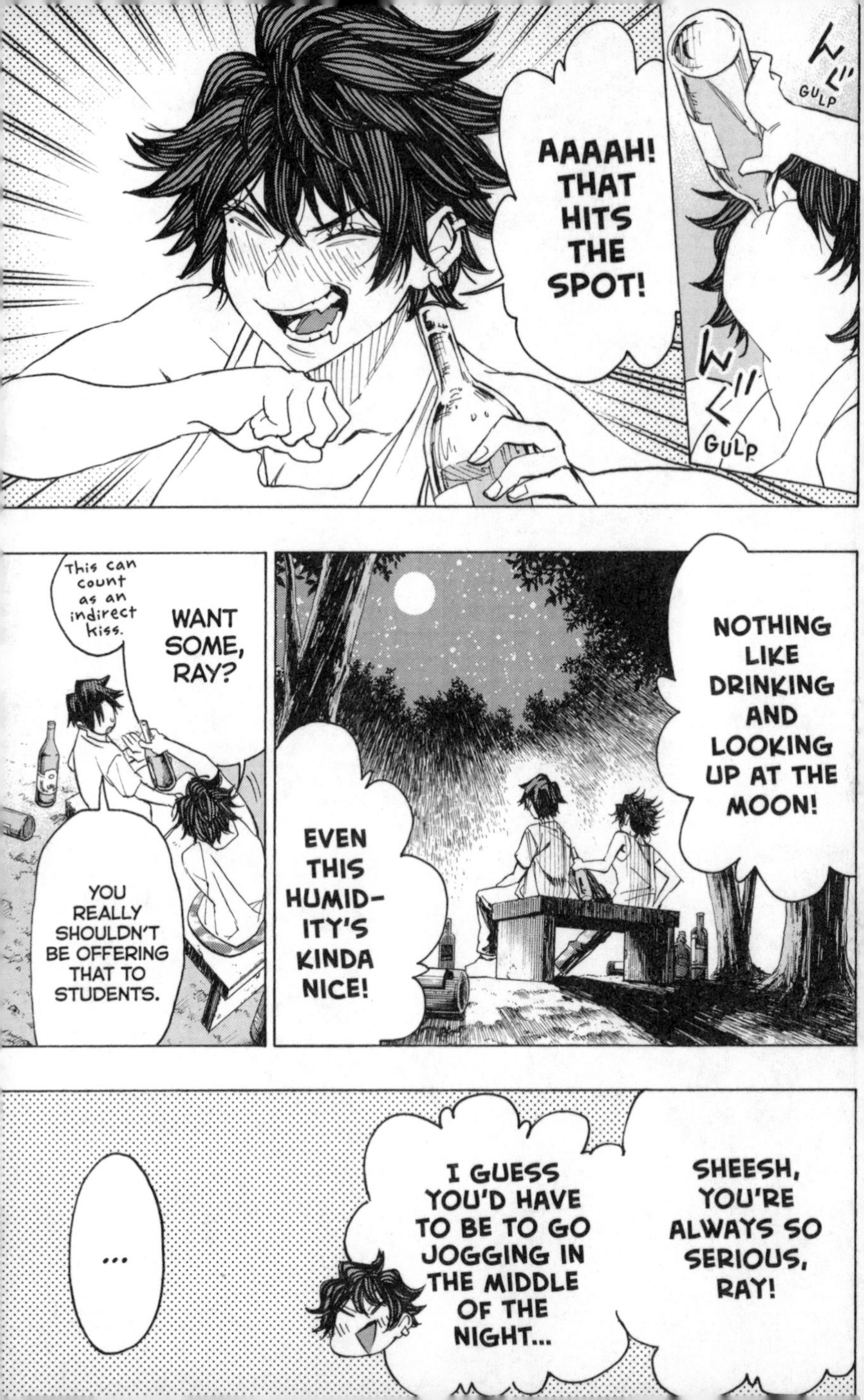
GULP
GULP
AAAAH! THAT HITS THE SPOT!
NOTHING LIKE DRINKING AND LOOKING UP AT THE MOON!
EVEN THIS HUMID-ITY'S KINDA NICE!
WANT SOME, RAY?
This can count as an indirect kiss.
YOU REALLY SHOULDN'T BE OFFERING THAT TO STUDENTS.
SHEESH, YOU'RE ALWAYS SO SERIOUS, RAY!
I GUESS YOU'D HAVE TO BE TO GO JOGGING IN THE MIDDLE OF THE NIGHT...
...

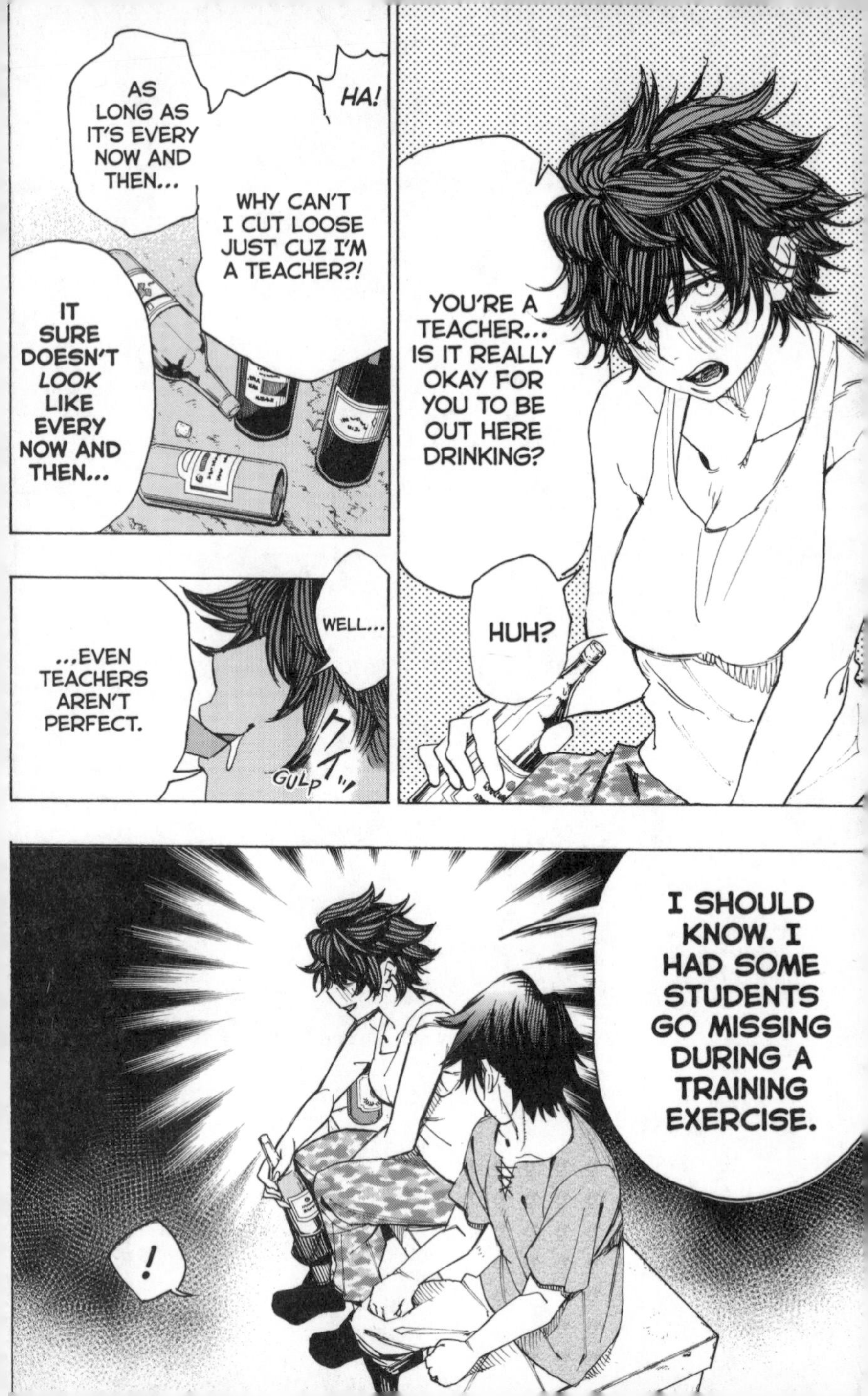
YOU'RE A TEACHER... IS IT REALLY OKAY FOR YOU TO BE OUT HERE DRINKING?
HUH?
HA!
WHY CAN'T I CUT LOOSE JUST CUZ I'M A TEACHER?!
AS LONG AS IT'S EVERY NOW AND THEN...
IT SURE DOESN'T *LOOK* LIKE EVERY NOW AND THEN...
WELL...
GULP
...EVEN TEACHERS AREN'T PERFECT.
I SHOULD KNOW. I HAD SOME STUDENTS GO MISSING DURING A TRAINING EXERCISE.
!

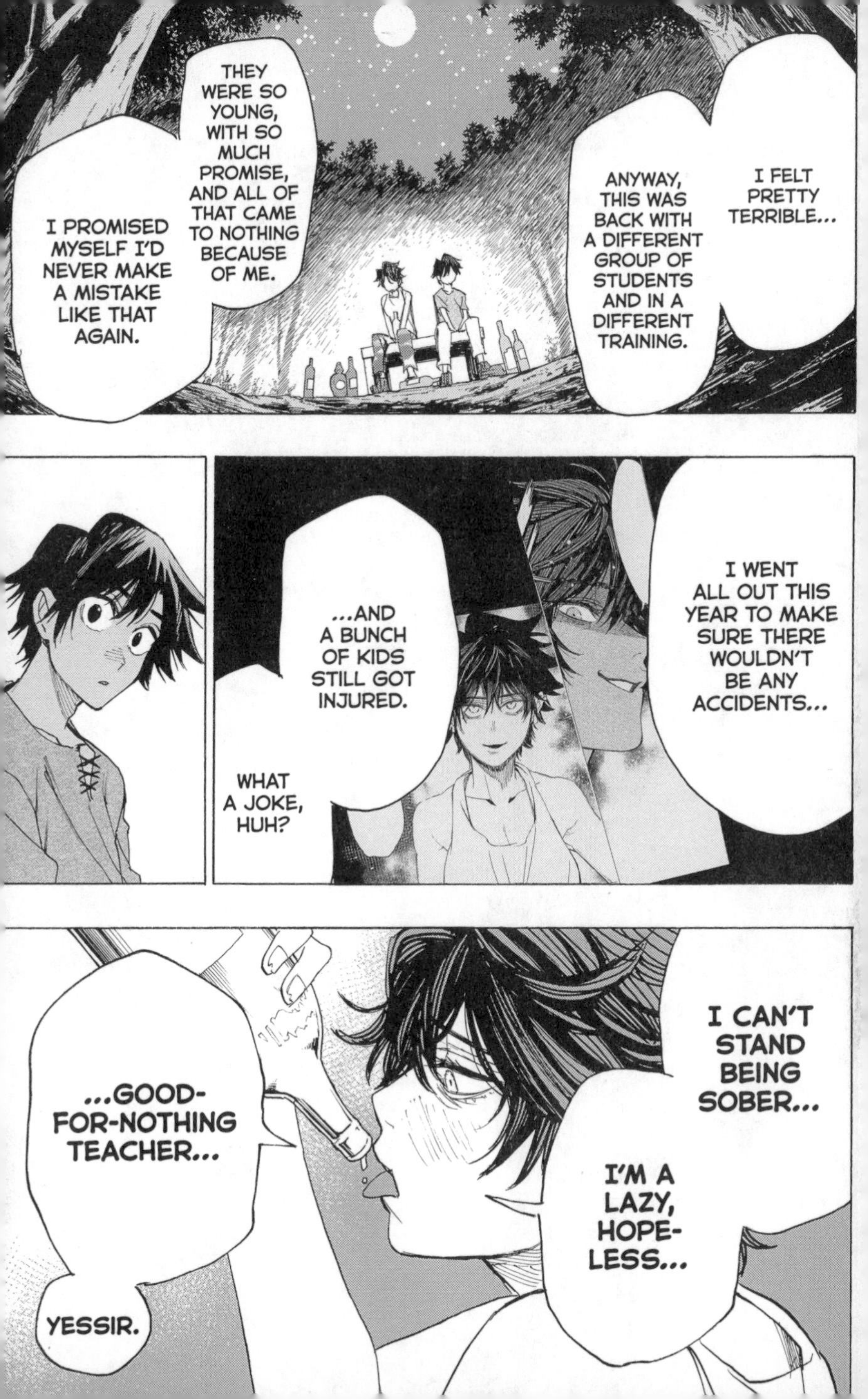
I FELT PRETTY TERRIBLE...
ANYWAY, THIS WAS BACK WITH A DIFFERENT GROUP OF STUDENTS AND IN A DIFFERENT TRAINING.
THEY WERE SO YOUNG, WITH SO MUCH PROMISE, AND ALL OF THAT CAME TO NOTHING BECAUSE OF ME.
I PROMISED MYSELF I'D NEVER MAKE A MISTAKE LIKE THAT AGAIN.
I WENT ALL OUT THIS YEAR TO MAKE SURE THERE WOULDN'T BE ANY ACCIDENTS...
...AND A BUNCH OF KIDS STILL GOT INJURED.
WHAT A JOKE, HUH?
I CAN'T STAND BEING SOBER...
I'M A LAZY, HOPE-LESS...
...GOOD-FOR-NOTHING TEACHER...
YESSIR.

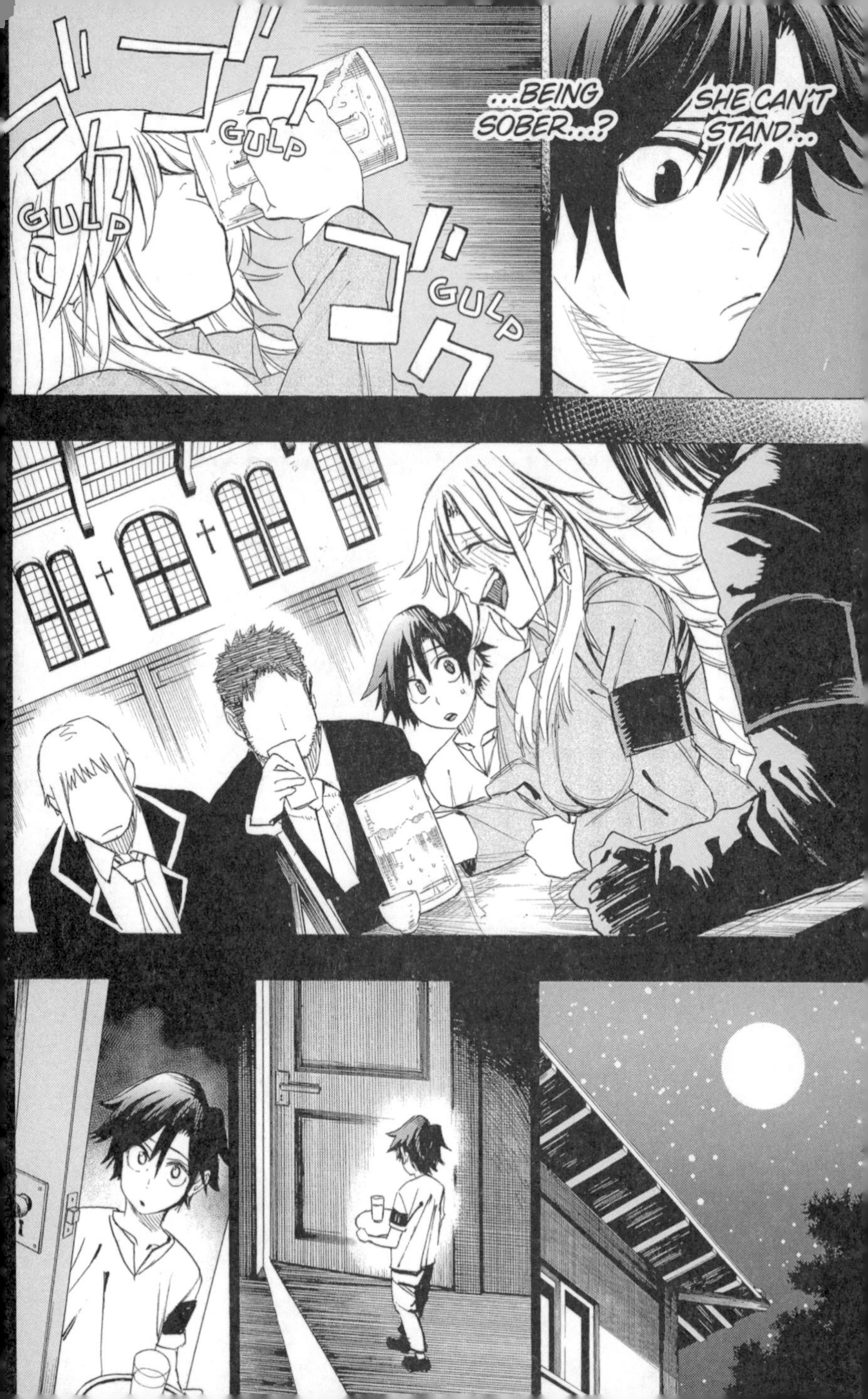
SHE CAN'T STAND...
...BEING SOBER...?
GULP
GULP
GULP

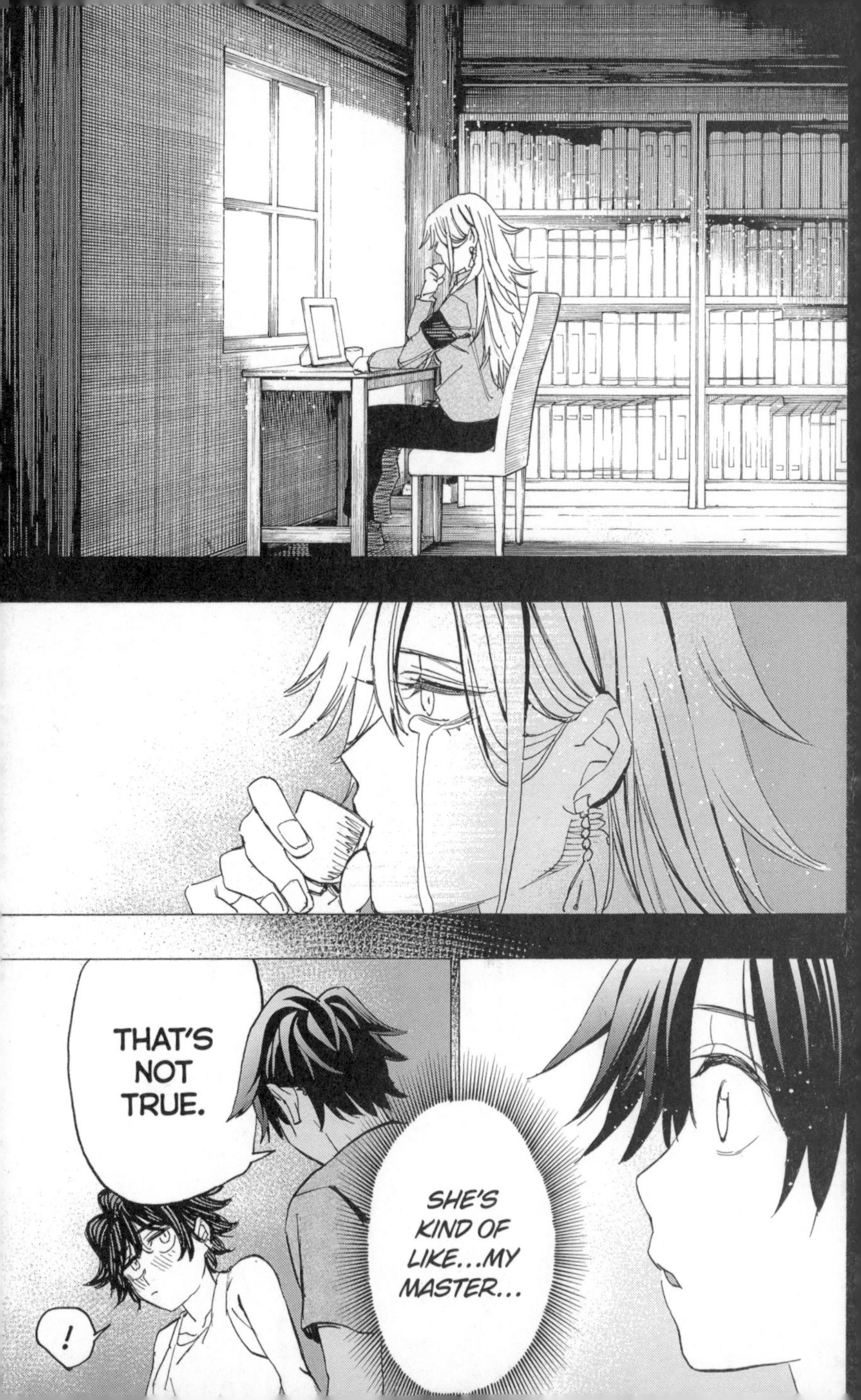
SHE'S KIND OF LIKE...MY MASTER...
THAT'S NOT TRUE.
!

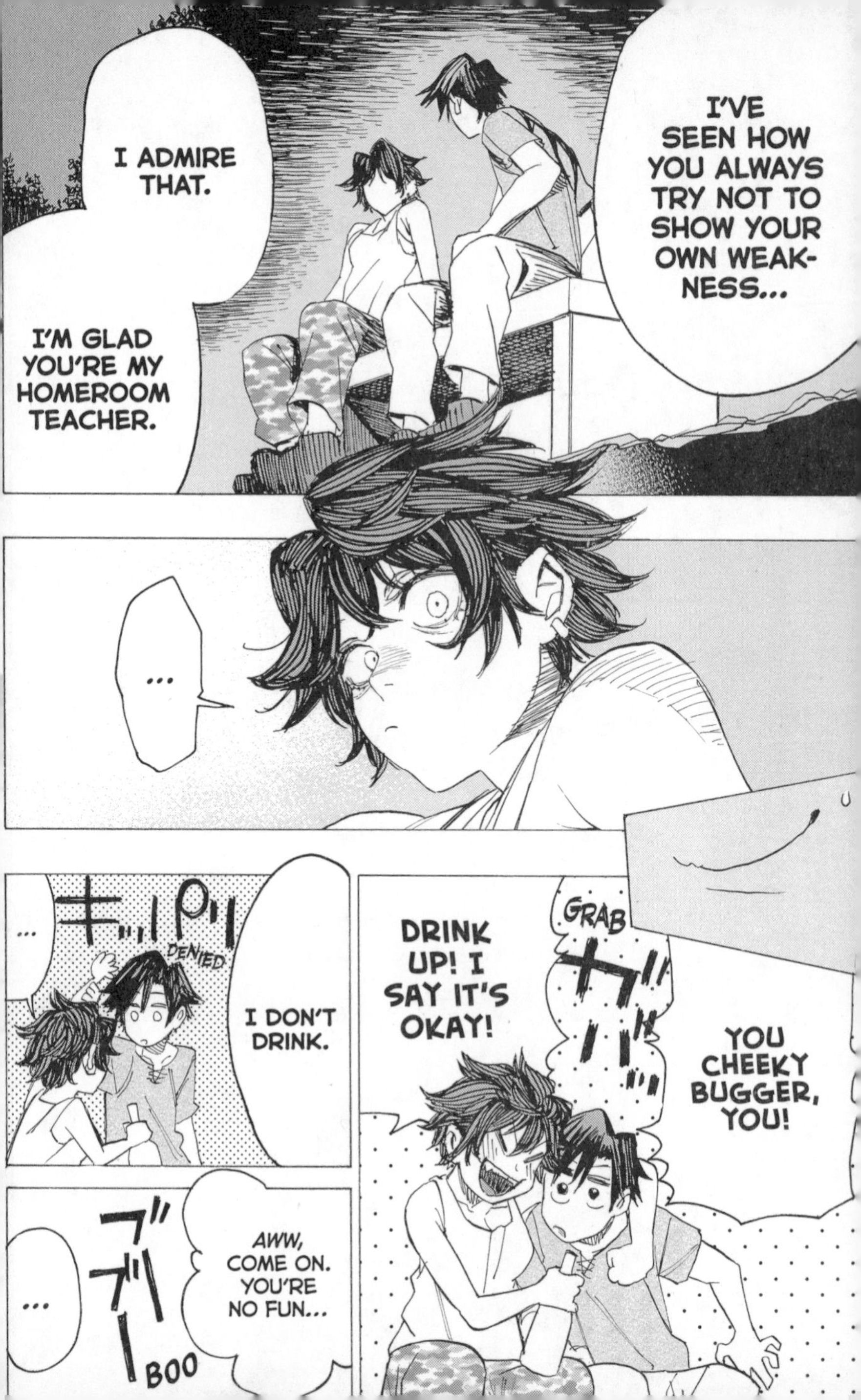
I'VE SEEN HOW YOU ALWAYS TRY NOT TO SHOW YOUR OWN WEAK-NESS...
I ADMIRE THAT.
I'M GLAD YOU'RE MY HOMEROOM TEACHER.
...
GRAB
YOU CHEEKY BUGGER, YOU!
DRINK UP! I SAY IT'S OKAY!
I DON'T DRINK.
DENIED
...
AWW, COME ON. YOU'RE NO FUN...
BOO
...

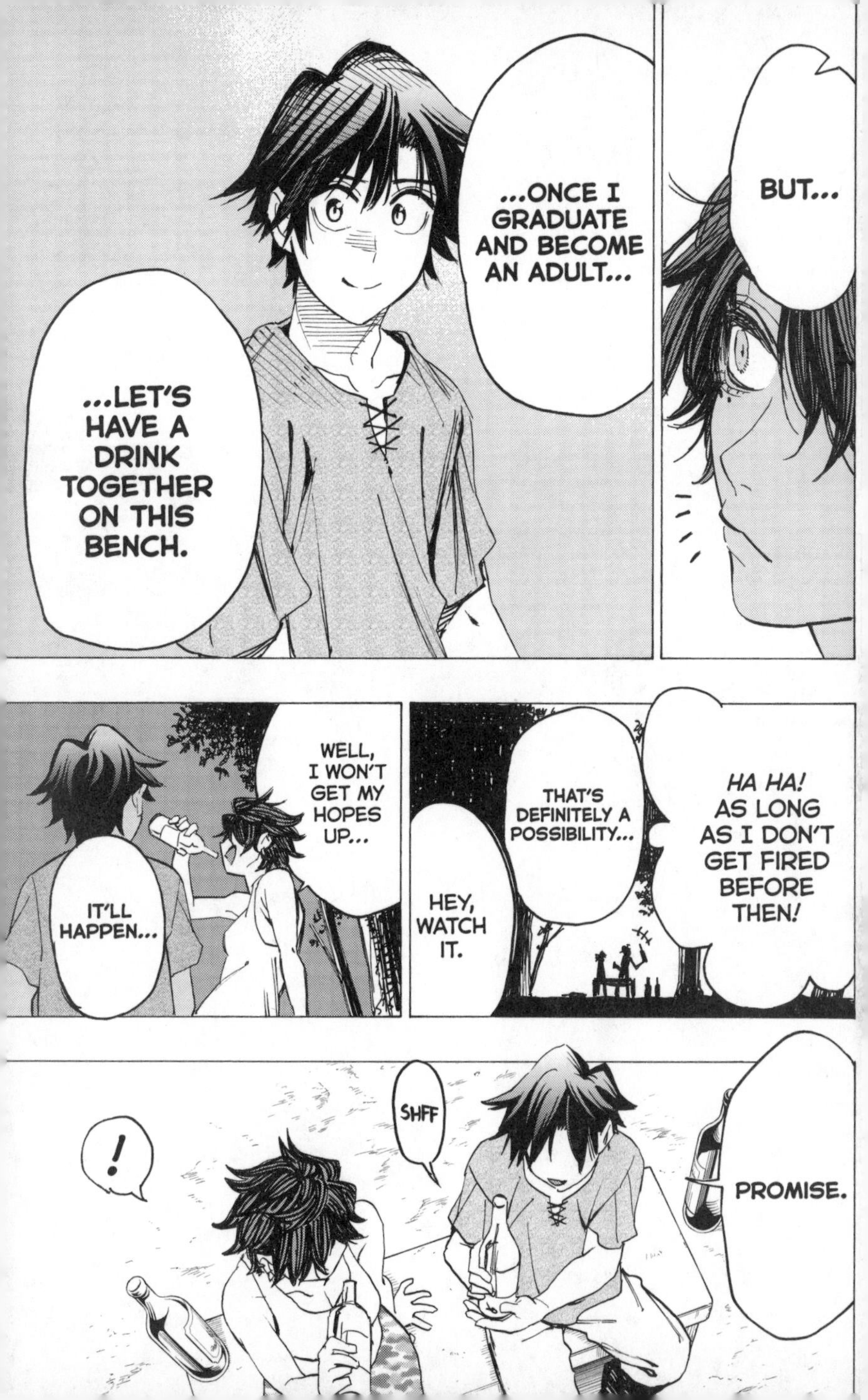
BUT...
...ONCE I GRADUATE AND BECOME AN ADULT...
...LET'S HAVE A DRINK TOGETHER ON THIS BENCH.
HA HA! AS LONG AS I DON'T GET FIRED BEFORE THEN!
THAT'S DEFINITELY A POSSIBILITY...
HEY, WATCH IT.
WELL, I WON'T GET MY HOPES UP...
IT'LL HAPPEN...
PROMISE.
SHFF
!

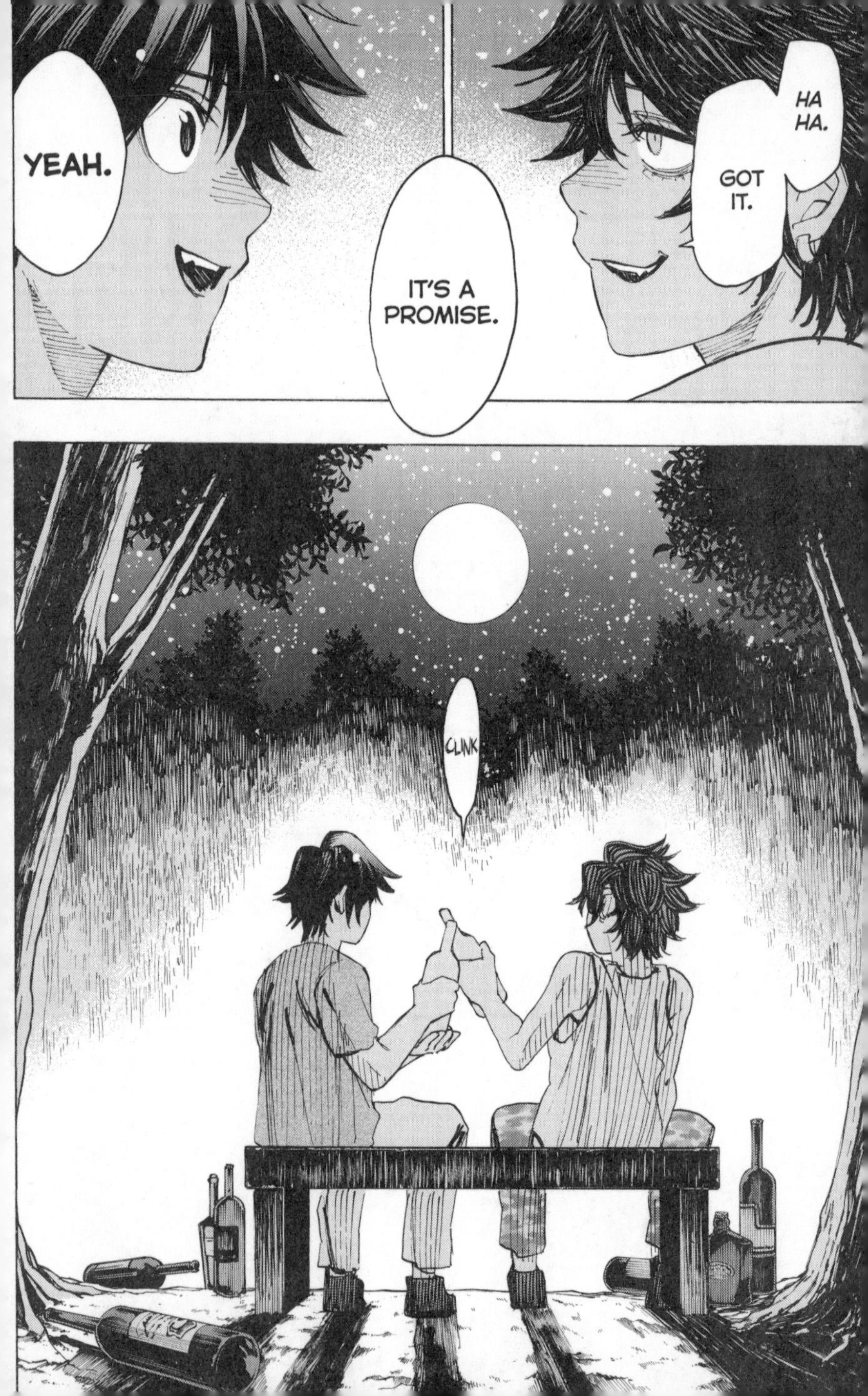
HA HA.
GOT IT.
IT'S A PROMISE.
YEAH.
CLINK

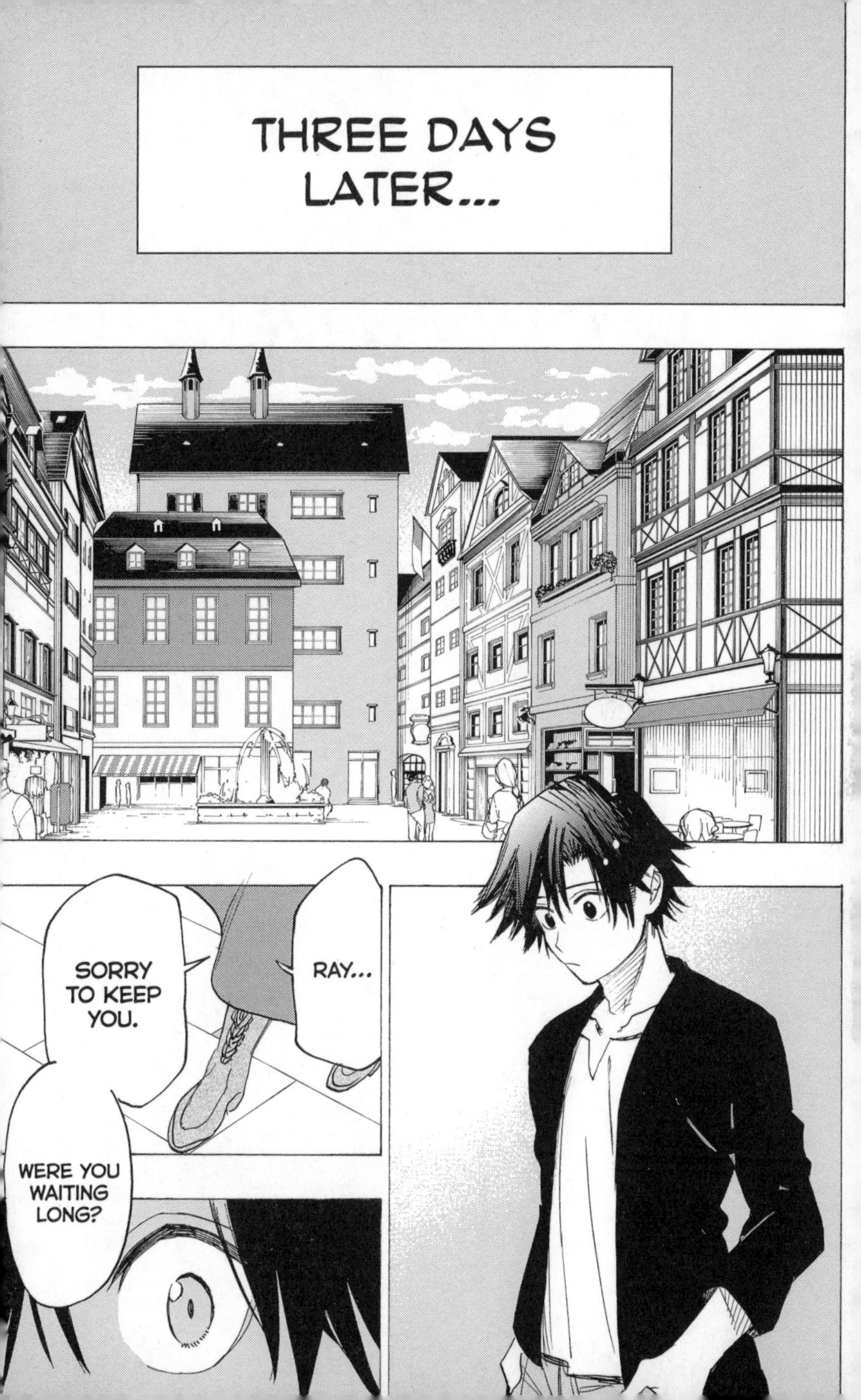
THREE DAYS LATER...
RAY...
SORRY TO KEEP YOU.
WERE YOU WAITING LONG?

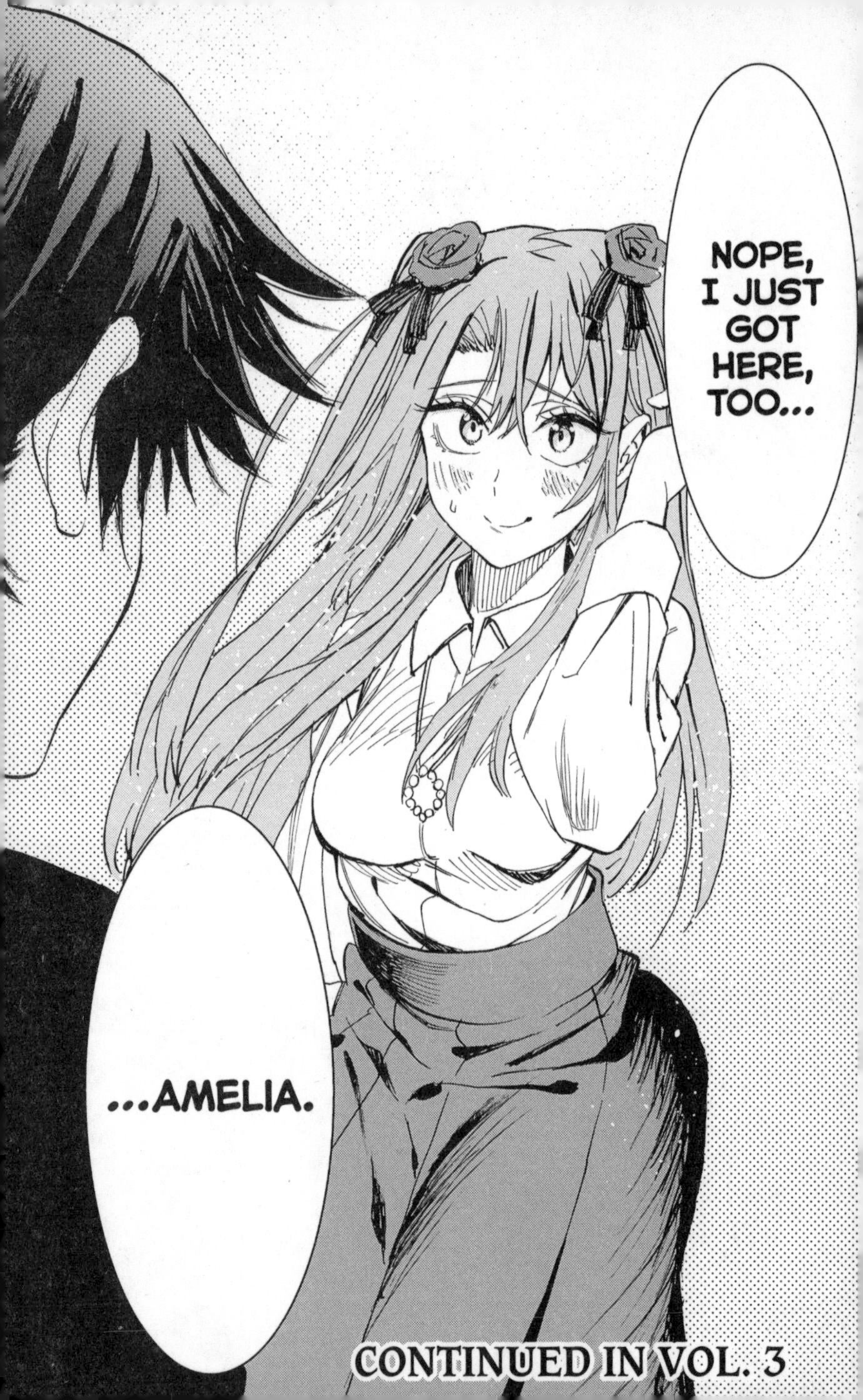
NOPE, I JUST GOT HERE, TOO...
...AMELIA.
CONTINUED IN VOL. 3

Sweet Time With Rebecca?

by Nana Mikoshiba

After managing to get permission to join both the Environmental Research Club and the Gardening Club, I threw myself into my after-school activities.

"You're early, Ray."

"Yeah, I've been looking forward to this!"

"*Hee hee.* I'm very glad to hear that."

Rebecca Bradley. Long, shiny black hair, a soft, straight nose, and plump lips. Her eyelashes were unusually long, making her beautiful, wide eyes look even more charming. What's more, a tiny mole under her right eye gave her a refined air beyond her years. I knew full well how beautiful Rebecca was.

"You're looking beautiful as usual today."

"Really, Ray... You always say that."

"No, honestly, you do."

"*Hee hee.* I do try to take care of my appearance, so I'm glad to hear you say that," said Rebecca, flashing a warm smile that looked more girlish than I would have expected.

"Seems like the other members are running late, huh?" I commented.

Usually, the other club members started coming in a little after classes ended, but nobody else had arrived. That got me wondering why Sella wasn't there yet. She was vice president of the club, and she looked up to Rebecca more than anyone. It was hard to imagine someone like her being late for a club meeting...

"Actually," said Rebecca, "it looks like none of the others will be able to join us today."

"Oh. Could it be some kind of... aristocrat thing?"

"Yes. Thankfully, I don't have to deal with that, but students from other noble families do have various responsibilities."

"I see. Got it."

Aside from myself, all the members of the Gardening Club were female. Plus, most of them were from noble families. It wasn't rare for one of them to miss this kind of meeting, but for the whole group to be absent...

"So it's just the two of us today?"

"Yes. Is... that a problem?" asked Rebecca, staring at me intently.

Of course being alone with her wasn't a problem.

"No, not at all!"

"Wonderful."

I'd often wondered at how Rebecca always seemed to have a smile ready. Maybe that was part of why everyone liked her so much. On top of that, she was the eldest daughter of the Bradley family, one of the Three Great Families, and there was something about her personality that drew people to her.

"Why don't we go water the plants together today?" asked Rebecca.

"Okay."

The two of us headed up to the roof, where the Gardening Club had its own flowerbed. There was just one problem with this setup: the roof didn't have a tap. In other words, we had to carry water up from a lower floor. The girls had managed it on their own until then, but now that I was there, I was happy to do it myself.

At that moment, I was carrying a bucketful of water from the tap; the rooftop flowerbed was pretty large. The Gardening Club had been around for a long time, and each successive generation had expanded the flowerbed. As a result, the current members had their work cut out for them watering all of the plants.

"Ray, thanks for always working so hard," said Rebecca.

"Just leave the heavy lifting to me!" I replied. "If there's one thing I'm confident about, it's my muscles."

Yes—even something like carrying water could double as weight training. I carried two buckets in each hand, making a total of four. The buckets had been filled to the top, so they were pretty heavy. In fact, this was such good training that I always took it upon myself to carry the water. I actually felt a little bad whenever Rebecca thanked me for it.

"Ray, there's something I've been wondering about... You're also in the Environmental Research Club, right?"

"Yeah."

Rebecca and I were walking next to each other, making small talk. She carried two empty watering cans—one for her, and one for me.

"All the guys in the Environmental Research Club are pretty big," Rebecca commented, "but you're not like that."

"That's true. But people often say that I look skinnier in a shirt. I'm actually pretty confident about my muscles."

Gulp.

For some reason, Rebecca had gulped loudly as she stared at my arms.

"Is something wrong?" I asked.

"Huh?! N-No… umm… it's nothing." She was definitely acting odd. She was looking everywhere but at me, and she kept fidgeting.

We finally reached the roof. I'd worked up a sweat on the way up, so I set the buckets down, took off my jacket, and rolled up my sleeves.

"Do… you want to touch them?" I asked.

"Huh?!"

Ahh. It looked like Rebecca was interested in my muscles.

"It's okay. You can touch them."

"Umm… are you sure?"

"Yeah."

She ogled at my arm. Seeing this, I was suddenly reminded of my master. She used to poke and prod at me all the time, saying things like,

"Whoa! You've gotten bigger, Ray!"

"Yeah."

"Come on, let me touch!"

"Fine, go ahead."

"Hmmm… Men's muscles really are different, huh!"

"You really think so?"

"Yeah! I think women are just instinctively drawn to muscles. Keep at it, Ray!"

"Yes, Master."

As I reminisced on that exchange from long ago, I wondered if Rebecca felt the same way as my master. Rebecca reached out a tentative hand and touched my bicep.

"Wow! You really aren't as skinny as you look!"

"Is that what other people say?"

"Ah, umm… well, yes. Some of the other Gardening Club members talk about you sometimes, Ray."

"Oh, really?"

"Yes."

As the only guy in a club full of girls, it seemed like I had drawn a good bit of attention. I'd spent a lot of time with Abbie, my master, and other women, so it didn't bother me, but maybe the girls from the Gardening Club weren't like them. I'd been careful about how I behaved around them, but now I started to worry that maybe I was making them uncomfortable.

"I'm not making anyone here uncomfortable, am I?"

"Not at all! It's nothing like that! Everyone is very fond of you, Ray. Even Dina has nice things to say about you!"

"Really? She does?"

"Yes. She says you work hard and always do a good job."

"That's... a little surprising."

Sella had accepted me into the club, but I felt like she still treated me a bit coldly. During one of my recent days off, she had asked me to go buy flowers with her. She then told me in no uncertain terms not to try anything funny with Rebecca or interfere with the club's way of doing things. Ever since then, I'd thought she didn't really care for me, but...

"I also think you're a hard worker, Ray," said Rebecca.

"Thank you."

I still hadn't quite figured out how to play the part of a student. I decided to join two clubs because I had heard that club activities were the best part of being a student, though I also made sure to join ones that I was actually interested in. Thanks to our "muscle talk," I'd been able to hit it off right away with the guys from the Environmental Research Club. On the other hand, I had all kinds of worries about the Gardening Club, so I was relieved to hear that those were unfounded.

"*Phew.* Well, umm... thank you for carrying these," said Rebecca.

"Of course. Feel free to ask anytime. These muscles aren't going anywhere!" I gave a wide grin, and Rebecca chuckled to herself.

"You really are an interesting guy, Ray."

Throwing caution to the wind, I asked her directly, "Is that a good thing or a bad thing?"

Rebecca put her hands together lightly, a mischievous glint in her eye. "Well, who can really say?"

Later, the two of us turned to watering the plants. We poured the water from the buckets into the watering cans and split up the watering between ourselves. I took the right half of the flowerbed, and Rebecca took the left. I'd done this countless times before, so we were finished before we knew it.

"Thank you for your help, Ray."

"No, thank you."

We sat down next to each other on a bench in the middle of the roof.

"Ah, come to think of it…" Rebecca began.

"What is it?" I asked. Rebecca looked like she had just remembered something.

"I just got some good black tea, so I thought I'd offer you some… but I forgot it in my room."

"Oh, really? Well, maybe some other time, then…"

Before I could continue, Rebecca shot me a glance. "Well… if you don't mind, would you like to go there now…?"

"Go where?"

"Umm… to my room."

"Huh…?"

The suggestion was about as shocking as you might expect. Officially, boys weren't allowed in the girls' dorms, but there were rumors about couples visiting each other's dorms.

"Is that really okay?" I asked.

"Yes, I'd like you to try some. If I go get it myself, it will already be dark by the time I get back. What do you say?"

"Well, I guess, if you're fine with it."

And so, in an unexpected turn of events, I found myself being invited into Rebecca's room.

"Please, come in," she said.

"Thanks…"

Rebecca had led me through the girls' dorm so that I wouldn't be spotted.

People said she wasn't too fond of special treatment, but being from one of the Three Great Families apparently meant that she got a room all to herself.

"Okay, please have a seat while I get the tea ready."

"Sure."

Rebecca went off to go brew the tea. Alone now, I took a look around the room. It was mostly white, with a few small objects set here and there. There were also stuffed animals and other cute objects; I was a little surprised to see that she liked that kind of thing. Maybe it was because she seemed so mature.

"Is something wrong, Ray?" asked Rebecca, setting the tea on the table.

"Your stuffed animals are cute."

"Yes, I like to collect cute things. It's a hobby of mine."

"They really suit you."

"*Hee hee.* Thank you."

We both took a sip of tea.

"Wow, this really is delicious!" I exclaimed.

"Isn't it? You always do so much to help, Ray, so I really wanted to share some with you."

The aroma of the tea drifted up into my nose; the taste was exquisite, too. I'd had plenty of tea in my life, but this was probably the best I'd ever tasted.

"Thanks for going to all this trouble for me. And for inviting me to your room."

"*Hee hee.* That'll be our secret." Rebecca flashed a grin, holding a finger up to her lips.

"*Ha ha,* good point," I said. "You're really popular, so it would be bad if word got out."

"I'm popular?"

"Yeah. Or, at least, I think so."

A cloud seemed to pass over Rebecca's face. Had I accidentally touched on a sensitive subject?

"I feel like people only like me because I'm the eldest daughter of one of the Three Great Families…"

"Maybe *some* people think that, but—" I stopped short and let out a small breath. Then, deciding I may as well tell her exactly what was going through my mind, I continued, "As for me, I think I'd like you just as much even if you weren't from a noble family. You're a really kind, beautiful person, Rebecca."

Turning a little red, Rebecca fixed her eyes on me. "You really are a charmer, Ray."

"I mean it!"

"That's what worries me... Are you so used to talking to women?"

"I don't know. I grew up surrounded by women, so maybe that has something to do with it."

Suddenly, there came a loud knock at the door, the sound reverberating around the room. Rebecca crossed directly to the door.

"Yes? Who is it?"

"It's Dina. Do you have a second, Rebecca?"

"Huh...? Dina?!" Rebecca looked as though she knew she'd sounded flustered.

"This... could be a problem," I thought to myself. I didn't dare to imagine what would happen if Sella found Rebecca and me in there together. After all, Sella had already warned me about trying anything funny with Rebecca. Not that I *had* tried anything, but who knew what Sella would think if she saw us.

"Hm? Is something wrong?" Sella asked from behind the door.

"N-No! Nothing at all!" Rebecca stammered.

"Then is it okay if I come in for a bit? I got some nice sweets today."

"S-Sure..."

"Are you not feeling well?"

Hearing this, Rebecca's face lit up as if to say, "That's it!"

"Y-Yes, actually..."

"R-Really?! I'll look after you! Please, let me in!"

"H-Huuuuh?!" cried Rebecca helplessly. However, it seemed like Sella wouldn't take no for an answer.

As I was trying to work out what to do, Rebecca turned to me with a worried expression. My only options were either hiding in one of the dorm rooms or making a run for it. There were a lot of rooms to hide in, but there was still a chance that Sella would find me, so running seemed like the better option. Then again… we were only on the third floor. It might just be possible for me to jump out of the window.

Okay. It was time to take the window option. I gestured at Rebecca to explain the plan.

"Huh…?!"

Even as Rebecca cried out in alarm, I made a gallant leap out of the window. I used Inner Code to strengthen my body and reduce the shock from the impact.

Rebecca looked concerned as she stared out of the window, but I waved casually to show that I was fine. Then, melting into the night, I made my way back to my own room.

The next day…

"Come to think of it, there were two cups in Rebecca's room the other night…"

"O-Oh, really?" I asked.

In a case of poor timing, I found myself alone with Sella in the club room; the other members seemed to be running late. Sella met my eyes for a moment before turning away again.

"Hey, Ray…?"

"Y-Yes?"

"What did you and Rebecca do yesterday after finishing up with club stuff?"

"I… just went back to my room like always." I had no choice but to lie. Still, Sella was clearly suspicious.

"Funny," she said. "I found a hair in Rebecca's room that looked like it came from a guy. It wouldn't happen to be yours, would it?"

"…"

If Sella had found some of my hair, then there was nothing I could do. All that remained was for me to quietly accept my fate…

"Th-The truth is…" I began. Just then, the door flew open with a bang.

"It's... not what you think! He didn't do anything weird!" Rebecca's protests rang across the room as she strode toward Sella.

"Rebecca! If you're going to date someone, at least tell me first!" Sella cried. "I have to see whether or not they're good enough for you. I won't go easy on them—not even if it's Ray!"

"I-It's not like that!"

It took a few hours for Rebecca to convince Sella that there was nothing between us. The moral of the story is... don't do or say anything that could be misinterpreted... Yeah...

The
ICEBLADE
SORCERER
Shall RULE
the
WORLD

Young characters and steampunk setting, like *Howl's Moving Castle* and *Battle Angel Alita*

Beyond the Clouds © 2018 Nicke / Ki-oon

A boy with a talent for machines and a mysterious girl whose wings he's fixed will take you beyond the clouds! In the tradition of the high-flying, resonant adventure stories of Studio Ghibli comes a gorgeous tale about the longing of young hearts for adventure and friendship!

The boys are back, in 400-page hardcovers that are as pretty and badass as they are!

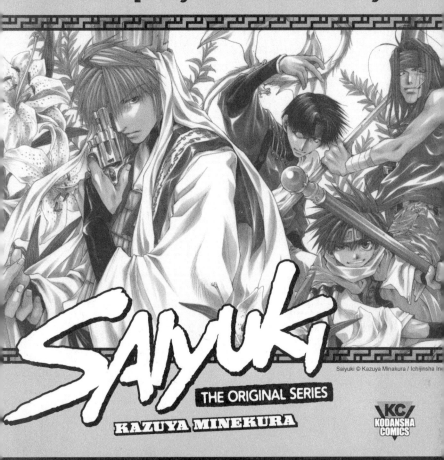

Saiyuki © Kazuya Minakura / Ichijinsha Inc.

SAIyuki
THE ORIGINAL SERIES
KAZUYA MINEKURA

KC KODANSHA COMICS

"AN EDGY COMIC LOOK AT AN ANCIENT CHINESE TALE." —YALSA

Genjo Sanzo is a Buddhist priest in the city of Togenkyo, which is being ravaged by yokai spirits that have fallen out of balance with the natural order. His superiors send him on a journey far to the west to discover why this is happening and how to stop it. His companions are three yokai with human souls. But this is no day trip — the four will encounter many discoveries and horrors on the way.

FEATURES NEW TRANSLATION, COLOR PAGES, AND BEAUTIFUL WRAPAROUND COVER ART!

The adorable new odd-couple cat comedy manga from the creator of the beloved *Chi's Sweet Home*, in full color!

Sue & Tai-chan

Konami Kanata

Sue is an aging housecat who's looking forward to living out her life in peace... but her plans change when the mischievous black tomcat Tai-chan enters the picture! Hey! Sue never signed up to be a catsitter! *Sue & Tai-chan* is the latest from the reigning meow-narch of cute kitty comics, Konami Kanata.

KC
KODANSHA
COMICS

A Kodansha Trade Paperback Original

Published in the United States by
Kodansha USA Publishing, LLC, New York.

Publication rights for this English edition arranged through
Kodansha Ltd., Tokyo.

First published in Japan in 2021 by Kodansha Ltd., Tokyo.
as *Hyouken no majutsushi ga sekai wo suberu*, volume 2.

ISBN 978-1-64651-625-4

Printed in the United States of America.

9 8 7 6 5 4 3 2 1

Translation: Nate Derr
Lettering: Darren Smith
Additional lettering: Sara Linsley
Editing: Jordan Reynolds, Andres Oliver
YKS Services LLC/SKY JAPAN, Inc.
Kodansha USA Publishing edition cover design by My Truong and Matt Akuginow

Publisher: Kiichiro Sugawara

Director of Publishing Services: Ben Applegate
Director of Publishing Operations: Dave Barrett
Associate Director of Publishing Operations: Stephen Pakula
Publishing Services Managing Editors: Alanna Ruse, Madison Salters,
with Grace Chen
Senior Production Manager: Angela Zurlo

KODANSHA.US

KODANSHA